Two Can Play That Game

Two Can Play That Game

Manipulation, Counter-Manipulation, and Recognition in John 21 through the Eyes of Genesis

D. Eric Lowdermilk

FOREWORD BY
R. Alan Culpepper

◥PICKWICK *Publications* • Eugene, Oregon

TWO CAN PLAY THAT GAME
Manipulation, Counter-Manipulation, and Recognition in John 21 through the Eyes of Genesis

Copyright © 2016 D. Eric Lowdermilk. All rights reserved. Except for brief quotations in critical publications or reviews, no part of this book may be reproduced in any manner without prior written permission from the publisher. Write: Permissions, Wipf and Stock Publishers, 199 W. 8th Ave., Suite 3, Eugene, OR 97401.

Pickwick Publications
An Imprint of Wipf and Stock Publishers
199 W. 8th Ave., Suite 3
Eugene, OR 97401

www.wipfandstock.com

PAPERBACK ISBN: 978-1-4982-0846-8
HARDCOVER ISBN: 978-1-4982-0848-2
EBOOK ISBN: 978-1-4982-0847-5

Cataloguing-in-Publication data:

Names: Lowdermilk, D. Eric.

Title: Two can play that game : manipulation, counter-manipulation, and recognition in John 21 through the eyes of Genesis / D. Eric Lowdermilk.

Description: Eugene, OR : Pickwick Publications, 2016 | Includes bibliographical references.

Identifiers: ISBN 978-1-4982-0846-8 (paperback) | ISBN 978-1-4982-0848-2 (hardcover) | ISBN 978-1-4982-0847-5 (ebook)

Subjects: LCSH: Bible. John, XXI—Criticism, interpretation, etc. | Bible. Genesis—Criticism, interpretation, etc.

Classification: LCC BS2615.52 L75 2016 (print) | LCC BS2615.52 (ebook)

Manufactured in the U.S.A.   12/16/16

Unless otherwise noted, scriptural quotations are from the *ESV® Bible* (*The Holy Bible, English Standard Version®*), copyright 2001 by Crossway, a publishing ministry of Good News Publishers. Used by permission. All rights reserved.

Scripture quotations taken from the New American Standard Bible®, Copyright © 1960, 1962, 1963, 1968, 1971, 1972, 1973, 1975, 1977, 1995 by The Lockman Foundation. Used by permission. (www.Lockman.org)

Scripture taken from the New King James Version®. Copyright © 1982 by Thomas Nelson. Used by permission. All rights reserved.

Scripture taken from the Common English Bible®, CEB® Copyright © 2010, 2011 by Common English Bible.™ Used by permission. All rights reserved worldwide. The "CEB" and "Common English Bible" trademarks are registered in the United States Patent and Trademark Office by Common English Bible. Use of either trademark requires the permission of Common English Bible.

To JonLuc

Contents

Foreword by R. Alan Culpepper | ix
Preface | xi
Acknowledgments | xv
Abbreviations | xvii

Chapter 1: Introduction | 1
  Statement of Problem · 1
  Connections between Genesis and Johannine Anagnorisis · 6
  Scope · 13
  The Design of the Research · 14
  Summary · 15

Chapter 2: Literature Review | 16
  John 21 in Relation to John 1–20 · 17
  The Treatment of Peter in the FG · 23
  Johannine Anagnorisis · 31
  Genesis, Hebraic Recognition, and Scholarship · 43
  Conclusion · 51

Chapter 3: Methodology | 52
  Narrative Criticism · 54
  The Scholar's Bias · 77

Chapter 4: A Theory of Manipulation and Recognition | 79
  Defining Manipulation and Recognition · 79
  Six Kernels of Manipulation · 90
  Summary · 113

Chapter 5: Patterns in Genesis Manipulation and Recognition | 119
  Selection of Narrative Units and Rationale · 119
  The Chosen Manipulator in the Character Development Process · 123
  Disempowerment of the Manipulated and Empowerment of the Manipulator · 134
  Evocative Déjà Vu Motifs · 138
  From Manipulator to Manipulable: The Effect of Counter-Manipulation · 149
  Summary · 166

Chapter 6: Applying a Manipulation Perspective to John 21:1–14 | 168
  Introductory Matters · 168
  Manipulation Kernels · 177
  The Disciples Go Fishing (John 21:1–5) · 183
  Faded Diminutives? . . . An Excursus · 204
  Little Ones Wrestle with a Great Catch (John 21:5–9) · 217
  Breakfast by a Charcoal Fire (John 21:9–14) · 228

Chapter 7: One Little Sheep Becomes a Shepherd: John 21:15–19 | 237
  The Significance of *Lex Talionis* · 238
  The Synonyms for Love, Feed, and Sheep · 240
  More Than These? · 249
  You Know and Understand Everything · 251
  Truly, Truly, You Shall Lay down Your Life · 256
  "A Need for Change within Peter Himself" · 267

Chapter 8: Conclusion | 269
  The Theory of Manipulation in Genesis and John · 269
  Assessing the Characteristic Patterns · 271
  The Effect of Understanding Diminutives · 275
  Conclusions, Implications, and Questions · 276

Bibliography | 279
General Index | 295
Scripture Index | 303

Foreword

In this volume Eric Lowdermilk departs from current scholarship on the recognition scenes in the Gospel of John by interpreting them in the light of the trickster motif in Genesis rather than recognition scenes in Greco-Roman literature. Reading the characterization of Peter and Jesus in John against this background—as any ancient Christian reader familiar with the Genesis accounts would—demonstrates the value of manipulation as a rubric for analyzing character interactions, which is especially appropriate for literature produced in an ancient, agonistic society. Lowdermilk shows how both Peter and Jesus seek to manipulate each other. In this context manipulation can be either positive or negative, and manipulators can either reveal or conceal, empower or disempower. Hence the title, "Two Can Play that Game."

Lowdermilk's extensive work on the trickster motif and recognition scenes in Genesis opens fascinating insights into these themes. Parallels emerge between Jesus and Joseph, Peter and Judah. Just as Joseph and Judah manipulate others in Genesis, so Jesus and Peter seek to manipulate one another in the latter half of the Gospel. First, Peter objects to Jesus's talk of death and pledges to lay down his life for Jesus. Then, he seeks to manipulate others through withholding his identity in the courtyard in John 18. In return, Jesus seeks to bring Peter to recognition, understanding, and faith. First, Jesus seeks to manipulate Peter by means of his rebuke, assuring Peter that he would deny Jesus that night, then through withholding his own identity at the great catch of fish, and finally through his questions and commands to Peter: "Do you love me, . . . feed my sheep." Character interaction, therefore, follows a pattern of manipulation and counter-manipulation through several recurring stages. The result is a fascinating exploration of the conventions of character interaction that are drawn from the trickster motif we encounter in Genesis.

This volume is particularly instructive for all who are interested in Genesis and the Gospels, the influence of the Hebrew Scriptures on early Christian writings, the dynamics of character interactions in ancient literature, the influence of the trickster motif and the recognition scenes in Genesis on later Jewish and Christian literature, and the place of John 21 in the narrative of the Fourth Gospel. Along the way Lowdermilk offers fresh insights into textual features in John 21, such as the use of diminutives, variants, and the relationship between John 21 and the body of the Gospel.

R. Alan Culpepper

Professor and Dean Emeritus
McAfee School of Theology
Mercer University

Preface

Research is much like a long hike through the woods.

Several years back, my older son JonLuc and I headed out for our first backcountry hiking experience. We were to spend a week in the Blue Ridge Mountains of Appalachia. We started with a three-day jaunt. It was a loop trail, beginning and ending at Cosby Creek Campground near the Tennessee and North Carolina border. Being rookies, we were a little nervous about being out on our own for the first time (*though I never admitted such to my sixteen-year-old son!*). On the second day, near the end of the seven-mile hike, we were both exhausted and ready for rest. We kept looking at the trail map and wondering when the designated camp site would appear beyond the bend. To make matters worse, I had rationed our food very carefully, and stubbornly refused to stop for an extra refueling before dinner—I had to stick to the plan. *Yay dad!*

While scouring the map for the campsite, I noticed a short spur trail in our vicinity that supposedly offered a beautiful overlook. Now, I've never been one to be able to ignore what *might* be out there. So, I persuaded my reluctant, weary son to follow me off the main trail. The side trail was heavily overgrown with tall, wild blueberry bushes and very difficult to follow. However, it was also surprisingly short—just about thirty yards or so long. When we came to the end of it, the view suddenly opened up to a breathtaking sight of a sprawling valley, with no trace of civilization for miles. We stood there in silence. Suddenly, I remembered our food rationing "wildcard." I had packed a jar of peanut butter, just for such an occasion. Too tired to dig through our packs for our spoons, we whipped out our hiking knives and devoured the entire jar, all the while soaking in the amazing vista of God's beauty. When we resumed the hike, we discovered our campsite only about seventy-five yards further down the main trail, literally just around the bend. Had we not gone off trail and explored, we would have missed what has become one of our most cherished father-son moments.

John 21 portrays the end of the disciple's long journey with Jesus in the Fourth Gospel and their "miraculous draught of fishes." Led by Peter, seven of them fish all night and catch nothing. In the morning, a stranger on the shore instructs them to cast their net again. The disciples surprisingly fail to recognize him. However, after an amazing catch and subsequent breakfast, there is no doubt in their minds who this stranger is. Jesus then questions Peter three times about his love and commissions him to feed and tend Jesus' sheep.

When I set out to examine John 21:1–19, I had an aim that is a bit uncommon in doctoral work. I wanted to take a broad approach to these 19 verses, allowing the text to offer to me what it had. While I specifically zeroed in on the failed recognition scene in the opening verses, I did not feel I could walk away from the text without answering some nagging questions. These side trails were, I felt, key to hearing and seeing all of what this story journey had to offer. What resulted, in effect, was three studies. First, in order to complete a thru-hike in John 21, I had to explore Genesis recognition scenes as a back drop for reading John 21. So I left the path and spent considerable time studying what I herein call "manipulation" in the so called "trickster" narratives. The first four chapters of this work then, represent that first study, culminating in a "manipulation theory" which is formulated in chapter four below. I then resumed the trail in order to apply this to John 21. However, I was interrupted by a lingering question among scholarship on this chapter; the Greek text uses five diminutives other scholars have deemed "faded," thus indicating the terms carry no semantic differences from their primitive lexical forms. However, without following this spur trail, I did not feel as though I could fully explore the vistas that the recognition motif held in the chapter. In a sense, this section constitutes the second study. Finally, I resumed the trek through to John 21 and the failed recognition there, applying what I had gleaned from the first two studies.

Readers of this work will no doubt come to the trailhead with differing agendas. If a reader uses this work to continue the discussion on trickster scenes in the Hebrew Bible, then chapters one through five will be most beneficial (and portions of the Literature Review in chapter two that address the Gospel of John may be easily omitted). Likewise, readers interested solely in work on Greek diminutives should by-pass the early chapters and pick up the walk partway through chapter six with the section titled "Faded Diminutives? . . . An Excursus." Finally, readers with intentions similar to mine, may wish to begin at the beginning and follow the entire journey as it unwinds through these side trails, culminating in these nineteen verses in John 21.

For me, the entire expedition has been a fruitful one. Through the application of Narrative Criticism, I have asked, "How would a reader, well acquainted with Genesis, understand recognition in John 21?" The journey has expanded my view of the horizon beyond Genesis and John, and thus refined my understanding of characters and characterization in the narratives found in both Testaments. It has sharpened my understanding of the plot found not only in John, but in similar plots in other places as well, such as the footpath of failed recognition in the Gospel of Mark.

The conclusion of this study, therefore, argues that in John 21, Jesus, much like characters in Genesis, actively withholds his identity in ironic counter-manipulation, mirroring Peter's earlier denials in John 18. The disciples' lack of recognition underscores their dullness, especially Peter's. Jesus' three questions to Peter continue the ironic counter-manipulation, paralleling Peter's earlier three denials. All this Jesus does to affect a turning in Peter. Finally, Jesus predicts that Peter will glorify God in his death, indicating his future turn toward ideal discipleship.

Ultimately, it is my hope that the path my readers and I take through this research ends not only with the gaining of academic knowledge, but that we will then apply internally what we glean from these stories of Jacob, Judah, Joseph, Peter, and Jesus. As we look within, we too may find a few manipulator tendencies as they did. May we each then continue our journey, and cry as Luther did, *Simul iustus et peccator*!

December 2015
Orlando, Florida

Acknowledgments

First, I thank God for the forgiving grace of Jesus Christ and for divine guidance during this work. Many times when I was about to give up, events changed in a strikingly timely and encouraging manner which I find quite difficult to explain simply by natural means. Thank you Father for your infinite goodness: *I do not deserve any of it.*

Next, I owe my immediate family—Patty, her mom Peggy, Rachel, JonLuc, William, and Nick—a massive debt of time and love. My wife Patty understands the sacrifice this has taken better than anyone. Countless times when I should have been home with them, my family would encourage me with texts, phone calls, etc., cheering me to push on. Nothing is sweeter than to be sitting in the office, begrudgingly plowing away on a dissertation chapter wondering if I "have what it takes," only to receive a text message from my daughter 700 miles away, plowing away on her own undergrad paper, but writing to me saying: "You've got this dad! You are my example!" How could I quit then?

To my parents Roy and Jeanette Lowdermilk: I love you and thank you for your many years of precious nurturing and guidance; you laid the foundation. To my now passed father-in-law Dr. Robert J. Terrey: Thank you for setting the standard.

To my good friend, Dr. Martin W. Mittelstadt: You are the one who pushed me to start the program. Thank you.

I wish to also express my deep gratitude to my advisors, the ever patient Dr. Maretha Jacobs of UNISA and Dr. Alan Culpepper of the McAfee School of Theology. Dr. Jacobs has answered countless emails and given tireless feedback on my chapters. As to Dr. Culpepper agreeing to be co-advisor, not least among those moments of divine guidance I refer to above is when I of all students, was granted to be instructed by one of the most respected Gospel of John scholars today—just because I asked. Thank you Alan. I hope you enjoy your time off . . . and that the fish always are biting.

Neither can I omit the late Dr. Richard Lemmer who began as my advisor before his untimely death. He was the encourager who forbade me to voice my self-doubt in my communications with him. I would have surely quit early on had it not been for his patient replies.

To those in my West Palm Beach circle I also owe gratitude. To Steve Thomas and Gerald Wright, my mentors and confessors I say thank you. To Nathan and Kathy Maxwell for constant tips and encouragement, thank you. To Randy Richards for telling me in May of 2009 regarding my first dissertation topic idea, "If I were on your committee . . . I wouldn't approve it!" Without his blunt kindness, I would have settled for less. Thank you Mark Kaprive and MaryAnn Searle for your flexibility as supervisors. Next to last, there is not a better interlibrary loan officer in the entire world than Nerolie Ceus. I so appreciate your cooperation in this project, along with your co-workers in the library at Palm Beach Atlantic University.

Finally, to two Sunday School classes at First Baptist Church of West Palm Beach, and First Baptist Church of Delray Beach: Thank you for hearing all of my strange ideas and readings of Genesis, the Gospels of Mark and John, and for the biblical community you have provided for us.

Abbreviations

ANF   Ante-Nicene Fathers
Apoc. Pet.   Apocalypse of Peter

Aristotle

Poet.   *Poetica*
Rhet.   *Rhetorica*

Aulus Gellius

Noct. att.   *Noctes atticae*

BD   Beloved Disciple

Cicero

De Or.   *De oratore*

Eusebius

Hist. Eccl. *Historia ecclesiastica*

ESV   English Standard Version
FE   Fourth Evangelist
FG   Fourth Gospel
Ign. *Smyrn.* Ignatius, *To the Smyrnaeans*

Josephus

Ant.	*Jewish Antiquities*
JSNT	*Journal for the Study of the New Testament*
JSOT	*Journal for the Study of the Old Testament*
Jub.	*Jubilees*
KTAV	KTAV Publishing House
NET	New English Translation

Pseudo-Philo

L.A.B	*Liber antiquitatum biblicarum*

Plutarch

Ag. Cleom.	*Agis et Cleomenes*
Ant.	*Antonius*
Comp. Ag. Cleom. cum	*Comparatio Agidis et Cleomenis cum*
Comp. Demetr. Ant.	*Comparatio Demetrii et Antonii*

Diog. Laert	Diogenes Laërtius

Quintilian

Inst.	*Institutio oratoria*

Rhet. Her.	*Rhetorica ad Herennium*

RRENAB	*Charte du Réseau de recherche en Narratologie et Bible*
SBL	Society of Biblical Literature
SPCK	Society for Promoting Christian Knowledge Publishing

Tertullian

Praescr.	*De praescriptione haereticorum*
Scorp.	*Scorpiace*

T. Levi	Testament of Levi
TDNT	*Theological Dictionary of the New Testament*
TDOT	*Theological Dictionary of the Old Testament*
WBC	Word Biblical Commentary

1

Introduction

*R*ecognition is a literary device that scholars have come to identify in a variety of literary genres, including ancient Hebrew narrative, Greco-Roman literature, and modern Western literature.[1] The purpose of this study is to gain a better understanding of recognition as it operates in John 21:1–19. In this final chapter of the Gospel of John, the disciples fish all night without results. In the morning, Jesus addresses them from the shoreline, yet the disciples do not *recognize* Jesus. After a miraculous catch of fish and a subsequent meal on the shore, Jesus thrice asks Peter about his love for him. After hearing three affirmative answers and instructing Peter to feed and tend his sheep, Jesus informs Peter of his future fate.

Recently in *Recognizing the Stranger: Recognition Scenes in the Gospel of John* (2008), Kasper Bro Larsen examined recognition scenes in the Gospel of John through the works of classical Greco-Roman literature, especially the *Odyssey*.[2] The following analysis will further an understanding of recognition by peering through the lens of Genesis to see how a first-century reader, well acquainted with that text, might interpret these nineteen verses in John.

Statement of Problem

To begin with, Aristotle addresses recognition, or ἀναγνώρισις, in his *Poetics*.[3] He presents a taxonomy of recognition and arranges different kinds of

---

1. Sternberg, *The Poetics of Biblical Narrative*, 177–78; Aristotle, *Poet.* 1452a. Even in Coptic texts, there is a very distinct recognition scene between Peter and Jesus in *The Acts of Peter and the Twelve Apostles*, found in the Nag Hammadi collection, Meyer, *The Nag Hammadi Scriptures*, 258, 364–65; Cave, *Recognitions*, 8.

2. Larsen, *Recognizing the Stranger*.

3. Aristotle, *Poet.* 1452a.

recognition or "discovery," from the least to the greatest kinds. The lowest kind requires a minimum amount of skill by the author. It is mere recognition by fabricated token, without other elements.[4] Tokens are objects that reveal the identity of the unrecognized. They may be traits one is born with, or marks attained over time, such as Odysseus's scar.[5] They may also be items, such as a boat, a letter, or even as Aristotle says, "the voice of the shuttle," which was a message the character Philomela weaves into fabric because her tongue had been removed.[6] Larsen states, "In Aristotle, the token is called σημεῖον (*Poet.* 1454b20; 1455a19), but this term seldom echoes in narrative or drama, where other designations dominate."[7] Larsen notes that tokens can also include: "scars . . . signet rings, footprints, pieces of cloth, locks of hair, necklaces, birthmarks, knives and swords, bands with inscriptions, cloaks, ornaments, toys, amulets, holy twigs, etc."[8] Terrance Cave's work reaffirms the token as an integral component of recognition scenes in Western texts since Aristotle: "We can now claim with greater emphasis that signs, marks or tokens are a distinguishing feature of recognition plots—their signature perhaps."[9] However, in his analysis of recognition, Aristotle states that scenes in which the discovery takes place by means of tokens are the "least artistic."[10] He especially dislikes "artificial tokens, like necklaces," as opposed to when the story produced a token that was "likely," in the normal course of events.[11] Stories in which the character makes the discovery due to memories or extrapolation, rather than by any token, evidence a greater level of artistry.[12]

Ultimately, for Aristotle, the most aesthetically pleasing forms of recognition scenes are those that occur in conjunction with *peripeteia*. These two distinct literary features, the discovery of someone's identity and the reversal of events contrasting with the character's previous fortune, combine to create a supremely pleasing moment in a complex plot:[13]

4. Aristotle, *Poet.* 1455a.
5. Aristotle, *Poet.* 1454b.
6. Aristotle, *Poet.* 1454b; Aristotle, *Aristotle in 23 Volumes*, 61n95.
7. Larsen, *Recognizing the Stranger*, 67.
8. Ibid., 68. Larsen points out that Jesus showing his scars to Thomas, "belongs to a long motif-tradition in ancient recognition literature . . . where bodily features like scars and wound marks . . . imply a dramatic story about threats to the observed one's somatic existence." Ibid., 67–68, 115–16.
9. Cave, *Recognitions*, 250.
10. Aristotle, *Poet.* 1454b; Aristotle, *Aristotle in 23 Volumes*, 59.
11. Aristotle, *Poet.* 1455a.
12. Ibid.
13. Aristotle, *Poet.* 1452a.

> A recognition (ἀναγνώρισις), as the name signifies, is a change from ignorance (ἀγνοίας) to knowledge, and so to either friendship or enmity in those determined to good fortune or misfortune. Recognition is most beautiful when it arises at the same time as reversal, as does the recognition in the *Oedipus*.[14]

Since Aristotle's time, scholars have repeatedly noted recognition scenes in literature, and Terrance Cave speaks of their ubiquitous nature.[15] Since recognition exists in so many genres, it has its rightful place as a building block of poetic structures. Therefore, on this basis, and for reasons stated below, we are not surprised to find instances of recognition in the Hebrew Bible.[16] Anthony Lambe notes recognition's fascinating role in the Joseph novella:

> The climax of the story, however, is constituted by the recognition scene or anagnorisis, which is followed by a peripeteia or reversal. Here occurs a transformation in Judah's character and behavior. Judah's ignorance and alienation are overcome in a moment of enlightenment and self-discovery that foreshadows his future role as spokesman in the Joseph story.[17]

In John 21:1–14, the reader is presented with the final recognition episode in the Gospel. Not only is this a scene of ἀναγνώρισις, but it is also one of reversal. Many scholars refer to this story and Jesus' three questions to Peter in the subsequent section as that disciple's restoration.[18] Larsen's monograph (based on his doctoral dissertation), is a fine analysis of such scenes from the perspective of Greco-Roman literature. Larsen's work hearkens back to the *Odyssey* and Aristotle's reference to Odysseus's scar as the "*locus classicus*" of the recognition scene in Greek literature.[19] Larsen makes a great contribution by examining Johannine recognition very closely, identifying "five moves: the meeting, cognitive resistance, the display of

---

14. Ibid.
15. Cave, *Recognitions: A Study in Poetics*, 10.
16. In using the phrase "Hebrew Bible," I am referring to the Old Testament, not specifically to the Hebrew or Masoretic Text. Since my methodological approach is to analyze Genesis narratologically from the vantage point of a first-century reader, I am not limiting my analysis to the Hebrew text. I will therefore note differences in the LXX when they are significant—as variations or alternate versions of the narratives in the Hebrew Bible.
17. Lambe, "Judah's Development," 57.
18. Pfitzner, "They Knew It Was the Lord," 68; Gaventa, "The Archive of Excess," 248–49; Keener, *The Gospel of John*, 2:1096.
19. Aristotle *Poet.* 1454b; Larsen, *Recognizing the Stranger*, 1.

the token, the moment of recognition and finally, the attendant reactions and physical (re)union."[20] He, moreover, sees recognition as a polarizing moment, dividing those who recognize from those who ultimately do not, because recognition "discloses the observers' true orientation toward things above."[21] Larsen hints at recognition's transformative power because "Johannine recognitions, unlike in some of the tragedies, are always euphoric, since they change apparent disadvantages into eternal life."[22]

Although the works of Larsen and others serve as critical pieces of the research puzzle, the Jewish canon should also be used to analyze ἀναγνώρισις in John 21. Roland Meynet argues that the Gospels are heavily dependent on the Hebrew Bible for their literary artistry. He has also shown that the awareness of this connection is nothing new to scholars.[23] The Fourth Evangelist (FE) repeatedly quotes, alludes to, or utilizes motifs from Genesis. Beginning with Jerome and leading up to 2012 with Maarten Menken's chapter "Genesis in John's Gospel and 1 John," a host of scholars have pointed out these allusions in the Fourth Gospel (FG).[24] There is, moreover, sometimes a lack of explanation of Jewish customs in the FG, indicating that the FE may have expected implied readers to bring some degree of awareness of the Hebrew Bible to their reading.[25] Connections to Genesis include the intertextuality between the prologues (Gen 1:1 and John 1:1), the reference to Jacob in the introduction of Nathanael (Gen 27:35 and John 1:47), the ascending and descending of angels on Jacob's ladder and the Son of Man (Gen 28:12 and John 1:51), the mention of Jacob in Shechem by the Samaritan woman (Gen 33:18–20 and John 4:12), the direct mention of Abraham (John 8:56), and the breathing on the disciples (Gen 2:7 and John 20:22).

Regarding the presence of recognition in the Hebrew Bible, Meir Sternberg suggests that the Jewish canon has been underappreciated as a possible origination point for this literary phenomenon:[26]

20. Ibid., 71. I will discuss Larsen's work more closely below.

21. Ibid., 219.

22. Ibid.

23. Meynet, *Rhetorical Analysis*, 173. See chapter 2, "Literature Review," below.

24. Menken, "Genesis in John's Gospel and 1 John," 83–98. See also Brooke, "4Q252 and the 153 Fish of John 21:11," 256; Culpepper, "Cognition in John," 259; Davis, "The Johannine Concept of Eternal Life as a Present Possession," 161–69; Dodd, *The Interpretation of the Fourth Gospel*, 349.

25. Note that the FE explains terms, such as ῥαββί in John 1:38, Γολγαθα in 19:17, and ραββουνι in 20:16, but not some feasts such as Passover or the Feast of Booths in 6:4; 7:2. Translating Hebrew terms but not explaining some Jewish feasts may indicate a Greek-speaking audience with Jewish awareness, such as proselytes or the Diaspora. See also Köstenberger, *A Theology of John's Gospel and Letters*, 132–37.

26. Larsen indicates his awareness of the recognition scene of Joseph and his

With surprisingly few exceptions, however, in each tale at least one character goes through a drama of discovery, complete with *anagnorisis* if not with a whole series of them, and none ends as unenlightened as he began. The passage from ignorance to knowledge, one of the great archetypes of literature, is another Hebraic innovation, for which the Greeks got all the credit.[27]

This last statement by Sternberg may be subject to debate, but he makes a good point. In Genesis, Pharaoh and Abimelech fail to recognize Sarah and Rebekah as the wives of Abraham and Isaac. Isaac fails to recognize Jacob posing as Esau. Jacob fails to recognize he has married Leah. Laban fails to recognize that Rachel has hidden his gods. Jacob wrongly recognizes the implications of Joseph's robe. Tamar forces Judah to recognize his own belongings. Finally, Joseph's brothers fail to recognize their lost brother as the vizier of Egypt. Recognition, including failed recognition, therefore, functions as a significant narrative mechanism in Genesis.

By focusing mostly on classical Greek literature to interpret Johannine recognition, previous analyses have not detected the role of deception and manipulation surrounding recognition.[28] Consequently, this leads to an understanding of recognition that does not delve deep enough into the nature of characters, their deceptive behaviors, and their reversals. Moments of biblical recognition often facilitate reversals. In this regard, Eric Auerbach writes: "Odysseus on his return is exactly the same as he was when he left Ithaca two decades earlier. But what a road, what a fate, lie between Jacob who cheated his father out of his blessing and the old man whose favorite son has been torn to pieces by a wild beast!"[29] Further, he concludes: "Humiliation and elevation go far deeper and far higher than in Homer, and they belong basically together. The poor beggar Odysseus is only masquerading, but Adam is really cast down, Jacob really a refugee, Joseph really in the pit and then a slave to be bought and sold. But their greatness, rising out of humiliation, is almost superhuman and an image of God's greatness."[30]

In Homer and other such classics, the *peripeteia* rarely brings a change in moral character. By analyzing Genesis, we will see that recognition often functions as a component of a process I shall call manipulation and

---

brothers. Larsen, *Recognizing the Stranger*, 2.

27. Sternberg, *The Poetics of Biblical Narrative*, 176.

28. Culpepper has initiated examinations of recognition in the Hebrew Bible, but an extended examination of recognition in Genesis has yet to be completed. See chapter 2, "Literature Review," below.

29. Auerbach, *Mimesis*, 17.

30. Ibid., 18.

counter-manipulation. Genesis contains several instances of characters misleading one another using varied shades of deception. These have been termed "trickster" episodes. I intend to reconfigure the trickster language used in scholarship to discuss these narratives in Genesis. In the chapter on manipulation theory below, I describe how the term "manipulation" lends theoretical flexibility to the description of these "trickster" behaviors in Genesis. I use the term "counter-manipulation" to describe what happens when another person manipulates a manipulator (trickster) by methods very similar to the original manipulation. Especially within counter-manipulation, moments of recognition mark a *peripeteia*, a sudden turn of events. When the reversal does occur in Genesis, the character sometimes transforms for the better. This transformation is not merely one of fortune, but is rather along ethical lines, in accordance with the values of the story world. Sometimes this change is only incremental, but the text marks that modification with devices such as speech, inner life, and actions. Understanding a theory of manipulation in Genesis will therefore be fruitful for understanding recognition, its effect on characters, and their reversals. This is the nature of recognition in Genesis and in John 21—it not only signifies a change in plot, but also a change within the characters.

Connections between Genesis and Johannine *Anagnorisis*

There are several connections between Genesis and the Fourth Gospel related to *anagnorisis* that are important to survey. First, Sternberg treats Hebrew *anagnorisis* in conjunction with his broad understanding of characters moving in varied states from "ignorance to knowledge."[31] While Sternberg's main concern is with characters' perspectives and points of view, some instances in Genesis of characters moving from ignorance to knowledge are clearly scenes of one character recognizing another character, as with Isaac recognizing that he has blessed Jacob and not Esau. However, other scenes involve a character's recognition of something with greater ramifications than merely the identity of another person. Judah finally realizes not only that the prostitute is Tamar but also that "She is more righteous than I" (Gen 38:26).[32] These characters learn the knowledge necessary for their corrected

---

31. Sternberg, *The Poetics of Biblical Narrative*, 176.

32. Regarding the suggestion that chapter 38 is an interpolation into the Joseph story rather than being a part of the unity of the narrative, see Ackerman, "Joseph, Judah, and Jacob," 103–4; Alter, *The Art of Biblical Narrative*, 3–11; Fentress-Williams, "Location, Location, Location," 20.1–8; Lambe, "Judah's Development," 53–54; Wenham,

role in the plot line of Genesis instead of following their own plans, often rooted in ignorance.[33] Though these scenes are not all *recognition scenes* in the sense of the recognition of a lost character, most do portray a movement from ignorance to knowledge, even if only in the recognition of a piece of information. Therefore, these recognition scenes are important to note in the analysis.

Jacob's recognition of Joseph's coat can be termed an *ignorance scene*, in that Jacob wrongly recognizes the *coat* of his son Joseph, because in fact, he is deceived and ignorant as to the meaning of the blood on the coat (Gen 37:32–33);[34] but Jacob does not recognize the identity of a person. The story of Judah and Tamar, however, fits both the narrower understanding of a recognition scene as well as Sternberg's definition, because in the end, Judah is deceived regarding the identity of the temple prostitute, the identity of the man (himself) by whom Tamar is impregnated, *but also deceives himself about his own morality and failure to fulfill family obligations* (38:25–26).[35] This will hold true of Peter as well in John 21. Sternberg ventures that recognition, ignorance, and plot all intertwine, and he notes that modern critics also see this connection: "No ignorance, no conflict; and no conflict, no plot."[36] In these narratives in Genesis, as well as the last chapter of the FG, the reader finds ignorance, recognition, conflict, and mechanisms of plot.

Second, "knowing" as a concept by itself is a connecting point between John and Genesis. As is discussed below, the patriarchs are constantly involved in scenes where someone's ignorance is highlighted, whether Isaac at the hands of Jacob in Genesis 27 or Judah and his brothers at the hands of Joseph in Genesis 42. When the story takes the reader to Egypt, the knowledge/ignorance theme is even more apparent. Alter notes that the primary biblical example of this contrast between knowing and ignorance is the story of Joseph circuitously confronting his brothers with their past, calling Joseph "the magisterial *knower* in this story."[37] Note that in the FG, Peter

---

Genesis 16–50, 363–65.

33. Sternberg, *The Poetics of Biblical Narrative*, 176. Regarding the "reader" and the issue of orality, ancient "readers" did not read individually in silence, but most were rather "listeners." A text "would typically have been read out from a scroll to some sort of assembled audience (many of whom would presumably not have been literate) rather than passed around to be read in our sense." Alter, *The Art of Biblical Narrative*, 90. The same was true in the FG. Since John is the primary text of examination, I will discuss orality and culture in chapter 6, "Applying a Manipulation Perspective to John 21:1–14."

34. Ibid., 4.

35. Ibid., 11.

36. Sternberg, *The Poetics of Biblical Narrative*, 173.

37. Alter, *The Art of Biblical Narrative*, 159; emphasis added.

says to Jesus, "Lord, you *know* everything" (John 21:17). Indeed, knowledge is a prominent theme in the FG to which this study shall return repeatedly.

This link will become more apparent as we explore each unit of text. Knowledge in Genesis and John then becomes a *fulcrum* of empowerment and disempowerment. Those most often connected with deception in Genesis realize the empowering and disempowering effects of knowledge, ignorance, deception, and recognition. Moreover, they attempt to use these for their own gain.[38] The same pattern becomes clear in the FG as Peter manipulates his accusers' lack of knowledge for his own gain in chapter 18.

Moreover, the theme of knowledge in the FG is more apparent when compared with the Synoptics. The term γινώσκω occurs 222 times in the New Testament.[39] Fifty-seven of these instances are in the FG. By comparison, the Synoptics total sixty, with Luke having the most—only twenty-eight.[40]

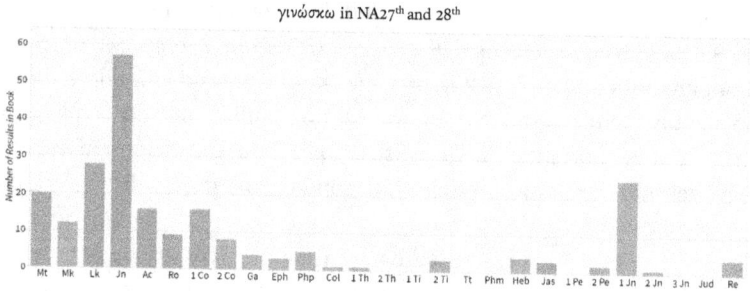

Thus the FG has twice the occurrences of γινώσκω as any one Synoptic Gospel. Likewise, οἶδα occurs 318 times in the New Testament. Eighty-four of those instances are in John, twenty-five are in Luke, twenty-four are in Matthew, and twenty-one are in Mark. With οἶδα then, the FG has three times the occurrences as any other canonical Gospel:

---

38. Similarly in 2 Bar. Lied, "Recognizing the Righteous Remnant?," 334.

39. These word counts were performed using *Logos Bible Software*. The texts used were the 27th and 28th editions of Aland et al., *The Greek New Testament*, and Logos Research Systems, *Septuaginta*.

40. γνωρίζω occurs twenty-five times in the NT, the Synoptics only having two occurrences in Luke, three in John and the most, six, are found in Ephesians. γνῶσις does not occur in the Fourth Gospel. ἐπιγινώσκω occurs forty-four times in the NT, six times in Matthew, four times in Mark, seven times in Luke, but does not occur at all in John. προγινώσκω occurs five times in the NT, and καταγινώσκω occurs only three times in the NT, but neither is found in the Gospels.

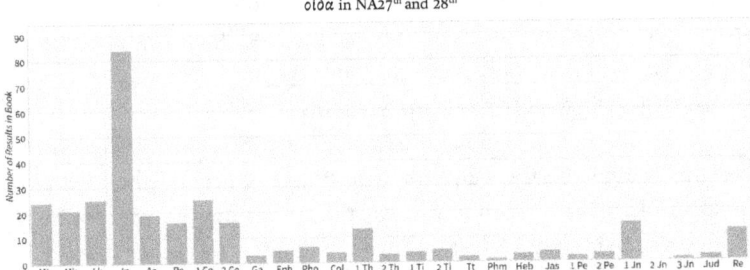

οἶδα in NA27th and 28th

"Knowing" is therefore a marked aspect not only of Genesis but also of the FG.

Third, the opening chapter of the FG establishes an interesting connection between *anagnorisis* and deception, as well as ignorance and knowledge. The character Nathanael first appears in the latter part of John 1:

> The next day Jesus decided to go to Galilee. He found Philip and said to him, "Follow me." Now Philip was from Bethsaida, the city of Andrew and Peter. Philip found Nathanael and said to him, "We have found him of whom Moses in the Law and also the prophets wrote, Jesus of Nazareth, the son of Joseph." Nathanael said to him, "Can anything good come out of Nazareth?" Philip said to him, "Come and see." Jesus saw Nathanael coming toward him and said of him, "Behold, an Israelite indeed, in whom there is no deceit!" (1:43–47).

Jesus makes a statement about Nathanael that some scholars consider an allusion to Genesis 27:35: "Your brother came deceitfully, and he has taken away your blessing."[41] In the LXX, the term "deceitfully" is translated μετὰ δόλου—with deceit. Jesus in John 1:47 states that Nathanael is one "ἐν ᾧ δόλος οὐκ ἔστιν." Moments later, in verse 51, Jesus again references the story of Jacob with a second allusion, namely, to the ladder of angels Jacob sees in

---

41. I am indebted to my doctoral co-advisor, Alan Culpepper, for first pointing this out to me. John Walvoord and Roy Zuck also note this with the short comment, "(*dolos*, 'deceitful') unlike Jacob." Walvoord et al., *The Bible Knowledge Commentary*, John 1:47. See also Beasley-Murray, *John*, 27; Bennema, *Encountering Jesus*, 66; Keener, *The Gospel of John*, 1:485–86; Trudinger, "An Israelite in Whom there is no Guile," 117–20. Psalm 32:2, which also uses *dolos* "deceit," in the LXX, may also be the target of the allusion, but in the Hebrew the passage shows no affinity to the name "Jacob." Koester argues, "The Evangelist expected the readers to catch the allusions to the Jacob story in order to make sense of the narrative." Koester, "Messianic Exegesis and the Call of Nathanael (John 1:45–51)," 23–26. But see also Schnackenburg, *The Gospel according to John*, 1:316.

his dream in Genesis 28:12.[42] Cornelis Bennema notes the significance of the first reference to Jacob: "If this allusion is intended, then Nathanael is *contrasted* to Jacob in that Nathanael represents the new Jacob or true Israel."[43] Paul Trudinger suggests the following reading: "Look, Israel without a trace of Jacob left in him."[44] Bennema, responding to Trudinger's insight, observes that Nathanael's identification of Jesus is significant: "Thus Nathanael responds to Jesus' revelation in the way the author desires, namely, he *perceives* Jesus' true identity."[45] Gerald Janzen also interprets Jesus' statement as Trudinger does, that Nathanael was "an 'Israel' in whom there is no 'Jacob.'"[46] In support of this, Janzen explains that there is significant attention given in the Hebrew Bible regarding deceitfulness between Israelites.[47] He concludes that the Hebrew text of Jeremiah 9:4 contains a play on Jacob's name and deceit (עָקוֹב יַעְקֹב), similar to Esau's statement in Genesis 27:36: "Jeremiah, by playing on the name, accounts (like Hos 12:3–6) for his own generation's behavior by referring to their ancestor Jacob."[48] This is important because it shows that the Jewish understanding of deceit was tied to the patriarch Jacob. Thus, Jesus sets the stage in the FG for themes related to deceit or guile. Below I will demonstrate that in much of Jacob's life, deceit intertwines also with the recurring theme of recognition.[49] In John 18, Peter will three times demonstrate his δόλος, lying about being a disciple of Jesus, and in John 21, he does not recognize Jesus.

The FE, therefore, alerts the reader to view coming material in light of these themes. Indeed this continues throughout the Gospel, as recognition occurs in the beginning (Nathanael and John the Baptist in John 1:34), middle (Martha in 11:27, who "is able to respond in faith to Jesus and recognize him for who he is") and end of the Gospel (the Beloved Disciple

---

42. This is well known, though the word "ladder" is not used. Keener, *The Gospel of John*, 1:489–91. "John seems to play upon an ambiguity caused by the masculine gender of the Heb. pronoun that stands for 'ladder.' As Jesus evokes the imagery of the entire Genesis scene, he himself becomes the place of God's revelation and dwelling (cf. John 1:14) as ancient Bethel had been." Mays, *Harper's Bible Commentary*, John 1:35–51.

43. Bennema, *Encountering Jesus*, 66–67; emphasis added.

44. Trudinger, "An Israelite in Whom There Is No Guile," 117.

45. Bennema, *Encountering Jesus*, 67; emphasis added. At this point Nathanael probably only *partially recognizes* Jesus' identity. The titles "Son of God" and "King of Israel" do not necessarily indicate Nathanael's complete recognition of Jesus' divinity. See ibid., 66–67; Koester, "The Death of Jesus and the Human Condition," 27.

46. Janzen, "How Can a Man be Born When He Is Old?," 334.

47. Ibid., 334n7.

48. Ibid.

49. Trudinger, "An Israelite in Whom There Is No Guile," 117.

[BD] and, finally, Peter).[50] As Bennema points out, the *ideal* is one who *perceives* who Jesus is. By referring to Nathanael as one in whom there is no guile, no deception, Jesus appeals to the pattern conversely—Nathanael is the opposite of Jacob, especially the early Jacob, who was involved in multiple scenes of deception and recognition. Yet reading on, one finds that the next words from the mouth of Nathanael indicate a connection with recognition as well: "Rabbi, you are the Son of God! You are the King of Israel!" Nathanael is able to recognize Jesus, at least by titles. These titles imply recognition of Jesus as Messiah, but they do not imply that those who used them fully understood Jesus and his kingdom. Acts 1:6 implies that the disciples, even after the resurrection, were looking for an earthly Messiah and an earthly kingdom. Qumran literature also suggests that ancient Jewish messianic expectations may not have included divinity.[51] We find an example of this in 4Q246, in the text referred to as *The Son of God*, where the Messiah is spoken of in nationalistic tones, but the text does not imply deity. The "Great God" will assist the "son of God" as he makes war, but the idea of a divine Messiah is not explicit.[52] Other scrolls indicate a "warlike" and "nationalist king figure" as well.[53] Nevertheless, even if he does not understand Jesus fully, Nathanael has made at least a partial recognition of him and this furthers the connection between deception, ignorance, and recognition in Genesis and the *anagnorisis* theme in John.

I have now explained a rationale for using the Hebrew Bible, specifically Genesis, as a lens for examining recognition in John. Additionally, a

50. Bennema, *Encountering Jesus*, 67, 147.

51. The divinity of the Johannine Jesus is indicated by phrases such as "And the word was God," (John 1:1) and "Truly, truly, I say to you, before Abraham was, I am" (John 8:58).

52. 4Q246 II 1, 7–8; Eisenman and Wise, *The Dead Sea Scrolls Uncovered*, 70–71. See also Painter, *John: Witness and Theologian*, 12, who asserts that the FG reinterprets the role of the Messiah.

53. But see Bauckham, *The Testimony of the Beloved Disciple*, 125–36. *The War Scroll*, for instance, presents such a Messiah. See Eisenman and Wise, *The Dead Sea Scrolls Uncovered*, 69. Although I would not argue that that the FG exhibits a direct literary dependence on Qumran, the Dead Sea Scrolls give us an indication of the ancient Jewish cultural milieu. Comparisons, therefore, are profitable. Price, "Light from Qumran upon some Aspects of Johannine Theology," 10–11. See also Thomas, "Meaning of the Terms Life and Death," 200; Coetzee, "Life (Eternal Life) in St John's Writings and the Qumran Scrolls," 48; Charlesworth, "Qumran, John and the Odes of Solomon," 107–36; Charlesworth, *John and the Dead Sea Scrolls*; Charlesworth, "A Critical Comparison of the Dualism in 1QS 3:13–4:26 and the 'Dualism' Contained in the Gospel of John," 76–106. Painter also explains: "Even those who believed in Jesus misunderstood him in terms of expectations within Judaism. Clarification always occurs in the context of Jewish misunderstanding. Thus 'Christ' (Messiah) and 'Son of God' are reinterpreted in the Gospel." Painter, *John: Witness and Theologian*, 12.

cursory reading of John and Genesis yields several parallels between Jesus and Joseph, as well as between Peter and Judah. However, I should make clear that I am not suggesting that in John 21 the FE intended to allude to Joseph and Genesis 41–45. The rationale here is that literary parallels exist, intended or not.[54] These parallels, along with the intertextuality indicated above, justify a theoretical comparison of the two texts.

In Genesis 41:55, Pharaoh says to the Egyptians: καὶ ὃ ἐὰν εἴπῃ ὑμῖν, ποιήσατε, "*whatever he says to you do it*" (LXX). In John 2:5, at the miracle at Cana (possibly also a scene of recognition, since the disciples begin to believe in Jesus there), one finds nearly the same command: ὅ τι ἂν λέγῃ ὑμῖν, ποιήσατε.[55] Another parallel is that in both Genesis 41–45 and John 21:1–19, there is an initial lack of food or sustenance. Menken has recently argued that the allusion implies that "faithfully carrying out the commands of Joseph and Jesus leads to the removal of a lack of food or drink, while Joseph and Jesus differ in that the former brings salvation by wise government and the latter by performing a miracle."[56] Both Jesus and Joseph had experienced some type of denial or betrayal by a central character. This character was also a part of a group that had been slow to recognize the supplier of food (Judah and his brothers, Gen 37:26; 44:3–45:3; Peter and his companions, John 21:4, 7 and 12).[57] Both Peter and Judah demonstrate a noticeable delay in grieving in situations where a reader might expect it. Judah does not grieve when a brother or father would be expected to mourn (Judah neither grieves over the loss of Joseph, contrasted with Reuben, Gen 37:29, nor over the loss of his own sons in Gen 38.);[58] and of the four Gospels, only the FG ominously lacks the record of Peter's grief at his denial (John 18:27).[59] Moreover, for both characters, full and complete grief is only indicated (or hinted at in the case of Joseph's brothers) *after* they *recognize* who is supplying the life-giving sustenance in the story (John 21:7, 12, 17;

---

54. See the diagram of the "spectrum of intertextual reading influence" in chapter 6, "Applying a Manipulation Perspective to John 21: 1–14," below.

55. Culpepper, "Cognition in John," 252. Menken notes this allusion. Menken, "Genesis in John's Gospel and 1 John," 90.

56. Ibid., 90.

57. Lambe, "Judah's Development," 57. "And of course down to Pascal at least, the Christian tradition has read Joseph as a prefiguration of Christ himself." Boitani, *The Bible and Its Rewritings*, 33.

58. Lambe, "Judah's Development: The Pattern of Departure-Transition-Return," 55–56.

59. Though the Synoptics all record Peter's grief at the point of the realization of denial (Matt 26:75; Mark 14:72; Luke 22:62), the FE may have intentionally delayed this for literary purposes. See chapter 7, "One Little Sheep Becomes a Shepherd: John 21: 15–19," below.

Gen 45:3). Both groups, the seven disciples and the eleven brothers, resist speaking to Jesus and Joseph respectively in the awkwardness of the failed recognition.[60] Both Peter and Judah begin by being assertive and impulsive (John 13:37–38, 18:10; Gen 37:26–27; 38:16), and move toward relinquishing control of their own self-preservation (John 21:19; Gen 44:33).[61]

Finally, Joseph *actively chooses* to make himself unrecognizable to his brothers and *chooses* when to reveal himself (Gen 42:7; 45:1–3).[62] This parallels V.C. Pfitzner's argument that the lack of recognition in John 21 was due to Jesus' own delay in manifesting himself to them.[63] Thus, the question becomes, can the text adequately demonstrate that Jesus actively *chose* to disguise himself? If so, what was his purpose? What is the relation between active withholding of recognition and a failed recognition? Does a failed recognition *emphasize* dullness on the part of Joseph's brothers and Jesus' disciples? Are they out of step with where they should be in relation to Joseph and Jesus? Does their ultimate recognition force the *peripeteia* and begin their transformation of moral character? Interesting parallels do exist between Jesus and Joseph, as well as Peter and Judah. Therefore, an examination of recognition in Genesis can elucidate Johannine recognition, especially in this episode of the "miraculous draught of fish."

Scope

Since recognition in this study is regarded as a component of manipulation narratives, I will focus primarily on a number of manipulation narratives in Genesis, beginning with Jacob's deception of Isaac and Esau in chapter 27, continuing through the lives of Jacob, his sons—especially Judah, and ending with Joseph in Egypt.[64] In Genesis, these narratives culminate in the recognition between Joseph and his brothers in Egypt (Gen 41:38–45:28). Therefore, the analysis of Genesis grows toward that culminating scene. As an apex at the end of a series of recognition scenes in the Genesis saga, the reunion of Joseph and his brothers will serve as a lens through which to view the culminating recognition scene in John 21.

---

60. Judah does demonstrate some semblance of grief before he knows who Joseph is in Gen 44:16–34, but the text hints at a greater level of grief in 45:3–5, when Joseph entreats them not to grieve.

61. Ibid., 59.

62. Ibid., 61.

63. Pfitzner, "They Knew It Was the Lord," 72.

64. See chapter 4, "A Theory of Manipulation and Recognition," below.

In the FG, I limit the study mainly to the role of recognition in John 21:1–19, as opposed to pursuing other items, such as the question of the symbolic nature of 153 fish, the validity of John 21 as epilogue versus appendix, etc., on which a vast quantity of work already exists. Other than summarizing research on these issues, this study will not address them.

The Design of the Research

In order to examine John 21 through the lens of Genesis this study will proceed along the following steps:

After dealing with the literature review and methodology in chapters 2 and 3, I present a theory of manipulation and *anagnorisis* in chapter 4. Scholarship has yet to treat these two literary phenomena together in a theoretical manner. I argue that manipulation and *anagnorisis* function interdependently, because lying, deception, and other forms of manipulation create a lack of recognition. This lack of recognition comprises one character's ignorance of another's identity or some other truth that is important to the scene. Thus, these two ideas must be treated together in a theoretical fashion.

I explore this in more detail in chapter 4, but at this stage, it is sufficient to say that recognition is often intricately associated with the "trickster" motif. In the act of concealing their identity, "tricksters" manipulate others, often deceptively, in order to achieve a desired outcome.[65] I begin chapter 5 by explaining the rationale for the selection of the units examined in this study and briefly examine research on the trickster motif. Understanding what other scholars have said will broaden our understanding as we treat manipulation alongside recognition.[66] Space, however, will not permit me to address all the manipulation episodes in Genesis (beginning with the serpent's lying and the recognition in chapter 3).[67] Continuing in chapter 5, I delineate a set of themes that span across manipulation narratives in Genesis. In working through the Genesis stories, I have found certain patterns. These are not the component parts or "kernels" identified below in chapter 4 in the taxonomy of any given manipulation narrative, but rather themes that extend across the many manipulation narratives. Therefore, it is important to explain each theme in order to demonstrate how it relates to the use of recognition and manipulation in these stories. I will then use the themes to analyze and seek further understanding of manipulation and

---

65. Such as Gen 27:33, which reads, "And he did not recognize him, because his hands were hairy like his brother Esau's hands. So he blessed him."

66. Nicholas, *The Trickster Revisited*.

67. Mleynek, *Knowledge and Mortality*, 5, 12; Williams, *Deception in Genesis*, 14, 22.

recognition in John 21:1–19. Tracing these patterns through John 21 will bring to light certain nuances regarding Johannine recognition and will highlight the journey of Peter's character as it evolves in that chapter. I argue that Jesus' manipulation of Peter, by delaying the disciples' recognition of him, is a response to Peter's manipulation of his accusers in chapter 18. Jesus' manipulation of Peter also contributes to Peter's transformation. This transformation is a positive development according to the values set forth in the Gospel of John—values centered around Jesus and the recognition of him: belief versus unbelief, following versus not following, and knowing versus ignorance. Peter ultimately recognizes Jesus and that he, not Peter, knows all things. Finally, I will summarize the findings for a fresh reading of John 21:1–19.

Summary

Recognition is a topic that has attracted growing attention in Johannine scholarship over the last three decades. Research heretofore has examined Johannine recognition from a Greco-Roman perspective. An examination from a Hebrew perspective can further that understanding. Genesis stands on valid intertextual grounds for increasing an understanding of the FG, especially since it is situated in a Jewish-Christian milieu. Finally, there are thought provoking parallels between key characters in the final recognition scenes in Genesis and the Gospel of John. These reasons warrant a comparison between the recognition scenes in Genesis and recognition in John 21.

2

Literature Review

The beginning of modern Johannine scholarship may be marked around 1925, with the early works of Rudolf Bultmann and Walter Bauer.[1] Indeed, in the twentieth century alone, the study of the Gospel of John has journeyed through many stages. From early debates over dating, authorship, and Hellenistic or Jewish origins, to recent arguments over whether this Gospel is anti-Semitic, the FG has had its fair share of scholarly attention.[2] On the one hand, Wayne Meeks argues for a disjointed text in John that contains "glaringly bad transitions between episodes at many points;"[3] on the other hand, Jeffrey Staley complains that the historical methods of Western scholars have "vivisected the biblical text and sucked out its readerly impulse."[4] Sandra Schneiders and others ask if the text is "hopelessly antiwoman," or if it still has "liberating potential."[5] Yet each contribution probes deeply the Johannine text, suggesting new ways for understanding it and often difficult new questions as well.[6] Nevertheless, until the last two decades, scholarship had focused very little on Johannine recognition scenes as a literary phenomenon.[7]

---

1. Bauer, *Das Johannesevangelium*; Bultmann, "Die Bedeutung der Neuerschlossenen Mandäischen und Manichäischen Quellen," 100–146; Ashton, *The Interpretation of John*, 8–9.

2. Boomershine, "The Medium and Message,", 118; Culpepper, "The Gospel of John as a Document of Faith,"; Kelber, "Metaphysics and Marginality in John," 60; Meeks, "The Man from Heaven," 170, 174–75; Sloyan, *What Are They Saying about John?*, 8, 11.

3. Meeks, "The Man from Heaven," 172.

4. Staley, "Reading Myself, Reading the Text," 61.

5. Schneiders, "The Encounter of the Easter Jesus with Mary Magdalene," 239–41.

6. For an examination of Johannine scholarship in general, see Ashton, *The Interpretation of John*; Sloyan, *What are they Saying about John?*

7. Larsen, *Recognizing the Stranger*, 6.

The following pages will examine recent scholarship on four main issues pertinent to this dissertation. The first section looks at John 21, and its relationship to the first twenty chapters. Second is a discussion of the role of Peter and the FG's characterization of him. The third section focuses on research related to Johannine *anagnorisis*, which has come to the fore in the last few decades. Finally, since this study will examine Johannine *anagnorisis* through the lens of Genesis recognition, this chapter concludes with the so-called Genesis "trickster," or as I shall term it, "manipulation" material as it relates to recognition.

John 21 in Relation to John 1–20

John 21 brings its own critical issues to the table. Scholars have asked whether it extends and completes John 1–20 or represents extraneous material and, if so, how one is to treat this in relation to the first twenty chapters. Since my method, laid out in the following chapter, includes reading the Gospel as a coherent whole from chapter 1 through chapter 21, I am surveying the scholarly treatment of this issue as it has arisen in the last century, and have therefore chosen scholars who have made substantial contributions, representative of specific trends in research.

The list of those who have questioned the role of chapter 21 in the Gospel is quite long.[8] As early as the turn of the twentieth century, F. R. M. Hitchcock was cautious about the role of chapter 21: "Its contents are, as Aristotle would say, 'outside the tragedy.'"[9] Bultmann was clear about his position: "The only question is from whom this postscript was derived. That the Evangelist himself added it ... is extraordinarily improbable."[10] Bultmann reasoned that the writing and terminology were too dissimilar from the first twenty chapters.[11] He was confident that someone added it after the original author's death and that this final chapter itself was not cohesive. It contained material from disparate sources.[12]

By the time Raymond Brown published the second installment of his two-volume commentary, the consensus was that chapter 21 was indeed an addition. Brown believed that most scholars did not view the chapter as original.[13] Yet he also asserted that it was better united to the first twenty

---

8. Minear, "The Original Functions of John 21," 85.
9. Hitchcock, "Is the Fourth Gospel a Drama?," 316.
10. Bultmann, *The Gospel of John*, 700.
11. Ibid., 700–701.
12. Ibid., 702, 704.
13. Brown, *The Gospel according to John (XIII–XXI)*, 1078.

chapters than the longer ending of Mark's Gospel was to its main body, and that scholars should consider John 21 as at least a part of the Johannine *writings*, even if from a redactor. Notwithstanding, Brown noted that even the renowned scholar F.C. Baur changed his opinion on the chapter, eventually accepting it as from the same hand as the rest of the work.[14]

Recently, the number of scholars who see chapter 21 as functioning within the entire Gospel is increasing. Some are changing their opinion and argue for interpreting the whole Gospel with chapter 21, regardless of the prehistory of either.[15] Carsten Claussen argues that according to literary theory, opening and closing portions of a text guide the interpretive process, and therefore John 21 is very important to understanding the rest of the text.[16] Claussen also continues to stress that there is no existing proof that the FG ever circulated without this last chapter.[17] Readers who approach the FG as a unity must therefore observe that the chapter stands in a "dialectical relationship" to the first twenty chapters.[18] The final chapter assists the reader in understanding the earlier portions of the Gospel. This is important even if chapter 21 was a later addition that readers utilized to make their interpretive decisions. Acknowledging the argument that a redactor added it at a later stage, Jan van der Watt argues that it is nevertheless an intriguing and important addition to the Gospel.[19]

This movement to include the last chapter of John in interpretive approaches has continued to grow for some years. In 1974 Stephen Smalley conceded, "On the surface, it seems difficult to maintain the view that John xxi was an original and intended part of John's Gospel."[20] He then went on to explain that this surface impression was not his position.[21] Smalley's reasoning was that intratextual connections between chapters 1–20 and chapter 21 were simply too strong to ignore.[22] Additionally, the theology of the Gospel

---

14. Ibid., 1078–80. Brown appears to base his reasons on Bultmann's list. Bultmann, *The Gospel of John*, 700–704.

15. Claussen, "The Role of John 21," 57. See also Fortna, "Diachronic/Synchronic," 396–97, who asks, "Can we after all make our reading dependent on a prior understanding of how the text arose?"

16. Claussen, "The Role of John 21," 58.

17. Ibid., 59.

18. Ibid.

19. Watt, *An Introduction to the Johannine Gospel and Letters*, 20.

20. Smalley, "The Sign in John XXI," 275.

21. Ibid., 276.

22. Ibid., 277.

"reaches its climax" in chapter 21 and connects the epilogue to the prologue and body by a pattern of "statement, sign and witness."[23]

Paul Minear is another scholar who over two decades ago began changing his position.[24] He reminds scholars that there is no evidence to suggest that the FG existed without this chapter. He also argues that there are not enough grammatical differences to warrant a "separate origin."[25] He posits that 20:30–31 was intended as a conclusion to the Thomas narrative, rather than to the Gospel as a whole. Additionally, he notes the resumptive use of "Simon Peter" in chapter 21, a name that was first used in chapter 1, and one that is present in chapter 21 to indicate fulfillment of the predictions Jesus made about Peter and himself in chapters 13 and 14.[26] Finally, Minear directs us to the recommencement in chapter 21 of the recognition motif that began with Jesus and Nathanael in chapter 1, and the resonance with themes of boats, feeding, and fish found in chapter 6.[27]

Lars Hartman also connects chapter 21 to the rest of the Gospel by using structural and linguistic techniques. He argues that the literary context unites chapters 20 and 21 by the opening words of 21: "after these things."[28] Hartman describes "recurring concepts and motifs" with his term "isotopies," and identifies several continued themes established earlier in the Gospel. Among these are food, love, shepherding, "the leadership of Peter," and "the BD's intimacy with the Lord."[29] He, like Minear, also identifies connections between chapter 21 and chapters 13 and 18.[30]

Pfitzner believes chapter 21, as well as the opening eighteen verses of the FG, were added in the revision process, but before "publication": "There cannot be the slightest suggestion that the gospel ever appeared in any form but that in which it has been passed down to us. It is generally accepted by scholars that both the Prologue (John 1:1–18) and the Epilogue (21:1–25) are editorial additions appended to John's Gospel before its final 'publication.'"[31] However, even with this, Pfitzner is cautious: "And if there are any redactional additions to the gospel, they come from one who knew

---

23. Ibid., 280.

24. Minear, "The Original Functions of John 21," 85.

25. Ibid., 86. Brown notes that there is a fifth or sixth century Syriac manuscript without chapter 21, but it appears to have lost its final pages. It ends abruptly, even before concluding chapter 20. Brown, *The Gospel according to John (XIII–XXI)*, 1077.

26. Minear, "The Original Functions of John 21," 92–93.

27. Ibid., 96.

28. Hartman, "An Attempt at a Text-Centered Exegesis of John 21," 30.

29. Ibid., 33.

30. Ibid., 38.

31. Pfitzner, "They Knew It Was the Lord," 64.

perfectly the mind of the master who originally witnessed in this gospel, and who conceived its theological structure and message."[32] Pfitzner also provides a list of thirteen distinctive Johannine features, one of which is "the motif of misunderstanding."[33]

Although Schneiders argues for a complex Johannine composition history, she also believes that chapter 21 was intended by the Johannine circle to move the readers from those who "see and believe" to those who "believe without having seen."[34] She holds that "chapter 21 is an integral part of the Gospel in fundamental theological continuity with chapters 1–20."[35] In her opinion, 20:30–31 closes out the pre-resurrection story of Jesus and serves as, "the conclusion of the account of what happened during the life and paschal mystery of Jesus."[36] Chapter 21 is forward-looking and serves as a treatise for the ones whose choices were belief or no belief, though not seeing. Thomas (John 20:29), then, is "the last of the seers."[37] She concludes that the miraculous catch "is neither an afterthought nor a correction but a symbolic presentation of the life of the church in the time after the Resurrection."[38]

Fernando Segovia also exemplifies the type of scholar who, regardless of the text's composition history, interprets the FG from an approach inclusive of the last chapter and is, "not at all interested in diachronic concerns."[39] He argues that 20:30–21:25 is a "farewell type-scene" after the manner of ancient biography, which includes a farewell speech in 21:15–23.[40]

In a 1992 article, John Breck asked whether John 21 was an appendix, epilogue or conclusion and answered by saying that it was indeed the conclusion of the FG.[41] Breck has not been satisfied with arguments that the author of chapter 21 used similar themes and style. He establishes his argument by making several proposals with regard to chiasm in the FG. Chiefly, he argues that the FE set the entire Gospel in one large chiasm. Sections of chapter one function in parallel to sections of chapters 20 and 21. Specifi-

---

32. Ibid., 74.
33. Ibid., 68.
34. Schneiders, "John 21:1–14," 70.
35. Ibid., 70.
36. Ibid., 21.
37. Ibid., 73–74.
38. Ibid., 75.
39. Segovia, "The Final Farewell of Jesus," 167.
40. Ibid., 169–70, 186–87. Segovia is critical of the "reception and application in history" of the shepherding metaphor and cautions against its use as a tool of "oppression" by the "colonizing and missionary church." Ibid., 187.
41. Breck, "John 21" 28.

cally, the verses in 20:24 through 21:14 are set in parallel to 1:43–49, where Jesus calls the disciples at Galilee, including Nathanael, who appears in the entire New Testament only in these two chapters.[42] Nathanael's confession parallels Thomas' confession.[43] Breck also believes this chapter complements themes that the FE established earlier.[44] "Following" is a theme "central to the Gospel" which reaches resolution in the final verses, particularly in the double "follow me" statements to Peter (John 21:19, 22).[45] Likewise, the rivalry between the BD and Peter is "left hanging, begging for a conclusion" if one stops at chapter 20.[46] In particular, the race to the tomb is a scene that "cries out for a conclusion."[47] The recognition by the BD in 21:7, and the subsequent affirmation of his "eyewitness" perspective in 21:24, forms that conclusion.[48]

Richard Bauckham doubts that an element such as style alone was sufficient to establish chapter 21 as original and proposed some elaborate Johannine arrangements of his own.[49] He notes the parallel statements in 20:30 and 21:25, but with a slight variation. While the former speaks of "'many other *signs*' that 'Jesus did,'" the latter reads "'many other *things* that Jesus did,'" and the slight difference between the two shows an intentional demarcation between the summary of Jesus' signs from the end of the entire Gospel.[50] Bauckham goes on to draw on Maarten Menken's relatively unknown dissertation of 1985 regarding numerical devices in the FG and argued for the inclusion of chapter 21 based on "numerical patterning" using gematria and the number of syllables or words in a given section.[51] Though Bauckham's argument is quite detailed, this statement perhaps is the simplest explanation of it: "John's Gospel does not have two endings, but a two-stage ending, the two parts of which (20:30–31 and 21:24–25) frame an epilogue (21:1–23). The numerical data help to make this clear.

---

42. Ibid., 37–38. An obvious limitation to this argument is that the section in chapter 1 is only nine verses, whereas the suggested paralleled section in chapters 20–21 is twenty-three verses long.

43. Ibid., 37.

44. Ibid., 39.

45. Ibid., 43.

46. Ibid., 49.

47. Ibid., 46. But this works two ways. Crying out for a conclusion certainly could motivate a later editor to add such a conclusion if the abrupt ending was the last words of a manuscript, as in, e.g., Mark 16:8.

48. Ibid., 45–46.

49. Bauckham, *The Testimony of the Beloved Disciple*, 272–73.

50. Ibid., 274; emphasis added.

51. Ibid., 275; Menken, *Numerical Literary Techniques in John*.

The sections 20:30–31 and 21:24–25 both consist of forty-three words. We have already noticed that the prologue to the Gospel (1:1–18) consists of 496 syllables. The epilogue shows its correspondence to the prologue in that it consists of 496 *words*."[52] Bauckham lists other phenomena of gematria, including the significance of the 153 fish and that "John" was the hidden name of the BD.[53] Regardless of whether scholars decide that this numerical encoding is legitimate, Bauckham is just one of many scholars who of late has championed the inclusion of chapter 21 into the FG.[54]

Many others are in this camp, yet the debate is far from closed. Respected scholars still question the compositional history of the FG and propose that an editor added chapter 21 at a later stage.[55] Larsen, whose excellent work gave rise to this dissertation, sees chapter 21 as a "secondary postscript added to the Gospel's original ending in 20:31."[56] Nor do all narrative scholars regard chapter 21 as included in the original edition of the Gospel.[57] Paul Anderson has recently proposed a "Two-Edition theory of composition," which involves the later addition of chapter 21.[58]

Although the objective of this dissertation is not to advance an argument for the original inclusion of chapter 21, current trends in research do clearly support a *method of interpretation* that considers the last chapter of the FG as part of a literary unit with the first twenty, and this study reads the text that way.[59]

---

52. Bauckham, *The Testimony of the Beloved Disciple*, 277; emphasis Bauckham.

53. Ibid., 278–82. See also Menken, *Numerical Literary Techniques in John*, 21–22.

54. See the review by Brouwer, "The Testimony of the Beloved Disciple," 399, who, though otherwise highly laudatory of Bauckham's work, says of the final chapter on numerical patterns: "[T]he whole enterprise appears to be a wild house of fantasy where all who know live, and all who do not, cannot." See also Beasley-Murray, *John*, 403, for a generally negative position on gematria.

55. But see also Köstenberger, *A Theology of John's Gospel and Letters*, 147. Culpepper moderates the position he took in *Anatomy of the Fourth Gospel*, 96, and moves toward viewing the FG as "a literary unity, regardless of what its compositional history may have been." Culpepper, "Designs for the Church in the Imagery of John 21:1–14," 369.

56. Larsen, *Recognizing the Stranger*, 211.

57. Spencer, "Narrative Echoes in John 21," 64.

58. Anderson, *The Riddles of the Fourth Gospel*, 69–70, 143–44. See also Waetjen, *The Gospel of the Beloved Disciple*, 8; and Collins, *These Things Have Been Written*, 38.

59. See also Gaventa, "The Archive of Excess," 248–49.

The Treatment of Peter in the FG

The way that scholars have understood Peter in the Gospel of John is also important to this study. Researchers' positions on Peter tend to fall into two groups, according to their understanding of the FE's characterization of him and his portrayal as compared with the BD. What follows is by no means an exhaustive treatment but rather highlights important early scholarship and some notable recent work on this issue.

The first group includes scholars such as Graydon Snyder, and tends toward anti-Petrinism.[60] Arthur Maynard also argues that the FG is very anti-Petrine.[61] He interprets the portrayal of Peter in John 21 as "very different," considering the section an appendix designed to "reconcile the Synoptic tradition of Peter's pre-eminence with the Johannine stress on the Beloved Disciple."[62] Maynard may in fact put forth one of the strongest pro-Beloved Disciple/anti-Petrine positions.[63] Regarding the narrative unit in chapter 19 where Mary is passed to the BD he states: "[I]t seems to say clearly that the Beloved Disciple is the earthly successor to Jesus."[64] Thus, scholars also offer varied interpretations of the BD's relationship to Peter and of whether or not the FE portrays these two figures in some type of rivalry.[65]

Some scholars are difficult to categorize squarely in either group. Bultmann sees in the evangelist's portrayal of Peter and the BD, evidence of tensions within the early church, and surmises a rivalry between "Gentile Christendom" and "Jewish Christendom."[66] This is why this suspected "rivalry" between Peter and the BD is still important. Following Bultmann, scholars often contend that these two characters represent competing early

---

60. Snyder, "John 13:16 and the Anti-Petrinism of the Johannine Tradition," 5.

61. So much so that at one time, he "assumed that this was one of the few agreed upon conclusions of Fourth Gospel Research." Maynard, "The Role of Peter in the Fourth Gospel," 531, 542.

62. Ibid., 544. See also Drogue who concludes that Peter in the FG "is a man who has come dangerously close to being placed beyond the Johannine pale." Droge, "The Status of Peter in the Fourth Gospel," 311.

63. But see also Snyder, "John 13:16 and the Anti-Petrinism of the Johannine Tradition," 5–15.

64. Maynard, "The Role of Peter in the Fourth Gospel," 539. Earlier Maynard reasoned that Peter "therefore has no claim to leadership in the later church." Ibid., 537.

65. Blaine, *Peter in the Gospel of John*, 7. See also Quast, *Peter and the Beloved Disciple*, 8, 12.

66. Bultmann, *The Gospel of John*, 484. Bultmann was not the first to propose that Peter and the BD symbolized certain groups. Brown notes that Gregory the Great also detected symbolism, but believed the BD stood for "the Synagogue," and Peter stood for "the Church." Brown, *The Gospel according to John (I–XII)*, xciv.

Christian traditions or communities.[67] In Bultmann's view, the BD is an "ideal figure" rather than a historical one and the FE uses the BD to symbolize Gentile Christianity, whereas Peter symbolizes Jewish Christians. The tension between these two signifies the movement of Christendom away from Judaism into Christendom's own religious identity:

> The self-awareness of this Christendom, emancipated from the ties of Judaism, shows itself in two scenes 13.21–30 and 20.2–10, where the beloved disciple appears beside Peter, the representative of Jewish Christendom. It is he and not Peter who reclines in Jesus' bosom, and can mediate Jesus' thought. And the relation between Jewish and Gentile Christendom is portrayed in characteristic fashion in 20.2–10, where each in his own way, by using the term in two senses, can claim to be "in front of" the other.[68]

Bultmann's position is an example of how a scholar's view of John 21 can often play a role in one's view of Peter.[69] As noted, for Bultmann chapter 21 is a "redactional appendix" in which the BD, different than in the first twenty chapters, "stands for a particular historical figure, clearly an authoritative one for the circle which edits the Gospel and one whose authority is placed side by side with that of Peter."[70] Despite his take on chapter 21 as an appendix, one might not characterize Bultmann's position on the first twenty chapters as completely anti-Petrine. He sees the footrace at the end of the FG as a reconciling of the two different yet equal roles of these figures and the communities they represent within the early church, without giving "precedence of the former over the latter."[71]

Another scholar who is difficult to categorize is Brown. Brown reminds us that there are indeed problematic passages in the FG regarding Peter that scholars cannot avoid. The FE is the only Gospel writer who identifies Peter as the disciple with the sword at Jesus' arrest.[72] Only in this Gospel is Peter told he cannot follow Jesus now, but afterward he will follow

---

67. See the discussion of Brown and Quast below.

68. Bultmann, *The Gospel of John*, 484–85. Bultmann sees the scene at the cross in 19:26 where Jesus "hands his mother over to the beloved disciple" as a symbolic movement, and that the symbolism can "scarcely be doubted."

69. Culpepper, "Peter as Exemplary Disciple in John 21:15–19," 166; Maynard, "The Role of Peter in the Fourth Gospel," 540.

70. Bultmann, *The Gospel of John*, 483, 701.

71. Ibid., 685.

72. Along with others, Brown et al., eds., *Peter in the New Testament*, 133.

(John 13:36).[73] Simon Peter sits "at a distance" from Jesus when compared to the BD (13:26).[74] Brown is, however, unwilling to say the FE intentionally denigrates Peter. If a rivalry exists at all, such an assumption "is probably an exaggeration, if it implies animosity, since that would not be true to the Johannine portrait of Simon Peter."[75] Nevertheless, Brown later moves toward acknowledging a tension between the two figures, saying, "The Johannine Christians, represented by the Beloved Disciple, clearly regard themselves as closer to Jesus and more perceptive than the Christians of the Apostolic Church."[76] Raymond Collins argues that the matter of their rivalry is vitally important and adds that Peter is often presented, "in a position subordinate to that of the Beloved Disciple."[77]

The second group leans toward a more positive view of Peter in the FG. Although firmly in this second group, Oscar Cullmann in his work *Peter: Disciple, Apostle, Martyr* argues that Peter was "unchallenged in the Synoptic Gospels," a position that might not be considered foreign to the anti-Petrine group.[78] Much later, Kevin Quast also lands firmly in the second group. He argues that "some who have seen a depreciation of Peter in the first twenty chapters of the Gospel now detect a reversal of attitude in John 21."[79] While focusing on an argument for the intentional anonymity of the BD, he also sees an ecclesiastical function in the role of the BD, but detects less of a rivalry between him and Peter.[80] Similar to Bultmann, Quast argues that each of these disciples "represents" their own stream of Christianity.[81] Quast also believes that Peter "fares well in comparison with the Synoptics."[82] Yet he states: "The Apostolic Christians do not have the

73. Ibid.

74. Ibid., 135.

75. "Should we speak of a rivalry in a sense whereby Peter would be deliberately depreciated in order to exalt the Beloved Disciple? Probably not." Ibid., 138–39.

76. Brown, *The Community of the Beloved Disciple*, 84.

77. Collins, *These Things Have Been Written*, 39. This question of rivalry between the two and the subordination of Peter may have been a significant idea as early as the late second century. In *The Acts of Peter and the Twelve Apostles*, after he asks Jesus (whom he has just recognized) how to feed the poor of the city, Peter is hesitant to inquire again of Jesus how to go about healing the sick: "Peter was afraid to take issue with the master a second time, so he motioned to John, who was next to him: 'You say something this time.'" Meyer, *The Nag Hammadi Scriptures*, 365. For a recent examination of Peter in the early church, see Bockmuehl, *The Remembered Peter*.

78. Cullmann, *Peter: Disciple, Apostle, Martyr*, 28.

79. Quast, *Peter and the Beloved Disciple*, 137–38.

80. Ibid., 12.

81. Ibid., 170.

82. Ibid., 166.

intimacy which the Johannine Christians experience. Nevertheless, they too are disciples of Christ although over dependent upon empirical evidence for their limited insight and faith."[83] Quast concludes, "[T]he Beloved Disciple validates Peter's role," and "Peter is portrayed in a positive light in ch. 21. Furthermore, this attitude does not contrast with the general picture of Peter encountered in the earlier chapters. Chapter 21 certainly cannot be regarded as a 'reversal.'"[84]

Francois Tolmie, whom we also may classify in the second group, makes an important contribution to the study of Peter when he emphasizes the difference between a *static view* of characterization and a *dynamic view* of characterization. In a static understanding, an interpreter weighs the "relative importance of [all] the various traits" of a given character, to reach the "full picture" a reader might arrive at when she reaches the "end of the narrative." In Tolmie's *dynamic view*, the interpreter is concerned with the "*process* whereby these traits are revealed step by step as the narrative progresses."[85] One might call this a "diachronic" approach to character. In this way, the character develops and changes in story time and in the reader's conception.[86]

Tolmie's approach frees him from actively choosing sides in the anti-Petrine debate. He traces the development of Peter's character throughout the Gospel apart from this polarity. Charting this disciple's character, Tolmie points out that Peter "took a negative turn in chapter 13."[87] Like other scholars, Tolmie concludes that the FG pairs Peter next to the BD.[88] However, Tolmie specifies that Peter is, even before chapter 21, "nevertheless portrayed as fulfilling some kind of leading role among the disciples."[89] In the end, Tolmie argues that the FG's comparison is between Peter and the Good Shepherd rather than Peter and the BD.[90] Peter thinks himself a good shepherd, but the comparison shows that he is not.

Richard Cassidy asks how readers at Philippi would have understood the canonical Gospels' presentation of Peter. He choses Philippi because as a Pauline community and Roman colony, readers would likely have been

83. Ibid. To me, this is an anachronistic post-enlightenment reading into the text.
84. Ibid., 148, 154.
85. Tolmie, "The (Not so) Good Shepherd," 356.
86. Tolmie's dynamic view is significant because after I completed the bulk of the research, I discovered that his method is similar to the sequential manner in which I treat certain characters below.
87. Ibid., 359.
88. Ibid., 360.
89. Ibid.
90. Ibid., 364.

more aware of the tradition of Peter's crucifixion. His choice of Philippi was also because scholars have not asserted that any evangelist penned a canonical Gospel there.[91] According to Cassidy, Peter serves as a hireling in chapter 18, "virtually fleeing" from Jesus, and "who abandons the Good Shepherd at the time of danger."[92] Cassidy also argues that by likening Peter to a hireling, the FE casts him, except for Judas, as the lowest of disciples.[93] He juxtaposed Peter against the "unwavering faithfulness manifested by the Beloved Disciple."[94] Yet Cassidy still leans toward a more positive view of Peter. Peter is "laudable" in that he is at least willing to follow Jesus to the courtyard of the high priest.[95] Using his construct of perceptive or "paradigmatic" readers, he concludes that "these four distinctive portrayals of Peter would, to varying degrees, have resonated positively with the members of the Christian community at Philippi."[96]

Bradford Blaine's *Peter in the Gospel of John: The Making of an Authentic Disciple* offers one of the more pro-Petrine positions: "This study has argued that Peter is portrayed very positively in the Gospel of John" and "throughout the Gospel he often teams up with BD . . . to follow and express devotion to Jesus."[97] Blaine admits such a positive view is "not widely held" in Johannine scholarship.[98] He pursues this track, arguing that the BD and Peter serve two different functions: "Whereas the BD achieves distinction in the Gospel for . . . showing the reader what a loving relationship with Jesus *looks* like, Peter demonstrates how discipleship is *crafted*."[99] Despite seeing Peter more favorably, Blaine views the confession "Holy one of God" in 6:69 as a lesser title based on Peter's limited understanding of Jesus. Peter's confession is secondary to Thomas' proclamation of "My Lord and My God" (John 20:28). Nevertheless, Blaine was willing to concede that Peter is "all over the map" in his manner of discipleship.[100]

Cornelis Bennema examines Peter's character in *Encountering Jesus: Character Studies in the Gospel of John* and in *A Theory of Character in New*

---

91. Cassidy, *Four Times Peter*, 109.

92. Ibid., 99, 107.

93. Ibid., 101.

94. Ibid., 107.

95. Ibid., 100.

96. Ibid., 126. Paradigmatic readers are those "who could have plumbed each Gospel for the subtle nuances its narrative contained."

97. Blaine, *Peter in the Gospel of John*, 183.

98. Ibid., 184.

99. Ibid., 183.

100. Ibid.

Testament Narrative. Yet because of his treatment of all the characters in the FG (and in the second text, in Mark and in Acts), he is only able to devote ten pages to Peter in the first tome (just a few more than that to the BD), and eight pages in the second.[101] Bennema states that "Peter's true significance is revealed only in John 21—an account only preserved in this gospel."[102] Contrary to the opinion of Blaine, Bennema characterizes Peter's confession of Jesus as the "Holy one of God" in chapter 6 in this way: "Peter displays traits of perceptiveness, outspokenness, zeal and loyalty."[103] Bennema believes some positions of anti-Petrinism are "too harsh."[104] Yet he concedes comparisons between the BD and Peter in which the FE portrays the BD in a more positive light.[105] He attributes the comparison not to Bultmann's idea of differing early Christian communities but, similar to Blaine, he believes these characters are portraying "corresponding rather than competitive roles."[106] He adds, "While the Beloved Disciple is the paradigm of loyal and credible witness for Jesus ... Peter exemplifies self-sacrifice in following Jesus."[107] Yet he is unwilling to go as far as Blaine, stating that Blaine was "perhaps too positive, minimizing [Peter's] misunderstandings, failures and instability."[108]

Finally, of late, Culpepper moves toward understanding Peter's character in the FG as having a positive, if not ironic role: "That Peter, who had denied Jesus three times, could become the shepherd of the flock paradoxically confirms Jesus' love for his own ... Peter is the gospel's affirmation that there is 'a future for failures.' Precisely the one who had denied Jesus three times becomes the exemplary disciple."[109]

Though I am not convinced that the FG is anti-Petrine, Maynard does make a convincing argument that the BD, when portrayed lying on Jesus'

---

101. Bennema, *Encountering Jesus*, 53–63, 171–82; Bennema, *A Theory of Character in New Testament Narrative*, 133–40.

102. Ibid., 53.

103. Ibid., 55. See Snyder, "John 13:16 and the Anti-Petrinism of the Johannine Tradition," 11.

104. Bennema, *Encountering Jesus*, 55–56n15, 16. See also Droge, "The Status of Peter in the Fourth Gospel," 307–11, whose work Bennema points out and who takes an anti-Petrine position.

105. Bennema, *Encountering Jesus*, 57, 60.

106. Ibid., 61. Quast notes, "Among scholars who see such a contrast are those who attribute the same basic role or function to both Peter and the Beloved Disciple with respect to their communities." Quast, *Peter and the Beloved Disciple*, 8.

107. Bennema, *Encountering Jesus*, 61.

108. Ibid., 62n37. Bennema, *A Theory of Character in New Testament Narrative*, 138n70.

109. Culpepper, "Peter as Exemplary Disciple in John 21:15–19," 178–79. He argues that in the FG Peter is in fact "exemplary," but not given "primacy." Ibid., 165.

bosom, is intentionally paralleled to Jesus in the bosom of the Father (John 1:18; 13:23).[110] In my judgment certain observations pose a serious challenge to those who conclude that John is anti-Petrine, such as the fact that the Synoptics portray Peter's boasting more harshly than the FG does, and that Peter is told that he *will* eventually follow Jesus (13:36). Nevertheless, while I agree with Quast that Peter is not portrayed as negatively as some contend, I shall argue below that Peter's *anagnorisis* in chapter 21 results in a reversal and a significant moment in the ongoing transformation of his character.

Thus, the FG traces the development of Peter as a growing disciple. The FE might have intended the contrast between Peter and the BD, perhaps to demonstrate hope for imperfect or "fallible followers," a phrase Elizabeth Malbon uses in her analysis of the Gospel of Mark.[111] The significance of Peter in the FG is his developmental characterization. He transitions from a boastful disciple (John 13:37), to one who lies and denies his discipleship three times (18:16–27), and then back to a restored disciple. The narrator tells us that after this story concludes, Peter will later "glorify God" in his death (21:19).

Therefore, Tolmie's view of Peter resonates with my argument. His *dynamic view* of characterization meshes well with my interpretation of the serial aspect of recognition scenes. Later I examine related characteristics of recognition in Genesis and argue that what I shall call manipulation narratives occur in series, focused upon a particular character in the story. This *serial aspect*, where several episodes centered on the same character are linked together, is important in Genesis as well as in the FG. By tracing the series, one finds movement and change within a given character, such as Judah in Genesis, or Peter in the FG. Tolmie's dynamic view is similar in that it allows a character to change throughout the story. Neither Jacob, nor Judah, nor Peter is the same at the story's conclusion, as when their stories began.

Setting simple classifications aside, Tolmie's treatment of Peter and the BD is consistent with how I view Johannine characterization. As I shall argue, most characters in Genesis, as well as those in the FG, do not fit into neat compartments or categories, and certainly not flat ones: Jacob is, for example, a deceiver as well as a chosen servant of God. Codifying characters into only two categories obscures the fact that authors sometimes use characters to mimic what readers already know of human life: that we

---

110. Maynard, "The Role of Peter in the Fourth Gospel," 536. See also Collins, "From John to the Beloved Disciple," 367; Conway, *Men and Women in the Fourth Gospel*, 176–77.

111. Malbon, *In the Company of Jesus*, 41–45. See also below in the next chapter, the treatment of Hylen, *Imperfect Believers*. In this sense, it is possible that the BD serves as a foil to Peter who may model the complex journey of human discipleship.

sometimes lead lives in which our behavior is conflicting, complex, and disturbing. The historical Peter may have been a very enigmatic figure indeed, just as the evangelists portray his character in all four of the Gospels, only more pointedly so in the FG. Therefore, when considering Tolmie and Cassidy's characterization models, I prefer Tolmie because he charts the decline of Peter's standing, beginning with Peter's boast in chapter 13, whereas Cassidy does not.[112]

Another perspective is that the differences between the Gospels' treatments of Peter may be due to differing literary and dramatic effects. I depart from Cullmann's position that Peter met little resistance in the Synoptic Gospels, because scholarly attention on Peter in the FG likely has caused some blindness to less than flattering Petrine passages in the Synoptics. All three of the Synoptics portray Peter's denials. Mark 14:29 and Matthew 26:33 register Peter's boasting more sharply than in the FG.[113] The same two Gospels record his curse upon himself, thus: "But he began to invoke a curse on himself and to swear, 'I do not know this man of whom you speak'" (Mark 14:71; Matt 26:72–4).[114] Thus while in the Synoptic denial scenes Peter claims he does not know Jesus at all, in the FG, he only claims he is not a disciple.

We should also note that in the FG, Peter voices his denials with the Johannine οὐκ εἰμί. This act characterizes him in a role that is cast opposite of Jesus. Combined with Peter's failure to grieve after the third denial in the FG (in contrast to the Synoptics, Matt 26:75; Mark 14:72: Luke 22:62; cf. John 18:27), this does indeed appear anti-Petrine. Yet perhaps this lack of remorse has a literary function as well, which I will address in chapter 7 below.

Concerning a possible rivalry, this study deals with the characters in the story world of the FG, rather than the particular historical individuals or communities that gave rise to the text.[115] Moreover, Blaine is also correct

---

112. Cassidy, *Four Times Peter*, 108; Tolmie, "The (Not so) Good Shepherd," 362. See further the discussion of theories of character in the next chapter.

113. Culpepper, "Peter as Exemplary Disciple in John 21:15–19," 172.

114. Brown et al., *Peter in the New Testament*, 164. There is also the identification of Peter with Satan in Matthew and Mark (Matt 16:23; Mark 8:33).

115. However, I lean toward a more pro-Petrine stance. I concede that since I approach the text from a narrative point of view, this lessens the chance that I will choose the anti-Petrine side of the fence, for with this approach I treat John 21 as integral to the Gospel, and much of the negativity surrounding Peter springs from the first twenty chapters. Brown, Donfried, and Reumann may have had the correct description when they state "this community has placed its apostolic figure (the Beloved Disciple) on a pedestal." Brown et al., *Peter in the New Testament*, 139. Culpepper holds a similar view in, Culpepper, *John, the Son of Zebedee*, 84, where the BD is "legitimizing and

when he observes that within the story world, "Peter has proven himself to be such a close supporter of Jesus that he warrants special observation and harassment from Jesus' enemies," and yet there is no need to declare one a winner and one a loser in the race to the tomb.[116] Thus, while I am far from anti-Petrine, I focus less on this polarity and the possible rivalry, and instead concentrate on the developmental characterization of Peter in the FG, especially as regards recognition and manipulation narratives.

In the next section I examine the last century's work on Johannine *anagnorisis* in which Peter, in chapter 21, is a central character.

Johannine *Anagnorisis*

One of the long-running questions about the FG is whether it is primarily Hellenistic or Hebraic.[117] In recent decades, scholars have begun to emphasize that even though the Gospel has Hebraic characteristics, the FE writes in the Greco-Roman milieu.[118] This development has fueled the suspicion that there is more to learn about Johannine *anagnorisis*.[119] Already around the turn of the last century, some scholars began associating the FG with Greek drama and more specifically, tragedy. Additionally, in the shift from the critical to post-critical paradigm in biblical research, more academics are moving toward interpreting Gospels as the products of literary skill.[120]

---

authorizing the distinctive teaching of the Johannine community."

116. Blaine, *Peter in the Gospel of John*, 188.

117. Larsen, *Recognizing the Stranger*, 7; Alter and Kermode, *The Literary Guide to the Bible*, 440. Probably the most important figure in this debate is Bultmann, who by supposing heavy Mandean Gnostic influences, asserts the FG's Hellenistic nature. One of the weaknesses of his argument is his overlooking the Semitic influence. Bultmann, *The Gospel of John*, 24–28; Meeks, "The Man from Heaven," 37; Sloyan, *What Are They Saying about John?*, 8, 11. Sloyan summarizes the status of this issue, stating that there is growing agreement that the Gospel is predominately from a Semitic origin but has a "thin Hellenistic overlay." However, just how "thin" the overlay is might be challenged by Tilborg's work, which considers how readers may have read the Gospel in Ephesus or as if written from the same. Ibid., 97; Tilborg, *Reading John in Ephesus*. See also Moloney, "Who Is 'the Reader' in/of the Fourth Gospel," 229; Dahl, "The Johannine Church and History," 148, 152, 167.

118. Sloyan, *What Are They Saying about John?*, 97. See also Tilborg, *Reading John in Ephesus*.

119. Stibbe, *John's Gospel*, 10–13, 72; Larsen, *Recognizing the Stranger*, 8.

120. Vorster, "The Historical Paradigm—Its Possibilities and Limitations," 104–23; Mouton et al., *Paradigms and Progress in Theology*; Thiselton, *New Horizons in Hermeneutics*, 313–67. That is not to say that no scholars view the Gospels as literary works before the shift. Redaction criticism focused on literary skill in the redaction process as well.

In the following section I survey the exploration of *anagnorisis* based on its association with ancient Greek literature. Moreover, I explain how scholars are recently examining recognition in ancient Hebraic literature and that some are therefore beginning to link this with the FG.

Just after the turn of the century, Hitchcock published on this topic with "The Dramatic Development of the Fourth Gospel," and followed later with, "Is the Fourth Gospel a Drama?"[121] He held that the Gospel contains five acts found in Aristotle's paradigm.[122] In *A Fresh Study of the Fourth Gospel* (1911), he wrote of the garden scene in chapter 18, "The Recognition scene in the Garden is one of the most pathetic and realistic in all of literature. It is a transcript from the [sic] life, a masterpiece from a master-hand, an idyll inimitable and touching, described with a marvelous self-restraint and simplicity."[123] Indeed, one may well say that Hitchcock was insightfully ahead of his time. However, though he was the first to direct research toward Johannine recognition (or failed recognition), Hitchcock did not pursue this device as a phenomenon unto itself.[124]

After decades of virtual scholarly silence on the topic of recognition, Culpepper, drawing on Northrop Frye's analysis, argues that the use of Aristotle's categories would be helpful for tracing the plot of the FG, because "*anagnorisis* permeates the plot."[125] Though other scholars have pointed in this direction, "they did not have in mind the highly developed art of narrative criticism . . . the existence of which they were barely aware."[126] In his examination of the FG, Culpepper employs aspects of literary criticism that are regularly used to analyze fictional works.[127] He studies the components now common to narrative criticism such as point of view, narrator, narrative time, plot, characters, implicit commentary, implied reader, and implied author.[128] Seeing *anagnorisis* as central to the entire plot, he argues,

---

121. Hitchcock, "The Dramatic Development of the Fourth Gospel," 266–79; Hitchcock, "Is the Fourth Gospel a Drama?," 307–17.

122. Ibid., 306–7.

123. Hitchcock, *A Fresh Study of the Fourth Gospel*, 140.

124. Larsen, *Recognizing the Stranger*, 10; Hitchcock, "Is the Fourth Gospel a Drama?," 307–17.

125. Culpepper, *Anatomy of the Fourth Gospel*, 83. However, Lee, in his 1954 "The Drama of the Fourth Gospel" had kept the idea of the elements of Greek tragedy alive. Lee, "The Drama of the Fourth Gospel," 173.

126. Sloyan, *What Are They Saying about John?*, 51.

127. Wead, *The Literary Devices in John's Gospel*, had laid the groundwork.

128. Sloyan, *What Are They Saying about John?*, 51; Culpepper, *Anatomy of the Fourth Gospel*, 81–84.

"In the Gospel of John, Jesus, who has descended from the world above, is unrecognized except by a privileged few."[129]

Mark Stibbe revived Hitchcock's work in *The Gospel of John as Literature*.[130] A year later he again aligned the Gospel with Greek tragedy,[131] returning to Hitchcock's analysis of tragedy in his monograph, *John's Gospel*. He detected five acts or stages in the Gospel, with chapter 20 serving as the fifth act and chapter 21 serving as an epilogue.[132] Stibbe traced Jesus' *anagnorisis* in the FG and argued that Jesus conceals himself from some characters who look for him.[133] Later Stibbe added that "the great challenge of the gospel is to recognize who [Jesus] really is."[134] Readers perceive things about Jesus that characters in the story never catch. The irony of Johannine failed recognition centers around the Jews who miss the very Messiah whom they await.[135] Stibbe also applied some of the techniques of Robert Alter, Shimon Bar-Efrat, and Meir Sternberg to the Fourth Gospel, and he noticed the narrative similarities between Genesis, the Hebrew Bible, and John. He argued that, though Hellenistic, the FG is also very similar to the "stories of Moses and other Jewish, charismatic heroes."[136] He also treated recognition in his commentary, *John*, where he asserted that many characters must figure out who Jesus is.[137] Stibbe concluded that *anagnorisis* is foundational to John's plot.[138] Yet, Stibbe does not explore the similarities of recognition between the FG and Genesis.

Though not in the category of biblical recognition, Terrance Cave's *Recognitions: A Study in Poetics* plays a role in the development of an understanding of *anagnorisis* in many genres. Larsen and other contributors utilize Cave as a modern foundation and reference point. Cave examines how theorists since Aristotle define and used the concept of *anagnorisis* in

---

129. Ibid., 83.

130. Stibbe, *The Gospel of John as Literature*, 15–24.

131. Stibbe, *John's Gospel*, 35–36; Culpepper, "The Plot of John's Story of Jesus," 349. Other subsequent scholars have also aligned the FG with Greek drama: Connick, "The Dramatic Character of the Fourth Gospel," 159; Conway, "The Production of the Johannine Community," 480; Keener, *The Gospel of John*, 1:10–11.

132. Stibbe, *John's Gospel*, 35–36. This is not the only instance of Stibbe referring to Hitchcock's analysis. See also ibid., 1, 64, 67.

133. Ibid., 15.

134. Ibid., 30.

135. Ibid., 65.

136. Ibid., 10–13, 72. On the techniques of Alter, Bar-Efrat, and Sternberg, see chapter 3, "Methodology."

137. Stibbe, *John*, 30.

138. Ibid., 203.

their work. He limits much of his analysis to a history of how theorists address recognition, rather than a history of how authors use the device. Cave presents a twofold argument. First, he posits that the Aristotelian definition in *Poetics* has been lost, as demonstrated by a diverse usage since *Poetics*: "If anagnorisis is still to be used in critical practices, the dispersal of its meanings has to be accepted *fait accompli*."[139] Second, he reasons that recognition does not provide the final closure that some have proposed: "Recognition may easily turn out to be an imposter, claiming to resolve, conjoin and make whole while it busily brings to the surface all the possibilities that threaten wholeness. The progression from negative to positive which recognition plots articulate is as radically unstable as a mirage."[140] However, Cave's work does not speak to the primary texts examined here, despite his ancillary references to Genesis' brilliance in recognition scenes.[141] Since he analyzes Western texts written after Aristotle had become a common tool for interpretation, Cave does not focus on Genesis or John.[142]

In her work, *The Poetics of Revelation*, Diana Culbertson argues that recognition is the fulcrum of transformation and that it "functions as the model for the apprehension of revelation."[143] She examines recognition in classical, Western, and Gospel literature, devoting one chapter to the FG and its pattern of recognition. In her view, the question, "What do you seek?" (John 1:38) is the theme of John. This question occurs in the opening chapter and, ironically, with the soldiers in 18:4, as well as with Mary in 20:15.[144] She points out that, just as foretold in the Hebrew canon, those who do not believe are often those who have recognition (and thus revelation) withheld from them (Wis 6:12–16; Prov 1:24–28). She notes this motif in John 8:59 where, "Jesus no longer conceals his identity; unbelief

---

139. Cave, *Recognitions*, 221. "The *Poetics* then appears as a set of malleable sentences on which future commentaries erect more or less flimsy structures in languages other than Greek." Ibid., 27.

140. Ibid., 487.

141. In a footnote, Cave mentions Dutch renaissance scholars, the theologian Vossius, and the poet Heinsius, and their reference of the Joseph story. Cave writes: "[F]or Heinsius (*De trag. const.* pp., 71–72, ch.6), this story 'is immensely superior to everything in the tragic poets' in its skillful handling of peripeteia and anagnorisis, indeed no action more suitable for tragedy can be found.'" Cave also directs his readers to Thomas Twinning's *Aristotle's Treatise on Poetry* (1789), which "produced English translations of the *Poetics* accompanied by more or less full annotations . . . He occasionally cites non-classical examples: the 'discovery' of Joseph by his brethren is 'the most beautiful and affecting example that can be given,'" ibid., 80n67; 139.

142. Ibid., 8.

143. Culbertson, *Poetics of Revelation*, 1.

144. Ibid., 157, 161–63.

hardens into hostility; and they pick up stones to throw at him. We read then that 'he hid himself and left the temple' (8:59)."[145] She calls to mind Isaiah 64:6–7: "For you hid your face from us and gave us up to the power of our sins" and clarifies that "The hiddenness of Jesus is the objectification of the blindness of [Jesus'] audience."[146] She concludes that Greek recognition serves as a "function of plot," and not a device used to facilitate "character transformation."[147] I shall argue that if read from the viewpoint of Genesis, recognition in John 21 is but one component of what may be classified as a manipulation narrative. Recognition moves beyond plot alone and serves as a tool to transform the character of Peter.[148]

Culpepper, in "The Plot of John's Story of Jesus," argues that recognition is one of the "distinguishing features" of the FG.[149] He points out that in chapter 21, "it is the Beloved Disciple who recognizes the risen Lord first," but Culpepper does not pursue the recognition motif further.[150] Later, in *The Gospel and Letters of John*, he notes that not only are there similarities between the Fourth Gospel and Greek tragedies, but with Hebrew Bible and apocryphal recognition scenes as well.[151] Picking up Hitchcock's analysis, he observes the presence of *lysis, anagnorisis, peripeteia,* and *pathos*.[152] He examines *anagnorisis* as a type-scene, devoting several pages to their treatment.[153] This is important because he initiates the comparison with recognition in the Hebrew Bible. He points to recognition in Genesis 18, where Abraham meets the three strangers and recognizes one of them as divine, and in Judges 6, where Samson's parents recognize the messenger as "the angel of the Lord."[154] Culpepper argues these recognitions "often occur at the unveiling of a divine or angelic being."[155] Also important is his analysis

---

145. Ibid., 160–62.

146. Ibid., 163. Her scripture citations are from the Jerusalem Bible.

147. Ibid., 2.

148. But she is on unsure ground when she says, that "those who recognize Jesus are those who search for wisdom." Though she is correct that disbelief prevents recognition in the FG, there is little to show that characters like the Samaritan woman and Peter were proactively seeking wisdom when Jesus comes on the scene. Ibid., 159.

149. Culpepper, "The Plot of John's Story of Jesus," 353.

150. Ibid., 356.

151. Culpepper, *The Gospel and Letters of John*, 76.

152. Ibid., 63.

153. Ibid., 72–86.

154. Ibid., 75. See also Reinhartz, "Samson's Mother," 25–37; Reinhartz, *Why Ask My Name?*, 164–65.

155. Culpepper, *The Gospel and Letters of John*, 77. Reinhartz notes this as well, *Why Ask My Name?*, 165.

that recognition occurs on multiple levels. First, the "recognizer" recognizes the "identity of the recognized." Second, the recognizer recognizes the "implication of the recognition," and third, the reader recognizes "the implied author's implicit purpose."[156] His "Designs for the Church in the Imagery of John 21:1–14" explores the connections between recognition and meals, and their significance for a paradigm shift for the church.[157] The *anagnorisis* in chapter 21 is a transitional device in the plot. Culpepper views the recognition of the disciples and their great catch as a transformation "to those who would be drawn to Jesus and invited to eat with him without seeing him."[158] He differs with some in that he interpreted John 21 as a true *anagnorisis* scene.[159] This lack of agreement, as to whether the miraculous draught fishes constitutes an actual recognition scene, may account for why it has received little attention in research.[160]

Piero Boitani has produced two monographs, both addressing *anagnorisis*, but mostly in medieval or later literature.[161] In so doing, he briefly touches on both Genesis and Johannine recognition. Approaching post-biblical texts from an ontological perspective, he sees in the texts "a fundamental need of human beings—a need for anagnorisis."[162] According to Boitani, the recognition of God requires revelation.[163] When we as humans recognize God, we rewrite and live out the stories of recognition already embodied in biblical texts. He states, "*to recognize God is to rewrite the Scriptures.*"[164] In his first work, *The Tragic and the Sublime in Medieval Literature*, Boitani is concerned with "what poems, narratives, and plays written over five hundred years ago mean to us today, whether what they say and the way in which they say it are still relevant to modern readers."[165] Two of his chapters specifically addressed the "medieval 'thirst' for recognition," narrowing his focus in the second of those chapters to the writings of Dante.[166] Important for this study is his proposition that "[d]epending on

---

156. Culpepper, *The Gospel and Letters of John*, 73.
157. Culpepper, "Designs for the Church in the Imagery of John 21:1–14," 369–402.
158. Ibid., 378.
159. Ibid.
160. See also Pfitzner, "They Knew It Was the Lord," 20.
161. Boitani, *The Tragic and the Sublime in Medieval Literature*; Boitani, *The Bible and its Rewritings*.
162. Boitani, *The Tragic and the Sublime in Medieval Literature*, 126.
163. Ibid., ix, 30.
164. Boitani, *The Bible and Its Rewritings*, 203–4; emphasis Boitani.
165. Boitani, *The Tragic and the Sublime in Medieval Literature*, ix.
166. Ibid., 130.

what is being recognized and to which end it is being known, the effect... will differ."[167] I must agree, because recognition functions differently from text to text. Exploring how recognition functions in Genesis, apart from Dante, Homer, etc., to see what particular effect(s) it achieves in Genesis is important for this study. From that, we can then ask how this function influences a reading of John.

Boitani also uses scripture in his analysis of writers like Dante and Klopstock. In doing so, he identifies parallels important for this study: "Joseph, a traditional *figura* of Jesus, manifested himself to, and was recognized by his brothers, who believed him dead—after resurrection, Jesus appears, is recognized, and 'believed in' by the apostles."[168]

In his second tome, *The Bible and Its Rewriting*, Boitani studies how specific works *rewrite* biblical texts and how this happens within Scripture itself: "Rewriting takes place within the Bible itself: Genesis rewrites Genesis, John rewrites Genesis, and the whole of the New Testament rewrites the Old, with the intention of 'fulfilling' it."[169] Recognition of God is a "central theme," and this process requires "exceptional means, or individuals, like Abraham, Jacob, Joseph, Moses, Job, the Prophets, and, later, the Apostles."[170] Boitani argues that in some texts, including scripture, failed recognition is due to moral deficiency: "The eye of the flesh, of the flesh that has sinned and is frightened, can no longer recognize the divine messenger at first glance... His light dimmed by sin and the shadow of death, man learns to recognize what is sent from God."[171] I will make a similar argument below. Boitani also takes a broad view of recognition and included Abraham's encounter with God in Genesis 18 as a recognition scene and Joseph's general recognition of God's intervention in his plight to/in Egypt as a recognition motif.[172] The recognition of God is "the very *telos* or aim of the narrative."[173] The plot builds toward the climactic moment of recognition. Similar to this

---

167. Ibid., 116. For instance, in Dante's *Hell*, "Recognition is the only chance of being remembered—of living—and at the same time of being damned forever in human memory," ibid., 110.

168. Ibid., 121.

169. Boitani, *The Bible and Its Rewritings*, vii.

170. "Throughout the Old Testament (more than seventy times in Ezekiel alone) there runs the 'formula of recognition', whereby God proclaims: 'they may know that I am the Lord' (the human response to this is the expression of faith and adoration ...)." Ibid., 12.

171. Ibid., 15. Reinhartz makes a similar statement about Samson's father. Reinhartz, "Samson's Mother," 25–37; Reinhartz, *Why Ask My Name?*, 165.

172. Boitani, *The Bible and Its Rewritings*, 3–16, 31.

173. Ibid., 16.

study, Boitani sees cognition as a device that brings about moral change. Recognition "awakens in the addressee self-knowledge, moral awareness, gratitude, and confession (Judah at Tamar's evidence, and again when the goblet is found in his brother's sack; the brothers when accused of spying and when asked to fetch Benjamin)."[174]

Perhaps Boitani's most relevant contribution to this study is that he occasionally, though briefly, links the Hebrew Bible, Genesis, and John via the FE's use of *anagnorisis*.[175] The FG re-writes Greco-Roman texts and "the Hebrew Bible for good measure."[176] Boitani devotes a measured portion of the first chapter to an explanation of Genesis. However, his real aim in the first chapter is to examine Thomas Mann's rewrite of Genesis in his work *Joseph and his Brothers*.[177] Therefore, his treatment of Genesis is referential, and only in relation to Mann's work. Later, he briefly discusses the "recognition of God," both by characters within the story world, as well as by readers of Genesis and the FG.[178] Ultimately, he does not offer a systematic treatment of recognition scenes as Larsen has done for John, or as I offer here for Genesis. Thus, a more substantial examination of recognition scenes in Genesis is still lacking, the results of which can then inform a reading of John.

Jo-Ann Brant in *Dialogue and Drama: Elements of Greek Tragedy in the Fourth Gospel*, takes up *anagnorisis* and argues that other scholars have slighted its plot function in favor of its effect on characters.[179] She also notes that in John, Jesus obscures his identity either for dramatic effect or to let a character move through a transition such as grief.[180] This point is important for this study because I will argue that recognition in Genesis as well as John is significant for character development. Brant also argues that recognition involves a re-alignment of a character and that, often, the character was powerless to stop the march of the plot.[181]

Stan Harstine's short article, "Un-Doubting Thomas: Recognition Scenes in the Ancient World" first surveys Thomas' doubting scene and then briefly examines other recognition scenes in John. He examines recognition through the lens of the *Odyssey*, where neither Odysseus' nursemaid nor his wife, Penelope, recognize him at first. He perceives that the "recognition of

---

174. Ibid., 30.
175. Ibid., 151–56.
176. Ibid., 145.
177. Ibid., 34–56.
178. Ibid., 119, 145, 148, 152, 159.
179. Brant, *Dialogue and Drama*, 57.
180. Ibid., 50–53.
181. Ibid., 51, 57.

an individual was critical for the acceptance of their authority."[182] Similar to Cave, Harstine sees the displaying of some unique, personally identifiable object or piece of information as integral to the recognition scene and necessary for the recognition to occur. Concerning Mary's recognition at the tomb he writes: "Only when she is called by name does she recognize this one as Jesus (John 20:11–16)."[183] He argues that an examination of all the recognition scenes in this Gospel "reveals this basic pattern of a recognition scene: The initial negative response by the character is followed by the disclosure of information specific to that individual and replaced by an affirmative recognition."[184] He clarifies that the negative response can also be, "a negative response to or lack of acceptance of the apparently dead individual (Jesus/Odysseus)."[185] Finally, the scene must also have "an embracing confession for the one seemingly brought back from the dead (Jesus/Odysseus)," such as Mary Magdalene in 20:16 saying "*rabboni*," or the BD stating, "It is the Lord!" in 21:7.[186] Harstine also examines the term "unbelieving," ἄπιστος, which is found in the recognition scenes of both Thomas and Odysseus. In the latter, Odysseus's wife Penelope is described by the nurse as having a heart that is "ever unbelieving."[187] Harstine argues the term should hinge on the lack of loyalty, that is, the withholding of loyalty. Penelope is simply too loyal to give in to a man until she is sure it is Odysseus.[188] Harstine uses these observations to argue that Thomas "would be understood by a first-century reader as that of a loyal and faithful servant, a servant who is waiting for a sign of recognition that only his true master can provide."[189]

The most thorough work of late on *anagnorisis* in the FG is that of Larsen (2008).[190] Larsen's concern is that few have studied *anagnorisis* through an Aristotelian lens, and "even fewer have studied anagnorisis in its capacity as a type-scene or a microgenre in John's narrative."[191] Much of this is because until recent decades, many New Testament scholars held

---

182. Harstine, "Un-Doubting Thomas," 439.
183. Ibid., 440.
184. Ibid., 441.
185. Ibid., 443.
186. Ibid.
187. Ibid., 446.
188. Ibid., 447.
189. Ibid., 442.
190. A monograph of his 2006 dissertation, "Recognizing the Stranger: *Anagnorisis* in the Gospel of John."
191. Larsen, *Recognizing the Stranger*, 6.

the "notion of an insurmountable divide between Judaism and Hellenism."[192] Larsen gives the *Odyssey* prominence in his work, though he admits that *anagnorisis* occurs in numerous other locations in ancient Greco-Roman texts. He includes in that acknowledgment biblical narratives such as the road to Emmaus (Luke 24) and the story of "Joseph's reunion with his brothers (Gen 42–45)."[193]

Larsen considers that in the Gospel of John "anagnorisis is *the* ultimate moment of coming-into-presence, as it, within a split second of realization, eliminates the distance between the recognizer and the recognized."[194] More specifically, he contends "that the recognition scene is a recurring, generic vehicle in John, which serves to host and thematize central problems in the Gospel concerning the knowledge of God through Jesus, as well as the believers' access to Jesus in his physical presence and absence."[195]

Larsen argues that texts signal recognition through three different "modes." The first is "*Showing* . . . by means of nonlinguistic signs."[196] The second is "linguistic *telling*" in which the unrecognized, in this case Jesus, communicates his identity verbally.[197] In John, this is the nature of the "I am" statements.[198] Finally, the story indicates recognition through "*whispering* . . . the act of letting selected observers know in advance, so that the recognition does not happen on the basis of what is told or shown during or after the encounter with the observed."[199] Larsen also contributes to the understanding of the token as a device to create recognition and revelation.[200] Earlier I noted his observation that "In Aristotle, the token is called σημεῖον (*Poet.* 1454b20; 1455a19)."[201] Later Larsen adds : "In a literary work like the Fourth Gospel consisting of a number of recognition scenes, it is obvious to take the sign as recognition token. In this connection, it is quite remarkable that the Johannine terminology regarding Jesus' miracles is comparable to the one being used by Aristotle when describing the type of recognition

---

192. Ibid., 8.

193. Ibid., 2.

194. Ibid., 6.

195. Ibid., 219.

196. Ibid., 49.

197. Ibid.

198. Ibid., 148.

199. Ibid., 50.

200. Ibid., 48, 67–68.

201. Ibid., 67. I have reproduced Larsen's variation in accents between σημείον and σημεῖον.

LITERATURE REVIEW

that takes place by means of tokens (διὰ τῶν σημείων, *Poet.* 1454b20)."[202] He reiterates that Greco-Roman literature "used a variety of terms ... and the exact same term (σημεῖον) only appears on occasions."[203] This constitutes a major contribution to scholarship and the understanding of the FE's treatment of miracles as "signs" in the FG.

Also important among Larsen's contributions is that recognition scenes go through five moves: "the meeting, cognitive resistance, the display of the token, the moment of recognition, and finally, the attendant reactions and physical (re)union."[204] He argues that recognition is also a "carrier of ideology ... giving expression to relational and social understandings of identity in terms of honor ... it negotiates social roles and thematizes social expulsion and integration."[205] To put this another way, recognition causes "embarrassment," a sense of a gap in the recognizer's knowledge. It is this missing knowledge that requires the *anagnorisis*.[206] Larsen then divides the FG into three sections, or stages of recognition: 1) "Anagnorisis and arrival (John 1–4)," where Jesus arrives on the scene; 2) "Recognition in Conflict (John 5–19),"[207] where Jesus "is met with real opposition and severe cognitive resistance";[208] and 3) "Recognition and Departure (John 20–21),"[209] where Jesus is finally recognized, culminating in Thomas' climactic declaration, "My Lord and my God!" (20:28).[210]

Larsen's closing pages set up the present study because they suggest two gaps. First, Larsen does not give John 21 as lengthy a treatment as he gives episodes in the first twenty chapters, devoting less than two pages to chapter 21.[211] Second, since Larsen's work approaches recognition scenes from classical Greco-Roman works, there awaits a closer exploration of how a reading of Genesis may influence a reading of Johannine recognition. Earlier in his study, Larsen makes short forays into the Genesis scenes. He states: "[A]t the end of the Joseph-novella, when Joseph reveals himself to his brothers ... The scene constitutes the turning point toward the fam-

---

202. Ibid., 116.
203. Ibid.
204. Ibid., 71.
205. Ibid., 71–72.
206. Ibid., 33.
207. Ibid., 22–23.
208. Ibid., 145.
209. Ibid., 23.
210. Ibid., 208. Larsen also discusses a "forensic type of anagnorisis, which is played out in a trial setting." Ibid., 222.
211. Ibid., 211–13.

ily reconciliation, though actually the recognition is played down as the brothers believe in him *right away*—no tokens required."[212] When discussing the move of cognitive resistance, he notes:

> In fact, without this move of *agnoia*, the recognition scene becomes a mere reunion scene with only faintly articulated, cognitive implications, as in Biblical examples like the reunion of Joseph and his brothers in Gen 42–45.... Such immediate recognitions, however, are significant exceptions that often aim to emphasize the actors' close relationship—so close that recognition becomes unnecessary or as easy as falling off a log.[213]

Failing to recognize Joseph over the course of two trips to Egypt with four encounters,[214] including a meal, is a much longer and difficult single recognition process than Larsen realizes.[215] This misunderstanding suggests the need for further analysis of the role of recognition in Genesis that subsequently may be applied as a lens for the FG.

Finally, Larsen also calls for a more thorough analysis of the shepherd discourse in relation to *anagnorisis* saying, "the shepherd discourse, with its treatment of recognition between actors that are interconnected, presents itself as a text to be further studied in the light of anagnorisis."[216] Though not the primary aim of the present study, I will briefly discuss a connection between the recognition of John 21 and the shepherd discourse and how that connection further clarifies the character of Peter and his fellow disciples.[217]

Larsen's work caps the emergence of scholarship on recognition in the FG. Since scholarship is beginning to see "Hellenism as an overall descriptive concept under which both the Judaisms and the Christianities of the period appear as subsets,"[218] should we not therefore ask what bearing does Genesis have on Johannine recognition? Additionally, since recognition is so prominent in Genesis, and given that the FG demonstrates intertextuality

---

212. Ibid., 56; emphasis added.

213. Ibid., 64–65.

214. Gen 42–43. Five encounters, if one considers that Joseph left to regain his composure and then returned to the meal scene (43:30–31).

215. Larsen also speaks of a "failed recognition scene" when Jacob and Rebekah "trick the old, blind Isaac into blessing Jacob." Ibid., 56.

216. Ibid., 223.

217. See also on *anagnorisis* MacFarlane, "Aristotle's Definition of Anagnorisis," 367–83; Browne, "Types of Self-Recognition and Self-Reform in Ancient Drama," 163–71; Sylva, "Dialogue and Drama: Elements of Greek Tragedy in the Fourth Gospel (Review)," 604–7.

218. Larsen, *Recognizing the Stranger*, 8.

with Genesis,[219] this presents an ideal topic for research. The present study picks up at precisely this point. By examining these episodes in Genesis, I will set forth a theory of manipulation narratives, of which recognition *is but one component*. I will then demonstrate a set of recurring patterns in manipulation narratives in Genesis that will serve as a lens through which to re-read or, perhaps, re-hear the manipulation narrative in John 21. Before turning to that question, I here briefly survey pertinent scholarship on Genesis recognition and trickster themes.

Genesis, Hebraic Recognition, and Scholarship

A number of scholars have wrestled with the recognition scenes in Genesis and other Hebraic texts. Many of the recognition scenes involve one character using deception to swindle another character out of some desired object or position, such as when Jacob disguises himself to obtain Esau's blessing (Gen 27). Some scholars approach these narratives by examining the theme of deception. They frequently identify these as "trickster scenes" or as scenes characterized by the "deception motif."[220] Others utilize the category of recognition when studying them.[221] Some wrestle with the moral implications of each scene,[222] issues of gender and power in the text,[223] as well as cross-cultural, anthropological, and folklore comparisons to the biblical examples.[224] What follows is a survey of recent major works on the topic of recognition and deception in Genesis.

The specific connection between recognition and deception motifs in Genesis begins in 1981 with Robert Alter's *The Art of Biblical Narrative*. Alter treats certain scenes in Genesis together, connected not by the motif of deception or trickery, but rather as recognition type-scenes.[225] However, his book is a methodological approach to Hebrew narrative in general. Alter uses some recognition scenes to illustrate the literary methods of

---

219. Such as John 1:1, 47–51.

220. Sternberg, *The Poetics of Biblical Narrative*, 9, 497.

221. Alter, *The Art of Biblical Narrative*, 4–5, 159–60, 163.

222. Williams, *Deception in Genesis*.

223. Robinson, "Wife and Sister through the Ages," 103–28; Steinberg, "Israelite Tricksters, Their Analogues, and Cross-Cultural Study," 1–13; Babcock-Abrahams, "A Tolerated Margin of Mess," 147–86; Clines, *What Does Eve Do to Help?*; Farmer, "The Trickster Genre in the Old Testament"; Fuchs, "For I Have the Way of Women," 68–83; Bowen, "The Role of YHWH as Deceiver in True and False Prophecy."

224. Niditch, *Underdogs and Tricksters*.

225. Alter, *The Art of Biblical Narrative*, 4–5, 159–60, 163.

ancient Hebrew narrative, but he does not attempt an analysis of this motif. Rather, he focuses on those scenes that illustrate his analysis of repetition, *Leitwörter, Leitmotiv,* implicit commentary and the like. His contribution is pointing out the connection between recognition, deceit, and ignorance versus knowledge. He considers the Joseph novella the finest example of this nexus:

> The preeminent instance of biblical narrative as a fictional experiment in knowledge is the story of Joseph and his brothers, for in it the central actions turn on the axis of true knowledge versus false, from the seventereen-year-old Joseph's dreams of grandeur to his climactic confrontation with his brothers in Egypt twenty-two years later. This theme of knowledge is formally enunciated through the paired key-words, *haker*, "recognize," and *yado (a,* "know," that run through the story.[226]

Sternberg's *The Poetics of Biblical Narrative* broadens the category even further.[227] He explores *anagnorisis* in a manner somewhat similar to Aristotle's characters moving from "ignorance to knowledge" but reminds his readers that recognition is a "Hebraic innovation."[228] He also argues that biblical characters rarely stand alone as static examples of virtue. Instead, the text holds them up for the reader as those who *change*, who demonstrate an aptitude to progress in their understanding of God, even if they do not progress in a direct, uninterrupted path. In fact, many biblical characters slip backwards into a state of ignorance:

> All biblical characters lapse, but many live to relapse as well. Instead of marking a reversal of character and often fortune too, as in Greek tragedy or the classical novel, biblical discovery, like Joycean epiphany, comes up as a momentary illumination that may well be followed by a backsliding into darkness ... But the most telling example rounds off the Bible's longest and most excruciating drama of recognition, namely, Joseph and his Brothers. The fraternal ordeal apparently a thing of the past, it suddenly resurges after Jacob's death, when the brothers voice the fear that Joseph is at last free to take his revenge (Gen 50:15–18). No wonder Joseph bursts into tears. It is as though the whole ordeal has been in vain: if they have learned anything about him beyond externals—and the fear may well have haunted them all those years—the effect has evaporated.

---

226. Ibid., 159.
227. Sternberg, *The Poetics of Biblical Narrative.*
228. *Poet.* 1452a; Ibid., 176–77.

God-like to the last—and himself among the handful of genuine learners—Joseph repeats his assurances in the hope of implanting the knowledge for good. Only a hope, this time, since he has just discovered the biblical rule ("Hard come, easy go") concerning the problematics of discovery.[229]

Thus for Sternberg, recognition or "discovery" is a device that marks not only the characters' development, but one which marks lapses and relapses as well—a "drama of discovery" in their moral progression.[230] Different biblical characters can demonstrate evidence of this process, whether the character is Judah, finally willing to sacrifice himself, or the rest of Joseph's brothers wrestling with whether he will seek retribution. This is a salient point, for I shall argue that Peter in the FG is in a similar process of development, and one marker along his journey occurs when he finally acknowledges to Jesus, "Lord, *you* know all things" (John 21:17).

Sherryll Mleynek in *Knowledge and Mortality:* Anagnorisis *in Genesis and Narrative Fiction*, also addresses the topic of *anagnorisis*, but unlike those before her, Mleynek examines *anagnorisis* using the Fall of Adam and Eve as the prototypical recognition scene for Western literature.[231] She argues that Adam and Eve's "discovery" is a transformative move toward awareness of mortality. *Anagnorisis* "is a synecdoche for mortality."[232] The insatiable desire "to know" leads to the inevitability of death. She then proceeds to analyze three major works of the nineteenth century and how *anagnorisis* functions in them, stemming from its usage in Genesis. A step removed from Cave's opinion that recognition scenes do not resolve plots, Mleynek argues that *anagnorisis* brings both closure as well as destabilization to narratives. It brings closure because the knowledge of our own impending death is "the most stable knowledge," and it brings instability because the awareness of death has the greatest force of change upon "human consciousness."[233] Thus, she states, "In fiction, *anagnorisis* forces closure through its transformative knowledge by establishing the appearance of a stable universe, after which the fiction must close or risk destabilization by another moment of *anagnorisis*."[234] In this way, Mleynek uses recognition in Western literature as a tool for understanding human existence, how we comprehend our reality and our end. *Anagnorisis* causes a desire to return

---

229. Ibid., 177–78.
230. Ibid., 176.
231. Mleynek, *Knowledge and Mortality*, 10–11.
232. Ibid., 3, 13, 90, 128.
233. Ibid., 127.
234. Ibid., 92, 127.

to a previous state of ignorance, such as the *anagnorisis* associated with grief: one longs to return to a pre-grieving innocence.²³⁵

At this juncture I should pause and make clear a point that is crucial to understanding this study: scholars such as Cave and Mleynek examine *anagnorisis* in Western literature, either as a universal literary device that crosses texts and genres or as a tool to further an ontological understanding of human existence.²³⁶ These methods of analysis are valid, but different from the present study.²³⁷ I argue that *anagnorisis* functions differently from text to text, and sometimes, from scene to scene.²³⁸ I analyze how recognition functions within Genesis and John and how it operates *within the story world* of these texts. *Anagnorisis* in Genesis, according to Mleynek, marks a move to a loss of innocence.²³⁹ However, Mleynek narrows her analysis to Adam and Eve and does not reflect on later narratives in Genesis. I argue that characters such as Jacob, Laban, Judah, and Joseph manipulate, wield, and conceal knowledge. The manipulation serves as a fulcrum on which they broker power. The withholding of recognition from others often sheds light on a character's moral lack. Eventually, these "manipulators" are also disempowered. In the final manipulation, or "counter-manipulation" which I shall explain in chapter 5, someone checks their misuse of power. The manipulator changes and displays new character traits.²⁴⁰

Lambe's article, "Judah's Development: The Pattern of Departure-Transition-Return," is also very important for this study.²⁴¹ Lambe sees both trickster as well as *anagnorisis* themes in Genesis 37–45.²⁴² In chapter 38, Judah demonstrates a moral lack in his failure to grieve at the loss of

---

235. Ibid., 12.

236. Ibid., 109, 114–15, 125.

237. For example, by using *Pride and Prejudice*, Mleynek argues that recognition can lead to greater self-awareness. Ibid., 91.

238. Also of late is Kennedy and Lawrence, *Recognition: The Poetics of Narrative: Interdisciplinary Studies on Anagnorisis*, which analyzes several different genres, but ever so scantly mentions Gen and the Gospel of John (one sentence on the latter). Its approach of examining texts from many genres, "demonstrates the varied and mottled nature of recognition." Ibid., 5. These recent interdisciplinary works attest to *anagnorisis*' enduring power as a literary motif and as a fulcrum of human understanding.

239. Mleynek, *Knowledge and Mortality*, 5, 12.

240. Reinhartz argues that unnamed characters can contribute to that characterization. The servants in the Joseph story fade as "Joseph interacts directly with his father and brothers, indicating that the relationships have been restored." Reinhartz, *Why Ask My Name?*, 35.

241. Lambe, "Judah's Development," 53–68.

242. Ibid., 56–57.

his sons and in his "impulsive sexual desire."[243] The scenes of Tamar's deception of Judah and his subsequent recognition use repeated terms and motifs from the previous chapter. These signify that Judah experiences a "flickering memory of his prior deception of his father and injustice to Joseph."[244] The point when Judah recognizes his own moral lapse "is followed by a *peripeteia* or reversal."[245] At that moment, "*anagnorisis* is self-revelation."[246] This begins his return to familial obligations and to his role as family spokesperson.[247] The text marks the change in character by Judah's self-sacrificial offer to save his half-brother Benjamin: "The old Judah sold his youngest brother into slavery: the new Judah sacrifices himself for his youngest brother."[248] Lambe reasons that the previous scenes where Judah is involved with *anagnorisis* (Gen 37–38) tie together his moral progression in a "network of interconnected meaning."[249] The episode with Tamar, preceding the brothers' Egyptian encounters with Joseph, is a move in Judah's moral development: "Judah thus comes to know himself in a way that he did not know before, making the transition from impulsive and destructive behavior to reflection and understanding."[250] Lambe titled the entire process as "departure-transition-return."[251]

Lambe's work is important because he demonstrates that the recognition scenes in the life of Judah sit at the doorsteps of moral transition. Joseph withheld his identity as a means of testing and moving forward the honorable changes needed in Judah. Such will be important when we examine the Johannine Peter, who, without recorded remorse, denied that he was a disciple of Jesus with the words "I am not" and therefore demonstrated that he was in need of honorable changes. Later I shall argue that Jesus withheld his identity as a means of moving forward the positive character development needed in Peter.

Also regarding recognition and ancient Hebraic texts, Liv Lied analyzes the recognition/judgment episode in 2 Baruch 50–51 and concludes with findings similar to the present study. She argues that "the righteous minority, those who know, and the wicked majority, those who do not know" are

---

243. Ibid., 56.
244. Ibid., 59.
245. Ibid., 57.
246. Ibid., 58.
247. Ibid., 57, 61.
248. Ibid., 64.
249. Ibid., 55.
250. Ibid., 59.
251. Ibid., 55, 67.

"contrasting groups."[252] The judgment episode is one of finality in which the recognition constitutes a reversal where the wicked and their power are "no longer inconsistently elevated."[253] Additionally, the bridging of the cognitive gap between the wicked and the righteous indicates the wicked are "forced to acknowledge their own failure."[254]

Finally, in the last decade, two authors have made major contributions to the area of deception and trickery in Genesis. Michael Williams' *Deception in Genesis* serves as a catalogue of deception stories, rating them on a basis of whether the text evaluates them morally positive or negative.[255] Dean Nicholas, in his more recent *The Trickster Revisited: Deception as a Motif in the Pentateuch*, explains the trickster motif in terms of deception, departure, return, and a subsequent increase in status.[256]

Williams' work may be the most comprehensive treatment of deception stories in Genesis. Lamenting disparate and suspect motivations in previous studies, he notes, that "there has been no careful, thoroughgoing analysis of the phenomenon of deception, either in the Bible as a whole or in Genesis in particular, to determine the criteria for the varying evaluations of deceptive behavior."[257] Williams' study challenges the "presumption that all deception is morally negative." Instead, his work sought "to discover the criteria the biblical narrators themselves use to evaluate the deception accounts they describe."[258] Williams questions whether a "one-size-fits-all" approach" to the so-called trickster scenes is sufficient, arguing that a characteristic approach to the phenomenon assumes wrongly that the Bible is "diachronically uniform" on the topic.[259]

He approaches the issue on five different fronts. First, he analyzes the scenes, catalogs them, and assesses the "narrative evaluation" of each within its context. The catalog includes identifying the "perpetrator," "victim," "type of deception," "motive," the "specific vocabulary used," and the source or "narrative strand" of each unit.[260] For instance, his assessment of

252. Lied, "Recognizing the Righteous Remnant?," 322.

253. Ibid., 334.

254. Ibid., 329.

255. Williams, *Deception in Genesis*. Indeed this is a struggle that interpreters have wrestled with ever since Augustine. See Robinson, "Wife and Sister through the Ages," 112.

256. Nicholas, *The Trickster Revisited*.

257. Williams, *Deception in Genesis*, 4.

258. Ibid., 3–4.

259. Ibid., 5.

260. He also analyzes whether the perpetrator and victim each have a "high" or "low" social standing. Ibid., 13–29, 50–52.

Isaac's deception of Abimelech in Genesis 26 reads, "[A]n implicit negative assessment of Isaac's actions is provided by Abimelech's unanswered final rebuke of Isaac."[261] For his analysis of *types* of deception, he relies on Stith Thompson's vast six-volume *Motif-Index of Folk-Literature*—a resource well-known in the world of folk literature.[262] Williams reasons that the text judges the deception positively if the deception reverses the wrongful loss of "previous status quo."[263]

Second, Williams analyzes other deception episodes in the Hebrew Bible to see if his paradigm applies to episodes outside of Genesis. Third, he examines how extra-biblical Jewish literature evaluates the Genesis deception scenes. Sources such as the Midrash and Targumim often agree with the narrative evaluation Williams detects within the pages of Genesis.[264] Fourth, Williams turns to Ancient Near Eastern literature to look for parallels to the deception type-scene and to determine if other cultures influenced the Genesis material.[265] Finally, Williams examines folk narratives of different cultures to see if, "the view of deception manifested in Genesis and the rest of the biblical materials is unique to that corpus or is shared by other cultures, not clearly in the stream of biblical tradition."[266] Williams concludes that Genesis evaluates deception positively when the trickster lies to someone who had originally deceived and wronged someone else. In summary, deception is "justified when it functions to restore *shalom*."[267]

Nicholas analyzes deception scenes in the entire Pentateuch and does so through the lenses of anthropology's cross-cultural understanding of *rite de passage*, liminality, the history of Israel, and its formation of canon and national identity during the period of exile.[268] Eschewing source-crit-

---

261. Ibid., 17.

262. Ibid., 13–29, 194, 213; Thompson, *Motif-Index of Folk-Literature*. I do not use Thompson's massive work as a source in my study but it is important to mention for understanding the extensiveness of Williams's analysis.

263. Williams, *Deception in Genesis*, 56.

264. One such example is the positive evaluation of Tamar's deception of Judah. Josephus, however, tends to "present the Jews to others in the best possible light." Ibid., 26, 108, 121, 131.

265. But he concludes that in Ancient Near Eastern literature there "are no cases in which a person uses deception to restore his/her situation to what it was before some personal harm was suffered" Ibid., 223. This is the opposite of the in-text evaluations of the Gen narrative accounts themselves, where the text implicitly condones deception when it restores *shalom*. Ibid., 151, 221–23.

266. Ibid., 6, 193.

267. But he concludes that this criterion changes in other biblical accounts to deception that is justified when it is used to protect Israel. Ibid., 221.

268. Nicholas, *The Trickster Revisited*, 35–36, 85–86.

ical methods, Nicholas attempts to analyze the "stories as they now exist embedded in the text."[269] He also uses cross-cultural and folktale analysis.[270]

Nicholas' findings are contrary to Williams': "[T]he major thrust of the deception motif in the Pentateuch is simply that deception leads to success/raise in status, and is usually a function of the patriarchs and matriarchs."[271] He argues the exile had a tremendous effect on the inclusion of such stories in the canon and that they "carry not only the narrative weight, but the ideological weight, in light of the Exile experience." He reasons that those in exile resonated with the "liminal period, the marginal 'betwixt and between,'" when the trickster had to go through a "change of place" leaving the safety of home, before returning in an elevated status. He calls this process "separation/marginalization/reaggregation."[272] There is an element of to-and-fro regarding dwelling in the promised land that often coincides with deception, liminality, and return. Abraham and Jacob both deceive and leave, only to return more wealthy men. The Genesis writer often pens this progression as "a foreshadowing of the Exodus account."[273]

I concur with Williams, that the text's evaluation of these narratives is sometimes negative and sometimes positive, depending on whether the deception sets aright a previous wrong. Additionally, this study argues that these narratives of deception are set in a series where a main character experiences a process of change. The text often evaluates the initial narratives negatively. In the final episode, another character tricks the trickster, transforming the trickster by actions similar to those he used to deceive others. I call this manipulation and counter-manipulation. Counter-manipulation, when carried out in a way that is "measure for measure" similar to the original manipulation, should be seen as a catalyst for change. Yet, Nicholas only ventures near this conclusion when he writes: "When another incident of sibling rivalry and parental favoritism occurs, Jacob's sons decide to rid themselves of their youngest brother Joseph. But after selling him into slavery, they bloody his coat and use it to deceive their father into thinking a wild animal had devoured him. The trickster had again been tricked by a device that previously he had used himself."[274] Nicholas also argues that the trickster "is the perfect marginal character, carrying a liminal and therefore

---

269. Ibid., 72n10.

270. Ibid., 9, 21.

271. Nicholas, *The Trickster Revisited*, 81. I debated whether to reproduce Nicholas's words as "raise [sic] in status." But "raise" is his spelling, and he uses it often enough to suggest that it was his intention. See also ibid., 25, 62.

272. Ibid., 36, 40, 105.

273. Ibid., 47. See also pages 55–58.

274. Ibid., 59.

salvific function."[275] He concludes: "At some point, this connection between Israel, liminality, and the trickster is lost, leaving religious communities with simply scandalous ancestors/'heroes of faith,'" and the majority of the later theological readings simply "whitewash" the patriarchs, while modern readers vilify them.[276] Thus, my study aligns more with Williams, and reasons that Genesis, by means of sequential episodes focusing on main characters, moves the reader, in narrative time, through the negative (though valid) assessments of these characters, and on to moments in their positive transformation.

Conclusion

The preceding pages demonstrate that there is a growing body of work steadily engaging the topic of Johannine recognition. Solid scholarship on recognition and deception in Genesis is increasing as well. After surveying the work of Alter, Sternberg, Lied, Mleynek, Lambe, and Boitani, we realize that Hebraic recognition is a rich area of study. Moreover, given the FG's intertextuality with Genesis and Larsen's recent work on Johannine *anagnorisis*, we understand that the convergence of Genesis and Johannine recognition is an important one. However, to date, no one has completed an in-depth study of this intersection.[277] By examining the Jacob-Judah-Joseph recognition scenes in Genesis, this work attempts to begin filling the lacunae by providing a rubric of recurring themes and motifs in Genesis. We will find that counter-manipulation and moral development are important patterns in Genesis manipulation narratives. The nexus between manipulation, *anagnorisis*, and transformation will figure prominently later in the study and I will use them as a lens for re-reading recognition in John 21.

---

275. Ibid., 100.

276. Ibid., 105.

277. Boitani's discussion of the convergence of these two is very limited. Boitani, *The Bible and Its Rewritings*, 35, 119, 145, 148, 159.

3

Methodology

This study examines how ancient readers well versed in the book of Genesis might have interpreted the FG. These readers might have picked up on intertextuality between the two books, such as when the narrator in the FG states that Jesus sat on Jacob's well, near the plot of land that Jacob gave Joseph (John 4:5-6). However, those same readers might also have brought to the FG their method of reading Genesis and their interpretation of its form. As Alter notes in his examination of Hebrew Bible narrative, reading (or listening) in a different culture is distinct from reading in one's own and indeed takes training: "Reading any body of literature involves a specialized mode of perception in which every culture trains its members from childhood. As modern readers of the Bible, we need to relearn something of this mode of perception that was second nature to the original audiences."[1] Since I will be using these intertextual connections to examine how *anagnorisis* and manipulation can extend our understanding of characterization, I will use narrative criticism as the primary method.[2]

---

1. Alter, *The Art of Biblical Narrative*, 62. See below, where I address orality briefly in chapter 6, "Applying a Manipulation Perspective to John 21: 1-14."

2. Though this is by no means an interdisciplinary project, there are inevitable overlaps with other methodologies. I occasionally draw from the work of Robbins and his socio-rhetorical criticism, especially when dealing with my own presuppositions. Robbins, *The Tapestry of Early Christian Discourse*. I also draw from Malina and Rohrbaugh and their cultural reading of the Gospel of John. Malina and Rohrbaugh, *Social Science Commentary on the Gospel of John*. When I examine certain diminutives in John 21, I will also briefly utilize rhetorical criticism (or "classical" rhetorical criticism as Meynet describes it, Meynet, *Rhetorical Analysis*, 172), because I detect some important Greco-Roman rhetorical devices in the exchange between Jesus and the disciples. See Black, "The Words that You Gave to Me I have Given to Them," 220-39; Porter, *Handbook of Classical Rhetoric in the Hellenistic Period, 330 B.C.-A.D. 400*, 901. Finally, I also very briefly utilize textual criticism, especially in the latter half of John 21, where I discuss how and why I chose some variant readings and how these alternate readings color the interpretation of the narrative.

As I discuss below, reading Genesis meaningfully requires an understanding of how the Genesis writer used the tools of narrative such as economy of words, repetition, and implicit commentary. Accordingly, in examining both Genesis and the FG, my reading is guided by scholars whose narrative method is informed more so by the Hebrew Bible than the New Testament.

This will influence the way we read John. Meynet demonstrates that as far back as the early nineteenth century, scholars such as Thomas Boys and John Jebb worked with the New Testament texts with the critical assumption that they "obey the same organizational laws as those of the Hebrew Bible."[3] Meynet argues that the New Testament is "completely impregnated by Hebrew writings."[4] Thus, this study focuses primarily on the techniques of scholars who specialize in the reading of Hebrew narrative: Robert Alter, Shimon Bar-Efrat, and, to some degree, Meir Sternberg.[5] However, what follows does not ignore the guidance of New Testament narrative critics.[6]

---

3. Meynet, *Rhetorical Analysis*, 173.

4. Ibid., 12.

5. Earlier I note that Stibbe briefly mentions the narrative analyses of Alter, Bar-Efrat, and Sternberg and Stibbe's limited application of them to the Fourth Gospel and its similarities with Gen. Stibbe, *John's Gospel*, 10–13, 72.

6. On the criticisms and constraints of narrative criticism, see De Boer, "Narrative Criticism, Historical Criticism, and the Gospel of John," 35–48. De Boer argues that "historical and literary approaches need not be mutually exclusive," ibid., 47. He also questions interpreting a text in its assumed coherent final form without examining its compositional history, ibid., 43, 47. See also his concerns in De Boer, *Johannine Perspectives on the Death of Jesus*, 43–52. Stephen Moore, in *Literary Criticism and the Gospels*, also raises concerns, drawing comparisons and contrasts between narrative criticism and composition criticism. Both tend toward a "holistic preoccupation" and a "preoccupation with overarching authorial purpose," ibid., 54–55. Compositional critics, unlike the typical narrative critic, do examine the compositional history of the work, though they utilize the same analysis of literary conventions, ibid., 6. Somewhat contrary to de Boer, Moore claims, "Narrative Criticism had its roots in structuralist narratology, but it had its roots equally in historical criticism." Ironically, this now puts it "ahead of the narratological curve," as secular narrative theory has come full circle, back to "'rediscovery' of historical context." Moore, "Afterword: Things Not Written in this Book," 254, 257. Moore also censures *biblical* narrative criticism because later narrative scholars rarely delve into the primary sources of narratology, the study of narrative theory, or literary critics in general. Moore, *Literary Criticism and the Gospels*, 6, 51, 55; Moore, *Afterword*, 254–57. Narrative criticism has never been fascinated with the theory for theory's sake, but instead has "really only ever been interested in interpretation," ibid., 254, 256. He also points out that narrative criticism is somewhat a child of the new criticism, known for "its rejection of extrinsic approaches to the literary text–biographical, historical, sociological, philosophical–and its advocacy of an intrinsic criticism." But narrative criticism had not bloomed in the world of biblical study until literary theory had moved on, having left new criticism and its desire for a coherent reading of texts behind, ibid., 9, 11, 54. Finally, Moore points out that American narrative critics "domesticate French theory when they import it," and use

Narrative Criticism

Anagnorisis is an unquestionably significant part of ancient Greek *stories*, in particular, the dramas and tragedies.[7] It also has plenty to do with the turning of plot, an element of story.[8] Since the arrival of Culpepper's *Anatomy*, no examination of the components of *story* within the FG can ignore narrative criticism.[9] The ideas contained in a narrative approach spring from notions previously established in literary analysis.[10] Narrative criticism utilizes techniques used by scholars to analyze fictional stories.[11] Thus, some of the approaches I use here are those that have been employed by others to examine the works of Jane Austen, Charles Dickens, Victor Hugo, etc. This is not to assert that narrative criticism may be applied only to works of fiction. In fact, any narrative work is to some extent *fictive*, even historical ones. When reporting historical events, an author chooses which characteristics of a scene to record, from which point of view to tell the story, and with what words and styles to communicate. Thus, the author fictively shapes like clay that which the reader receives. An author can do this with or without an eye to historicity. Therefore, when we approach a text using narrative criticism, we are attempting to understand how that author has crafted the narrative. We ask, "What does the text imply about its readers? How do the individual narrative units relate to the whole? How is the story told? What is the plot?" We also look to see how characters are formed and how characterization is communicated to the reader. According to Mark Powell, the "goal of narrative criticism is to read the text as the implied reader."[12] To read this way, scholars generally do not separate the content of the story from the way it is constructed, but rather analyze them together.[13] This involves approaching the work as an entire unit, as one story, taking notice of things such as implied commentary, economy of detail, repetition, and irony, while listening to the story content as well. In the following pages, I examine some of these aspects upon which narrative critics focus.

---

the method to reassemble the text after decades of dissection. See also Moore, *Post Structural-Ism and the New Testament*, 5, 65–68, 78–80.

7. Browne, "Types of Self-Recognition and Self-Reform in Ancient Drama," 164.
8. Ibid., 164; MacFarlane, "Aristotle's Definition of Anagnorisis," 374–75.
9. Culpepper, "The Plot of John's Story of Jesus," 349.
10. Powell, *What Is Narrative Criticism?*, 1.
11. Resseguie, *Narrative Criticism of the New Testament*, 18.
12. Powell, *What Is Narrative Criticism?*, 20.
13. Resseguie, *Narrative Criticism of the New Testament*, 19.

METHODOLOGY

The Story as a Whole

While the efforts of Form and Source criticisms produce great amounts of scholarly work on the origins of the Gospels, narrative criticism approaches the text with the interpretive assumption that each Gospel is one complete, undivided story. According to Willem Vorster, in the critical paradigm of biblical interpretation, "knowledge is obtained by taking apart the New Testament material without studying sections or traditions as parts of a whole."[14] Narrative criticism however, attempts to ask, "What did this story intend to convey when presented in its entirety?"[15] "What was the intended effect of the 'final form'?"[16] Nicholas bemoans the former state of biblical criticism: "First, the atomizing tendencies of the historical critical method left the new literary critics a text that was so fragmented, one could rarely discuss an entire chapter; in many instances, a single verse was fragmented beyond recognition."[17] Powell notes that the predominant mindset of Historical-critical method seeks to find the reality behind the text, the *Sitz im Leben*, rather than the message conveyed in the story.[18] Narrative criticism seeks the communicative purpose of *each* individual story unit, intertwined *within* the entire book.[19] Narrative critics therefore argue that the stories were written "to be read from beginning to end."[20]

A Suspension of Disbelief

If we read the FG and Genesis as intended in their final form, our reading will include reading them from their *Weltanschauung* as well. This poses a problem for modern readers, for the worldview of many excludes the possibility

---

14. Vorster, "Towards a Post-Critical Paradigm," 35.

15. Larsen agrees, noting the critical period of biblical hermeneutics with its focus on methods such as source and form criticism leaves "less room for the Johannine genius to operate." Larsen, *Recognizing the Stranger*, 7.

16. Gaventa, "The Archive of Excess," 241–42. In a conversation with then colleague and narrative critic Dr. Martin Mittelstadt, Mittelstadt commented, "I simply don't waste my time with who wrote Luke. I'd rather spend my time with the story in the text." Mittelstadt, personal discussions about narrative form and techniques in the New Testament, 2000. See also Alter, *The World of Biblical Literature*, 70, 109.

17. Nicholas, *The Trickster Revisited*, 82. See also Bar-Efrat, *Narrative Art in the Bible*, 124–25; Sailhamer, *Pentateuch as Narrative*, 3.

18. Powell, *What Is Narrative Criticism?*, 2. Resseguie also notes the transition from the historical-critical method, *Narrative Criticism of the New Testament*, 17–19.

19. See also Moore, *Afterword*, 254. But note, not all of Moore's comments on this method are intended as praise.

20. Powell, *What Is Narrative Criticism?*, 2.

of supernatural phenomena.[21] Paul Ricoeur, in referring to the worldview of critical scholarship, laments, "In every way, something has been lost, irremediably lost: immediacy of belief."[22] He distills the very heart of the hermeneutical/*Weltanschauung* problem when he states, "We must understand in order to believe, but we must believe in order to understand."[23] This is fitting for interpreters of the FG, since belief is the goal of this Gospel, and the text itself censures unbelief. The implied reader of the FG however, is entreated to believe in the supernatural: "but these are written so that you may believe that Jesus is the Christ, the Son of God, and that by believing you may have life in his name" (John 20:31).[24] How are these different worldviews to be reconciled in relation to the text? Indeed, much of the critical period of hermeneutics deals primarily with matters of historicity, and the issue is still not settled. How should we therefore approach the text? Of course, the text may be approached in different ways, depending on one's interest. However, when aiming to understand a text as its original readers did, *choosing* to read the text *as* the implied reader will open a door for us. Powell writes: "To read in this way, it is necessary to . . . forget everything that the text does not assume the reader knows. The critic should . . . not be distracted by questions that the implied reader would not ask."[25] Powell refers to Samuel Taylor Coleridge, who foreshadows the intersection of differing worldviews in his approach to the romance of poetry. When writing poetry dealing with the supernatural, Coleridge choses a "willing suspension of disbelief for the moment, which constitutes poetic faith."[26] Such a suspension of disbelief, which of course may be distinct from personal religious belief, puts the real

---

21. Craffert, "Did Jesus Rise Bodily from the Dead? Yes and No!," 133–53; Craffert, "Jesus' Resurrection in a Social-Scientific Perspective," 126–51.

22. Ricoeur, *The Symbolism of Evil*, 351.

23. Ibid.

24. But not even all *ancient* readers, or characters within the story, believe easily. See below.

25. Powell, *What Is Narrative Criticism?*, 20.

26. Coleridge and Shawcross, *Biographia Literaria*, 6. This also requires a measure of "intellectual humility" to allow the text to speak to and "draw out" the critic, as if she were in the original audience, rather than a scholar standing apart from the text observing from a third-person perspective: "What is tacitly assumed, though rarely admitted, is a vantage point of cognitive superiority from which the modern investigator overviews the ancient text, and that assumption of superiority entails a sense of existential distance from the text. By contrast, the literary analyst, though he should certainly be aware of the differences of ancient mind-set and ancient literary procedures, presupposes a deep continuity of human experience that makes the concerns of the ancient text directly accessible to him." Alter, *The World of Biblical Literature*, 23, 204–6.

reader one step closer to the mind of the implied reader.[27] Some readers approach the text out of literary interest, some out of personal faith, and some read the FG for a combination of reasons. Moreover, much like characters within the text, those reading from a perspective of personal faith can yet wrestle with belief througout the reading process. For all of these groups, the "suspension of disbelief" offers a hermeneutical meeting ground. Thus, for Ricoeur, the goal is a "second naiveté:" "The second naiveté aims to be the postcritical equivalent of the precritical hierophany."[28]

Seymour Chatman may perhaps agree with Coleridge. Defending himself for interpreting a film through the eyes of its sexually voyeuristic characters, he makes the point that one must read, "imaginatively in a character's set of mind, even if that character is a nineteenth century lecher."[29] Narrative scholars can choose an open readerly stance during interpretation, because the FG implores readers to believe the accounts (John 20:30–31). In other words, narrative critics may read the text according to the implied author's "ideological" point of view.[30] Further, the FG itself provides an entry and exit point for that chosen point of view. Describing Boris Uspensky's, "function of framing in literature and pictorial art," Culpepper notes that the narrator speaks in the first person, both in the opening chapter ("And the Word became flesh and dwelt among *us . . . we* have received," 1:14–16) and closing chapters ("*we* know," 21:24) of the Gospel. This "framing" can serve the reader to "facilitate this transition from an external to an internal point of view at the beginning and from an internal to an external point of view at the conclusion."[31]

Narrative criticism thus brings everyone to the table, for in it, all can look *critically* at matters of dialogue, narration, plot, gaps, and point of view as analytically thinking scholars; but each can also enter for the moment into the world of John's readers and wonder at, for example, the miraculous catch. This is the perspective from which I endeavor to read: taking an investigatory point of view, but alongside the FE's implied readers.

---

27. This is nothing new to scholars. Kelber notes: "[M]iracles have long been assigned an indispensable locus in the plot construction of the narrative Gospels, as we read them with a postcritical 'second naiveté.'" Kelber, "The Quest for the Historical Jesus," 114.

28. Ibid., 351–52. Ricoeur calls this problem "the knot."

29. Chatman, "What Novels can do that Films can't (and Vice Versa)," 445–47.

30. Ibid. Adele Berlin drew upon Boris Uspensky's "Ideological Level." It is the point of view "according to which the events of the narrative are evaluated or judged." Berlin, *Poetics and Interpretation of Biblical Narrative*, 55.

31. Culpepper, *Anatomy of the Fourth Gospel*, 46.

Economy of Detail

We now turn to what Alter calls the "Bible's highly laconic mode of narration,"[32] and its "rigorous economy of biblical narrative."[33] When approaching Hebrew Bible narrative, one of its prominent characteristics is the tendency toward brevity of details. These Jewish storytellers simply avoid inessentials. This is also true of commentary, which often lies implicitly in the details, or in the omission of them, rather than in explicit narrative asides. This tendency also extends past the syntax level to the choice and inclusion of whole scenes. Most scenes advance the plot. Thus, close examination must ask what the purpose of each scene is. Of the remaining scenes, Bar-Efrat states: "The task of those incidents, which are not essential to the structure of the plot and could be omitted, is to emphasize aspects, expand situations, illuminate characters, deepen significance, etc."[34] Therefore, we are hard pressed to say that any given scene in Hebrew narrative can be omitted without altering subtle nuances to plot and characterization. The story of Judah traveling away from his brothers, attaching himself to a foreigner, and marrying a Canaanite is important to the plot (Gen 38:1–2). The narrative communicates to the reader that Judah has walked away from familial ties. This characterization conditions the reader's understanding prior to the upcoming turn of the plot, when Judah's recognition of his items brings reversal, and Tamar manipulates him back toward familial obligations. By including the previous scene where he "went down from his brothers," the author strategically chooses and places the scene for the reader to understand certain points about Judah's character. The scene therefore is important to both characterization and plot. It cannot be deleted without changing important nuances in the story.

Economy of detail also functions on an individual *word* level. When reading of Joseph traveling in captivity to Egypt and hearing of the Ishmaelites carrying "gum, balm, and myrrh" (Gen 37:25), the astute reader will suppose that these four words are not superfluous. The same reader is rewarded seven chapters later when she realizes that upon carrying their brother Benjamin down to Egypt, the brothers unwittingly and symbolically repeat the journey of Joseph, carrying these same items: "and carry a present down to the man, *balm* and a little honey, *gum*, *myrrh*, pistachio nuts, and almonds"(43:11).[35] The careful reader notes the parallel and remains

---

32. Alter, *The Art of Biblical Narrative*, 184.
33. Ibid., 61. See also Alter, *The World of Biblical Literature*, 102.
34. Bar-Efrat, *Narrative Art in the Bible*, 96.
35. Ackerman, "Joseph, Judah, and Jacob," 90–93.

observant for what will happen next. Alter states: "There is not a great deal of narrative specification in the Bible, and so when a particular descriptive detail is mentioned—Esau's ruddiness and hairiness, Rachel's beauty, King Eglon's obesity—we should be alert for consequences, immediate or eventual, either in plot or theme."[36] Therefore, cohesion and intratextuality exist within Genesis, even at the word level. The same holds true for the FG, and not only because of its intertextuality with Genesis. The economy of detail that we find so prominent in ancient Hebrew narrative was also praised by some in classical Greek.[37] The importance of this concise style will become apparent when I examine the significance of textual features in the FG.

The same economy in writing is in force when the Genesis writer elects to include that a patriarch chooses a sibling over a firstborn or when the details are provided in a dialogue between characters.[38] Such is the case when Judah initiates a sexual encounter with Tamar and completes the encounter nearly bereft of words altogether. This phenomenon almost escapes the reader until she encounters Joseph, who by contrast, resists a sexual encounter initiated by someone else and which was continually offered to him via a plethora of words (Gen 38:16–18; 39:10).[39] A close reading reveals a *contrast*, indicated by an economy of detail and words. Judah enters into a sexual liaison with Tamar, needing no invitation and with little words at all to narrate the scene, whereas Joseph abstains from a sexual liaison with Potiphar's wife, despite her unrestrained biddings. The FE narrates similar contrasts, specifically in the case of Peter. As a young disciple in chapter 13, he is constantly stating his mind, whether by refusing a foot washing (John 13:8), reversing that refusal and requesting Jesus to wash his hands and head (13:9), or boldly claiming that he would follow Jesus and back up that commitment with his life. He enters the dialogue five times in chapter 13, with a total of forty-five words, not including imploring the BD to ask Jesus who the betrayer will be. However, when the reader arrives in chapter 21, that same Peter utters only twenty-five words in the entire chapter, and he may

---

36. Alter, *The Art of Biblical Narrative*, 180.

37. Maxwell, "The Role of the Audience in Ancient Roman Theater"; Scodel, *Listening to Homer*, 131–32, 154; emphasis added. Larsen also briefly discusses oral delivery in reading: "The act of reading in Antiquity was often a social activity performed out loud by the reader, the so-called *lector* or ἀναγνώστης (*anagnōstes*). The only occurrence of the verb ἀναγινώσκω in John is when the *Ioudaioi* read the superscription on the cross (ἀνέγνωσαν, 19:20)." Larsen, *Recognizing the Stranger*, 213n58.

38. Alter, *The Art of Biblical Narrative*, 80.

39. "[I]t will be especially helpful to keep in mind the tendency of the biblical writers to organize dialogue along contrastive principles—short versus long, simple versus elaborate, balanced versus asymmetrical, perceptive versus obtuse, and so forth." Ibid., 183.

hope to appease Jesus' questions with one simple seven word response "ναὶ, κύριε, σὺ οἶδας ὅτι φιλῶ σε," ("Yes Lord, you know that I love you." 21:15b). If Jesus stops there, Peter will speak only nine words in the entire chapter.[40] A perceptive reader might notice a change in Peter's long-windedness and wonder if this is indicative of other changes in this prominent character.

Use of Repetition

Tied directly to economy of details is repetition. Alter argues that if readers should take note when a writer uses details sparingly, they should also remain vigilant for repeated words, sounds, actions, and speeches, as well as variations in these.[41] Repetitions can range from a three-consonantal root to a large narrative type-scene.[42] We see the use of repetition in even broader ways than just narrative units. James Price argues that the FG, in a manner similar to the Thanksgiving Hymns of Qumran (the Hodayoth or 1QH), uses repetition extensively to reinforce its theological themes.[43]

More important for this study is repetition of and within narrative units, especially type-scenes. Alter defines a type-scene as: "[A]n episode occurring at a portentous moment in the career of the hero which is composed of a fixed sequence of motifs. It is often associated with certain recurrent themes."[44] The repetition of type-scenes is evident in Genesis, where the pattern of the wife/sister deception occurs three times (Gen 12:10–20; 20:1–17; 26:1–10), the switching of siblings arises twice (27:1–46; 29:15–30), and the lack of recognition connected with some combination of garments and goats is repeated three times (27:1–46; 37:1–36; 38:1–30). I will however, slightly broaden this terminology and refer to units of varying sizes, noting repeated patterns found not only in scenes (denoting one action in one place and at one time between the same set of characters, e.g. Jacob feeding Isaac his stew, Gen 27: 18–29), but also in episodes (multiple scenes together, creating one story unit, e.g. Jacob and Rebekah's entire deception of Isaac and Esau, 27:1—28:5), and in longer narratives or cycles, where several episodes in a character's life together contain the repeated motifs and themes, and therefore constitute the "type" characteristics which Alter

---

40. The first two words are "I-am-going fishing," only two words in Greek.

41. Alter, *The Art of Biblical Narrative*, 183.

42. Alter calls this a "scale of repetitive structuring ... running from the smallest and most unitary elements to the largest and most composite ones." Ibid., 95.

43. Both documents use this technique, in Price's words, "to a point of monotony." Price, *Light from Qumran upon some Aspects of Johannine Theology*, 10.

44. Alter, *The Art of Biblical Narrative*, 96.

refers to. These repetitions serve a function for the reader, as *Leitwörter* and *Leitmotiv*, which the text leads the reader to connect.[45] Probably the most obvious example of repetition in Genesis relevant to this study is the recurrence of the root for *recognize*, נכר and all its forms.[46] This *Leitwort* ties narrative units together. Segovia notes a similar broad continuum of repetition in the FG as well, found at both the word and scene levels.[47] The FE repeats certain themes, namely fish, bread, sheep, and shepherding, unifying the narrative. This is also true of named persons, such as Nathanael. These repetitions alert the reader to make textual connections to prior chapters.

Implicit Commentary

This brings the discussion to implicit commentary, which Alter calls "the imaginative subtlety of biblical narrative."[48] The text suggests implicit commentary when the narrator offers no outright statements about nuances, such as the scruples of a character. The story instead entices the interactive reader to perceive these conclusions.[49] Genesis demonstrates implicit commentary in the above-mentioned contrast between Judah and Joseph in regards to their sexual behavior. Genesis readers may infer that Judah has less moral integrity than Joseph, but the biblical writer does not explicitly state this comparison. Such was the job of the ancient reader. The text implies a similar comparison between Jacob and Judah. When Jacob's sons lead him to infer the supposed death of Joseph, the reader is presented with two verses (twenty-nine words in the Hebrew text) describing Jacob's outward display of grief. When reading of Judah losing his two sons, the reader encounters no grieving at all.[50] The implicit commentary is that Judah is somehow callous to the death of his offspring, whereas Jacob's very life is bound up in his (favorite!) children, which is explicitly stated later (Gen 44:30).

We also find implicit commentary in the birthright narrative of Jacob and Esau (Gen 25). By portraying Esau's focus on his hunger, Jacob's stew (Esau "pantingly, calling it 'this red red stuff.'"), the willingness to forfeit

---

45. Ibid., 95. See the discussion of these in the analysis of Gen below, in the section "Evocative *Déjà Vu* Motifs."

46. Ibid., 4–5, 159–60, 163. See the treatment of נכר below under "Evocative *Déjà Vu* Motifs."

47. Segovia, "The Final Farewell of Jesus," 170. See also Anderson, "From One Dialogue to another," 96.

48. Alter, *The Art of Biblical Narrative*, 88. See also Alter, *The World of Biblical Literature*, 47–84.

49. Osborne, *The Hermeneutical Spiral*, 161–62.

50. Lambe, "Judah's Development," 55–56.

his birthright, and the short staccato explanation of his eating and departure ("and he ate and he drank and he rose and he went off"), the writer of Genesis presses the reader to infer the negative assessment.[51] Alter states, "Esau, the episode makes clear, is not spiritually fit to be the vehicle of divine election, the bearer of the birthright of Abraham's seed."[52]

Implicit commentary need not be limited to judgment of character. In Genesis 12:3 Abraham is told, "I will bless those who bless you, and him who dishonors you I will curse." That blessing is seen implicitly when, after lying about his wife, Abraham, not Pharaoh, walks off with a significant increase in material possessions—one that is described in many words: "And for her sake he dealt well with Abraham; and he had sheep, oxen, male donkeys, male servants, female servants, female donkeys, and camels" (Gen 12:16).[53]

Stibbe utilizes the works of Alter, Bar-Efrat, and Sternberg as he applies this method to John's Gospel: "The result is that the reader is forced to get at character and motive through a process of *inference* from fragmentary data, often with crucial pieces of narrative exposition strategically withheld."[54] Culpepper reminds his readers that irony is often a part of this process, noting that implicit commentary serves as, "'silent' communication between author and reader," in which "[t]he implied author smiles, winks, and raises his eyebrows as the story is told. The reader who sees as well as hears understands that the narrator *means more* than he says."[55] Daniel Marguerat, commenting on Culpepper's treatment of Johannine implicit commentary, observes that the pieces of the puzzle that the FE intends for the implied reader to infer, relate to three areas in the FG: "misunderstanding, irony, and symbolism."[56] An astute implied reader in the FG is therefore, "in the know," whereas certain characters, such as the Pharisees in John 9, do not know (9:29).

Gaps, Implied Reader, and Point of View

Narrative criticism of the Gospels also includes exploration into narrative gaps, the implied reader, and point of view. The implied reader is the

51. Alter, *The Art of Biblical Narrative*, 45.
52. Ibid.
53. Nicholas, *The Trickster Revisited*, 46.
54. Stibbe, *John's Gospel*, 10–11.
55. Culpepper, *Anatomy of the Fourth Gospel*, 151, 165–66.
56. "[L]e malentendu, l'ironie et la symbolique." Marguerat, "L'exégèse biblique à l'heure du lecteur," n.p. I am grateful to my colleague Dr. Craig Hanson for assistance with this article, since I am not a student of French.

personification of the way the author desires the real readers to respond. For Martin De Boer, the implied reader is a "construct of the text" and the "role of the [implied reader] is to feel or to achieve what perhaps may be called the 'implied intention' of the implied author."[57]

Narrative gaps, therefore, may indicate areas where the author assumes something already known by the implied reader. For instance, there was no need for the FE to explain why the disciples are shocked that Jesus is speaking to the woman at the well. The implied readers should know why—it was socially unacceptable for a man to speak to a woman in that setting, especially a Samaritan and one who came at that time of the day alone to the well.[58] A gap may also occur where the narrator or a character refers to something that has not yet been explained, as in John 2:4, when Jesus says, "My hour has not yet come."

The overall point of view of the narrator in the FG is one of omniscience.[59] This is clear where, in John 21:4, the disciples do not know that the man on the shore is Jesus, but the narrator knows and informs the readers of Jesus' identity (John 21:4). Sometimes the point of view of the narrator is juxtaposed against that of a character in the dialogue.[60] In John 2:20–22, those in dialogue with Jesus regard the "temple" as a building. The narrator counters that Jesus was speaking of his body. In chapter 7 below, I will clarify where the narrator's point of view, signified by the words used to describe the 153 fish in contrast to Jesus' words, adds significance both to the catch of 153 fish, as well as to Jesus' dialogue with the disciples.

The omniscient narrator also gives a rare peek into the interior feelings of Peter when Jesus questions him. However, the FE leaves the reader a gap by not explaining specifically what aspect of the third question has grieved Peter (John 21:17). The nuance may have been lost over time, or the FE may have intended the gap in order to build intrigue. When a text performs in this second way, with intentional ambivalence, Sternberg terms this "indeterminacy."[61] Textual indeterminacy occurs in Genesis and in the FG. Such ambivalence of meaning may serve dramatically to draw the reader further into the story and build suspense until the point where many of the pieces fall into place. I will return to textual indeterminacy periodically in

---

57. De Boer, "Narrative Criticism, Historical Criticism, and the Gospel of John," 303. See also Moore, *Literary Criticism and the Gospels*, 46.

58. Bailey, *Jesus through Middle Eastern Eyes*, 201–2, 212.

59. Culpepper, *Anatomy of the Fourth Gospel*, 21.

60. The narrator, Michal, and David each have a different description and point of view of David's dancing before the Lord in 2 Sam 6:14–21. Berlin, *Poetics and Interpretation of Biblical Narrative*, 72.

61. Sternberg, *The Poetics of Biblical Narrative*, 118, 177, 285, 303–4.

the discussions of Genesis as well as the FG, where passages leave the reader wondering, perhaps intentionally, what the characters were thinking.

Irony

Irony occurs when the narrative provides a "contrast of appearance and reality," and the difference is portrayed as "a confident unawareness (pretended in the ironist, real in the victim of irony), that the appearance is only an appearance."[62] Irony often includes a "comic effect," in that the victim is unaware of the double meaning, but should be.[63] When the author uses irony, made apparent by the omniscient point of view of the narrator, the intended effect is that the implied reader would see the irony and respond differently than the characters in the text. For instance, the implied reader should recognize that Jesus is "greater than our Father Jacob" in 4:12.[64] David Ball argues that irony is inseparable from the "I am" sayings and is often the key to seeing the divine point of view that the narrator desires the implied reader to have. The use of irony may challenge readers to see a revelation that would not otherwise be obvious. John 8:33 is entrenched in irony in the fact that the *Ioudaioi* are, in the narrator's perspective, the opposite of what they themselves believe: claiming to be descendants of Abraham—but spiritually they are not, claiming bondage to no one—but in bondage to sin.[65]

Sjef van Tilborg points out a striking irony when the chief priests shout, "We have no king but Caesar (John 19:15)," a statement that is ironically more true than the priests realize, as the chief priests are voicing chants of worship which Ephesian listeners would have thought natural for priests of emperor worship.[66] In fact, Charles Connick notes that "nearly every

---

62. Muecke, *Irony*, 35.
63. Culpepper, *Anatomy of the Fourth Gospel*, 167.
64. Moloney, "Who is 'the Reader' in/of the Fourth Gospel," 220–28.
65. Ball, *"I Am" in John's Gospel*, 85, 256–60.
66. The temple priests were responsible to assert the emperor's divine cult status. When that information comes to bear on John 19:15, where the Jerusalem priests assert, "we have no king but Caesar," they "not only renounce their political independence but they also no longer profess that God is the only king of Israel." Readers in Ephesus might have caught this and, more importantly, that the Jerusalem high priests put themselves in the position of emperor cult high priests. They not only affirm a political alliance but, ironically, an Ephesian reader may also have seen them as proclaiming the divinity of the emperor himself. Tilborg writes, "Anyway, people in Ephesus will not have found it strange that precisely the high priests of the people are presented as the advocates and spokesman of the divine kingship of the emperor." The irony of this abandonment of divine loyalty may have been surprising, especially if there were Jewish Ephesian readers. Tilborg, *Reading John in Ephesus*, 173, 217.

word that Caiaphas utters is ironical."[67] Irony frequently involves a negative inference toward the victim of the irony. As Douglas Muecke states, "Other things being equal, the greater the victim's blindness, the more striking the irony."[68] The ironies in the FG can therefore be "corrective" and serve to demonstrate the dullness of the one who believes the appearance is the reality.[69] In Genesis, Judah and his brothers deceive their father into arriving at a wrong conclusion. With the words "Please identify," they induce Jacob to believe that a wild animal devoured Joseph (Gen 37:32). Judah and his brothers deceive their father and believe that they can easily dupe him. Ironically, in the next chapter, Judah is the one deceived. He must *recognize* not only his items of personal identification, but also the reality that Tamar is *"more righteous than I"* (38:26). The double irony begins with Judah deceiving, but then the tables are turned and the chapter ends with this, Judah's own explicit statement about his lack of moral character in comparison to Tamar. The FG often characterizes the victims of irony with their own words. This is true of Peter, who ironically says at the trial that he is not Jesus' disciple, and who later, moreover, does not know his shepherd's voice (John 21:4–5). Peter's claim was truer than he realized. Misunderstanding is likewise intertwined with irony as characters in the FG, including the Samaritan woman, Nicodemus, the disciples, and Martha, repeatedly find that they are confused. The narrator, however, grants the implied reader an omniscient point of view, which exposes the misunderstanding and the ironic truth of the scene.

Characters and Characterization

Since *anagnorisis*, as it functions within manipulation narratives, informs a reader's understanding of a character's development, I now turn to an extended focus on characters.

---

67. Connick, "The Dramatic Character of the Fourth Gospel," 166. Connick points to what is perhaps the most poignant of Caiaphas's irony, John 11:50, "[I]t is better for you that one man should die for the people, not that the whole nation should perish." Ibid.

68. Muecke, *Irony*, 28–29.

69. Culpepper, *Anatomy of the Fourth Gospel*, 168.

Theories of Character

Analysis of characters is an oft-neglected component of narrative analysis.[70] Yet scholars have not overlooked characters completely. E.M. Forster sparked the discussion when he posited that characters are either flat or round.[71] Flat characters for the most part have a "single idea or quality," and rarely, if ever, surprise the reader.[72] They are, "easily recognized whenever they come in—recognized by the reader's emotional eye, not by the visual eye, which merely notes the recurrence of a proper name."[73] Round characters are Foster's title for the opposite kind, full of surprise and complexity, closely resembling the internal conflicts in humanity.[74] Nevertheless, flat characters might not always remain flat. Great authors can surprise even with a normally one-dimensional character.[75] Flat characters can slip into roundness, and back out, as in the case of the Jane Austen character, Fanny.[76] Forster tends to favor round characters, unless the author is also a genius at flat characters, types, and caricatures, such as Dickens. Round characters are preferred because that complexity allows them to come closer to the *mimesis* of the complexities of life, and therefore capable of causing deep emotions in the reader.[77]

Auerbach argues that characters in Greco-Roman literature are static or flat, whereas characters in Hebrew literature are round and show a progression.[78] In the course of his examination of elevated styles of narrative used by authors in the mimetic portrayal of life, Auerbach observes the lack of complexity and development in characters in Homer. Homer's characters stand in contrast to the reversals of fortune, the intricacies "on the verge of dissolution," and conflicting desires and motives of the Old Testament characters.[79] For Auerbach, the Markan Peter "is the image of man in the highest and deepest and most tragic sense."[80] Ironically, although the biblical characters are far more complex, the reader must infer much, with the

---

70. Chatman, *Story and Discourse*, 107. See also Rimmon-Kenan, *Narrative Fiction*, 29; Bennema, *Encountering Jesus*, 2.
71. Forster, *Aspects of the Novel*, 100–118.
72. Ibid., 103–4.
73. Ibid., 105.
74. Ibid., 107, 118.
75. Ibid., 116.
76. Ibid.
77. Ibid., 109, 112, 116–18.
78. Auerbach, *Mimesis*, 17.
79. Ibid., 18.
80. Ibid., 41.

biblical style so bereft of extraneous details. Conversely, according to Auerbach, the Homeric style is quite full of descriptors, but rarely demonstrates complexity and development.[81] The biblical style portrays characters that throughout life are molded by God in such a way that later "produces from them forms which their youth gave no grounds for anticipating."[82] Thus, they surprise the reader with "layers of consciousness and conflict."[83] For Auerbach, these features are representative of the two genres: complex and developing characters described with little detail in biblical narrative, and static but generously depicted characters in Homeric narrative. Later theorists, do however, challenge this second categorization.

William Harvey continues Auerbach's quest for a theory of mimetics, but does so by focusing on a theory of characters.[84] He, too, uses categories, but speaks of "end[s] of the scale" and of "fluidity" between his definitions—the best artists can blend characters' traits so well as to render categories ineffective.[85] He identifies not two but three main types: protagonist, background, and intermediate characters. He then subdivides the intermediate type into cards and ficelles. For our purposes here, protagonists are synonymous with Forster's round characters.[86] Second, background characters are very flat, and at the extreme, they represent an "unreal stereotype," which never provokes the reader.[87] However, like Forster's flat character, Harvey's background character can slip into a moment of vividness that "is only one arc of the circle that if fully drawn would make up the rounded character."[88] Third, Harvey extracts from Forster's flat category intermediate characters, whom he subdivides into either cards or ficelles. Both sub-types are more than simple flat characters with one trait. They have a functional purpose in the story. The card's singular trait (often negative) evokes an amusing response in the reader. The text produces a conflicted dislike or pity for the card. Thus, while Forster describes Charles Dickens' Mr. Micawber as flat,

---

81. Ibid., 17–18.
82. Ibid., 18.
83. Ibid., 13.
84. Harvey, *Character and the Novel*, 23. When speaking of theories of characters, I am referring to how scholars classify characters into categories, such as flat, round, ficelle, card, and even static and developmental. When I use the term "characterization," I am referring to the manner in which the author "communicates character traits to the reader." Bennema, *Encountering Jesus*, 66–67. Harvey draws similar distinctions, *Character and the Novel*, 30.
85. Ibid., 56, 63, 68.
86. Ibid., 54–55.
87. Ibid., 53.
88. Ibid., 55.

Harvey sees him as a card.[89] For Harvey, cards grip the reader because their comical singularity is true to life. Most readers know a Mr. Micawber—someone they have characterized by one trait or another. They exclaim, "What a character!"[90] Likewise, ficelles are also intermediate characters of one trait. They serve secondarily to the protagonist, but do so without an imposing intrusion into the plot.[91] For Harvey, the "danger" of the card is that he or she is, "liable to grow out of all proportion." That of the ficelle, however, is of becoming too flat and serving "merely a function."[92]

Robert Scholes and Robert Kellogg emphasize not only characters, but also the types of art they typify: representational (or mimetic), illustrative and esthetic types.[93] Representative art and characterization remain "highly individualized" and attempt to "duplicate reality," whereas the illustrative aims to highlight only one facet of it.[94] Illustrative art and characters are more fictive and serve to symbolize the emotions that drive the plot forward but do not mimic life.[95] Scholes and Kellogg continue Auerbach's position that Greco-Roman characters are rarely complex, conflicted, or developing, whereas the characters in the Hebrew Bible change and are multifaceted.[96]

Chatman furthers our understanding of character. Beginning with Forster's categories, he argues that round characters are open-ended. Thus, classifying modern round characters is nearly impossible.[97] Round characters are open-ended because they can surprise the reader with unpredicted behavior. Since they are open-ended, Chatman argues for an understanding of characterization which allows the reader and/or critic to "infer and even speculate" *into* that open-endedness.[98] As I explained above, economy of detail and implicit commentary in biblical narratives call for the reader to do just what Chatman proposes. Nevertheless, Chatman offers a method for separating "the worthwhile from the trivial."[99] Citing Bradley's method, he advises a re-reading of the text, taking note of what the character "does and

---

89. Forster, *Aspects of the Novel*, 104, 111; Harvey, *Character and the Novel*, 59.

90. Ibid., 58.

91. Ibid.

92. Ibid., 62–63.

93. Scholes and Kellogg, *The Nature of Narrative*, 84, 102.

94. Ibid., 84, 103. The representational, illustrative, and esthetic types are also not exclusive and the author may at times combine them within a character. Ibid., 100.

95. Ibid., 102–3.

96. Ibid., 164, 166, 169, 176.

97. Chatman, *Story and Discourse*, 112.

98. Ibid., 117.

99. Ibid., 120.

does not do, does and does not say, what is said to and about him, to 'read out' and speculate about these data"[100] to build a "paradigm of traits."[101]

Shlomith Rimmon-Kenan picks up where Chatman left off, arguing that readers should explore characters beyond the surface of the text, but also hoping to create some resolution regarding a theory of characters.[102] Characters that change in a way the reader does not expect have "directional dimension."[103] Suggesting that Chatman's paradigm is too static, she continues the move away from only two categories of characters and draws on Joseph Ewen's "continuum" of characters and his three axes upon which to plot them: "complexity, development, [and] penetration into the 'inner life.'"[104] Using this method, critics may chart characters with only one trait or with a number so high as to suggest "infinite degrees of complexity."[105] Characters that do not change do not necessarily possess only a single trait but can also be complex.[106] The consideration of a character's inner thought life permits the analysis to differentiate between a complex character with whom we have little view of the interior, as with Abraham or Jacob, and one with whom we have a vast view of their mind, as with Fyodor Dostoevsky's Raskolnikov.[107] This is important, because later Bennema uses these axes to classify the characters in John.[108] Rimmon-Kenan also theorizes on the process of characterization, noting "direct definition" and "indirect presentation."[109] The first occurs with direct statement, such as "John was angry." The second is equivalent to implicit commentary, and happens when the author describes the character's behavior and allows the reader to infer

---

100. Ibid., 134–35.

101. Ibid., 126. Chatman argues this method in opposition to formalism and some structuralism positions that view open-ended exploration of what characters "'are' by some psychological or moral measure" as an "erroneous" exercise. Ibid., 111. See also Conway, *Men and Women in the Fourth Gospel*, 50.

102. Rimmon-Kenan, *Narrative Fiction: Contemporary Poetics*, 31–35, 44.

103. Ibid., 41.

104. Ibid., 42–43; Ewen, "The Theory of Character in Narrative Fiction," 7; Ewen, *Character in Narrative*, 33–44. Ewen's works are available only in Hebrew.

105. Rimmon-Kenan, *Narrative Fiction: Contemporary Poetics*, 43.

106. Ibid.

107. Ibid., 83–84.

108. Bennema, *Encountering Jesus*. Using these axes, he plots his characters on an "*aggregate* continuum," from least to greatest complexity, development, and inner life, as agent, type, personality, or individual. He therefore "places Peter on the character continuum as an individual." Bennema, *A Theory of Character in New Testament Narrative*, 86, 138.

109. Rimmon-Kenan, *Narrative Fiction: Contemporary Poetics*, 63.

the interpretation, e.g., John "got up, banged the door, and left the house."[110] The character commits certain actions and omits others that perhaps they should not have. A character's speech, appearance, and environment also paint a picture. Finally, authors use a variety of analogies to communicate information about the character, using their name (Dickens' "Gradgrind"), surroundings, and other characters to whom they are compared and contrasted, and therefore paint the reader's perception of the character.[111]

The rigorous discussion on characters and characterization has led in recent decades to a growing body of work on characters in the Hebrew Bible and the Gospels. Sternberg maintains that biblical narratives are terse in detail for two important reasons. First, the brevity draws the reader into the story and forces her to create a fuller character in the process of "gap-filling."[112] Second, the lack of detail relates to a Hebrew understanding of an unfathomable God—details are hard to come by. Nevertheless, even though the narratives are terse, the human characters are complex and surprising, supplying evidence of their fallen and conflicted natures. God, in contrast, "remains static."[113] Alter likewise stresses the capacity and process of change in biblical characters, once again, in contrast to Greco-Roman ones.[114] Thus, a move toward complex and developing biblical characters has been growing. Nevertheless, not all rush to see them so complex and developmental.

Culpepper devots nearly fifty pages to characters in his narrative analysis of the FG.[115] He explores the convergence of historical and fictional criticism and argues that analysis of fictional works should not be alien to Gospel analysis. Whether authors write historical works or fiction, all do so with "an element of selectivity."[116] Choosing which characters to include, determining how to represent them, deciding which details to communicate and how to convey them, are all parts of a creative process: "Even if the figure is real rather than 'fictional,' it has to pass through the mind of the author before it can be described."[117]

Culpepper agrees with others that Greek characters are typically static and Hebrew characters develop throughout the narrative. While he

110. Ibid., 111. See also pages 63–65.

111. Ibid., 61–72.

112. Sternberg, *The Poetics of Biblical Narrative*, 186–88, 222–30.

113. Ibid., 324.

114. Alter concedes that Greek characters sometimes change, but Achilles changes "in feeling and action, not in character." Alter, *The Art of Biblical Narrative*, 127. See also Bennema, *A Theory of Character in New Testament Narrative*, 35–44.

115. Culpepper, *Anatomy of the Fourth Gospel*, 100–148.

116. Ibid., 105.

117. Ibid.

posits that the FG "draws from Greek and Hebrew models of character development,"[118] using Harvey's model he argues that nearly all of the FG's characters are ficelles and have a functioning "representational value" and are "particular ethical types," having only a "single-trait."[119] Yet as Culpepper works through the characters in the pages that follow, he cites many character complexities in the FG. Though the character of Jesus is "static," Culpepper nonetheless speaks of Jesus with Harvey's notion of "mystery," that is, Jesus is "never fully exposed" or "'penetrated.'"[120] While the disciples have representational roles, they also follow, misunderstand, and even desert Jesus. They believe, but do not believe in him.[121] This way of describing Johannine characterization hints at the need for biblical scholars to either create or adopt a method that analyzes characters beyond the two or three categories of Forster and Harvey. As Rimmon-Kenan has pointed out earlier, characters, including biblical ones, can be static and complex at the same time.[122]

Another New Testament scholar who has been applying theories of character to the Gospels is Elizabeth Struthers Malbon. In her book, *In the Company of Jesus: Characters in Mark's Gospel*, she examines Forster's two categories. While she also briefly considers Adele Berlin's three categories (full-fledged character, type, and agent), Harvey's three categories, and Baruch Hochman's eight sets of criteria, she choses to remain with Forster's two-fold analysis.[123] She, however, does not work with impermeable categories and often refers to a continuum on which flat and round designations can be plotted.[124] Many times, the assumed characterization readers hold for certain characters is challenged by turns in the story. At times the crowd surprisingly follows Jesus, while the disciples abandon him.[125] Many of the followers of Jesus are "fallible followers."[126] Surprise and juxtaposition are

---

118. Ibid., 103.

119. Ibid., 102. Raymond Collins and Margaret Davies take a similar approach. Collins, "The Representative Figures of the Fourth Gospel," 26–46; Davies, *Rhetoric and Reference in the Fourth Gospel*.

120. Culpepper, *Anatomy of the Fourth Gospel*, 112; Harvey, *Character and the Novel*, 71.

121. Culpepper, *Anatomy of the Fourth Gospel*, 115–25.

122. Rimmon-Kenan, *Narrative Fiction: Contemporary Poetics*, 41–44.

123. Malbon, *In the Company of Jesus*, 159–63, 184–85; Hochman, *Character in Literature*, 88–89; Berlin, *Poetics and Interpretation of Biblical Narrative*, 23. Specifically for her consideration of Berlin's work, see Malbon, *In the Company of Jesus*, 159n52.

124. Malbon, *In the Company of Jesus*, 197.

125. Ibid., 97.

126. Ibid., 41–45.

therefore considerable elements in her theory of characters. Similar to Cassidy's and Tolmie's views of Peter's character, which I discussed above, she also points out that readers build characters through a series of events, as the characters act and interact with one another.[127]

In her more recent book, *Mark's Jesus: Characterization as Narrative Christology*, she refines her method of plumbing Markan character.[128] She does not focus so much on a general theory of biblical characters, but rather specifically on Jesus. She analyzes two types of story events: saying and doing.[129] Thus, she examines "what Jesus does," "what others say," "what Jesus says in response," "what Jesus says instead," and "what others do."[130] In so doing, she finds that Markan Christology is one of juxtaposition and surprise. Separating the narrator's voice from that of Jesus, she argues that Jesus often deflects the appellations the narrator places on him and turns the attention toward God.[131] Minor characters have their surprises as well. They are far from the flat "monolithic stereotypes" readers have assumed them to be. Readers' perceptions of character *groups* such as the "Roman authorities" and religious authorities are challenged by the positive actions of their individual *members* like the centurion and Joseph of Arimathea (Mark 15).[132] Thus, Malbon advances her theory of characters beyond a simple two-part categorization of flat and round.

Colleen Conway also moves in this direction, drawing upon the work of Seymour Chatman and Hochman. She argues for a theory of characters that combines both the mimetic and the functional view of character, thus allowing a deeper exploration of characters. Hochman maintains that the process of characterization happens in relation to other characters. Conway uses this theoretical platform to launch her dissertation on gender and character in the FG. She argues that building a characterization of given characters in the FG "in isolation from one another" is impossible.[133] In chapter 9, the blind man is characterized as admitting he does not know Jesus at first but later recognizing him (John 9:38). This characterization works only in contrast to the Pharisees who inversely, claim they can see but who admit,

---

127. Ibid., 53.

128. Malbon, *Mark's Jesus: Characterization as Narrative Christology*.

129. Ibid., 15.

130. Ibid., 18–22.

131. Ibid., 70. She also argues that the Markan Jesus and the Markan narrator "are not always in agreement." Ibid., 79.

132. Ibid., 123.

133. Conway, *Men and Women in the Fourth Gospel*, 66.

"we do not know where he comes from" (9:29).[134] Conway also aligns herself with Chatman and Rimmon-Kenan when she notes that the reader's understanding of Peter has to do with what he does in the garden, wielding a sword and demonstrating his misunderstanding of Jesus' kingdom.[135] She greatly assists our understanding of minor characters in the FG by pushing beyond Culpepper's original analysis and noting their ambiguity.[136] She contributes one of the more convincing arguments against the idea that the FG contains mostly flat characters. Since so many scholars disagree on what the "single trait" is for a given character, especially minor ones (e.g., Nicodemus), she responds by asking how scholars can categorize the character as flat.[137] Yet Conway describes the BD and Jesus as flat characters.[138] This contrasts with Scholes and Kellogg, who uses the example of Jesus' cry of abandonment on the cross as an example of complexity and conflict.[139]

Susan E. Hylen carries ambiguity in characterization even further. She laments that since many scholars classify Johannine characters as flat, their reading obscures the understanding of the FG. She also reminds her readers that modern scholars in classical studies are beginning to question whether Greco-Roman characters are "flat, static and opaque."[140] Thus, she continues the move toward a more nuanced theory of characters and characterization. She also leans away from a purely mimetic theory of characters, viewing them more as "creations of literary work."[141] Like Conway, she demonstrates that characters in the FG previously assumed to be flat have much contradiction: the Jews believe in Jesus, some of the disciples do not believe, the BD does not understand that Jesus must rise from the dead, and Nicodemus adequately understands Jesus' origin.[142] Her goal was to show that such ambiguity is not problematic, but rather clarifies a Johannine understanding of discipleship as an imperfect process, with followers that stumble along the way.[143] Even in imperfect faith, the Samaritan woman, whose "testimony

134. Ibid., 134–35.

135. Ibid., 174.

136. Conway, "Speaking through Ambiguity"; 328; Conway, *Men and Women in the Fourth Gospel*, 51; Culpepper, *Anatomy of the Fourth Gospel*, 102.

137. Conway, *Speaking through Ambiguity*, 328–29; Hylen, *Imperfect Believers*, 4, 23; Bennema, *Encountering Jesus*, 7.

138. Conway, *Speaking through Ambiguity*, 330.

139. Scholes and Kellogg, *The Nature of Narrative*, 163.

140. Hylen, *Imperfect Believers*, 4.

141. Ibid., 5.

142. Ibid., 28, 26, 62, 83, 101, 118. Another benefit is that it also allows her to read the FG in a way that "affirms Judaism." Ibid., 128, 155.

143. Ibid., 72–73.

about Jesus' identity as the Messiah is exploratory rather than confessing," is able to usher her entire town to Jesus.[144] Hylen's method is important because she deflates the notion of single trait characters in John, making room for more ambiguous characters that develop and change. I concur. Significant characters in Genesis as well as John sometimes go through a journey of significant moral change.

Notwithstanding, New Testament scholarship does not depart completely from types and a representational view of character in the FG. Following Aristotle's four criteria for characters, Peter Dschulnigg espouses a view that many characters in John's Gospel are not complex portraits, but are rather representational. This allows readers to identify with characters by what the characters symbolize.[145] At the same time, the FE paints them in a mimetic way, indicating certain faith responses to Jesus. Some characters, such as Peter and Nicodemus, appear negatively, only to overcome their weaknesses later on. The reader, challenged by the types, can then change his or her orientation toward Jesus based on each character.[146]

Bennema also has not shunned the representational value of characters in the FG, but treated the representational aspect in a different way. Probably more so than any other Johannine scholar, Bennema has expressed dissatisfaction with a simple typical flat versus round theory of characters.[147] Like Hylen, he argues biblical scholarship has not kept pace with specialists in Greco-Roman writings.[148] From their work, he promoted "that character can be more complex and take on more dimensions than Aristotle has us believe."[149] Greek characters "tend" toward the flat, but some like Ajax do develop, change, and some offer glimpses of their inner life, such as Euripides' Medea.[150] He also draws from Richard Burridge's assertion that some characters in Plutarch's *Lives* go through changes.[151] He concludes: "from

---

144. Ibid., 54–55.

145. Dschulnigg, *Jesus Begegnen: Personen und ihre Bedeutung im Johannesevangelium*, 1–2, 88–89.

146. Ibid., 1.

147. Bennema, *Encountering Jesus*, 2–3, 13.

148. Bennema, "A Theory of Character in the Fourth Gospel . . .," 378. Among other scholars, Bennema is also critical of Tolmie's view of character, whom I discuss in the section on Peter in the previous chapter. Ibid., 11–12.

149. Ibid., 383.

150. Ibid., 385, 420. Contra Scholes and Kellogg, *The Nature of Narrative*, 164. See also Berlin, *Poetics and Interpretation of Biblical Narrative*, 23, who calls their assessment of "primitive stories" as "flat and opaque" a "gross oversimplification."

151. Bennema, "A Theory of Character in the Fourth Gospel . . .," 387; Burridge, *What Are the Gospels?*, 178.

classical tragedy to comedy to biography, historiography and novel, there are significant instances where character can be complex, change, have inner life and even show personality."[152] Like Culpepper, Bennema applies modern analysis of fictive characters to the biblical text, citing Frank Kermode that "constructing character" happens by "'inferring ... from other texts and from life.'"[153] He terms this approach "a form of historical narrative criticism, taking a text-centered approach but examining aspects of the world outside or 'behind' the text if the text invites us to do so."[154] Bennema therefore combines the mimetic and autonomous view of character. As long as scholars are careful, realizing that one can adapt contemporary concepts and ideas to analyze biblical characters, they can draw from other texts, from modern understandings of characters, and from life itself.[155] The point of view of the FE positions the reader in an "evaluative" stance, soliciting him or her to make judgments on each Johannine character's faith response.[156]

In his monograph, *Encountering Jesus: Character Studies in the Gospel of John*, Bennema asks how the FE can "present characters as being unstable, complex and ambiguous" in the FG's dualism of "belief and unbelief."[157] He answers this by taking Rimmon-Kenan's use of Ewen's three axes of "complexity, development and penetration into inner life," and analyzes each Johannine character on each axis, while also uniquely maintaining Culpepper's and Collins' type and representational analysis.[158] He examines each character via these axes, but the character's faith *responses* he places into the two categories of adequate or inadequate.[159] Characters may move back and forth between adequate and inadequate, thus showing development.[160] This affirms a character's complexity, despite never developing an adequate faith response (e.g., Judas).[161] Likewise, there are characters assumed to be flat who bring tension and complexity to the story, such as the BD when he presumably falls short of "resurrection faith" at the tomb.[162] Bennema

---

152. Bennema, "A Theory of Character in the Fourth Gospel...," 395.

153. Ibid., 399. Contra Stibbe, *John as Storyteller*, 24.

154. Bennema, "A Theory of Character in the Fourth Gospel...," 401.

155. Ibid., 396.

156. Ibid., 410, 414.

157. Bennema, *Encountering Jesus*, 18.

158. Ibid., 13–14, 208.

159. Ibid., 14–15, 207; Bennema, "A Theory of Character in the Fourth Gospel...," 399, 415.

160. Ibid., 418.

161. Bennema, *Encountering Jesus*, 135.

162. Ibid., 172–73.

also says that Peter is, "unstable and presents conflicting traits, making room for considerable character development" but with only a measure of penetration into the inner life.[163] Bennema's theory of characters blends a mimetic and autonomous approach, because each character not only has a historical referent, but also serves a representative literary function, beckoning the reader to identify with and respond in faith.[164] In his conclusion, Bennema states: "Although Collins and Culpepper have rightly noticed the representative value of the Johannine characters, they have wrongly assumed or concluded that John reduces his characters to their belief-responses and hence makes them types."[165] Differing from Conway's assertion that in the FG minor characters undercut the dualistic worldview of the text, which only allows for adequate or inadequate belief responses, Bennema embraces the FE's dualism of belief versus unbelief, but also responds by saying, "Life is complex, unstable and ambiguous and so are people."[166] Finally, in *A Theory of Character in New Testament Narrative*, Bennema applies this theory of characterization to Mark, John, and Acts to demonstrate is efficacy for the entire New Testament.[167]

Petri Merenlahti also sees biblical characters in contrast to Homeric ones, arguing that Peter is a highly mimetic, complex and ambiguous character that "reacts in a way the reader might think anyone would."[168] Nevertheless, Merenlahti's approach is unique in that he transforms the theory of biblical characters by arguing Gospel characters develop across the Gospels.[169] Taking a position of Markan priority, he suggests that characters develop from the earliest Gospel to the latest ones (Luke and John), and that the characters lose distinctive features that are problematic for hegemonic ecclesiastical interpretations of Jesus.[170] This means that the evangelists reinterpret the stories to fit their growing doctrinal agenda. The woman who has been hemorrhaging for twelve years in Mark 5:30 is able to touch Jesus without his knowing who touched him. However, according to Merenlahti, Matthew's version minimalizes this and portrays Jesus catching her in the

---

163. Ibid., 61–63.
164. Ibid., 13, 208.
165. Ibid., 208.
166. Ibid., 211; Bennema, "A Theory of Character in the Fourth Gospel . . .," 413; Conway, *Speaking through Ambiguity*, 325.
167. Bennema, *A Theory of Character in New Testament Narrative*.
168. Merenlahti, "Characters in the Making," 56.
169. Ibid., 61.
170. Ibid., 51, 71.

act—thus removing any scandal of Jesus' lack of omniscience (Matt 9:22).[171] Merenlahti's work therefore demonstrates the growing consensus that Gospel characters are far from flat or static—"all static, comprehensive and harmonious interpretations of these characters [are] problematic."[172]

This study contributes an understanding of just one component of biblical character development: how *anagnorisis*, as a component of manipulation in Genesis, informs a reading of characters and their reversals. This analysis in turn informs an understanding of Peter's characterization in the Gospel of John. Chatman argues that narrative events are like dots connecting and punctuating the turns of a story.[173] Manipulation narratives are just such events. At each turn, when one character hides the truth and manipulates another, the reader sees another facet of the character. Manipulation events serve not only to help the reader see the character more fully, but also within the story world, that these events sometimes transform and move the character one step closer toward a surprising new type of person.

The Scholar's Bias

Although this is not an interdisciplinary project, Vernon K. Robbins' socio-rhetorical criticism also influences my work.[174] In particular, Robbins' fourth textual layer lends itself well to handling the biases and presuppositions of not only the biblical author and any redactors, but also of the interpreter. Robbins calls this ideological texture, that is, how the interpreter's worldview affects the interpretation:[175]

> Since one of the characteristics of scientific (*wissenschaftliche*) analysis is to hide its ideological foundations, it is natural that New Testament interpreters have been reluctant to evaluate their deepest commitments programmatically and to submit them to public scrutiny. Socio-rhetorical criticism calls for interpretive

---

171. Ibid., 66–68.
172. Ibid., 71.
173. Chatman, *Story and Discourse*, 44, 53–54.
174. Though not enthusiastically, Moore notes the convergence of Robbins's third layer of "social and cultural texture" with narrative criticism since narrative critics "have always been deeply attentive to context, thanks to the heavy drag of historical criticism on their scholarly sensibilities," and the realization of this convergence will only "merit a yawn from New Testament narrative critics." Moore, *Afterword*, 257.
175. Robbins, *The Tapestry of Early Christian Discourse*, 36, 192, 201, 215.

practices that include minute attention to the ideologies that guide interpreters' selection, analysis and interpretation of data.[176]

For my perspective on bias, I blend Robbins' approach with the work of philosopher Hans Georg Gadamer. Gadamer's analysis assists me as I attempt to objectivize what experiences I as a researcher bring to the reading of these texts.[177] One must carefully think through such experiences to critically examine how they shade the reading and discern when one's presuppositions facilitate or hinder the overall objective: to inch closer to a better understanding of "original authorial intent" of the FE in chapter 21 via the lens of Genesis. I readily acknowledge that we can never know for certain if and when, we have reached "original authorial intent," or, for that matter, if it is even possible to fully do so, living in a different age, culture, and worldview. Indeed, original intent is difficult to discern even in face-to-face dialogue. People bring their own pre-judgments and ideologies to conversations, and this is no less true of readers and texts, if not more so. Yet the author's intended message is still the target for which I aim, acknowledging that these epistemological limitations obscure the target. This is why scholars now speak of "valid" or "adequate" readings.[178]

Thus, as one reads my work, one should note that I approach the text as an American, white male, who has served in various protestant churches and Christian colleges. As an Evangelical Christian, the significance of the stories in Genesis and John deeply guide my faith and how I see the world. Simply said, these texts are sacred to me—they are inspired, authoritative, and inform my metanarrative, my worldview.

---

176. Ibid., 201.

177. Each interpreter carries his or her presuppositions about the world to the text. Gadamer's point is to dispense with the fruitless goal of objective interpretation. So much lies beyond that plateau. Gadamer, *Truth and Method*, 101–98; Weinsheimer, *Gadamer's Hermeneutics*, 12, 161, 248. For an explanation of reader response theory on the other end of the spectrum, one that leans more toward accepting readings dictated by the reader's own presuppositions and responses, somewhat regardless of original authorial intent, see Tate, *Biblical Interpretation*.

178. On the topic of multiple meanings of a text and a "valid reading," or "adequate" reading, see Boomershine, "The Medium and Message," 113; Combrink, "Multiple Meaning and/or Multiple Interpretation of a Text," 26–37; Staley, "Reading Myself, Reading the Text," 65; Tate, *Biblical Interpretation*, 158–59; Thiselton, *New Horizons in Hermeneutics*, 495–99. Admittedly, this is easier said than done. It is at odds with and in contrast to the goals of some literary scholars (e.g., Moore, *Literary Criticism and the Gospels*, 54). See previous footnote for a critique of narrative criticism.

4
A Theory of Manipulation and Recognition

Seymour Chatman aptly states, "[T]heory is not criticism. Its purpose is not to offer new or enhanced readings of words, but precisely to '*explain what we all do in the act of normal reading, with unconscious felicity.*'"[1] The problem with ancient texts is that modern readers do *not* necessarily know how to read them with unconscious felicity. Much has been lost of the cultural codes that inform the reading. The following theory of manipulation, and how *anagnorisis* works within manipulation, attempts to bring back to the surface and explain what the implied readers of Genesis may have gleaned with "unconscious felicity" when reading these manipulation narratives.

Defining Manipulation and Recognition

In chapter 2 we examined research regarding not only Johannine recognition, but also Hebraic recognition and the related literature on trickster characters in Genesis. Central to my argument is that recognition is a *component* of manipulation: these two literary phenomena neither function alone, nor are they identical. In both Genesis and the FG, recognition and manipulation often function together, with recognition operating as just one component of the larger phenomenon of manipulation.

Defining both recognition and manipulation, then, is important to this study. As indicated earlier, manipulation is a term I have chosen in order to describe much of what others have called "trickster scenes." Nicholas explains that Daniel Brinton, in *The Myths of the New World* (1868), first

---

1. Chatman, *Story and Discourse*, 55; emphasis added.

coined the term "trickster."[2] However, this term clouds a sharper understanding of the narratives in Genesis. The following delineates why.

First, my examination of the Joseph recognition story prompted me to look at several narrative units throughout Genesis. I included some of these episodes in my analysis because of the *Leitwörter* embedded in the stories.[3] I treat *Leitwörter* more thoroughly below, but here it is sufficient to say these are repeated words or roots in a series of narrative units that sometimes support the values in the stories (as in the play on the *Leitwörter blessing* and *birthright* throughout Genesis and the emphasis on God's distinctive blessing as opposed to primogeniture[4]). These recurring terms provide a noticeable framework, tipping off the reader that the stories containing the words are connected.[5]

When looking at the Joseph story, a careful examination makes us aware that we should include in the analysis several scenes from Jacob's life. The *Leitwort* "recognize," הכר and its root נכר, demonstrate this.[6] The most conspicuous usage is in 42:7–8: Joseph *recognized* his brothers, but because he "made himself a stranger," or *concealed* himself from them, they *did not recognize* him (Gen 42:7).[7] I will return to this verb root below and examine it more closely. For now, let us note that this same word appears at the beginning of Jacob's life when he and his mother Rebekah dupe Isaac and Esau out of the blessing: "and he did not *recognize* him" (27:23). Through the repetition of this group of words from the root נכר, the following units emerge as scenes to be included in the analysis: Isaac not recognizing Jacob (Gen 27),[8] Laban not recognizing that Rachel had his stolen gods (Gen 31),

---

2. Nicholas, *The Trickster Revisited*, 9; Steinberg, "Israelite Tricksters, Their Analogues, and Cross-Cultural Study," 2. The term may also be related to תָּעַ֖ע in Gen 27:12, which the *English Standard Version* (ESV) translates "mocking" but which can also be defined as "trick," as in the NIV. See תָּעַ֖ע in Swanson and Logos Research Systems, *Dictionary of Biblical Languages with Semantic Domains: Hebrew (Old Testament)*.

3. See Alter, *The Art of Biblical Narrative*, 92–93, who borrows the concept of *Leitwort* from Buber, *Werke 2, Schriften zur Bibel*, 1131. See also Fishbane, *Text and Texture*.

4. Sailhamer, *Pentateuch as Narrative*, 130; Alter, *The Art of Biblical Narrative*, 6, 94–95.

5. Ibid., 94.

6. There is disagreement as to whether this word group arises from one or two roots. See my discussion of the issue in the following chapter. I will at times refer to the consonantal roots without vowels, since the root is what is repeated in the text.

7. Ibid., 4–5, 159–60, 163. See also Sarna, *Genesis* בראשית: *The Traditional Hebrew Text with New JPS Translation*, 292n7, who states that the phrase "he recognized them but he acted like a stranger" is probably a play on words: "Hebrew . . . *va-yitnakker—va-yakkirem* . . . is perhaps playfully allusive to Gen 37:18—*va-yitnakklu*, 'they conspired.'"

8. "The verb (*hqr*) is in this instance not so much 'knew, recognized' as 'discovered, unmasked.'" Speiser, *Genesis*, 209n23.

Jacob recognizing Joseph's bloodied robe (Gen 37), Judah recognizing his signet ring, cord, and staff in the hands of Tamar (Gen 38),[9] and, finally, the culminating Genesis recognition text, when Joseph recognizes his brothers but they do not recognize him (Gen 42).[10] Are these recognition scenes or trickster scenes? Perhaps this should not be an either/or question.

When Joseph makes himself strange to his brothers (Gen 42:7), the story certainly demonstrates an element of deception and trickery. Working backward through the text, we find that this component is highly consistent with the Jacob נכר narratives. Tamar deceives Judah into living up to his legal duty (Gen 38), and Judah and his brothers deceive Jacob into recognizing Joseph's robe and drawing the wrong, but expected, conclusion (Gen 37).[11] Moving further, the motif of deception continues, even beyond scenes that involve the strict recognition of persons only. Jacob's sons deceive the men of Shechem into enduring the injury of circumcision, which renders them ineffective for battle (Gen 34). Next, Rachel lies and deceives Laban into thinking her innocent of stealing the household gods (Gen 31). Also with Laban, there is an element of veiled maneuvering in Jacob's divinely instructed husbandry, which he practices in order to obtain the striped and speckled goats (Gen 30).[12] Moreover, Laban deceives Jacob into marrying both daughters (Gen 29).[13] Finally, with the all-important blessing, Jacob reluctantly, but with the help of his mother Rebekah, deceives and tricks his father Isaac and brother Esau, thus living up to his name (Gen 27). Trickery and deception are very consistent elements coupled with the נכר recognition motif in Genesis.

Yet after careful examination, I have come to believe that we can improve upon the term trickster to describe the characteristics that unify these scenes. On the one hand, there are episodes in which the deception is bold, blatant, and painted negatively by the text, such as when Joseph's brothers allow their father to believe the lie but later pathetically claim, "We are honest men" (Gen 42:11). On the other hand, there are episodes in which the deception leaves the reader wondering how the text evaluates it and speculating just how much deception, if any, is actually occurring. In these cases,

---

9. Williams notes the connection of *haker* in both Gen 37 and 38. Williams, *Deception in Genesis*, 128–29.

10. Alter, *The Five Books of Moses*, 142n23, 171n32, 212n32, 219n25, 240nn7–8.

11. Alter, *Genesis*, 7.

12. As explained and reported by Jacob himself when he recounts the husbandry methods to Rachel and Leah in the field (Gen 31:10–13).

13. A manipulation that becomes important for the formation of the nation of Israel in that Leah gives birth to Judah, from whose line comes King David and other kings (Gen 29:35).

it may be simply *artful maneuvering* of people and situations, such as Jacob's breeding of the flock, or, as we shall see below, Joseph's masterful work to bring Judah to the point that he is ready to sacrifice himself for Benjamin. In the first example, the brothers are lying and clearly characterized negatively by the text. In the second two examples, there is no outright lie, but instead artful maneuvering of people and circumstances. Kenneth Burke, in discussing his suggested indexing of any given subject for analysis in a literary work, proposes a certain tenacity in labeling a given phenomenon: "We must keep prodding ourselves to attempt answering this question: 'Suppose you were required to find an over-all title for this entire batch of particulars. What would that be?'"[14] I argue then that the term "trickster" does not have the semantic breadth and dexterity to account for the varied behaviors that are found in these recognition-deception motif stories.

Additionally, the description of tricksters in cross-cultural work can be misleading when approaching Genesis.[15] Some characteristics that scholars have attributed universally to tricksters do not occur in the Genesis text. Scatological associations are part of cross-cultural descriptions and yet no such connections exist in the Genesis stories.[16] Some have indicated that tricksters use their trickery to "expose the dirty bottom" of society.[17] In Genesis, there are some manipulators who expose the dirty bottom of society, such as Tamar.[18] However, there are other deceivers, such as Laban, or the younger Judah, who are themselves near the moral bottom of society. Additionally, Barbara Babcock-Adams points out that tricksters, studied cross-culturally "frequently exhibit some mental and/or physical abnormality, especially exaggerated sexual characteristics."[19] This characteristic is also not present in Genesis.

---

14. Burke, *Terms for Order*, 154.

15. Williams, *Deception in Genesis*, 6.

16. Nicholas, *The Trickster Revisited*, 9, 13. Nicholas also speaks of "voracious appetite—both gastronomical and sexual" as trickster characteristics. Though Judges contains the scatological element in the story of Ehud, this is the characteristic of the person manipulated (tricked)—Eglon, not Ehud. This is true also of the eating appetite of Esau—not Jacob.

17. Steinberg, "Israelite Tricksters, Their Analogues, and Cross-Cultural Study," 3; Pelton, *The Trickster in West Africa*, 265. Pelton refers to a moral bottom, not a low social status.

18. Though Tamar is on the lower rung of social status in that society because she has no husband, she is not the "dirty bottom" to which Pelton refers. The "bottom" is a moral indicator of the "underside of life." Tamar rather exposes Judah's moral error, his underhanded dealing in the episode.

19. Babcock-Abrahams, "A Tolerated Margin of Mess," 159–60.

Thus, a new term can enhance the analysis of this phenomenon in Genesis.[20] For this reason, I use the word group of *manipulate, manipulator,* and *manipulative,* instead. Shimon Bar-Efrat briefly but skillfully applies these terms to describe the transition in the life of Absalom, who moves from "being manipulated" to being the "manipulator."[21] After Amnon rapes Tamar, Absalom murders Amnon and then flees Jerusalem (2 Sam 13). To demonstrate a chiastic narrative structure, Bar-Efrat points out Absalom's transition as the story progresses. Absalom moves from someone Joab manipulates and maneuvers (along with King David for Absalom's return to Jerusalem for reconciliation with David, 2 Sam 14:1–28), to the one maneuvering and manipulating Joab for his own selfish ends (14:28–33).[22] Joab begins by circuitously manipulating David with the woman of Tekoah, to have the king summon Absalom to return. However, the unit concludes with Absalom manipulating Joab to get David to summon Absalom directly into his presence by setting Joab's field afire (14:31). The story continues with Absalom's manipulative quest to usurp his father's throne (2 Sam 15–18). Thus, Bar-Efrat uses the modern term to describe this ancient literary phenomenon. Joab and Absalom both use either indirect or deceptive means to manipulate someone for a desired result.

My work uses these terms instead of "trick" or "trickster" because they allow for greater theoretical clarity when analyzing each of the related narratives in Genesis. This is true whether one views the action as negative or positive. The modern semantic range of this word group is quite flexible: one can employ it when discussing certain arts, as when manipulating a medium such as clay or fabric, and one can use it in discussing organizations in the sense of "to manage or utilize skillfully."[23] These are two examples of the positive nuances the word group can provide. However, its meaning can also convey deceptive trickery, such as "to control or play upon by artful, unfair, or insidious means especially to one's own advantage."[24] By expanding to and using the broader manipulation word group, we can include and analyze

---

20. Steinberg calls for new terminology on the basis that one term cannot span the cultural diversity of tricksters in different societies. Steinberg, "Israelite Tricksters, Their Analogues, and Cross-Cultural Study," 4, 10.

21. Bar-Efrat, *Narrative Art in the Bible*, 102. After I completed the majority of my analysis and writing, I found that Heather McKay had used the same terminology in a brief article to analyze the manipulation of Isaac by Rebekah and Jacob (Gen 27), and Tamar by Jonadab and Amnon (2 Sam 13). McKay, "Lying and Deceit in Families," 28–41. Her analysis in Gen however, was limited to just one scene.

22. Bar-Efrat, *Narrative Art in the Bible*, 102.

23. Merriam-Webster Dictionary, "Britannica Online," http://www.britannica.com/.

24. Ibid.

some *manipulation* narratives that previous scholarship has not regarded as trickster narratives. When Judah uses ambiguous language ("Remain a widow . . . till Shelah my son grows up," Gen 38:11) and omits telling Tamar that he was not going to give her to Shelah, he manipulates Tamar, keeping her from his seed and removing her from his family. Rather than directly refusing to allow Tamar permission to marry his third son, he circuitously goes about reaching his desired goal—the preservation of Shelah (38:11).[25] We should treat his manipulative behavior, though not typically identified as trickery by scholars, in the same category as the trickster narratives: i.e., Jacob's manipulation of Isaac and Laban, Laban's manipulation of Jacob, and most importantly Tamar's manipulation of Judah.[26] As a lexical category, manipulation offers greater flexibility when dealing with each narrative, since scholars disagree as to whether characters such as Jacob, Joseph, and others act in a negative or positive manner.

Moreover, since blatant deception and trickery are of course manipulative, modern discussions of manipulation, ethics, and lying can also, in a qualified way, inform the choice of this term and extend theorizing regarding this ancient phenomenon. The following articles especially highlight that manipulation need not include direct deception and can rather operate based on privileged information to manipulate a victim. However, I acknowledge that concerning content, the phenomena of ancient and modern manipulation differ widely by time and culture.

In a paper on deception and trickery, Barry O'Neill sets out to present "clear definitions" of different forms of deception.[27] He then places these against the backdrop of deception scenes in Genesis. First, O'Neill notes the position of the victim when a trick is involved. The victim may be morally lacking, or mentally dull and naïve. Moreover, deception may be associated with sin. As O'Neill points out, "in Yehuda's case it is lust, in Jacob's case love . . . and in Shekhem's case it is greed for the goods of Dinah's family."[28] Second, he offers two definitions of manipulation. The first definition includes, "inducing someone to do something while withholding information

---

25. "He does so under the pretense of Shelah's adolescence, but he has no intention of subjecting his son to Tamar's string of misfortune." Mathews, *Genesis*, 717.

26. For example, Williams, *Deception in Genesis*, 25. Likewise, Williams does not treat Shechem's attempted manipulation of Jacob's sons (Gen 34) in his categorization of deception, ibid., 23.

27. O'Neill explains that the idea for this paper began as an informal talk in 2000 at the Jerusalem Conference on Biblical Economics at Hebrew University., O'Neill, "A Formal System for Understanding Lies and Deceit."

28. Ibid.

relevant to their decision, information that they would want to know."[29] Here we see that deception can be a part of manipulation. Jacob lies to Isaac about his identity, claiming to be Esau, and in the process, withholds the truth that he is instead Jacob (Gen 27:19). O'Neill's second definition entails a more subtle form of maneuvering: "manipulation occurs when one persuades another using knowledge of their particular psychology, rather than rational means. Both of these touch on the idea that the manipulator is using broader knowledge than the victim."[30] In O'Neill's evaluation, the taking of Esau's birthright is the prime biblical example, for no lie or deception of *any kind* is present:

> Jacob knew when to approach Esau to buy his birthright—when he was hungry and weary after working in the field. It was not a matter of withholding information, more of knowing which "version" of the person to approach, to get to do something that the other versions would regret. Manipulation involves the truth that the same person can face the same situation and make a decision in different ways.[31]

Some scholars make the mistake of assuming all manipulations and tricks in Genesis were acts of deception, but as we see in this story between Jacob and Esau, this is not the case.[32]

Also helpful is the work of Joel Rudinow in his 1978 article "Manipulation."[33] Rudinow's contribution is that he too explains manipulation in such a way that it may or may not include deception. He defines manipulation as "an attempt to get someone to do or omit doing something he might not otherwise do or omit." Note that deception is not at the crux of his definition. To elaborate manipulation further, Rudinow contrasts coercion with manipulation and argues that coercion is different. It consists of simple brute force used to change behavior. Manipulation, however, is much more artful. Similar to O'Neill, Rudinow asserts that the manipulator may choose not to lie but instead only wield certain knowledge of the situation

---

29. Ibid.
30. Ibid.
31. Ibid.
32. See for instance Anderson's discussions of deception in Anderson, "Jacob, Laban, and a Divine Trickster?," 3–23. O'Neill gives another example of manipulation without deception: "An interesting manipulation is Jacob's ploy when he learns of the advance of Esau's troops. He tries to placate Esau with gifts of goats, sheep, camels, cattle and asses, but instead of sending them all forward to Esau at once, he divides them into herds." O'Neill, *A Formal System for Understanding Lies and Deceit*, n.p.
33. Rudinow, "Manipulation," 338–47.

or victim, in order to manipulate the same into a desired response.[34] Thus, one can begin to see that in the absence of outright dishonesty, the ultimate moral problem with manipulation often lies in the lack of concern for the victim.[35] The actions of a manipulator who does not outright deceive may appear "delicate, sophisticated, even artful in comparison with the hammer-and-tongs crudity of coercion."[36]

Rudinow offers several examples of artful manipulation that may or may not involve deception. One example is when a wife manipulates her husband to stay at home on a particular evening by using alluring attire and enticing words without resorting to deception, even though, as Rudinow is careful to explain, both the husband and wife clearly know that what the wife actually wants is his companionship, irrespective of sexual activity. Both are aware of the ploy of manipulating the husband's desires and, therefore, no deception is involved. Nevertheless, manipulation occurs. I would add to this explanation that at the least, the wife is *indirect and circuitous* regarding her true motives, even if the husband is aware of them. The point that both O'Neill and Rudinow agree upon is that direct deception need not be a part of manipulation (Gen 25:29–34).[37] The wife plays on the husband's desires, in a way that is analogous to Jacob playing on Esau's desire for food.[38]

Rudinow also explains that when analyzing manipulative behavior, the examination of *detail* and *context* is important. Without understanding the relationships, desires, and power deficits of the characters in a given situation, an accurate analysis of manipulation narratives is restricted:

> Since the manipulator's behavior is normally either deceptive or predicated on some privileged insight into the personality of his intended manipulee, the precise nature of his behavior and its relation to his goals and intentions will very often be obscure to an observer whose vantage point is not also specially privileged.

---

34. Ibid., 346.

35. Ibid., 347. So too Fallis, "When people are deceived (i.e., when they are led to have false beliefs), they often do not make the same choices that they would have made based on accurate information about the world. Such manipulation can easily cause people to make choices that are harmful to them and, even if no other harm results, arguably still violates their autonomy." Fallis, "Lying and Deception," 38–39.

36. Rudinow, "Manipulation," 339.

37. Alter calls Jacob a man of "legalistic calculation," who has "carefully weighed" each word to obtain the birthright. Alter, *The Five Books of Moses*, 131n31.

38. Though the text does not indicate that Esau is aware that Jacob is manipulating him as the husband in the example is.

Thus, the [interpretation] depends to a large degree upon the detail—and length—of their descriptions.[39]

In Genesis, as well as the FG, the readers (with the help of an omniscient narrator) have a point of view that is "specially privileged." Because of the reader's knowledge of the details of the story of Judah, the reader realizes that Tamar is manipulating Judah's sexual appetite and callousness without ever issuing an outright lie. In fact, at that instance of sexual brokerage, Tamar is in reality a prostitute, taking payment for sex.[40] Nevertheless, Rudinow aptly cautions that "it is only to be expected that deception plays a role in the great majority of cases of manipulation."[41] If, however, the victim's desires are strong enough, the manipulator needs little or no deception:

> Now, if I am prepared (able and willing) to offer you irresistible incentives, I need neither disguise my project nor base it on any very deep insight into your personality. I can reasonably expect the incentives, since they are so strong, to accomplish my ends without the addition of dissimulation or subtlety of any other sort. But if I want to accomplish the same ends in the same circumstances without recourse to irresistible incentives, I cannot reasonably expect to succeed unless I am either deceptive or know or believe that there are some incentives which, though not in themselves irresistible, you will find irresistible, that is, unless I know or think I know a weakness of yours.[42]

Jacob's manipulation of Esau over a bowl of red lentil stew, without any deception at all, demonstrates Rudinow's point—no deception was needed. Jacob and the reader of the Genesis narrative realize that a simple bowl of hot stew is an "irresistible incentive," appealing enough to manipulate Esau to give up his costly birthright. This is a subtle way of illustrating Esau's character.[43] Rudinow's explanation that sometimes incentive alone is not enough, elucidates our analysis of Tamar's manipulation of Judah, where some form of deception was needed. This is because the reader should surmise that Judah would not have slept with the prostitute had he realized she was his daughter-in-law.[44]

39. Rudinow, "Manipulation," 346.

40. "She set aside her widowhood for the demeaning status of a prostitute." Mathews, *Genesis*, 718.

41. Rudinow, "Manipulation," 347.

42. Ibid., 347.

43. Alter, *The Five Books of Moses*, 131n30.

44. Sarna, *Genesis* בר־אשית: *The Traditional Hebrew Text with New JPS Translation*, 268n15.

In an article wrestling with mental health therapists' alleged tendency to wrongly stereotype and label certain patients as "manipulative," Nancy Potter argues that there is great ambiguity in this label in clinical circles. In her analysis, she contends that in "broader society," "manipulative" covers a variety of behaviors, some morally wrong, some not.[45] Some of these behaviors are nothing more than the indirect means of persuasion that are culturally acceptable.[46] Others may be acceptable according to context, such as a flight attendant who pretends to enjoy her work in order to increase passengers' compliance with flight safety requirements.[47] Other uses of the term in the broader context include "efforts to control others," indirect or circuitous behaviors to negatively influence others,[48] "using deception for personal gain without concern for victims,"[49] and even "do-not-speak-to-me-behaviors."[50] She also notes that "trust development" is a tool of manipulation.[51] She cautioned, however, that "what counts as indirect or covert is culture-bound."[52] Manipulation may be an appropriate means of action "[w]hen power imbalances exist and the more powerful party refuses to negotiate."[53] Her contribution is relevant because she argued that the popular definition of manipulation covers quite a broad variety of behaviors, some of which are morally wrong while others are either socially accepted means of indirect persuasion or the appropriate means of defense in a situation of powerlessness. Thus manipulation, at least in the general public usage (as opposed to a strictly negative clinical definition Potter offers), is a term that

---

45. Potter, "What is Manipulative Behavior, Anyway?," 142. Though the purpose of her article was to correct the use of this broad definition, negatively, in a clinical setting. Ibid., 148.

46. Such as the presentation of only one's best, or even exaggerated, attire in courtship. Ibid., 144. Also important here is that Potter was trying to narrowly define manipulation clinically, as a named psychologically dysfunctional or morally wrong behavior. Thus, she does not categorize such behavior in courtship as clinical manipulation. However, due to its broad usage, I am using the term to describe behaviors that could be classified good or bad, and her explanation of the broader usage of manipulation contributes to the discussion.

47. Ibid., 143.

48. Ibid., 142.

49. Ibid., 145. See also McKay, "Lying and Deceit in Families," 34.

50. Potter, *What is Manipulative Behavior, Anyway?*, 142. Here one thinks of a similar effect when Joseph imprisons his brothers for three days, thus cutting off all communication with the one who holds their fate, increasing their angst (Gen 42:17).

51. Ibid., 143.

52. Ibid., 148.

53. Ibid., 144. Though again, this behavior does not fit her clinical negative definition of "manipulativity."

provides semantic dexterity for describing many behaviors, whether these are the morally wrong lying and controlling of others, or some indirect or roundabout means of persuasion, regardless of whether they are socially acceptable or not.

With these discussions as a theoretical backdrop, I understand a manipulation narrative in Genesis as when person or group "A" (the manipulator) carries out certain actions, in an indirect, masked, or camouflaged manner, in order to obtain a desired objective. "B" (the victim) does not know or recognize that "A" has acted this way. With time however, "B" almost always recognizes the manipulative behavior.[54] This differs from Larsen's definition of *anagnorisis* type-scenes where the "overall *telos* is recognition of a hidden truth."[55] The overall *telos* of Genesis manipulation narratives, as understood here, is intentional secrecy to *obtain a desired benefit*. The hiding of the truth is a means to an end, and Larsen's "recognition of a hidden truth" by the victim is but one possible outcome of the manipulation. I also argue that the desired benefit is something other than the desired "test" frequently found in Greco-Roman *anagnorisis*.[56] Often the manipulator, "A," intends the secrecy in order to change circumstances over which the victim, "B," has control. The manipulation changes the power balance so that "A" may obtain the goal. Jacob manipulates Isaac to force him to bless him, Laban manipulates Jacob so that he can force Jacob to marry both daughters, and so forth. Sometimes this manipulation is justified, as with Tamar manipulating Judah. Sometimes it is not, as with Simeon and Levi.

Turning now to my analysis of the structure of a manipulation narrative, I would like to point out that as was true in Larsen's taxonomy of five moves of *anagnorisis*, the classification described below is composed of "stock devices," which most consistently occur in manipulation narratives.[57] However, there are manipulation narratives where the story unveils certain components differently or omits them entirely.[58] An example of this is the aforementioned story of Jacob and Esau and the bowl of stew, where deception or concealed behavior is not apparent, but the episode contains enough of the other elements to constitute a manipulation narrative.[59]

---

54. Larsen speaks of a "delusive mask" in recognition scenes. Larsen, *Recognizing the Stranger*, 46.

55. Ibid., 59.

56. Ibid., 133.

57. Ibid., 59.

58. Ibid., 63.

59. Deception may yet be present. The reader may wonder if Jacob has been secretly scheming to present the offer to Esau based on his knowledge of Esau's weaknesses.

Six Kernels of Manipulation

In defining the components that make up manipulation narratives, I have chosen to label these as "kernels" following the work of Seymour Chatman. Deriving his definition from Roland Barthes, Chatman describes a kernel as a "major event" that "advances the plot by raising and satisfying questions."[60] Kernels are the units in the story that if removed, would damage the plot structure.[61] They are "hinges" or "branching points" at which the story can take two or more different courses. Characters make decisions, circumstances go one way rather than another, and the story marks out a course. Furthermore, according to Chatman, "proper interpretation of events" depends on "the ability to follow these ongoing selections, to see later kernels as consequences of earlier [ones]."[62] Using this approach, I have carefully examined Genesis, and identified and labeled six kernels of manipulation. I find these kernels to be the most consistent and elemental to the Genesis manipulation narrative. They are: 1) The desired benefit, 2) The manipulation, 3) The benefit achieved, 4) The moment of recognition, 5) The statement, or challenge in response to the manipulation, and 6) The effect of the manipulation on the plot or characterization. I will discuss each in turn.

The Desired Benefit

The desired benefit is a goal the manipulator is trying to achieve by his or her action toward the victim. Frequently, but not always, this goal benefits the manipulator and not the manipulated victim. The text communicates the desired benefit to the reader by different means, such as character statements, narrator explanations, implications, or any combination of these. In the case of Jacob and Rebekah manipulating Isaac and Esau out of the blessing (Gen 27), the desired benefit is clearly portrayed on the lips of characters three times: Isaac proclaims to Esau the reason for the meal is "that my soul may bless you before I die" (27:4). Rebekah also states it in her first explanation to Jacob, but she adds a divine component to her version of

---

60. Chatman, *Story and Discourse*, 53. Larsen's "moves" are very similar, and are "minimal narrative units," the "trajectory elements of a type-scene." Larsen, *Recognizing the Stranger*, 59n74.

61. Satellites are minor narrative units that if deleted would not affect the structure of the story. Chatman, *Story and Discourse*, 53. Considering Auerbach's discussion of description in the Hebrew Bible and his statement that what is included is "necessary for the purpose of the narrative, all else is left in obscurity," there may be no true satellites in Gen. Auerbach, *Mimesis*, 11.

62. Chatman, *Story and Discourse*, 53.

Isaac's instructions: "that I may eat it and bless you *before the LORD* before I die" (27:7). Rebekah again states the goal after Jacob's rebuttal: "so that he may bless you before he dies" (27:10).

In some instances, the desired benefit is less clear to the reader, or its identification is delayed and only made known to the reader at the same moment the manipulator makes it known to the victim. When Laban manipulates Jacob into marrying both daughters, the narrator explains early in the story that Leah was older, and less beautiful than Rachel was (Gen 29:16–17), but Jacob is unaware of the impending substitution.[63] When Jacob responds in shock, Laban explains that it is not the custom in his land to marry the younger before the older.[64] However, even this explanation leaves the reader to notice a further implication: Laban perhaps wanted both daughters married in order to secure fourteen years of labor from Jacob instead of only seven. The reader also later learns that Laban has determined that the LORD blesses him by means of Jacob's presence (30:27). In some manipulation narratives, the desired benefit is simply uncertain. In the case of Rachel stealing Laban's gods, the story never makes this at all clear, at least to modern readers. Perhaps the possession of the gods evokes or symbolizes material blessings,[65] or perhaps Rachel's theft and act of sitting on them disgraces and contrasts Laban's *teraphim* with the *Elohim* of Abraham, Isaac, and Jacob (31:42).[66] We note the point of view of the narrator, who disparagingly calls them הַתְּרָפִים (31:19, 34, 35) but Jacob and Laban call them אֱלֹהֵי (31:30, 32).[67] Even still, the desired benefit of the manipulation is textually indeterminate. In Joseph's reunion with his brothers in Egypt, the desired benefit is also undecided. Is this to test the brothers to see if they are the same as they were, or to see if they have harmed Benjamin?[68]

---

63. Although Rashi suggests that Jacob suspected this type of behavior of Laban, and therefore clarified, "Rachel, thy *younger daughter*," lest Laban marry Jacob to a "Rachel out of the street." Silbermann, *Chumash with Targum Onkelos, Haphtaroth and Rashi's Commentary*, 1:137.

64. McKay calls Laban "the wily family manipulator." McKay, "Lying and Deceit in Families," 28.

65. Speiser states that in Nuzi customs, the ownership of the gods was a cultural signal indicating "legal title to a given estate," thus, Rachel lays claim to some of Laban's property for her husband. Speiser, *Genesis*, 250.

66. Alter, *The Five Books of Moses*, 172n34.

67. Ibid., 171n30. Regarding the pejorative sense of *teraphim*, see Sarna, *Genesis* בראשית: *The Traditional Hebrew Text with New JPS Translation*, 216n19.

68. Although Joseph outwardly states, "By this you shall be tested" (Gen 42:15), the text requires the reader to consider closely whether inwardly Joseph is carrying out these maneuvers in order to test the brothers, to exact suffering, to bring contrition, to cause them to change, or some combination of these. See below.

Alternatively, is Joseph trying to cause the brothers to suffer for their crime, or even to bring about their contrition and confession, thus transforming them morally? The uncertainty draws the reader into the story.[69]

The Manipulation

The next kernel in the manipulation narrative is perhaps the most important and most consistent. The manipulator carries out an action that typically obscures some bit of information from the victim's field of knowledge. Almost without fail, this is some form of masking or camouflage. Masking can be a physical concealment, such as with Jacob's covering of goatskins. Laban masks both his intentions and his daughter's identity with the natural darkness of the day's end: "And when it was evening he took his daughter Leah and brought her to Jacob . . . And in the morning, behold, it was Leah!" (Gen 29:23, 25). Masking can also be verbal, when the manipulator uses words to mask the truth, as with Jacob's sons lying to him about Joseph's robe: "This we have found" (37:32). The brothers did not "find" the robe, and the lie masks the truth of Joseph's fate.[70] In this case, the robe accompanies the lie and is a false token. Jacob himself used false tokens with his father, also in the form of garments.[71] Manipulators may also physically mask their behav-

---

69. I interpret Joseph's motives as either indeterminable in the text or as working to produce remorse and reconciliation, rather than seeking revenge. One indication of this in the text is when Joseph's steward replies to the brothers' appeal that they had brought back the misplaced silver: "Peace to you, do not be afraid. Your God and the God of your father has put treasure in your sacks for you. I received your money" (Gen 43:23). If Joseph was seeking only revenge, it is neither likely that his servants would treat the brothers this way (while also invoking God as the source, just as Joseph later does to his brother as the cause of his demise in 45:5, 8), nor that the writer would include an indication such as this in the narrative. Interpretation of a compassionate Joseph can also be found in the Midrash *Bereishit Rabbah*: "He treated them as a brother when he had the upper hand, but they did the reverse." Freedman and Simon, *Midrash Rabbah*, 91:7n3. "Only before their eyes did he bind [Simeon], but as soon as they left, he brought him out, gave him to eat and drink, and bathed and anointed him," (ibid., 91:8). Likewise, the Midrash *Tanhuma*, on Gen 44:34, when Joseph instructs his servant to overtake and challenge the brothers, reads "See, he is confounding them with words, now harshly and now gently." Townsend, *Midrash Tanhuma*, 10:13. But other rabbinic traditions portrayed both Joseph as well as his brothers in a more negative light, calling Joseph and Judah a "bull and a lion trying to gore each other" until the point where Joseph fears for Egypt's safety and begins to relent. Bialik et al., *The Book of Legends = Sefer Ha-Aggadah*, 55:107.

70. "The brothers baldly lie." Mathews, *Genesis*, 700.

71. "[T]he brothers used an article of [Joseph's] clothing in order to deceive their father (37:26–33), just as Jacob years before had used Esau's clothes to mislead Isaac." Sarna, *Genesis* בראשית: *The Traditional Hebrew Text with New JPS Translation*, 398.

ior by distance (e.g., three days, 30:36; 31:46), distraction (e.g., during sheep shearing, 31:19; 38:12–13), or by hiding or altering objects (e.g., Rachel hiding the gods, 32:34, or the brothers bloodying Joseph's robe, 37:31).[72]

The question of recognition first comes into play within the manipulation kernel, for it is at this point that the manipulator often *prevents* the victim from recognizing someone or from recognizing what the manipulator is doing. We must remember that *anagnorisis* and manipulation are not equivalent. Rather, the manipulative masking prevents or delays recognition. Later, when the ruse unravels, recognition proper occurs when the victim realizes what has transpired. This is the recognition kernel, which I discuss below.

Jacob's sons manipulate their father by masking Joseph's true fate and guiding his incorrect interpretation of Joseph's bloodied robe, thereby foiling his recognition of Joseph's fate. Jacob's correct recognition of that fate is delayed until his sons return from their second trip to Egypt (Gen 45:25–28). The entire process, spanning over two decades, can be understood as a manipulation cycle, in which the manipulation kernel is found early on in the narrative (Gen 37), and the recognition kernel is located nine chapters later (46:28–30).

Earlier in Jacob's life, in his manipulation of Isaac and Esau, the manipulation kernel occurs when Jacob enters Isaac's presence and deceives him. Jacob's physical and verbal masking of his identity prevents Isaac from recognizing his identity. The writer communicates the verbal masking to the reader with a series of three character lies from Jacob: "I am Esau your firstborn. I have done as you told me," (Gen 27:19); "Because the Lord your God granted me success," (27:20); and when Isaac asks, "Are you really my son Esau?" Jacob answers, "I am" (27:24). These lies impede the recognition. In this case, Jacob is able to delay the recognition only briefly, until the moment where he departs and Esau returns (27:30–35). The entire process is a manipulation episode, but the manipulation kernel (27:5–29) and the recognition kernel (27:30–40), are two components of the overall narrative. The manipulation kernel includes Jacob, Rebekah, and Isaac, and the recognition kernel includes Esau and Isaac. Moreover, the subject matter that manipulators camouflage is *not* restricted to individuals, but may be objects or the truth about a given situation: later in life Jacob masks his plans to escape Laban by sending for and talking to his wives in the field (31:4),

---

72. In the case of Laban putting three days distance between himself and Jacob, the text implies that three days distance (30:36) was to mask these animals from Jacob's view or control. However, there is little doubt Jacob was already aware of the marked animals since he was in charge of Laban's herd.

Rachel masks Laban's recognition of the whereabouts of his gods (31:32), and Jacob's sons mask the reality of Joseph's fate (37:31–32).[73]

Switching is another common device of manipulation. A switch involves a transfer of something—property, persons, etc. The transfer is often reciprocal, meaning that the manipulator reverses the position or possession of two items or people. A switch might not be as blatant as theft, such as when Jacob switches himself *for* Esau, and Leah herself *for* Rachel. A theft, however, is the taking of someone's property or persons without permission. Rachel does not switch, but rather blatantly steals Laban's gods. Jacob *switches* siblings in the *theft* of the blessing. He both switches and steals. Other Genesis manipulation narratives also involve a switch. Laban agrees to give Jacob the marked animals (Gen 30:32, 35–36),[74] but then takes them for himself, and Joseph switches the silver from his possession, back to his brothers' sacks repeatedly (42:27–28, 35; 44:1).

More shrewdly, manipulators are masters of using words to hide their actions. There is the obvious lie, as just noted with Jacob lying to Isaac three times, but clever manipulators often stop short of an outright lie and instead trick their victims, either with omissions of the truth or with ambiguous language.[75] Laban does not lie when he states, "It is better that I give her to you than that I should give her to any other man; stay with me" (Gen 29:19). However, this statement is ambiguous.[76] Laban does in fact plan to give Rachel to Jacob, but only after Leah and seven more years of labor. By using this ambiguous statement, and omitting other parts of the truth, Laban

---

73. Larsen establishes that *anagnorisis* is not limited to recognizing individuals, but chose to restrict his analysis to such. Larsen, *Recognizing the Stranger*, 59.

74. The text does not specify "Laban" in verse 35, though some English translations supply it. However, in the next verse "he" put three days distance between himself and Jacob, making clear who removed the animals. Note that Alter suggests this was to prevent cross breeding. Alter, *The Five Books of Moses*, 164n35–36. However, Laban's intentions move beyond that. He removes the very animals that he has just agreed to let Jacob select. In verse 32, "Let me pass" is in the first person in Hebrew. Laban agreed to let *Jacob* complete this task, and then violates the agreement and gives the animals to his sons (Gen 30:35). This is a clear switching of the animals. However, Laban might argue that his was not theft. His character could conceivably claim, "Jacob is still free today to go through my flock and remove any spotted/speckled/striped animal he finds!" Although morally wrong, readers in that culture might have seen in this an element of shrewd dealing. The LXX however, portrays Jacob's offer as having been for *Laban* to pass through the sheep, παρελθάτω πάντα τὰ πρόβατά σου σήμερον, καὶ διαχώρισον, "Let all thy sheep pass by to-day, and separate" (Brenton LXX). The "separate" is in the second person, "you separate." Logos Research Systems, *Septuaginta*.

75. See also McKay, "Lying and Deceit in Families," 28–41.

76. "Laban's reply is a piece of consummate ambiguity naively taken by Jacob to be a binding commitment." Sarna, *Genesis* בראשית: *The Traditional Hebrew Text with New JPS Translation*, 204n19.

skillfully manipulates Jacob into a position of entrapment, another ability of manipulators.[77] Laban never explicitly agrees to *only* seven years for only Rachel. He does in fact give her to him, for seven years labor, but with the previously unstated condition, that Jacob takes Leah first, for seven years as well. Though many readers may reach the "inescapable" conclusion that Laban is in the wrong,[78] Laban has used Jacob's deep desire for Rachel to put him in a position where he chooses to comply. Yet Jacob is a fast learner. Later, he is careful not to share his divinely supplied breeding insights with Laban, disclosed in Genesis 31:10–12. The narrator also explains that "Jacob tricked Laban the Aramean by *not telling* Laban he intended to flee" (31:20). Rachel, too, is skillful in the use of ambiguous language: "'Let not my lord be angry that I cannot rise before you, for the way of women is upon me.' So he searched but did not find the household gods" (31:35). Though the statement may have been true, it misleads Laban to believe that he cannot or at least out of decorum should not, search her saddle. He consequently believes that Rachel does not have the gods. In the next manipulation narrative, Shechem and Hamor omit to tell the men of the city one important point—that Shechem had raped Dinah (34:20–24).[79] This father and son team attempted to manipulate both the men of the city, as well as the sons of Jacob. The sons of Jacob, nevertheless, have the last word, manipulating Shechem and Hamor out of their very lives. However, their tactics were far less cunning. The brothers lie outright, saying, "Only on this condition will we agree with you—that you will become as we are by every male among you being circumcised. Then we will give our daughters to you, and we will take your daughters to ourselves, and we will dwell with you and become one people" (34:15–16). Also with Jacob's sons, we see three chapters later that ambiguous language can come in the form of questions. The inquiry, "Please identify whether it is your son's robe or not," certainly and carefully misleads Jacob to wrongly assume Joseph's death (37:32).

The resolution of the ambiguity created by the manipulation may take time to materialize, as was the case with Judah manipulating Tamar with the words, "Remain a widow in your father's house, till Shelah my son grows up" (Gen 38:11). At best, this is a misleading statement. It is close to an outright lie, strongly implying that he will give her to Shelah. Moreover, it is similar to Laban's ambiguous statement to give Rachel to Jacob. There is a stated time delay, after which someone is supposed to give a spouse. In addition,

---

77. Only after the marriage does Laban tell Jacob, "It is not so done in our country, to give the younger before the firstborn" (Gen 29:26).

78. Williams, *Deception in Genesis*, 20.

79. Mathews, *Genesis*, 605.

just like Laban, Judah omits an important point: he never intends to give Shelah to Tamar. Nevertheless, Tamar is quick, and manipulates Judah with her own ambiguity and omission. By asking Judah what payment he will offer, she leads him blindly to continue his assumption that she is only a prostitute (38:16). Then, she omits to offer her name. The two verbal strategies together lead him further from any notion that he knows her. Finally, her statement of, "If you give me a pledge, until you send it" (38:17), leads Judah to believe that at some point, she will receive payment and return his items. Nevertheless, she immediately leaves, removing his ability to make payment. Lastly, Joseph demonstrates his verbal skills as well by asking his brothers, "Where do you come from?" (42:8). He knows where they are from, but this furthers their ignorance of his identity. In addition, his omission of his name in the dialogue is an obvious verbal masking as well.

Manipulators in Genesis may also use a tactic noted by modern mental health therapists, that of trust building.[80] A manipulator may purposefully take action to build trust in the victim, thereby furthering the deception.[81] Laban enthusiastically acts the generous relative, proactively offering for Jacob to name his own wages (Gen 29:15; 30:28). He also continues the tactic when he attempts to engender trust by the response "Good! Let it be as you have said" (30:34). This quick response is too good to be true to come from the lips of the deceptive Laban. It should give Jacob pause as well as the reader. Rachel also, ever the prodigy of her father, engenders trust when instead of declaring, "I do not have your idols," rather calls him "lord" and asks for his mercy: "Let not my lord be angry that I cannot arise before you" (31:35). This may be a calculated move to build false trust, and further the deception. Jacob as well builds trust with his father Isaac by encouraging him to eat ("now sit up and eat of my game") and by claiming that the meal came as a blessing from God (27:19-20). Jacob's sons also employ trust building when they do not wait for Joseph's absence to be noticed, but instead proactively communicate to their father in a feigning of concern and offer the robe that they had "found" (37:32).

A manipulator may strategically position an object or person of desire to distract and lure the victim into blindness and may utilize such a person or object that is already present. Jacob conveniently has a bowl of stew just at the time when Esau comes famished from the field (Gen 25:29-34). Rebekah and Jacob, though prompted by Isaac's wish, provide the food Isaac

---

80. Potter, *What is Manipulative Behavior, Anyway?*, 143.

81. "Laban pretends to be concerned for Jacob's welfare." Sarna, *Genesis* בראשית: *The Traditional Hebrew Text with New JPS Translation*, 203. McKay speaks of "compliance," in which the manipulator presents an "apparent following of [the victim's] wishes." McKay, "Lying and Deceit in Families," 36.

loves, furthering the distraction. Laban conveniently allows Jacob to pursue Rachel, never mentioning the obligation to marry Leah first, but rather keeps Jacob's object of desire foremost in his mind. The men of Shechem use daughters and property as luring devices not only for Jacob's sons, but also for the men of the city, attempting their manipulation ploy with two groups at the same time. We can also argue that Jacob's sons use Dinah as a luring device to further the plan of having the men of Shechem immobilize themselves, all for a ruthless murder (Gen 34). Tamar obviously distracts Judah with the allure of sexual liaison (Gen 38). Finally, though not as deceptive or as clearly distracting, it is interesting to note that the missing Simeon is not enough to lure Jacob's sons back to Egypt. However, grain and the promise of life for their families are. Grain and life are objects of desire over which Joseph has complete control.

We could categorize several other devices of manipulation in the Genesis text, many of them occurring less frequently than those above do. These would include crafty husbandry (Gen 30:37–43), escape or flight (31:20, 27), rape (34:2), force of power (34:1–4,[82] 42:6–7, 9, 12, 14, 17,[83]), injury (by means of circumcision, 34:24–25), murder (34:25),[84] foreign language (42:23),[85] and tests (42:15, 18).[86]

---

82. This manipulation occurs by means of either political power, physical power, or both. The narrator implies this when calling him "prince of the land" but calls her a young woman. Additionally, Shechem calls her a "girl" to his father in contrast to calling her "young woman" to her family. In any case, she is in no position to challenge his "taking" of her. See Ibid., 234n6.

83. Joseph rattles off a series of threatening questions and accusations, ending in their three-day imprisonment. The swift verbal battery of questions culminating with this action underscores the power deficit, thus manipulating the brothers into a much less favorable position. The narrator explains that Joseph continues the power-plays: "They served him by himself, and them by themselves" (Gen 43:32).

84. Some in post-exilic Israel viewed the deception *via circumcision* worthy of censure, not simply the retribution for the rape of Dinah. "And my father heard these things and was wroth, and he was grieved in that they had received the circumcision, and after that had been put to death, and in his blessings he looked amiss upon us. For we sinned because we had done this thing against his will, and he was sick on that day," Charles, *T. of Levi* 6.6, "Testaments of the Twelve Patriarchs."

85. The use of the interpreter increases the figurative distance between Joseph and his brothers and furthers the masking. Mathews, *Genesis*, 780.

86. This is not a test in the Greco-Roman version of *anagnorisis*, where if the test is passed, the observed reveals himself. Note that Joseph, changing the conditions of the test from verses 15 to 18, increases the manipulative effect. The brothers now have reason to believe that the viceroy is unpredictable as well as angry and powerful. This is similar to a type scene in American films where a criminal requires the hero, usually a detective or law enforcement officer, to overcome a series of tests or obstacles, such as racing from one phone booth to another, answering a series of phone calls in a short

I have one final important point to make about the kernel of manipulation. Often the devices manipulators use result in an entrapment. The victim lands in a position that he or she would not have chosen had all the information been available. This final position is often a distinct disadvantage or disempowerment to the victim—a loss of a blessing (Isaac and Esau), the unwanted gain of three extra wives and years of extra labor (Jacob, Gen 29:23–24, 28–29), or the loss of livestock and idols (Laban). As the saga of manipulation continues, the stakes get higher, and victims are trapped into losing the security of marriage and family (Tamar), their seed and public honor (Judah), their freedom (Joseph), a child (Jacob), and even their lives (the men of Shechem).

The Benefit Achieved

After the manipulation, the manipulator typically obtains the results that he or she desired, and the text communicates the attainment to the reader. Once Isaac is satisfied that he is speaking to Esau, he blesses the camouflaged Jacob (Gen 27:27–29). This is important for the understanding of the function of the manipulation narrative. The writer does not merely state, "And [he] blessed him," but records the entire blessing in the next three verses. This indicates the power and importance of the blessing in the story. The text then refers to the blessing nine times in the next thirty-two verses (27:33 [twice], 36; 28:1, 3, 4, 6 [twice], 14–15). Then, Isaac repeats the very act of blessing in the opening verses of chapter 28, summarizing again God's favor on Jacob and his offspring.[87] Jacob the manipulator has won this round.

Laban realizes his goals as well when he manipulates Jacob in the next chapter. Immediately after the masking by the evening darkness, the narrator explains that Jacob consummates the marriage and soon thereafter, recognition occurs in the morning (Gen 29:25). After his reaction and Laban's explanation, Jacob relents and the narrator summarizes the benefit Laban was seeking: "So Jacob went in to Rachel also, and he loved Rachel more than Leah, and served Laban for another seven years" (29:30). Laban now has both daughters married and fourteen years of nearly free labor in addition. Laban the manipulator achieves his goal.

---

amount of time. If the hero fails any of the tests, the criminal will carry out whatever negative actions he or she has threatened, such as killing a hostage. The manipulation increases the sense of the manipulator's power and the victim's powerlessness.

87. Sarna, *Genesis* בראשית: *The Traditional Hebrew Text with New JPS Translation*, 195n1.

However, sometimes the manipulator does not win the prize. In the ensuing years, Laban and Jacob continue their craftiness. As discussed above, when Jacob is ready to depart with his family and possessions, Laban bargains with him to stay and agrees to allow him to have the marked animals, but then removes them himself from the flock (Gen 30:35–36). Nevertheless, Laban never achieves the multiplication of more marked animals. Though Laban does take into his possession the animals that day, Jacob is the one who truly achieves benefits by manipulation, when he uses divinely directed husbandry, which he never reveals to Laban. Jacob exceeded Laban in breeding, and the text reads, "So the feebler would be Laban's, and the stronger Jacob's. Thus the man increased greatly and had large flocks, female servants and male servants, and camels and donkeys" (30:42–43). In the following chapter, the narrator explains that Jacob heard Laban's sons bemoaning, "Jacob has taken all that was our father's, and from what was our father's he has gained all this wealth" (31:1). Jacob the manipulator has achieved his goal, but not Laban.

Sometimes the desired benefit is a change in circumstances, such as Jacob's desire to flee Laban with his family (30:25), which is realized in 32:1: "Jacob went on his way, and the angels of God met him." Jacob also reached a functional peace with, and separation from, Laban; a desired benefit readers learn of due the frustration that Jacob explained to his wives in the field and the command from God to "now arise, go out from this land, and return to the land of your kindred (31:4–13, 51–55).

Sometimes the victims have to infer the results themselves. Tamar realized by observation and deduction that Judah had obtained his goal, "for she saw that Shelah was grown up, and she had not been given to him in marriage" (Gen 38:14). At other times, directness of the text and the immediate action of the manipulator afterwards indicate clearly what goal the manipulator achieved: "and she conceived by him. Then she arose and went away, and taking off her veil she put on the garments of her widowhood" (38:18–19).[88] In agreement with the comments of Potter noted above, in the power imbalance, Tamar disempowers Judah against the future confrontation and accusation of whoredom when she takes the pledge of signet, cord, and staff, in place of the payment of a kid goat.[89]

---

88. Regarding the phrase "So he gave them to her and went in to her, and she conceived," Alter writes, "The last of the three verbs reveals that Tamar gets exactly what she has aimed for." Alter, *The Five Books of Moses*, 218n18.

89. "The dramatic denouement comes as Tamar, who has sustained her remarkable self-restraint until the very last moment, confronts Judah with the at once overwhelming and unimpeachable evidence. Yet her tactic of indirect accusation assures a minimum of embarrassment and so elicits a noble response." Sarna, *Genesis* בראשית: *The*

As discussed earlier, the text does not make clear what Joseph's desired goal was when he encountered his brothers in Egypt, but there were several possible objectives for his manipulation. If his intention was to cause suffering for their crime, Joseph achieved that goal. He put them in prison (Gen 42:17), bound and kept Simeon (42:24), secretly returned their money, which forced them to ask, "What is this that God has done to us?" (42:28), and caused them even more alarm upon finding all of their money returned in the embarrassing presence of their father (42:35). If Joseph's goal was proof that Benjamin was alive and had not suffered a similar fate, he achieved that goal as well (43:29–30). If his goal was to produce contrition, then contrition was produced: "Then they said to one another, 'In truth we are guilty concerning our brother, in that we saw the distress of his soul, when he begged us and we did not listen. That is why this distress has come upon us.' And Reuben answered them, 'Did I not tell you not to sin against the boy? But you did not listen. So now there comes a reckoning for his blood'" (42:21–22, see also 42:13; 44:16). And ultimately, if the goal was to see an actual change in actions to accompany the contrition, that too Joseph achieved. Judah, the very brother who opportunistically suggested making a profit on his capture, was the one who was willing to suffer loss, making the self-sacrificial offer. At the moment of crisis he stepped up to Joseph and said, "Now therefore, please let your servant remain instead of the boy as a servant to my lord, and let the boy go back with his brothers. For how can I go back to my father if the boy is not with me? I fear to see the evil that would find my father" (44:33–34).

This speech by Judah is the last effect achieved before Joseph ends his manipulation and reveals himself to his brothers. Thus, it may be indicative of why he withheld his identity. A reader might also ask if Joseph was watching for this change of behavior toward familial obligations, or if the emotion was just too much for him to handle and continue a game of suffering and retribution. In my view, the text suggests that his motives at least included some desire to see a change in his brothers, or that at least a combination of conflicting motives existed that included this goal. The text favors this view in three ways: First, his weeping occurs three times (Gen 42:24; 43:30; 45:2), indicating that Joseph may have possessed compassion all along. Second, if he only wanted to cause them to suffer there was no need for the elaborate scheme. He had the power and means to achieve revenge instantly, or revenge in a drawn out process. Thus, once Benjamin was in view and safe, he could have separated Benjamin and then enacted revenge on the other ten, but he did not. Third, to release the other ten and keep Benjamin as a

---

Traditional Hebrew Text with New JPS Translation, 270.

slave would have been illogical if Joseph's goal was revenge or only revenge (44:17). Regardless of the degree of other motives, Joseph also wanted to see if his brothers had changed, if they would do some harm to Benjamin similar to what they did to him, given the perfect opportunity.[90] Once Judah proved that rather than doing so, he would sacrifice himself, the ruse was over—the manipulation had provoked, as well as demonstrated the positive character change. Alter notes the developmental effect: "Joseph's 'testing' of his brothers is thus also a process that *induces* the recognition of guilt and leads to psychological *transformation*."[91] All the planning and manipulating come to a rush of emotion in a moving moment of recognition.

The Recognition

Once the manipulator achieves the prize, the camouflaging ends. The recognition is immediate for Isaac and Esau. When the older Esau enters Isaac's presence seeking the blessing, the truth emerges. This moment is one of emotion as Isaac trembles at the recognition (Gen 27:33). In the story of Joseph also, this is immediate and emotional, by means of character statement, "I am Joseph! Is my father still alive?" and "I am your brother, Joseph, whom you sold into Egypt," (45:3–4). There is no longer any reason for the masking.[92] There is no token provided for either Isaac, or Joseph's brothers, other than the presence of Esau and Joseph themselves.[93] Tokens are less frequently a part of the manipulator equation and, for that matter, are not a chief concern of my theory. Isaac demanded no proof of the identity of the real Esau as he had of Jacob who was pretending to be Esau. Nevertheless, tokens do occur. Tokens force the recognition by Judah that saves Tamar's life (38:25–26). Sometimes the recognition is caused by the correct person arriving on the scene, as with Esau (27:30), or the wrong one, as with Leah, forcing Jacob to immediately recognize he has married the wrong daughter (29:25).[94]

90. Ackerman, "Joseph, Judah, and Jacob," 93.

91. Alter, *The Five Books of Moses*, 259n34; emphasis added.

92. Unlike some modern novels, the Gen reader is not kept in the dark for an extended period, as is the reader of Dickens's *Great Expectations*, who, later in the novel, suddenly learns along with Pip that the benefactor is the repulsive Magwitch. The Gen reader is aware of Joseph's identity and thus anxiously awaits the unveiling.

93. Though Jewish tradition holds that Joseph used a token of a physical mark on his body, "And they came near (XLV, 4). He showed them that he was circumcised." Freedman and Simon, *Midrash Rabbah*, 93:6.

94. That rabbinic tradition interpreted this not only as a scene of deception, but also as a recognition scene is evident. In the Megillah tractate of the Babylonian Talmud,

In some of the Genesis manipulation narratives, no explicit recognition occurs. Laban never has a moment where he recognizes that Jacob has secretly bred him out of a flock, nor does he ever recognize that Rachel has his gods. However, his sons do verbalize the loss of their wealth: "Jacob has taken all that was our father's, and from what was our father's he has gained all this wealth," (Gen 31:1). There is also no record of the men of Shechem recognizing the deception by Jacob's sons. The text is silent, emphasizing the finality of their deaths. Likewise, in the story world, Jacob's sons were never aware of Hamor and Shechem's plan to take their property, though the narrator and the reader are (Gen 34). In chapter 37, Jacob makes an incorrect recognition, still in the grips of his sons' manipulation. However, due to Joseph's manipulation of those same sons, Jacob has his moment of true and dramatic recognition: "And they told him, 'Joseph is still alive, and he is ruler over all the land of Egypt.' And his heart became numb, for he did not believe them. But when they told him all the words of Joseph, which he had said to them, and when he saw the wagons that Joseph had sent to carry him, the spirit of their father Jacob revived. And Israel said, 'It is enough; Joseph my son is still alive. I will go and see him before I die'" (45:26–27). Later, when Jacob finally sees Joseph face to face, he falls on his neck and weeps (46:29).

Because the moment of recognition represents such a dramatic reversal of events, great emotion frequently accompanies the moment, even if that emotion has to be expressed by the narrator's explanation of a character's silence. In Genesis 45:3, the moment strikes Joseph's brothers dumb because they are "dismayed at his presence." Recognition in manipulation narratives brings a consequent dramatic reversal of fortune. Sometimes the person or group responsible for the wrongdoing is in shock when the tables are turned, and they are the victims of the manipulation and recognition.

Rabbi Jonathan ascribed the following conversation between Jacob and Rachel: "Jacob said, 'In trickery I am your father's brother.' She asked, 'But is it proper for a righteous man to resort to trickery?' He replied, 'Yes, for we read: "With the pure thou dost show thyself pure, and with the crooked thou dost show thyself wily"' (2 Sam. 22:27). So he gave her certain tokens [by which to identify herself]. But when the wedding night came, Rachel said to herself: Now my sister will be humiliated. So she turned the tokens over to Leah. Hence it is said, 'And it came to pass in the morning that, Behold, it was Leah' (Gen. 29:25)." Rashi also reports the tradition. Silbermann, *Chumash with Targum Onkelos, Haphtaroth and Rashi's Commentary 5 Vols.*, 1:138; Bialik et al., *The Book of Legends = Sefer Ha-Aggadah*, 47:71.

Statement or Challenge in Response to the Manipulation

The fifth kernel, a statement or challenge in response to the manipulation, is quite common in Genesis manipulation narratives. Both Isaac and Esau respond verbally to Jacob's deception. First Isaac questions who he had indeed blessed (Gen 27:33). Then Esau responded "with an exceedingly great and bitter cry," asking that Isaac also bless him (27:34).[95] Isaac then responds, declaring the covert manipulation: "Your brother came deceitfully, and he has taken away your blessing" (27:35). Then Esau responds again with the well-known "Is he not rightly called Jacob?," recalling the earlier loss of the birthright and now this lost blessing (27:36). Finally, Isaac responds again with another affirmation of the blessing and a poetic pronouncement of Esau's position and future (27:37–41). The episode then continues with the narrator's explanation of Esau's hatred for Jacob and Rebekah's plans for Jacob to flee (27:41–46).

One common phrase victims voice in response to manipulation first occurs before our selected scenes, when God questions Eve after the serpent's deception, "What is this you have done?" (Gen 3:13). Later, in Genesis 12:18, Pharaoh responds to Abraham's deception regarding Sarah with, "What is this you have done to me?"[96] Abimelech responds similarly when both Abraham and his son Isaac repeat the wife/sister deceptions (20:8; 26:10). When Jacob awakes the morning after his wedding, he responds with the same phrase, "What is this you have done to me? Did I not serve with you for Rachel? Why then have you deceived me?" (29:25). When the sons of Jacob first discover the silver returned in their sacks, they, too, respond with this echoing phrase, "What is this that God has done to us?" (42:28). This kernel then serves as a signpost and confirmation of the indirect, circuitous, or outright deception of the manipulators. The victims would *not* have chosen the outcome if, at first, they had known fully what was occurring. This is what makes the narrative unit a manipulation narrative. Person or group "B," the victim(s), does not know or recognize that person or group "A," the manipulator(s), arranged these circumstances or actions in some indirect, masked, or camouflaged fashion to acquire the desired objective. Eventually though, "B" becomes aware of the manipulation and

---

95. "In the pathetic voice of a small child." Alter, *The Five Books of Moses*, 144n34.

96. Pharaoh challenges Abraham with not one but three questions: "What is this you have done to me? Why did you not tell me that she was your wife? Why did you say, 'She is my sister,' so that I took her for my wife?" Victor Hamilton characterizes the implication: "[T]he king's three questions addressed to Abram reveal that the pagan king indeed knows that adultery is a moral evil. In fact, Pharaoh exemplifies a higher degree of moral sensitivity than does the patriarch." Hamilton, *The Book of Genesis: Chapters 1–17*, 385.

cries out in protest against the loss. This is the nature of Genesis manipulation, where the goal of the manipulator was to change the balance of power and grasp something he or she desired.

The response, however, does not always follow this phrase exactly. When Jacob finally confronts Laban while fleeing, he unleashes a verbal defense, describing all that he had suffered for Laban. This includes the accusation of Laban's double handedness: "you have changed my wages ten times" (Gen 31:41), which summarizes and recaps the Rachel/Leah sibling switch for labor earlier. This defense was provoked and was in response to Laban's threatening response to Jacob covertly fleeing Laban's presence, "What have you done, that you have tricked me and driven away my daughters like captives of the sword?" (31:26). Laban continues with bravado, "It is in my power to do you harm" (31:29), with the accompanying challenge regarding the theft of the gods (31:30). But Laban cannot harm Jacob because of the warning from God in a dream (31:29).[97]

In some manipulation narratives, we never hear the challenge at all. Just as the reader never hears of the recognition, so, too, the reader never hears the challenge when Simeon and Levi silence the voices of Shechem (Gen 34). Jacob however challenges Simeon and Levi, when saying, "You have brought trouble on me by making me stink to the inhabitants of the land, the Canaanites and the Perizzites. My numbers are few, and if they gather themselves against me and attack me, I shall be destroyed, both I and my household" (34:30).[98] Tamar never verbally redresses Judah, but instead turns her own form of manipulation back on him (Gen 38). Judah however, does respond with the moment of self-recognition, "She is more righteous than I, since I did not give her to my son Shelah" (38:26). Observe however, that he offers no challenge or protest to the manipulation. This is a textual clue to the moral evaluation of her behavior—neither Judah, others in the scene, nor the narrator challenge her behavior.[99]

With Joseph's abduction and sale to the Ishmaelites, we hear no protest from him immediately, though we find out later from the brothers' mutual confession that "we saw the distress of his soul, when he begged us and we

---

97. The Midrash *Bereishit Rabbah* likens Jacob's innocence and defense to David's innocence, which he argues for in similar language to Jonathan in 1 Sam 20:1 "What have I done? What is my guilt? And what is my sin before your father, that he seeks my life?" Freedman and Simon, *Midrash Rabbah*, 74:10.

98. Jacob seems to have forgotten the protection of God's blessing and intervention that recently enabled him to flee from the forces of Laban (31:29).

99. The "others" in the scene are comprised of unnamed characters, who tell Judah of her pregnancy, bring her out on his command, and who send Tamar's message and items back to Judah (38:24–25).

did not listen" (Gen 42:21). Jacob, though, responds immediately to the loss of his son, and refuses to be comforted: "It is my son's robe. A fierce animal has devoured him. Joseph is without doubt torn to pieces... No, I shall go down to Sheol to my son, mourning" (37:33, 35).

Joseph's revealing in Egypt elicits several responses, but none of them rising to the level of a challenge, thus indicating that everything Joseph has done can be justified in light of the brothers' previous actions. Initially, his brothers respond with silence (Gen 45:3). Later they do speak to him (45:15), but this is still not evidence enough that they have put the matter behind them. In Genesis 50:15–21, after their father's death, the brothers entreat Joseph, possibly lying once again, claiming that Jacob had commanded them to ask for Joseph's forgiveness. However, this again is too much for Joseph, and he weeps and answers that God had intended the plan in order to provide for the family. The news of a living Joseph had also struck Jacob dumb (45:26). Upon further explanation of Joseph's words, and upon seeing the caravan, he recovers and responds, "It is enough; Joseph my son is still alive. I will go and see him before I die" (45:28), and repeats a similar phrase when seeing Joseph face-to-face (46:30). Here again however, the lack of any challenge is a textual indication that Joseph's actions are justified in the story world of the text.

The Effect of the Manipulation on the Plot or Characterization

We now turn to the last and perhaps one of the more telling kernels of manipulation—the effect of the manipulation on the story and characters.[100] Important to the Genesis form of manipulation and recognition, is that sometimes the deceptive behavior of the manipulator (equivalent to the "observed" in Larsen's work) effects a change, not only in the plot, but also in the characters, especially the victim.[101] We see this more often when the victim is a former manipulator. As we move through some examples, I will also note how the text characterizes certain characters in particular scenes.

When we observe Jacob and Rebekah's manipulation of Isaac and Esau, we see first that the manipulation effects a plot reversal. Jacob's theft of the blessing reverses Esau's good fortune of the coming blessing as first-born,

---

100. One might argue that this is not a kernel. Yet if we consider that kernels are essential to the plot, and that good analysis should "see later kernels as consequences of earlier [ones]," I believe the classification is appropriate. Chatman, *Story and Discourse*, 53.

101. Larsen, *Recognizing the Stranger*, 63.

and instead Esau must serve his younger brother. All the blessings, divine as well as material, are now gone. Jacob too experiences some reversal, not only from bad to good fortune, but also from being close to family to moving away from family. Nevertheless, despite the distancing, Jacob and Isaac experience measured reconciliation after the manipulation, as Isaac calls Jacob back and restates the blessing, along with the directions on where to find a wife. The narrator adds, "Thus Isaac sent Jacob away" (Gen 28:5).

The story characterizes Jacob as following his mother's lead, but also as deceptive and using that deception to manipulate the blessing away from Isaac. The manipulation characterizes Isaac as blind, not only physically but also in a spiritually perceptive sense, contrasted to Rebekah.[102] The story characterizes Rebekah ambiguously: she is deceptive (and willing to bear a curse in Gen 27:13),[103] but also spiritually inquiring and aware of YHWH's word regarding the older serving the younger (25:23). The previous story regarding the birthright had already characterized Esau negatively (25:29–34). Here the narrator explicitly states that Esau hates Jacob because of the theft (25:41). Esau also marries, but possibly in such a way as to displease his father.[104]

But when Jacob arrives in Paddan-aram, Laban turns the tables on him in what I will in chapter 5 describe further as "counter-manipulation," that is, when someone manipulates the manipulator, often in a fashion very similar to the original manipulation. This too results in a reversal, as initially Jacob does not marry Rachel but Leah, and not for seven years of labor but eventually fourteen for both. More importantly, the prolonged labor for someone he desires so much puts Jacob in a power imbalance with Laban.

The text portrays Laban as deceptive, manipulative, and greedy. Laban could just as well have given Jacob both daughters once Leah was recognized, without seven more years of labor. He also evades sole responsibility for his deception. Though the deal was between Jacob and Laban alone ("*I* will serve *you*" Jacob says, and Laban responds "It is better that *I* give her to *you*," Gen 29:18–19), note that Laban resorts to the use of "our" and "we" in verses 26 and 27, "It is not so done in *our* country ... Complete the week of this one and *we* will give you the other." When Laban's character speaks in the plural, the text characterizes him as avoiding sole responsibility for the switch, and he explains the reason for his deception by sharing the

---

102 Mathews, *Genesis*, 417.

103. "Upon me be (the responsibility for warding off) thy curse." Freedman and Simon, *Midrash Rabbah*, 65:15n1.

104. Alter, *The Five Books of Moses*, 148n4.

blame with compatriots and their customs.[105] However, Jacob also receives a negative characterization. By virtue of the fact that Laban used "evening," to mask Leah, and "morning" to reveal her, both of which are effects upon the eyes, the text may also portray Jacob as somewhat perceptually blind as his father was in the previous episode. Thus, not only is Jacob manipulated by a sibling switch, he is also ironically, victimized by darkness and some of his own blindness.[106] This episode also serves as a counter-manipulation.

In this episode, we may have the first positive change in the character of the original manipulator. Jacob the manipulator, who deceived his father and brother, possibly learns from a similar switch. When Laban explains that they do not "give the younger before the firstborn," (Gen 29:26), he echoes the firstborn/younger sibling switch Jacob performed earlier.[107] When he states Jacob must serve seven more years, the text records Jacob's response, that he did so and took Rachel, but it records no protest. Jacob is silent at this moment.[108] This subtle nuance may indicate his awareness that he has been manipulated in just the same way he manipulated his father, implying his awareness of guilt. The implication may be that Jacob is learning and transforming because of the counter-manipulation, because he complies with the new arrangements and does not respond verbally after Laban's answer.

In the next manipulation between Laban and Jacob, Jacob walks away with many more marked animals than Laban may have anticipated, despite Laban's violation of the agreement by removing the animals himself, rather than allowing Jacob to do so. He then distances his flocks from Jacob. Nevertheless, once again, there is a significant reversal of the events that one person had planned. Jacob counter-manipulates Laban, who ends up with fewer and feebler flocks. Jacob "increased greatly" (Gen 30:42–43). Moreover, instead of keeping Jacob and his skills, Laban loses them, and in a mini-*dénouement*, Jacob flees for home.

---

105. Philo, though allegorically, holds Laban accountable for blaming the customs of the time to marry the older daughter first: "Such a man as this the lawgiver calls labour, who, not perceiving the true laws of nature, falsely assents to those which are in force among men, saying, 'It is not the custom in our country to give the younger daughter in marriage before the elder.'" Philo, *Drunkenness* 47; *The Works of Philo*, 211.

106. "[Jacob] took advantage of his father's permanent darkness to misrepresent himself as his elder brother, so Laban makes use of the darkness to substitute elder sister for the younger." Sarna, *Genesis* בראשית: *The Traditional Hebrew Text with New JPS Translation*, 397.

107. Alter, *The Five Books of Moses*, 155n26; Sailhamer, *Pentateuch as Narrative*, 194.

108. "Jacob conceded the point." Ibid., 194.

The text characterizes Jacob as blessed by God and relentlessly harassed by Laban (Gen 31:7).[109] Laban is characterized as perpetually deceptive, manipulative, and once again greedy: "All that you see is mine" (31:43). This manipulation episode characterizes deities as well. The story belittles the power and effectiveness of Laban's gods to deliver over and against the power of Jacob's God to deliver Jacob's family.[110] In the first attempt, that of Laban attempting to manipulate Jacob out of the marked animals, there is no observed change in Jacob, the victim of the manipulation. This is no surprise since Laban is unsuccessful in his attempt to manipulate. However, considering Jacob's counter-manipulative breeding and escape, a careful observation reveals a Laban with an ever so slight degree of concession. He complies with Jacob's departure and upon setting up the marker, invokes Jacob's God as witness between them, rather than his gods, which at the moment, the narrator has explained, are unavailable—still under Rachel's saddle. He states, "The LORD (יהוה) watch between you and me" (31:49). This concession by Laban makes way for the functional reconciliation between the two.[111]

The important change observed in the victim of counter-manipulation is often a change along a path of *positive development, according to the values of the story world.*[112] In Genesis, those values fall along the axes of: entreating and responding to the God of Abraham[113] versus other gods,[114]

---

109. The Midrash *Bereishit Rabbah* characterizes Laban as recognizing that blessing when he speaks to the men he assembled for the wedding feast: "You know how we were short of water, and as soon as this righteous man came the water was blessed." Freedman and Simon, *Midrash Rabbah*, 70:19.

110. Sarna, *Genesis* בר־אשית: *The Traditional Hebrew Text with New JPS Translation*, 216n19.

111. The text implies that the two reconcile, and they agree to disagree, building a marker beyond which neither will pass. However, characters do not typically use markers when they are completely reconciled. The phrase, "The Lord watch between you and me," or its equivalent, occurs elsewhere between two persons who have a case against each other. See Gen 16:5 and 1 Sam 24:12.

112. Chatman speaks of the "norms of the narrative," which the implied author communicates to the reader: "The real author can postulate whatever norms he likes through his implied author." Chatman, *Story and Discourse*, 149. See also Rimmon-Kenan, *Narrative Fiction: Contemporary Poetics*, 83–84.

113. Who is YHWH, the LORD of Abraham (reading Gen from a narratological standpoint, in its final form, Gen 12:1). This is also the God of creation, according to the account beginning in 2:4, "These are the generations of the heavens and the earth when they were created, in the day that the Lord (יְהוָה) God made the earth and the heavens." Literary scholar Paul Borgman interprets both creation accounts together, but as having been crafted separately for literary purpose: "The one God in two aspects couldn't have been dramatized any more succinctly and powerfully than by having these two accounts of creation side by side." Mann, "All the Families of the Earth," 342. This does not mean that Gen 1–2 is without difficulties. Ibid., 351.

114. Borgman, *Genesis: The Story we Haven't Heard*, 38. The motif of responding

allegiance versus non-allegiance to family and its obligations,[115] truth versus deception,[116] vulnerability and self-sacrifice versus arrogance and self-promotion/preservation.[117] Thomas Mann in particular argues that the characters in the Abraham, Jacob, and Joseph cycles undergo a transformation that is "at once personal, social, and spiritual, and that takes place within the context of his respective family relations."[118] In the FG, the values all fall on axes focused on the protagonist, Jesus, and his ultimate recognition: belief versus unbelief,[119] following versus not following, and knowing versus

---

to YHWH is marked early in Gen 4:26, when "people began to call upon the name of the LORD." In 29:20–22, Jacob vows that, if God will be with him and return him to his father's house, "then the LORD shall be my God." See also Sternberg, *The Poetics of Biblical Narrative*, 177.

115. Petersen and Osiek, "Genesis and Family Values," 9–10. We see this in the negative characterization of one's turning away from family, as in the case of Judah in 38:1, and in the murder of a sibling, Gen 4. Borgman states that, in Gen, "families nearly self-destruct with subtle or shocking rivalries and one-upmanship." Borgman, *Genesis: The Story we Haven't Heard*, 39. The importance of allegiance to familial obligations is also seen in the negative assessment when "little ones" are taken or plundered (34:25, 29, 30), or in the positive affirmation of caring for little ones, even at the expense at times of an adult's safety (43:8; 45:19; 47:24; 50:21). Mann argues that "the primary resolution within the Joseph narrative takes place on this familial level: Jacob eventually must be willing (like his grandfather) to give up his beloved son Benjamin in order for the family to survive (cf. 42:36–38 and 43:13–15), abandoning a favoritism in which much of the family hostility was rooted." Mann, "'All the Families of the Earth,'" 349.

116. In Gen 3:14, the serpent is the first creature to receive a pronouncement of punishment for wrongdoing. The serpent's punishment is pronounced before Eve's. The serpent's crime was deceiving Eve (3:13). Note also that the "LORD God" (3:14) is the one who punishes the serpent.

117. Borgman argues that the characters God chooses in Gen "are ordinary human beings with normal dispositions toward self-aggrandizing choices." Borgman, *Genesis: The Story we Haven't Heard*, 21. Adam and Even chose "what forever will be the normal choices of self-aggrandizement. Ibid., 30. Westermann remarks that the temptation to be like God, which the serpent offered to Eve, was "concerned with a divine and unbridled ability to master one's existence." Westermann, *Genesis 1–11: A Commentary*, 248. Borgman argues that the dominant theme in Gen 1–11 is that God speaks into existence the created order, summing it up that it was "very good" (Gen 1:31; Borgman, *Genesis: The Story we Haven't Heard*, 24), only to have the characters' "lust to be number one" repeatedly degenerate humanity to the point where Lamech is "seventy and seven times" as bad as Cain (ibid., 34), and even the one righteous man available, Noah, becomes drunk after the flood, leading to a shameful moment with Ham and thus signals a "bad start to a second human race" (ibid., 36). This reaches a boiling point in the self-promoting construction of the tower of Babel (ibid., 36). There are other axes of values in Gen, such God's blessing versus birthright (Gen 17:18–19; 25:21–34).

118. Mann, "'All the Families of the Earth,'" 349. Buber recognizes the developmental nature of characters as part of the Gen agenda, beginning with God's choice of Abraham: "[W]ith Abraham what matters is not his character as God finds it, so to speak, but what he does, what he becomes." Buber and Glatzer, *On the Bible: Eighteen Studies*, 33.

119. Painter, *John: Witness and Theologian*, 77–85.

ignorance.[120] Here in Genesis, Laban suddenly makes a vow and calls upon the God of Abraham, Isaac, and Jacob, not his *teraphim*, to witness that vow. He also agrees to let Jacob go, and he departs peaceably. Even though he is not a patriarchal character of the promised blessing such as Jacob, Judah, or Joseph in the chosen line, the text evidences a subtle concession in this positive direction.

A positive change in a character may not show up immediately after the counter-manipulation. Although Judah's change is most clearly demonstrated at the moment he is willing to sacrifice himself for Benjamin in Egypt, his use of the term "pledge" (Gen 44:32), ties the episode to the episode of Tamar's counter-manipulation of him and the occurrence of "pledge" there (38:17–18). This *Leitwort* indicates for the reader that some part of the change in Judah, evidenced in Egypt in chapter 44, is linked to the previous manipulation by Tamar. Earlier in Genesis, Jacob also may have undergone a measured degree of change as a result of a counter-manipulation, which was demonstrated only after some delay. In chapters 32–33, after having been counter-manipulated by Laban by means of the ironic sibling switch, Jacob, on his return to meet Esau, refers to Esau as "my lord" or himself as "your servant" a total of nine times (32:5, 18, 20; 33:5, 8, 13, 14). Instead of stealing a benefit from Esau, he is offering gifts, and he expresses his desire to "appease" Esau: "For he thought, 'I may appease him with the present that goes ahead of me'" (32:20), a statement that may concede past guilt.[121] Although he puts his favorite wife and son in the rear for protection, he puts himself in the front, in harm's way (33:2–3).[122] While Jacob has not yet learned to be completely transparent (since he lies about where he will travel, 33:14–17), and the gifts may still be an attempt to manipulate, some change is noticeable.

In the manipulation between Jacob's sons and Shechem and Hamor, there is no noted change in character in a positive direction, but there is significant reversal and clear characterization. Hamor and Shechem are characterized as deceptive, manipulative, greedy, and opportunistic, but also as dull or blinded by their greed; unaware of the fate about to fall on them ("I will give whatever you say to me. Only give me the young woman to be my wife," Gen 34:12; "Will not their livestock, their property and all their beasts be ours? Only let us agree with them, and they will dwell with us," 34:23). Individually, Shechem is characterized as sexually unrestrained

---

120. Ibid., 86–100.

121. *The NET Bible First Edition*, Gen 32:20n44.

122. The *Midrash Bereishit Rabbah* reads "Let him harm me, rather than them." Freedman and Simon, *Midrash Rabbah*, 78:8.

and as a demanding young prince: "Get me this girl for my wife" (34:4).[123] Hamor is characterized as a father, conceding to an unrestrained demanding young prince, and Jacob is characterized as unresponsive when action is needed: "so Jacob held his peace until they came" (34:5).[124] He is also seen as over reacting when his sons take too severe of an action: "My numbers are few ..." (33: 30). Amidst all of this, a sweeping reversal occurs. Hamor and Shechem believe they will obtain all of Jacob's family's livestock, property, and beasts, but in fact, they lose not only their own livestock, but they lose their lives and their families are taken. In the end, all of Jacob's sons are characterized as deceitful and manipulative, and Simeon and Levi are characterized as murderers because they "came against the city while it felt secure" (34:25).[125] Jacob's other sons are characterized as plunderers, after the murder (34:27–29). In this story, no positive development in the characters occurs.

In the Joseph novella, the effect of the manipulation is certainly a reversal as well. Young Joseph sets out on a journey to check on his brothers, brags of dreams that indicate his family will do obeisance to him, but ends up in an Egyptian prison.[126] However, the injustice done to Joseph sets up a tension in the text, where the reader awaits the reversal that puts the brothers on the defensive in chapters 42–45. Whereas there is no positive character development in this manipulation, there is ample characterization of the players. By narrator explanation, we learn that Jacob plays favorites: "Now Israel loved Joseph more than any other of his sons" (Gen 37:3). The narrator also characterizes Joseph negatively, as a tattletale, bringing a bad report about his brothers (37:2).[127] Jacob is once again characterized as dramatic, saying that he will mourn his son's death until he enters Sheol (37:35). The narrator characterizes the brothers as deceptive and manipulative, hiding their behavior in order to secure their goal of ridding themselves of Joseph. By narrator explanation, we learn that the brothers hated Joseph and could not speak kindly to him (37:4), and were jealous of him (37:11). By narrator

---

123. Samson utters similar words in Judges 14:2, characterizing him in a similar manner, in a passage that likely alludes to this one. Additionally, *Jubilees* characterizes the rape even more negatively because it portrays Dinah as very young, "but she was little, only twelve years old." *Jub.* 30:2. Charlesworth, *The Old Testament Pseudepigrapha*, 112.

124. Mathews, *Genesis*, 597.

125. Ibid., 606.

126. Sarna calls Joseph's dream sharing a "highly egocentric vision of superiority and lordship" Sarna, *Genesis* בראשית: *The Traditional Hebrew Text with New JPS Translation*, 256.

127. Mathews, *Genesis*, 687.

explanation and implication, we learn that the brothers sit down to eat, implying casualness about their act of kidnapping.[128] Moreover, by his own words, we learn that Reuben is more concerned for himself than for Joseph. Reuben mourns for his fate, rather than Joseph's: "and I, where shall I go?" (37:30). And by implication we discern that Reuben goes along with his brothers' story and does not speak up as firstborn to inform his father of Joseph's true fate (37:32).

Judah's manipulative withholding of Shelah from Tamar affects the plot as well. Like the episode before, it establishes the power imbalance and tension between Tamar and Judah. A perceptive reader senses the injustice of Judah's lack of action toward Tamar. Likewise then, when she turns the tables on him, this constitutes a sudden *peripeteia* for Judah, when he realizes he is guilty of the crime for which he plans to execute Tamar. Thus, the text characterizes him negatively in a number of ways. First, he turns away from familial obligations, "went down from his brothers, and turned aside" (Gen 38:1).[129] The narrator explains that Judah also "saw" and "took" (יַּרְא and יִּקָּחֶהָ, 38:2) the woman, with the same two verbs that Shechem "saw" and "took" Dinah (34:2). "Took" is, moreover, the second verb used to describe Rachel's action when she "took" the gods (31:34). However, Judah does not "humiliate" Tamar as Shechem did with Dinah (34:2). In contrast to the family injunction against marriage outside the tribe (28:1), Judah takes a Canaanite wife. More importantly, Judah's manipulation by withholding Tamar from Shelah demonstrates his dishonesty, lack of responsibility toward his family obligations, and manipulative nature.

This is another episode that demonstrates the transforming effect of counter-manipulation on the original manipulator.[130] Judah's swift reversal is not just one of reversed fortune, but of character as well. His own words demonstrate this when he says, "She is more righteous than I" (Gen 38:26). The narrator's explanation of the withholding of further sexual liaison also shows the change. Finally, the reader must infer evidence of Judah's change by the fact that he withholds his judgment and death penalty for Tamar as the story continues to the birth of his twin boys.

When we analyze Joseph's manipulation of his brothers and their recognition of him, we find here a great reversal of events and character. This includes the very reversal foretold by Joseph's dreams (Gen 37:5–11), when they bow down to him (42:6). The brothers experience reversal when they are put in prison (42:17), mirroring Joseph's imprisonment (39:20).

---

128. Ibid., 697.
129. Lambe, "Judah's Development," 56–57.
130. This will be discussed in detail in the following chapter.

When they make the journey to Egypt with Benjamin in tow (43:11–14), the journey is a replay of the enslavement of Joseph (35:25–28). But this time, the situation is in reverse in that Joseph is in charge, rather than his brothers or the Ishmaelites. In addition, the positive change in the original manipulators is most dramatic. The brothers go through a change, evidenced by their admission of guilt (42:21–22), acknowledgment that God is responding to their guilt (42:28), and attitude toward Joseph once he is recognized. In 45:15, the narrator states, "After that his brothers talked with him," which is a clear change from the opening of chapter 37 that reads, "they hated him and could not speak peacefully to him" (37:4).[131] Judah evidences an even more significant change in character, moving from withholding actions in the episode with Tamar, to proactively taking actions of self-sacrifice, leadership, and family spokesperson on the behalf of others.[132] Reuben evidences the least change in character of all. In fact, when the text specifically names him in this story, Reuben is the same ineffective older brother he was years earlier, with plans to rescue someone that risk not a hair of his own head (42:37).[133] The previously histrionic, favorite-playing Jacob now releases Benjamin and only responds, "If I am bereaved, I am bereaved" (43:14).

Summary

Before examining the broad patterns that my theory of Genesis manipulation yields for an analysis of John 21, I would like to summarize what I have said thus far. Recognition in Genesis is in this study regarded as part of a larger mechanism I have termed "manipulation." "Manipulation" is, in my view, a more apt term for describing what happens in narrative units in

---

131. Also in Gen 37:18, they refer to Joseph as "dreamer." In 37:27, Judah does call him "brother," but in 37:22, in speaking to their father they refer to the robe as "your son's." Whereas in chapter 42, he is referred to as "our brother" (42:21), and "the boy" (42:22).

132. Alter, *The Five Books of Moses*, 259n34. This is an example of the drastic development of biblical characters, in contrast to Homeric characters, which Auerbach describes, saying God "continues to work upon them, bends them and kneads them, and, without destroying them in essence, produces from them forms which their youth gave no grounds for anticipating." Auerbach, *Mimesis*, 18. Though some rabbinic tradition interpreted Judah's attitude as belligerent, there was clearly a plurality of rabbis who viewed it as conciliatory, even reporting that Judah "broke out into sobs and cried out in a loud voice" when he drew near to Joseph." Bialik et al., *The Book of Legends = Sefer Ha-Aggadah*, 55:107.

133. "He is indeed a foolish firstborn!" Freedman and Simon, *Midrash Rabbah, Genesis*, 91:9.

Genesis previously called "trickster" scenes. As a term employed to facilitate narrative analysis, "manipulation" can better describe the broad array of behaviors and actions of these characters. As pointed out earlier, manipulation occurs when person or group "A" arranges matters in an indirect, masked, or camouflaged manner, in order to obtain a desired objective. Person or group "B" is initially unaware that "A" has done this. Frequently, "B" later recognizes this circuitous manipulative behavior. The semantic range of the word group "manipulate, manipulative, manipulation" includes blatant deception for personal gain that is morally wrong, artful indirect maneuvering to restore and correct an injustice, and many of the subtleties in between. As a theoretical term, manipulation is not a panacea, but it does add greater theoretical specificity than "tricking" does. I also assert that recognition is *not* equivalent to manipulation, but rather only one kernel in the manipulation "type" narrative. Manipulators thwart or delay recognition of information that, if known, would prevent the manipulator from obtaining a specific goal. Recognition happens after the manipulator has employed one or more of the devices described above, the ruse unravels, and the victim finally realizes the truth.

I have identified and labeled six kernels that frequently occur in manipulation narratives. They are 1) The desired benefit the manipulator is pursuing, 2) The actual manipulation, accomplished by means of a variety of devices, 3) The benefit achieved, 4) The moment of recognition, 5) The statement or challenge in response to the manipulation, and 6) The effect of the manipulation on the plot or characterization. These kernels clearly have a cause and effect aspect, but they may not always fall chronologically according to their numbered order here. Furthermore, not all manipulation narratives include all six kernels.

There are many devices a manipulator may use, ranging from murder and outright lying to artful positioning of a desired object or goal. They include physical masking of persons or objects (by clothing [false tokens], by environment, or by space), switches, and thefts. Manipulators may also ply their verbal masking by ambiguous language or statements and omissions. Finally, the manipulator may resort to distraction, trust building, positioning or use of an object of desire, flight, entrapment, crafty husbandry, force of power, rape, injury, murder, and avoiding or failing to fulfill an obligation. These devices sometimes overlap. For example, "force of power," and "rape" both describe the same behavior that Shechem takes against Dinah. Important here to understand is that preventing or thwarting recognition, whether by disguise, lying, or playing on the victim's dullness, is merely one *component* of what is really the issue at hand—*manipulation*.

A manipulation narrative can therefore be plotted with this classification of kernels and devices:

Genesis 27: Jacob & Rebecca manipulate Isaac & Esau

Kernel	Components and Devices
1) The Desired Benefit	Isaac's blessing, revealed by *character statements*.
2) The Manipulation	*Masking of Person (Thwarted Recognition by means of false tokens), Trust building, Lie, Switch, Positioning/Use of Object of Desire, Entrapment.*
3) The Benefit Achieved	Isaac blesses Jacob instead of Esau, revealed repeatedly by *character statements*.
4) The Recognition	By means of *the arrival of the correct person.*
5) The statement or challenge in response to the manipulation	"Your brother came deceitfully." "Is he not rightly named Jacob? For he has cheated me these two times."
6) The effect of the manipulation (or counter-manipulation) on the plot or on characterization.	Plot: Reversal of the blessing and primogeniture. Plot: Jacob is distanced from family, yet reconciles somewhat with Isaac before departure. Characterization - Jacob: Deceptive, manipulative, and following his mother's instructions. Characterization - Isaac: Blind, physically as well as spiritually-perceptually. Playing favorites. Characterization - Rebekah: Ambiguously deceptive, playing favorites, but also seeking a divine blessing for Jacob. Characterization - Esau: From the previous episode, a man driven by desires. Hates Jacob and marries to displease parents. Character Transformation: None.

The goal of this theory and classification of Genesis manipulation narratives is to contribute to the ongoing discussion of recognition in ancient Greco-Roman and Jewish literature. I am especially interested in sharpening our understanding of biblical manipulation and recognition in order to gain a more informed interpretation of recognition in John 21. The theory and taxonomy discussed above contribute to the discussion in the following ways.

First, as far as I am aware, this theory is the first to combine the two literary phenomena of tricking/manipulation and recognition in a systematic way for analysis of the relevant narratives. Aristotle's treatment of *anagnorisis* does not combine the two,[134] and whereas Culpepper and Larsen examine recognition in Greco-Roman contexts, they do not combine it with an extended examination of the trickster material. Auerbach's first chapter of *Mimesis* deals with Odysseus' recognition scene and God's command for Abraham to sacrifice Isaac, but his goal is to compare and contrast the rich, descriptive style of the Homeric poems and its "static" characters,[135] with the terse, non-descriptive style of the Hebrew Bible and its conflicted yet developing characters.[136] While the major contribution of his chapter is the contrasting of the two styles to serve as a foundation for his examination of how literature had treated "reality in European culture" during the past two millennia, Auerbach does not specifically analyze recognition comprehensively nor its component parts.[137] Williams supplies us with a classification of trickster scenes, but does not combine this with a close examination of recognition.[138] He examines these scenes primarily to discover the text's moral evaluation of them.[139] Likewise, in his examination of the trickster material, Nicholas does not develop the recognition component.[140]

I have approached these narratives from a narrative point of view to see what Genesis might offer when specifically focusing on both recognition and manipulation. I have also closely examined the kernels most consistent to manipulation narratives. What I have found is that in the convergence of manipulation and recognition, manipulators frequently withhold recognition from others in order to achieve selfish goals. Additionally, as I shall

---

134. Aristotle, *Poet.* 1452a–52b, 1454b, 1455a.

135. Auerbach, *Mimesis*, 21.

136. Ibid., 3, 5–6, 9–10, 13, 17–18, 23.

137. Ibid., 23.

138. Williams, *Deception in Genesis*. Williams's taxonomy also does not examine some manipulations scenes, such as Shechem's attempted manipulation of Jacob's sons and Judah's manipulation of Tamar. Ibid., 23–29.

139. Ibid., 221.

140. Nicholas, *The Trickster Revisited*, 55.

describe in the next chapter, counter-manipulators manipulate to correct the injustices created by the achievement of those selfish goals. Williams comes to a similar conclusion that tricksters are justified when restoring shalom.[141] However, when applying this theory of manipulation, the analysis demonstrates that in counter-manipulation, a reversal frequently ensues, which can often transform characters in a positive way, according to the values of the text. This will also have a bearing on the interpretation of recognition in John 21.

Larsen points out that in the Greco-Roman world, the observed often withheld recognition to create a test of loyalty.[142] Manipulators in Genesis have far more pointed motives than that. As I have explained, Genesis *anagnorisis* does not function alone but forms part of a grander scheme of deception and gain. Larsen, along with Jo-Ann Brant, argue that there has been "too much focus on the role of *anagnorisis* in John's delineation of character."[143] Culpepper as well focuses his examination of *anagnorisis* on plot.[144] However, this study of Genesis demonstrates that, in addition to plot, *anagnorisis* can certainly yield more information about characters, characterization, and their transformation. When we examine the desired benefit of the manipulator, each manipulation narrative yields information about the manipulator. Larsen's move away from characters may be due to the fact that he drew primarily from *The Odyssey* and other Greco-Roman narratives, which, until recently as we have discussed above, were thought to contain primarily static characters. Notwithstanding, there appears to be much more we can learn about characters by applying the above analysis to Genesis as well as Johannine *anagnorisis*. By studying Genesis, we see that at least in that text, manipulation and *anagnorisis* often create changes in characters, which readers can trace in the text. In the case of Joseph and Tamar, their manipulation tactics may include that goal—to change those who originally manipulated them. I have therefore given *anagnorisis* greater importance in my theory.

Additionally, this taxonomy allows other scholars to examine other recognition narratives further by means of the types of devices I have provided. It adds to Larsen's analysis of Greco-Roman literature by identifying strategies such as omission, switching, theft, trust building, and positioning/

---

141. Williams, *Deception in Genesis*, 221.

142. Larsen, *Recognizing the Stranger*, 63, 63, 68, 133. Recall that, in Larsen's terminology, the "observed" is analogous to the manipulator in my theory because the manipulator is the one whom the victim finally observes and recognizes, Ibid., 63.

143. Ibid., 17; Brant, *Dialogue and Drama*, 57.

144. Culpepper, *The Gospel and Letters of John*, 67–86, esp. 71.

use of objects of desire.[145] Larsen's analysis delivers to readers what Greco-Roman texts offer. The analysis of Genesis manipulation and recognition provides several new devices scholars can consider when analyzing similar narratives. Since Genesis is a text with a progressive series of manipulation narratives (which of course contain recognition and thwarted recognition as devices), this analysis should also contribute to the understanding of the FG, which Larsen demonstrates is a text with progressive recognition narratives, culminating in the last chapters. My hope is that by combining my analysis with that of Larsen, others that follow can increase our theoretical understanding of what is occurring in manipulation and recognition in the Fourth Gospel and beyond.

Finally, in addition to the term manipulation, in the next chapter I will explain more clearly the concept of "counter-manipulation," describing the corrective measures that manipulate the manipulator. The addition of the term counter-manipulator allows the reader to distinguish between initial manipulators, who tend to seek selfish ends, from those whose manipulative actions serve positive ends. This counter-manipulative action is the move of "turnabout is fair play" that transforms the original manipulator by actions strikingly similar to his own schemes. When someone manipulates a manipulator in a manner similar to his or her own original behavior, the maneuver catches the manipulator off guard and elicits either silence or statements such as "she is more righteous than I" (Gen 38:26). This "tit for tat" response is the "counter-manipulation." The transformation of the manipulator is therefore a key theme in the research below.

---

145. Williams does include "Victim lured by kind words." Williams, *Deception in Genesis*, 23.

5

Patterns in Genesis Manipulation and Recognition

In this chapter, I transition from discussing the kernels *within* a manipulation narrative, to describing the broad patterns that one sees spanning across these narratives. Here I provide what I have learned of themes that bridge and provide linkage between these narratives. Before delineating these patterns, however, I first address the selection of passages included in this study.

Selection of Narrative Units and Rationale

Genesis offers no shortage of manipulation/recognition narratives. In the patriarchal narratives of Genesis, there is an *extended pattern* of manipulation, deception, and recognition.[1] Since Joseph's reunion with his brothers is the culminating scene in a long sequence of manipulation narratives, my analysis in this chapter includes the following episodes, which lead up to the reunion of Jacob's family in Egypt: Rebekah/Jacob manipulate Isaac/Esau (Gen 26 and 27), Laban manipulates Jacob in matters of marriage and labor (Gen 29), Laban attempts ... but Jacob out-manipulates Laban by means of breeding the livestock (Gen 30),[2] Rachel manipulates Laban with stolen gods (Gen 31), Shechem attempts ... but the brothers deceive, manipulate, and murder Shechem (Gen 34), Judah and his brothers manipulate Jacob and Joseph (Gen 37), Judah manipulates Tamar, but Tamar counter-manipulates Judah (Gen 38), and, finally, Joseph reciprocates with

---

1. Or "failed recognition," as Larsen deems the Rebekah/Jacob versus Isaac/Esau blessing story, in Larsen, *Recognizing the Stranger*, 56.

2 Jacob does say to Laban, "point out (recognize -נכר) what I have that is yours."

119

the counter-manipulation of his brothers (Gen 42–46, with the *concealing* taking place in chapter 42 and the reunion proper taking place in 45).[3]

Another key reason for including these episodes is that they each fall into a *series of episodes* that center on a given character. There is a series of episodes focused on Jacob and a series of episodes that focus on Jacob's sons, with a growing emphasis on Judah. With regard to Jacob, there are the following series of episodes:

> *Jacob/Rebekah manipulate Isaac/Esau (Gen 26, 27)*[4]
>
> *Laban manipulates Jacob into marrying two daughters (Gen 29)*
>
> *Laban attempts, but Jacob rather manipulates him in the matter of the flocks (Gen 30)*
>
> *Rachel, Jacob's wife, manipulates Laban in the matter of the stolen gods (Gen 31)*
>
> *Judah and his brothers sell Joseph and manipulate (i.e. deceive) Jacob (Gen 37)*

Episodes focused on Jacob's sons, with an increasing emphasis on Judah:

> *The brothers manipulate and murder Shechem (Gen 34)*
>
> *Judah and his brothers sell Joseph, and manipulate and deceive Jacob (Gen 37)*
>
> *Judah manipulates and prevents Tamar from receiving his seed (Gen 38)*
>
> *Tamar manipulates Judah into giving her his seed (Gen 38)*
>
> *Joseph manipulates his brothers and Judah in Egypt (Gen 42–46)*

Thus, when examined in this manner, three key characters, Jacob, Judah, and Joseph, arise in these two manipulation series.[5] There is also some overlap. The episode where the brothers manipulate their father belongs in the manipulation series of Jacob as well as Judah and his brothers.

---

3. Or one could call it "dis-recognition." This unusual compound term conveys Joseph's *active* role, in disguising himself while preserving the Hebrew play on recognize (הכר).

4. Jacob purchasing Esau's birthright is certainly a manipulation narrative. However, due to space limitations and the need to focus the Gen examination toward recognition in John 21, there is no need to examine it further. As already stated it exhibits how manipulation occurs at times without lying or the thwarting of recognition.

5. Or character groups, since the brothers often function as a character group, alongside Judah.

In all the narratives, there are other characters, including Laban, Rachel, Shechem, Hamor, Tamar, and Rebekah. Though these characters are worthy of study in themselves, I will not examine them closely, since I argue below that the plot lines in the second half of Genesis mostly revolve around other key characters: Jacob, the brothers and Judah, and Joseph. Thus, we will discuss these characters only as they relate to the central characters.

This aspect of a *series* of manipulation narratives revolving around a specific character is an important characteristic of Genesis manipulation: multiple episodes of manipulation perpetuated by a character throughout his life. This *serial nature* of manipulation narratives, focused on a certain character, illuminates how the Genesis manipulation "type-narrative" functions. Each series of narratives—Jacob's manipulation narratives, Judah's manipulation narratives, Joseph's manipulation narratives—helps us to trace characterization through narrative kernels situated along the character's path of development, what Rimmon-Kenan calls "'directional' dimension."[6]

There are other episodes I could have chosen for discussion. The first and most obvious would be the serpent's deception and manipulation of Adam and Eve in Genesis 3. Other examples could include Abraham's manipulation of Pharaoh (Gen 12), Lot's daughters' manipulation of their father for his seed (Gen 19), Abraham's manipulation of Abimelech (Gen 20), and Isaac's manipulation of Abimelech (Gen 26).[7] Each of these narratives can also be analyzed using the six kernels identified in the previous chapter, keeping in mind that not all six kernels are present in all manipulation narratives. In Abraham's manipulation of Pharaoh in 12:13, the first kernel is present when Abraham states the benefit he hopes to achieve as a result of his manipulation of Pharaoh: "Say you are my sister, that it may go well with me because of you, and that my life may be spared for your sake."[8] The

---

6. Rimmon-Kenan, *Narrative Fiction: Contemporary Poetics*, 41.

7. One can see therefore, that Abraham and Isaac each are also involved in a series of narratives each, in which they, as key characters, begin as manipulators.

8. Bar-Efrat writes: "Modern scholars have claimed that at that time marriage between a step-brother and sister was still permitted (this view is based on the custom among neighbouring nations, particularly Egypt . . .)." Bar-Efrat, *Narrative Art in the Bible*, 240–41. See also Hamilton, *The Book of Genesis: Chapters 1–17*, 381–82. More recently, Nicholas and others address this, surveying publications dating back to the late 1800s, resulting from archaeological work on cuneiform tablets originating in ancient Nuzi. They find that Hurrian customs allowed the wife to be adopted also as a sister. However, dissension has arisen with this explanation and scholarship demonstrates that this may not have been directly tied with marriage and, in fact, is not a sufficient explanation for the wife-sister narratives in the Pentateuch. Nicholas, *The Trickster Revisited*, 4–6; Hamilton, *The Book of Genesis: Chapters 1–17*, 381–82. But see Hoffmeier, "The Wives' Tales of Genesis 12, 20 and 26 and the Covenants at Beer-Sheba," 81–100. Nicholas also surveys recent as well as older source critical approaches

second kernel, the actual manipulation, is implied by the following verse: "And when the princes of Pharaoh saw her, they praised her to Pharaoh. And the woman was taken into Pharaoh's house" (12:15). Here the narrator, by describing Sarah's relocation into Pharaoh's house, implies to the reader that the proposed lie, a verbal mask, has taken place. The third kernel follows on the heels of the second—for the benefit is attained quickly: "And for her sake he dealt well with Abraham; and he had sheep, oxen, male donkeys, male servants, female servants, female donkeys, and camels" (12:16).[9] Kernels four and five are conflated in Pharaoh's response to Abraham: "What is this you have done to me? Why did you not tell me that she was your wife?"[10] Here the victim of the manipulation both recognizes Sarah's true role in relation to Abraham and, at the same time, challenges the manipulator. The effect of the manipulation on plot and character, kernel six, is also present. Abraham, as the father of the forthcoming nation of Israel, continues forward, even though he has threatened the plot of the promised seed with his deceptive behavior.[11] He is characterized negatively by Pharaoh's threefold challenge.[12] In this regard Nachmanides points out, "Even if it were true that

---

to these narratives, and the idea that "Pentateuchal redaction was concerned to 'whitewash' biblical heroes," yet concludes, "But the ethical problems remain." Ibid., 7–8. Sacks remarks: "Abraham's excuse is weak . . . the words themselves are true. Sarah is in some sense his sister, but since the sentence itself was intended to imply that she was not his wife it was certainly a lie." Sacks, *A Commentary on the Book of Genesis*, 143. Along with Sacks, Fishbane and Sarna both interpret the journey through the text of the Jacob deception stories as offering a "moral critique" of these characters. Fishbane, "Composition and Structure in the Jacob Cycle (Gen 25:19–35:22)," 30; Sarna, *Understanding Genesis*, 183.

9. Ironically though, for Abraham, one can argue that the text implies that the favor he incurs from Pharaoh is not only due to his manipulation but also due to the blessing pronounced only fourteen verses earlier, "and I will bless you and make your name great" (12:2). Mathews notes, "'But the Lord inflicted' highlights the contrast between Abraham's welfare and that of Pharaoh." Mathews, *Genesis*, 129. The text underscores the wealth again in the transition to the next narrative unit in 13:1–2.

10. Which is in keeping with the verbal challenge of other manipulators we have discussed (Gen 20:8; 26:10; 29:25; 42:28). See Williams, *Deception in Genesis*, 15.

11. The SBL Publication, *Harper's Bible Commentary*, intended probably more for the layperson, labels this passage "The Promise Endangered." Mays, *Harper's Bible Commentary* in Logos Bible Software.

12. Hamilton, *The Book of Genesis: Chapters 1–17*, 385. Commentators have wrestled for centuries with how to frame the deceptive behavior of Gen characters, ibid., 381–82; Nicholas, *The Trickster Revisited*, 1. Robinson, referring to Abraham, Sarah, and Pharaoh, summarizes the broad spectrum of scholarly interpretation when he notes that "the same text has been read with precisely opposite appraisals of the character of the main actor." Robinson, "Wife and Sister through the Ages," 104. Cassuto argues that Abraham lied and did not trust God. However, he believes Abraham did this "only because he thinks that in this way he would be able to protect her honour

she was his sister and his wife, nevertheless when they wanted to take her as a wife and he told them, *She is my sister*, in order to lead them astray, he already committed a sin towards them by bringing upon them a *great sin*, and it no longer mattered at all whether the thing was true or false!"[13]

Other narratives omit certain kernels. For instance, in Genesis 3 we never hear of Adam and Eve challenging the manipulation of the serpent, just as a challenge is not evident when the brothers manipulate and murder Shechem (Gen 34).[14] Nevertheless, the general pattern of manipulation throughout Genesis can be analyzed by using these six kernels. For the sake of scope, I have chosen to limit this analysis to the Jacob-Judah-Joseph narratives. They demonstrate the series aspect of Genesis manipulation. Moreover, as the culminating manipulation narrative in Genesis, Joseph's manipulation of his brothers offers interpretive insights into the culminating manipulation episode in the FG, that of Jesus manipulating Peter and his fellow disciples in John 21.

The Chosen Manipulator in the Character Development Process

In any narrative, there are major and minor characters. This is true of Genesis as well. From very early in Genesis, the story traces a certain family lineage. A careful look at Genesis 5 reveals that the story is not about the "other sons and daughters." The phrase "sons and daughters" begins in verse 4, where Seth is the named son, but the text tells us that Adam had other offspring as well. The story goes on to trace the line of Seth, noting the other

---

more successfully than if he had to risk combat with the local inhabitants in a foreign land." Cassuto, *A Commentary on the Book of Genesis* 2, 350–53. Williams and Nicholas both argue for a negative evaluation of Abraham's behavior. Yet Nicholas also argues that "deception is always successful and brings about a raise of status in the deceiver."

Approaching the text from a narrative standpoint, I disagree, but in a qualified manner. I have argued that in the immediate aftermath of manipulation, in the third kernel, the manipulator achieves the desired goal. However, in the context of the larger Gen story, many narratives are evaluated negatively. Tamar's manipulation of Judah, for instance, implicitly corrects the wrong that Judah had committed toward her.

Therefore, although Gen implicitly appreciates certain manipulation narratives, transposing this evaluation to all such episodes is not faithful to the text. Thus, a "one size fits all" approach to these stories is problematic. Approaching each scene on its own merits yields different conclusions for each story. Nicholas, *The Trickster Revisited*, 25; Williams, *Deception in Genesis*, 27–29.

13. Chavel, *Ramban Commentary on the Torah. Genesis: (Nachmanides)*, 263–64. Though the quote is that of Nachmanides, the emphasis is added by Chavel.

14. Although God challenges in 3:11 with "Who told you that you were naked? Have you eaten of the tree of which I commanded you not to eat?"

offspring, but advancing to the next major character, which in this case, is Seth's son Enosh (Gen 5:6–11). The pattern continues, and the story highlights where one son is chosen and blessed by God over another. We see this, of course, with Jacob and Esau (Gen 27), and even at the close of the entire narrative, when Jacob blesses Ephraim with his right hand, as opposed to Manasseh, the firstborn (48:17–20). However, these characters are not in the forefront only because of an author's whim. We learn in chapter 12 that they all belong to a certain chosen lineage, central to the plot of Genesis.

The first pronouncement of the blessing to Abraham and his descendants occurs in Genesis 12, though the enacting of the covenantal ritual does not take place until three chapters later. This blessing and subsequent covenant become a resonating bell throughout the rest of the book. With each successive generation, God reiterates the covenant (Gen 13, 15, 17, 26, 28, 35). Genesis, moreover, closes with a recapitulation of the promise to Abraham that he would possess the land of Canaan, though it does not repeat the promise of numerous descendants and the blessing to other nations (Gen 50:24).

The story repeatedly reminds the reader that Abraham's descendants are the chosen key characters in the divine promise and thus in Genesis as a whole. Though this may seem overly simplistic, it is important for understanding key characters. This theme of the chosen manipulator will repeat itself over and over again in the subsequent narratives. The Genesis manipulation narratives are not centered on background characters, ficelles, or intermediary characters: those non-family or peripheral family members who function secondarily to the protagonists and have a lesser part to play in the creation of the nation of Israel. Each episode focuses on a *divinely chosen leader* in the national plot line.[15] Sometimes the deceiver is the *divinely chosen leader*, but sometimes the deceived is the one who is the *chosen one*, as is the case with Jacob and Laban (Gen 29). Other times both the deceiver and the deceived are *divinely chosen leaders*, as is the case in the Judah and Joseph story (Gen 42–46).[16]

Second, despite some poor decisions, these key leaders are in a process of character development. From a narrative perspective, assessing Genesis as one coherent whole, the text portrays many of these characters in their first manipulation episode as morally lacking. Jacob lies and steals a blessing,

---

15. Or one may call them a *factoring character*, a character that has a key role to play in the resolution of the plot scheme. In some ways, they are akin to pieces in a game of chess, other than the pawns. Each of these recognition narratives includes a rook, knight, bishop, queen, or king. One could say that nowhere in Gen does the reader encounter a "pawn on pawn" manipulation/recognition narrative.

16. Noting that Jacob prophesies the ruling line to come through Judah in 49:12.

Judah sells his own brother, and, although it is not an episode of him manipulating others, Joseph is early on portrayed as a bragging tattletale.[17]

However, though characters such as Jacob, Judah, and Joseph still need moral development, they stand in contrast to characters such as Esau, Laban, Shechem, Hamor, Potiphar, and Joseph's servants. These secondary characters are either not on the stage long enough to show any development, such as Joseph's servants, or for the period of time that they are present, they remain flat and undeveloped. Of these secondary characters, Laban comes the closest to a round character when, at the meeting at Gilead, he finally concedes to Jacob and ratifies their agreement by calling on YHWH (Gen 31:49) and *Elohim* (31:50) to watch between the two of them. Otherwise, we can best describe him as a card.[18] The intermediate characters of Rebekah, Rachel, and Tamar, who are also active manipulators, are important, but as shall become clear, they are not each in their own right the subjects of a *series* of manipulation narratives. Rebekah, Rachel, and Tamar all manipulate only once and are never "manipulated back," whereas Jacob and Judah (and perhaps Joseph at the occasion of the blessing of his sons) are involved in multiple manipulation narratives and are at turns the manipulators and the manipulated. This does not reflect negatively on the women in the story. They are not classed with the likes of Esau, Laban, and Shechem. In fact, they are often the heroines who save the day by rescuing the plotline. Even though deceptive, Rebekah positions Jacob to receive the blessing instead of Esau, and Tamar ensures that she will bear a child who eventually will produce the ruling line of Israel (49:8–12, esp. 10).

Returning to the primary character—the chosen manipulator in the character development process—the referenced development is along moral and spiritual lines, measured by the values set forth in the story world. In Genesis, those values fall along the axes of: entreating and responding to the God of Abraham versus other gods, allegiance versus non-allegiance to familial obligation, truth versus deception, vulnerability and self-sacrifice versus arrogance and self-preservation. We will see this pattern in almost every narrative unit to be examined, with almost every protagonist in each unit demonstrating all the points of this theme. It is a consistent and noteworthy pattern of manipulation and recognition narratives in Genesis. Sternberg identifies this development and speaks not only of a progression in adherence to God, but also the character's knowledge of the same: "Roughly speaking, so far as personal and national fortune goes by merit,

---

17. Mathews, *Genesis*, 687; Sarna, *Genesis* בראשית: *The Traditional Hebrew Text with New JPS Translation*, 256.

18. Harvey, *Character and the Novel*, 59.

then merit itself consists *less in innate virtue* than in the *capacity for acquiring and retaining knowledge of God's ways*: less in a state of being than in a *process of becoming*, by the trial and error of experience."[19] The "process of becoming," which Sternberg mentions, is a driving component of the plot. The tension in the plot of not knowing whether the protagonist will "get it" and finally come closer to the God of Abraham, allegiance to familial obligation, truth, vulnerability, and self-sacrifice, makes the story, or the plot, *work*. Sternberg calls this "plot intermediacy" and "plot indeterminacy" and argues that these two work together hand in hand.[20] The narrator stands betwixt God and humanity and, in so doing, leaves the plot indeterminate, unresolved—and this keeps the reader in suspense.[21] Scholes and Kellogg also spot this developmental progression and note that it occurs along ethical lines:

> The heroes of the Old Testament were in a *process of becoming*, whereas the heroes of Greek narrative were in a state of being. Process in Greek narrative was confined to the action of a plot. And even so, the action exemplified unchanging, universal laws; while the agents of the action, the characters, became as the plot unfolded only more and more consistent ethical types. Abraham, Jacob, David, and Samson, on the other hand, are men whose personal development is the focus of interest.[22]

That Abraham is chosen by God and is in a process of ethical development is clear from the announced blessing, followed by the lie in Egypt (Gen 12:2–3, 13). However, what about the other characters that we are most concerned with in this study? What can be discovered about the characters Jacob, Judah (in conjunction with his brothers), and Joseph?

First, concerning whether Jacob is chosen or not, Alter notes the repetition of the blessing pronounced by Isaac: "Although one must always guard against the excesses of numerological exegesis, it is surely not accidental that there are just seven scenes, and that the key word "blessing" (*berakhah*) is repeated seven times."[23] The issue of God's blessing residing on Jacob is

---

19. Sternberg, *The Poetics of Biblical Narrative*, 177. Emphasis added.

20. Ibid., 118, 177, 285, 303–4.

21. Farmer also notes, "The virtue of the trickster tale lies in the obliqueness of its message: it never counsels us overtly." Farmer, "The Trickster Genre in the Old Testament," 127.

22. Scholes and Kellogg, *The Nature of Narrative*, 123; emphasis added.

23. Alter, *Genesis*, 137–38. Determining or discussing theologically "why" persons such as Ishmael, Esau, and Reuben are not chosen leaders is beyond the scope of this work.

indisputable. Sarna declares that this is established at the oracle given to Rebekah, which textually separates the blessing from the deception: "His claim rests wholly and solely on God's revealed predetermination, and the presence of the oracle constitutes a moral judgment on Jacob's behavior."[24] The blessing is repeated to Jacob immediately after he flees for his life from Esau, both by Isaac, and then by God at Bethel:

> And behold, the LORD stood above it and said, "I am the LORD, the God of Abraham your father and the God of Isaac. The land on which you lie I will give to you and to your offspring. Your offspring shall be like the dust of the earth, and you shall spread abroad to the west and to the east and to the north and to the south, and in you and your offspring shall all the families of the earth be blessed. Behold, I am with you and will keep you wherever you go, and will bring you back to this land. For I will not leave you until I have done what I have promised you" (Gen 28:13–15).

That Jacob is also a manipulator is all too obvious. Esau echoes what future readers would notice for millennia: "Is he not rightly named Jacob," because, as Nicholas words it, "'He has *"jacobed"* me a second time' (27:36)!"[25] Jacob is probably the clearest example of a patriarch who repeatedly finds himself in deception stories. When in Haran, the tables are turned back on him when he receives Leah as a wife instead of Rachel—a deception that echoes his deception of his sibling and father. John Sailhamer directs our attention to the implicit commentary on Jacob's actions: "By calling such situations to the attention of the reader, the writer begins to draw an important lesson from these narratives. Jacob's deceptive schemes for obtaining the blessings did not meet with divine approval. God's will had been accomplished through Jacob's plans, but the writer is intent on pointing out, as well, that the schemes and tricks were not of God's design."[26]

With the deception continuing, readers at first do not know how Jacob was able to manipulate Laban's flocks into breeding favorably for his own gain, but in the end they learn, when Jacob reports to his wives, that God gave him the plan in a dream (Gen 30:25–43; 31:10–13). The back and forth manipulation between Jacob and Laban is dizzying. As Jacob and his tribe leave Haran, Rachel lies to Laban and manipulates him out of his household *teraphim* (31:22–35). Jacob, in terminology that will haunt him

---

24. Sarna, *Genesis* בראשית: *The Traditional Hebrew Text with New JPS Translation*, 397.

25. Nicholas, *The Trickster Revisited*, 54.

26. Sailhamer, *Pentateuch as Narrative*, 194.

(and eventually his sons), challenges Laban to recognize, הַכֶּר, his property.[27] Manipulation seems to find its way into Jacob's life regardless of where he lives or how old he is.[28]

Genesis also clearly portrays Jacob as moving forward in the character development process, even if we might assess the progress as painstakingly slow. Jacob, unlike characters such as Esau or Laban, interacts with and worships YHWH, the God of Abraham and Isaac (Gen 28:13). Moreover, he does this even amidst his deceptive schemes: "So early in the morning Jacob took the stone that he had put under his head and set it up for a pillar and poured oil on the top of it" (28:18). During the ongoing strife with Laban, Jacob attributes his blessings to God (31:5, 9, 11–13, 42). He concludes his parting negotiations with Laban with a sacrifice (31:54). Immediately thereafter, the angels of God appear to him and he calls on God as he prepares to face Esau. In his prayer, he acknowledges his own unworthiness of the blessing (32:10). He continues that encounter with the well-known scene in which he wrestles with God (Gen 32). His allegiance to his family, his vulnerability, and his self-sacrifice become evident in how he arranges for the meeting with Esau, for he puts himself in the front of the family, rather than behind (33:3).[29] He bows to the ground seven times (33:3) and repeatedly calls Esau "my Lord" (33:8, 13, 14, 15) and himself as "thy servant" (33:5, 14). The entire episode is one of reconciliation with Esau: "He himself went on before them, bowing himself to the ground seven times, until he came near to his brother. But Esau ran to meet him and embraced him and fell on his neck and kissed him, and they wept" (33:3–4). However, this *does not* mean that he has completed the character development process, as he still appears to mislead Esau concerning his destination (33:14–17). Eventually, though, Jacob is even willing to endanger his favorite son for the safety and well-being of the entire family, stating, "If I am bereaved of my children, I am bereaved." (43:14).

---

27. Here the reader observes Rachel as a member of Jacob's family acting, unknown to Jacob, on his behalf. Rachel is not an acting manipulator or manipulated character in a series of manipulation narratives of her own; Jacob is. Thus, Rachel is really acting in a way that ironically *assists* the key character's escape. Rachel is a member of the chosen family, and she deceives without Jacob's knowledge of it. However, Laban, unlike Rachel, is involved in a number of manipulation episodes. Nevertheless, Laban is not the chosen one. For analysis of the role of gender in these situations, see Fuchs, "For I Have the Way of Women," 68–83; and Steinberg, "Israelite Tricksters, Their Analogues, and Cross-Cultural Study," 1–13.

28. Alter, *Genesis*, 171. See Gen 27:23; 31:32; 37:32–33; 38:25–26; 42:7–8.

29. Freedman and Simon, *Midrash Rabbah*, 78:8; Mann, "'All the Families of the Earth,'" 349. Petersen and Osiek, "Genesis and Family Values," 20.

Judah and his brothers fit the chosen manipulator profile as well, but admittedly in different ways. The fact that all the brothers are chosen of God is apparent from the continued story of the Pentateuch as a whole.[30] These twelve brothers, plus the two sons of Joseph, go on to lead the twelve tribes of the new nation. Their role in the life of the nation is so important that an extensive narrative is dedicated to the dramatic story of their births and the strife among their mothers (Gen 29:31–30:24; 35:16–19). Once the youngest son Benjamin had arrived, the narrator rehearses with readers again the twelve sons, their names, and their mothers (35:23–26). That they are crucial to the story is obvious from the attention the narrator has placed on them, recounting their legacy. Genesis ends with Israel's pronouncement of things to come in the lives of his twelve sons. The author uses thirty-three verses to confirm that the blessings of Abraham, Isaac, and Jacob have now passed to the sons of Jacob, though not without some rebuke for earlier behaviors (49:1–27). In the narratives in the latter chapters of Genesis, Judah especially emerges as a noted leader among his brothers. Here the plot focuses and narrows to him, as the new leader among his brothers.[31] Sternberg notes the narrative specifically names Judah, while referring to the rest only as "the brothers" (44:14).[32] Thus, he is *key* to the story, a definite leader—for good or bad—among his brothers.

That the brothers manipulate needs little discussion, for when the family arrives in Shechem, the legacy of manipulation continues. The narrator summarizes the rape which precipitates the murders, giving three lines to the situation the brothers were in as "the men were indignant and very angry, because he had done an *outrageous* thing in Israel by lying with Jacob's daughter, for such a thing *must not be done*"(Gen 34:7).[33] The story clearly spells out their behavior: "The sons of Jacob answered Shechem and his father Hamor deceitfully" (34:13).[34] The reader hears the dramatic portrayal of the wrong against Dinah, but also the negative characterization

---

30. Sailhamer argues for a literary interpretation of the Pentateuch as a whole narrative. Sailhamer, *Pentateuch as Narrative*, 1–2.

31. Ackerman, "Joseph, Judah, and Jacob," 110.

32. Sternberg, *The Poetics of Biblical Narrative*, 305.

33. The careful reader later notes the contrast in Judah venturing to a prostitute only four chapters after his looting of Shechem for sexual sin against Israel, though granted Judah's sexual act with Tamar (with a prostitute that is) was consensual. The portrayal of the uncompleted character development *process* in this particular chosen son of Jacob is undeniable. See Lambe, "Judah's Development," 55.

34. In verse 14, rather than "They said to them," the LXX has, "And Simeon and Levi, the brothers of Dinah, said to them," thus, attributing the deceptive scheme to these two brothers from the start. Logos Research Systems, *Septuaginta*.

of the murders by the brothers.³⁵ The narrator's gratuitous explanation of Shechem's excited preparation, calling him a "young man," hints at his youthful naivete, perhaps portraying him a little less culpabile. Ultimately, this underscores the brothers' greater deceptive manipulation: "And the young man did not delay to do the thing, because he delighted with Jacob's daughter" (34:19). The text also records Jacob's clear condemnation of their behavior (34:30–31). However, there was evil on both parts. Note the line by Shechem when convincing the men of the city to agree to the conditions: "*Will not their livestock, their property and all their beasts be ours*? Only let us agree with them, and they will dwell with us" (34:23). Then the brothers fall on the city "while it felt secure" (34:25), which implies greater treachery and injustice.³⁶ The actual manipulation of the brothers selling Joseph and deceiving their father into believing that Joseph is dead is well known, and I will discuss that scene further below (Gen 37).

However, for now we turn for a closer look at the brothers' developmental aspect. This group is never recorded in the text as calling on God as Jacob does (Gen 28:19–22), but, in the end, they are moving toward *acknowledgment* of God in their lives, especially at the orchestrated direction of Joseph, unbeknownst to them (42:28).³⁷ But just how deeply involved in the character development process are they? When examining Judah more closely, one observes that his initial distance from the values of Genesis is perhaps greater than that of his father, grandfather, and great-grandfather. Anthony Lambe notes the subtlety of the text's indication of Judah's lack of family connectedness: "In sharp contrast to Jacob, who mourns fervently for his son Joseph, it is never recorded that Judah mourns Er and Onan."³⁸ This implies that Judah is withdrawn from his sons and that he is oblivious to their true characters, which the text states clearly (38:7–10).³⁹ That he drifted from his father and brothers is echoed in the choice of words "turned

---

35. As mentioned earlier, some in post-exilic Israel viewed the deception *via circumcision* worthy of censure, not simply the retribution for the rape of Dinah. "And my father heard these things and was wroth, and he was grieved in that they had received the circumcision, and after that had been put to death, and in his blessings he looked amiss upon us. For we sinned because we had done this thing against his will, and he was sick on that day," Charles, *T. of Levi* 6.6, "Testaments of the Twelve Patriarchs." *Jub.* 30, which exonerates the brothers for their behavior.

36. Sarna, *Genesis* בראשית: *The Traditional Hebrew Text with New JPS Translation*, 238. The *Targum Onkelos* seems to imply this as well. Aberbach and Grossfeld, *Targum Onkelos to Genesis*, 204n9. The LXX has ἀσφαλῶς, "safe, secure." Arndt et al., *A Greek-English Lexicon of the New Testament and Other Early Christian Literature*, 119.

37. Sternberg, *The Poetics of Biblical Narrative*, 297.

38. Lambe, "Judah's Development," 55–56.

39. Ibid., 56. See also Alter, *The Art of Biblical Narrative*, 7.

aside" to describe his journey to visit Hirah the Adullamite and his choice to engage the prostitute Tamar.[40] His choice of a wife from the daughters of Canaan stands in contrast to the directions of Isaac and the behavior of his father, Jacob.[41]

The first glimpse of Judah progressing in the character development process appears when he learns he has impregnated his daughter-in-law: "'She is more righteous than I, since I did not give her to my son Shelah.' And he did not know her again" (Gen 38:26). Second Temple Jewish interpretation contributes to our understanding, for *Jubilees* 41:23–25 considerably expands Judah's confession:

> And he knew that the deed which he did was evil because he lay with his daughter-in-law. And he condemned himself in his own sight. And he knew that he had sinned and gone astray because he uncovered the robe of his son. And he began to mourn and make supplication before the LORD on account of his sin. And we told him in a dream that it was forgiven him because he made great supplication and because he mourned and did not do it again.[42]

Thus, ancient readers of Judah's interlude with Tamar likely interpreted the episode as the beginning of the character development process. The final chapters of Genesis have even more to do with the turning of Judah toward family, vulnerability, admission of wrong, and self-sacrifice. Some scholars argue that chapter 38 is incongruent with the Joseph story and is, therefore, from a source critical approach, out of place.[43] However, scholars using literary approaches have shown that it is well situated within the Joseph story.[44] In chapters 37 and 38, Judah begins to emerge as a leading manipulator in the group of brothers and the plot line. He indeed voices the idea to sell Joseph off to Egypt behind Reuben's back, thus leading the brothers in this act of treachery and manipulation (Gen 37:26).[45] Nevertheless, when Joseph

---

40. Lambe, "Judah's Development," 56–57. When he actually engages Tamar the prostitute in the business deal, the LXX says, that "he went out of his way to her," "ἐξέκλινεν δὲ πρὸς αὐτὴν τὴν ὁδὸν" (Gen 38:16), Logos Research Systems, *Septuaginta*.

41. Mal 2:11; Townsend, *Midrash Tanhuma*, 9:9.

42. Charlesworth, *The Old Testament Pseudepigrapha*, 131.

43. Speiser, *Genesis*, 299.

44. Lambe, "Judah's Development," 53–54; Fentress-Williams, *Location, Location, Location*, Additionally, Johannine scholar Spencer states, "Intrusions, on the contrary, often occur in narrative genres, and, in many cases, provide important information to the reader." Spencer, "Narrative Echoes in John 21," 56.

45. Josephus interprets this as an attempt to relocate Joseph's death, this "barbarous act," away from Judah and his brothers and allow it to happen elsewhere. *Ant*. 2.3.32, in

boxes Judah and his brothers in a corner in Egypt, their characters begin to change. As a group they admit that they cannot escape the foreboding divine retribution: "At this their hearts failed them, and they turned trembling to one another, saying, 'What is this that God has done to us?'" (42:28). Then, on their second trip to Egypt, Judah himself begins to acknowledge that perhaps God is involved in their lives and they, as a group, need to be aware and respond: "What shall we say to my lord? What shall we speak? Or how can we clear ourselves? *God has found out the guilt* of your servants; behold, we are my lord's servants, both we and he also in whose hand the cup has been found" (44:16). Note also that though Joseph is addressing the alleged behavior of the one supposed culprit Benjamin, Judah responds in the plural. The perceptive reader notices the double meaning of Judah's words and its confessional nature concerning the brothers' harm to Joseph.[46] We will return to Judah later, but the scene indicates that Joseph has engineered a reversal for Judah and his brothers, with the result that Judah is changing, and the character development process is moving forward. Ultimately, the brothers echo the same "thy servant" language their father uttered to Esau. After Jacob dies, they send a message to Joseph saying, "And now, please forgive the transgression of the servants of the God of your father" (50:17). What follows is a moment of reconciliation similar to that of Jacob and Esau.

We see that Joseph, too, is a chosen manipulator in the process of development. That he was chosen by God comes from his own words, when he attributes his exile to Egypt as part of God's overall plan to save Israel (Gen 45:5–7). However, this was not always the case. In the beginning, when he is young and eager to share his dreams with his brothers, the idea of God being a part of the process is ominously missing in his speech (37:5–11).[47] Some have characterized his dream sharing as braggardly.[48] Following the narrative principle of repetition, we can discern the dramatic nature of Joseph's dream sharing, as he repeats the command "behold!" five times

---

Josephus and Whiston, *The Works of Josephus*. Philo however, interprets Judah's actions clearly in a positive manner: "[F]or in my opinion, he was afraid lest his brother might be treacherously slain by the others, who had conceived an irreconcilable hatred against him, and therefore he proposed that he should be sold, substituting slavery for death, the lighter evil for the greater." Philo, *Joseph* 4.15, in *The Works of Philo* (trans. Yonge).

46. Alter, *Genesis*, 262. "[H]ere agnition is not possible without a recognition of personal responsibility, without which the sign is open to misinterpretation and the agnition becomes *méconnaissance* and ultimately ruin." Boitani, *The Bible and Its Rewritings*, 30. Boitani uses the term agnition synonymously with recognition or acknowledgement. See ibid., 16–17, 30–31, 136, 145.

47. Sarna, *Genesis* בראשית: *The Traditional Hebrew Text with New JPS Translation*, 256.

48. Ibid.

in explaining the two dreams (37:5–9). However, after spending time in a dungeon, he characterizes his dreams a bit differently: "It is not in me; God will give Pharaoh a favorable answer" (41:16).[49]

Finally, when he eventually reveals himself to his brothers, Joseph is very clear that God has been directing his exile all along: "And now do not be distressed or angry with yourselves because you sold me here, for God sent me before you to preserve life" (Gen 45:5). Note also that one learns that *Elohim* is the planner behind this exile, for he is found no less than four times on Joseph's lips as he explains the omniscient divine causality to his brothers (45:5–9). The repetition is obvious.[50]

That Joseph manipulates his brothers is clear. As mentioned above, he actively *conceals* his identity from his brothers when they arrive in Egypt. As a youth he makes mistakes, which scholars have struggled to discern his motives as an adult in Egypt when his brothers arrive in his presence.[51] However, Joseph is characterized in a much more positive light than Judah and even Jacob when considering them as manipulators. Josephus interprets Joseph's actions in a positive light when stating: "Now this he did in order to discover what concerned his father, and what happened to him after his own departure from him, and as desiring to know what was become of Benjamin his brother; for he was afraid that they had ventured on the like wicked enterprise against him that they had done to himself, and had taken him off also."[52] Just a few lines further he adds that Joseph also did these things so as to "make trial of his brethren, whether they would stand by Benjamin when he should be accused of having stolen the cup, and should appear to be in danger; or whether they would leave him, and, depending on their own innocency, go to their father without him."[53] The author of *Jubilees* also read Joseph's actions as having a specific positive goal: "And Joseph thought of an idea by means of which he might learn their thoughts, whether they had thoughts of peace for one another."[54] Therefore, we may

---

49. "But a recurring motif is God's presence with Joseph in Egypt, whether he is in Potiphar's house or in Pharaoh's prison. The reader notes with satisfaction that Joseph's rise to power in Egypt results from a combination of pious behavior, divine help, and his wise advice at court." Ackerman, "Joseph, Judah, and Jacob," 86.

50. Ackerman notes that the Joseph story demonstrates "how human beings cannot thwart divine purpose." Ibid., 86.

51. Sacks, *A Commentary on the Book of Genesis*, 364. Ackerman speaks of Joseph's "apparent vengeance on his brothers" at their arrival in Egypt and then later says Joseph "changes his mind and allows the brothers to return to Canaan." Ackerman, "Joseph, Judah, and Jacob," 87, 90.

52. *Ant.* 2.99, Josephus and Whiston, *The Works of Josephus*.

53. *Ant.* 2.6.125.

54. *Jub.* 42:25, Charlesworth, *The Old Testament Pseudepigrapha*, 133. Though

plausibly say that Joseph's manipulation of his brothers may have been for a specific positive goal.

We conclude that Jacob, Judah, the brothers, and Joseph are chosen key characters. They repeatedly find themselves on either side of deceit and recognition. The reader repeatedly encounters them in a pattern as *manipulators*, who appear to be recipients of the Abrahamic blessing, and who are in varying stages of coming to terms with the implicit moral code and directives of God in the story world of Genesis. I now turn to the next pattern in these series of manipulation narratives.

Disempowerment of the Manipulated and Empowerment of the Manipulator

The analysis now turns to the pattern of empowerment and disempowerment in the Genesis narrative.[55] In this narrative, readers find much to do with goods, blessings, birthrights, flocks, and even household gods. Readers also find that in each narrative, the manipulator uses the manipulation exchange to wrestle something from the manipulated, and, in the end, often arrives at a position of greater power than before the deception. However, research has at times overlooked the power aspect in these narratives, while concentrating on the deception.[56] Kathleen Farmer is one who sees this power aspect and argues that these stories begin with an underpowered character, scheming for a way to gain power despite overwhelming odds.[57] Williams, in his catalog and analysis of fifteen deception scenes in Genesis, identifies the social position of the perpetrator at the beginning of the deception. In eleven of those scenes, he marks the perpetrator as standing in a lower position than the victim at the beginning of the scene.[58]

The Jacob cycle is replete with the constant imbalance of power and wealth. Beginning in Genesis 27, Jacob and Rebekah remove something of great power from the hands of Isaac and Esau—God's blessing. It is,

---

Pseudo-Philo condenses the Joseph novella greatly, it also characterizes Joseph's actions positively: "And Joseph recognized his brethren, but was not known by them. And he did not deal vengefully with them, and he sent and summoned his father from the land of Canaan, and he went down to him." *L.A.B.* 8:10, ibid., 314.

55. Lied notes a reversal of power and pride of the wicked in the recognition episode in 2 Bar 51. Lied, "Recognizing the Righteous Remnant?," 314, 322.

56. Fuchs, "For I Have the Way of Women," 69.

57. Farmer, "The Trickster Genre in the Old Testament," 122. McKay also notes this. McKay, "Lying and Deceit in Families," 30.

58. Williams, *Deception in Genesis*, 51. Again, Steinberg argues a similar position. Steinberg, "Israelite Tricksters, Their Analogues, and Cross-Cultural Study," 6.

moreover, a blessing with tangible benefits. Regarding Jacob's increase in goods and influence, Farmer states, "The blessings he so ardently pursues consist primarily of possessions, prestige, and power."[59] This is not news to the reader who in previous chapters has read of the blessing to Abraham and Isaac.

Tangled in the Jacob cycle is the tit for tat, back and forth manipulation between Laban, Jacob, and Rachel. In that maze one finds Laban exerting power over Jacob and vice versa. When Laban manipulates Jacob into seven more years of labor than Jacob had planned (Gen 29:21–30), he disempowers Jacob. The manipulator empowers himself to have a free servant (a blessed and prosperous servant at that) for an additional seven years. The same is true for Jacob. By omission, he never tells Laban of the divine instructions for breeding and thus disempowers Laban of the expected multiplication of his flocks. This empowers Jacob by delivering to him the desired benefit of wealth, frustrating Laban's labor-related swindling (30:43). The topic of power and blessing arises again, on the lips of Rachel and Leah, who say, "All the wealth that God has taken away from our father belongs to us and to our children" (31:16). Power again comes to the fore when Laban catches up with Jacob as he and his family flee. On that occasion, Laban states, "It is in my power to do you harm" (31:29), but God had interrupted Laban's plans in a dream and warned him not to harm the blessed Jacob. Power is in play. Jacob, by scheming to leave Paran undetected, demonstrated his intention to prevent Laban from thwarting his plans (31:20, 32). The story of power continues when the issue of the *teraphim* arises in verse 30. If in fact Laban can determine who has the gods, or where the gods are, he will have *power* over the thief as well as over the propagation of the family of Abraham, because of the threat of death upon the thief (31:32).[60] However, the deception and manipulation by Rachel removes that power from Laban's hands when she misleads her father with the words, "Let not my lord be angry that I cannot arise before you, for the way of women is upon me" (31:35). Jacob responds in anger with castigation, explaining that he is justified in leaving without being "hotly pursued" (31:36) and he concludes by noting the power of the blessing in verse 42.

The pattern continues with the brothers at Shechem. In this instance, the brothers lie and entrap the men of Shechem, clearly intending to disempower them by taking their very lives when they were most vulnerable. The men of Shechem are manipulated to undergo circumcision so that they will be too sore from the surgery to fight effectively (Gen 34:25). This is a

---

59. Farmer, "The Trickster Genre in the Old Testament," 103.
60. As the reader shall see, Benjamin is yet to be born of Rachel.

manipulation of the manipulators, because Hamor and Shechem were attempting to manipulate both the men of their own city as well as Jacob's sons. They implied that the procedure was warranted because the men of the city would gain the property of Jacob's family (34:23). Therefore, the power play is in the thoughts of both parties at the outset—the sons of Hamor and the sons of Jacob. In the end, though, the successful manipulators win, disempowering and killing all the males of Shechem (34:25–26).

The power struggle also occurs when the brothers manipulate Joseph and their father. At Dothan, they rob Joseph of years of his life that could have been spent with his family. They withhold from Jacob the knowledge of his son's real fate, and thus his chance to go after him (Gen 37:31–35).

Looking at Judah and Tamar, the turn from being in a position of power to disempowerment is very apparent. Scholarship recognizes this power imbalance especially with female tricksters. Naomi Steinberg points out that deception is used often when "other forms of power are lacking."[61] Nicholas states that "females, in an androcentric world, must resort to trickery to make a mark in society."[62] In Tamar's case, according to legal obligation and practice, she deserved Shelah as a husband and replacement for her previous two, wicked, but now dead, sons of Judah (Gen 38:8).[63] When Judah refused Shelah, he put Tamar in a state of lesser power. Considering she was a woman in the Ancient Near East, she was already in a position of less power than Judah. She was so disempowered that she had little choice but to turn to him to produce offspring.[64] Tamar skillfully manipulates the situation to reverse the power, wrestling from Judah what he should have given her through Shelah. In fact, she very effectively lessens Judah's power with both potential as well as realized shame and humility by the type of pledge she requests of him. Concerning the potential shame, Judah, upon the report from Hirah of not finding the prostitute, replies, "Let her keep the things as her own, or we shall be laughed at" (38:23). As to the pledge, Alter explains that the items taken in earnest were very valuable ones, thus removing power from Judah: "Tamar's stipulated pledge, then, is an extravagant one: taking the instruments of Judah's legal identity and social standing is something like taking a person's driving license and credit cards in modern society."[65] In the end, the pledge—and the manipulation—are ex-

61. Steinberg, "Israelite Tricksters, Their Analogues, and Cross-Cultural Study," 1.

62. Nicholas, *The Trickster Revisited*, 22.

63. Alter, *Genesis*, 218.

64. "If this could not be through Shelah, she had no alternative but that it should be through Judah." Silbermann, *Chumash with Targum Onkelos, Haphtaroth and Rashi's Commentary*, 187.

65. Alter, *Genesis*, 221.

tremely effective: "She (implicitly) leaves the community a childless widow (separation). In the marginal state, she deceives. She returns pregnant with twins of Judah's line, i.e. a raise in status."[66]

Finally, the culminating manipulation narrative is the quintessential reversal of power. Beginning in chapter 42, one finds the sons of Jacob already disempowered by the famine, and unknown to them but known to the reader, Joseph has risen in power greatly.[67] This is a complete reversal of events that transpired two decades earlier in chapter 37. Additionally, Joseph proves to be as skillful as Tamar in continuing that power reversal. The reader is aware that Joseph probably has the power either to take the lives of his brothers or at least to keep them in prison indefinitely. Joseph runs a manipulation scheme that keeps his brothers powerless against him for quite some time. Ackerman has argued that Jacob's clan is at the mercy of Joseph: "[T]he family will not survive if Benjamin is not sent to Egypt."[68] In Egyptian culture, those who could interpret dreams held great power over the one seeking the interpretation.[69] As members of a neighboring culture, this would explain the family's emotions, both of anger when Joseph shared his dreams as a young man (Jacob also rebuked him), as well as the dreadful fear that fell upon the brothers when Joseph revealed himself to them in Egypt (Gen 37:8, 10, 19–20; 45:3). Joseph, as the manipulator, was in *complete control*. He held the power of life and death over his entire family. The *Midrash Tanhuma* echoes this loss of power at the hands of Joseph, in God's response to Judah's plea in 44:18–34: "The Holy One said to him [Judah]: Behold, you have now let go of your former power, and spoken supplications."[70] Sternberg underscores Joseph's forceful manipulation of power against his brothers: "Throughout the drama of retrospection, Joseph figures as stage-manager as well as player, exploiting his superiority. . . . he

---

66 Nicholas, *The Trickster Revisited*, 62. However, I do not concur with Nicholas's overall thesis of the trickster's progression from marginality to a return with a "raise in status" as he presents it. As I explain below, Tamar is a counter-manipulator. Initial manipulators, while they do increase in power temporarily and obtain their desired goal, do not increase in status in the eyes of the text. A case in point is Laban, who, though surely a manipulator, never increases in status in the eyes of the reader.

67. Thus, I posit that Joseph does not here fit the role of "underdog," as has been put forth as characteristic of tricksters. It is often the case, as with Tamar, who had few to no alternatives. However, Joseph was free to do as he pleased. Compare Steinberg, "Israelite Tricksters, Their Analogues, and Cross-Cultural Study," 6.

68. Ackerman, "Joseph, Judah, and Jacob," 92. Note however, that Ackerman says "The last thing that Joseph can do, if he wants to reestablish his place as brother in the family, is to overwhelm his brothers with his power." Ibid., 96.

69. Miller, "Social and Political Elevation in Middle Kingdom Egypt."

70. Townsend, *Midrash Tanhuma*, 11.8.

gives them a taste of his own suffering—helplessness in the hands of a bully, false charge with death in the offing, imprisonment, abrupt commutation of sentence—by forcing them to go through it in experiential order."[71]

In summary, by working through selected narratives in Genesis, we observe the disempowerment of the manipulated and empowerment of the manipulator as a pattern. The character that manipulates, by a variety of manipulative acts, puts him or herself in a position of power while removing control from the victim.

Evocative *Déjà Vu* Motifs

Robert Alter writes considerably on *Leitwörter*, that is, words or root words repeated in a series of narrative units, which indicate to the reader that the author is tying certain stories together.[72] For the purpose of this study, I will note three different ways that *Leitwörter* function. However, I must first make clear that though different, these functions do not lie in completely separate categories. The Genesis writer utilizes some of these word repetitions in more than one manner.[73]

The first function occurs when the narrator utters the *Leitwörter* and only the reader hears them. By all indications in the text, the characters are not aware of them. The words do not occur within the narrative world. They serve as literary bookends or connectors. One example of this is the first word group mentioned earlier, namely "recognize," הכר or its root נכר. In some scenes, only the narrator uses it. In Genesis 27:23, regarding Isaac's failed recognition, the narrator states, "And he did not *recognize* him because his hands were hairy like his brother Esau's hands." As I noted earlier, this root is used frequently in the stories of Jacob's family, from his moment of blessing, in the Joseph story, continuing through to 42:8. In some of those instances, the word is uttered by one or more of the characters (Gen 37:32; 38:25). Nevertheless, in its last usage in Genesis, the term is again found only on the lips of the narrator, "but they did not recognize him" (42:8). These instances demonstrate how *Leitwörter* can serve to establish literary continuity from scene to scene.[74] All of these stories in the life of Jacob and his sons are intended to be read together.

---

71. Sternberg, *The Poetics of Biblical Narrative*, 294.

72. Alter, *The Art of Biblical Narrative*, 94.

73. I differ a bit here from Alter, who defines his categories more narrowly. Ibid., 95. See also Alter, *The World of Biblical Literature*, 61.

74. Mays, *Harper's Bible Commentary*, s.v. Gen 37:21. This is the case not only with individual roots, but also with similar phrases and thematic announcements, that is,

Second, Alter notes that a *Leitwort* is sometimes combined with a theme that reinforces the "value-system of the narrative—it may be moral, moral-psychological, legal, political, historiosophical, theological."[75] When a *Leitwort* combines with such a theme, it functions to reinforce the *substantive intent* of the story's content—its moral tale.[76] In this second function, the word highlights the meaning of the story.

When the brothers arrive in Egypt, the narrator once again underscores the themes of deception and recognition in Jacob's family. All four of the following italicized verbs are from the root נכר: "Joseph saw his brothers and *recognized* them, but he *treated them like strangers* and spoke roughly to them . . . And Joseph *recognized* his brothers, but they *did not recognize* him" (Gen 42:7–8). Alter has noted this term and its repetition:

> The opposition between Joseph's knowledge (which is also the narrator's) and the brothers' ignorance is focused through the insistence of a *Leitwort* that figured earlier in the story: he recognizes them, they recognize him not; and in a pun characteristic of *Leitwortstil*, he makes himself a stranger or seems a stranger to them, *vayitnaker*, a verb with the same root, nkr, as "recognize," haker.[77]

Here, the use of the *Leitwort nkr* (נכר) reinforces the theme that those who use deception to prevent recognition by others may in the end have the tables turned on them and be forced to recognize something about themselves. In this case, it is Jacob's sons, who manipulated and deceived Jacob by preventing a correct recognition of Joseph's robe. They are now ignorant, and do not recognize who Joseph is or what he is doing to them.

But how can the root in this passage mean both to recognize and something nearly its opposite, to make oneself not recognizable? The root נכר occurs extensively in ancient Semitic languages, and Hebrew lexicons differ regarding whether to categorize it into one or two roots.[78] The one

---

Leitmotiv. Note the sad irony of not only Jacob unknowingly pronouncing judgment on Rachel for the crime of theft in Gen 32:32 but also the same misguided verdict pronounced by the brothers unknowingly upon Benjamin in Gen 44:9: "If any of your servants is found to have it, he will die." Sternberg, *The Poetics of Biblical Narrative*, 304.

75. Alter, *The Art of Biblical Narrative*, 95.

76. Ibid.

77. Ibid., 163; underline emphasis added, italics emphasis Alter. Sternberg made the same analysis in Sternberg, *The Poetics of Biblical Narrative*, 288. See also Ackerman, "Joseph, Judah, and Jacob," 90; Lambe, "Judah's Development," 61.

78. Botterweck and Ringgren, *TDOT*, 9:424–25. Both Brown et al., *The Enhanced Brown-Driver-Briggs Hebrew and English Lexicon*, and Köhler et al., *The Hebrew and Aramaic Lexicon of the Old Testament* use two roots, but indicate through *sigla* the

root theory borrows from the principle in Arabic where a root may carry its regular sense, as well as its opposite.[79] The original denotation of the root is believed to have been "to inspect."[80] If this is correct, we can logically theorize that the term was used to indicate the various results of the said inspection. But modern Arabic tends toward the usage of "*failing to recognize*" something and uses the term to indicate "not to know," "pretend not to know," "deny, disown, disavow," and "disguise" or "mask."[81] Qur'anic usage of the term, likewise, renders the verbal forms as "to be unable to recognise something or someone" and "to deny, to refuse to accept, to disclaim."[82] Biblical Hebrew uses the term to indicate recognition, the apparent positive result of inspection (Gen 38:26), as well as failing to recognize or understand, a negative result (Deut 32:27). However, whereas in the Hebrew Bible these opposite meanings are represented by the same root and at times directly juxtaposed against one another (Gen 42:7-8; Ruth 2:10,[83]), modern and Qur'anic Arabic both use a different form, '*arafa*, to indicate to know or recognize.[84] Examining the Hebrew of Genesis 42:7, when Joseph *recognized* his brothers, we see that the term occurs in the Hiphil stem, וַיַּכִּרֵם. The same is true in verse 8, with both occurrences of the verb, but the second instance is simply negated by לֹא. However, in verse 7, when the text says that Joseph "treated them like strangers," the verb occurs in the Hitpael stem, וַיִּתְנַכֵּר. But the Hitpael is not an automatic indication of negated recognition. The same verb in Proverbs 20:11, "Even a child *makes himself known* by his acts," is in the Hitpael, and it is instances such as this

---

uncertainty of the etymology. Holladay and Köhler, *A Concise Hebrew and Aramaic Lexicon of the Old Testament*, based on Koehler and Baumgartner's work, uses one root.

79. Botterweck and Ringgren, *TDOT*, 9:424.

80. Köhler et al., *The Hebrew and Aramaic Lexicon of the Old Testament*, 699.

81. Wehr and Cowan, *A Dictionary of Modern Written Arabic*, 1170. I am grateful to colleague Dr. Wagdy Wahba for his repeated patient assistance, as I am not a student of Arabic. Though his discipline is not language, he is a native speaker of Arabic.

82. See *Sura* 11:70: "[H]e became doubtful about their identity"; 27:41 "Disguise her throne for her." Badawi and Haleem, *Arabic-English Dictionary of Qur'anic Usage*, 963.

83. The noun forms often indicate a foreigner, foreign land, or strange object. Consequently, the book of Ruth appears to intentionally contrast these two opposite connotations of the root: "Why have I found favor in your eyes, that you *should take notice* of me, since I am a *foreigner*?" See Botterweck and Ringgren, *TDOT*, 9:423-32, but especially ibid., 427-28.

84. *Sura* 16:83: "[T]hey recognise (*'arafa*) God's blessings, [but] then refuse to acknowledge (*yunkir* from the root *nkr*) them." Badawi and Haleem, *Arabic-English Dictionary of Qur'anic Usage*, 963. Gen 42:7-8, in an Arabic translation, also utilizes the two different roots, *The Holy Book*.

that may have motivated lexicographers to class the verb into two different roots.⁸⁵ Moreover, the positive as well as the negated meanings both occur in the Niphal (Prov 26:24; Lam 4:8)⁸⁶ and the Piel (Deut 32:27; Job 21:29) stems.⁸⁷ Therefore, it is not surprising that there is confusion regarding the derivation of the word group and how to classify it. Notwithstanding, it is noteworthy that the majority of the instances of negated recognition are with stems that are frequently associated with either passive,⁸⁸ reflexive,⁸⁹ or causative meanings.⁹⁰

Qumran literature also attests to both uses of the term, even within the same group of texts. In 4Q381, fragment 13, line 2, reads הלוא תכיר and has been translated "Will you not recognize."⁹¹ Fragment 45a of that same group, line 2, reads מתעבות הכרתי, and has been rendered "from abominations (which) I knew."⁹² But 4Q381 69 8, reads ולהנכר, and has been translated "and to act as a stranger."⁹³

Regardless of its history, the term serves well for underscoring a theme that runs through the narrative units. "Recognize" is combined with the theme that those who use deception to prevent recognition by others are ironically, in the end, forced to recognize something about themselves—typically their ethical failures and their own ignorance.⁹⁴ Ironically, Jacob

---

85. Brown et al., *The Enhanced Brown-Driver-Briggs Hebrew and English Lexicon*, 648–49, classifies the positive form of the verb, "to recognize" as the first root, and Prov 20:11 in that class, whereas the negative form, "to treat as foreign," and therefore Joseph's alienation of his brothers, is categorized as the second root.

86. Lam 4:8 is the positive meaning, but negated with the negative particle לֹא.

87. Köhler et al., *The Hebrew and Aramaic Lexicon of the Old Testament*, 699–700.

88. Niphal, "disguise oneself," Prov 26:24. Ibid., 699.

89. Hitpael, "to act as a stranger," Gen 42:7, second occurrence of the verb in the sentence. Ibid.

90. Piel, "make a false presentation," Jer 19:4, "and they have treated this place as foreign." This is not the ESV, but rather the translation rendered by Brown et al., *The Enhanced Brown-Driver-Briggs Hebrew and English Lexicon*, 649. My colleague, Dr. Wahba, tells me that in modern Arabic, the lack of recognition represented by the *nkr* root often carries a nuance that, if not a completely reflexive idea, is an action one at least partially carries out within oneself, namely, of denying that one knows another person or object, namely, "to pretend not to know."

91. Charlesworth et al., *The Dead Sea Scrolls*, 12–13. In instances where I have reproduced Hebrew text unvocalized, I have done so in keeping with sources that provide it unvocalized, or, because I am referring to the consonantal root alone.

92. 1Q381 45a 2. Ibid., 23–25. But the verb may be כרת, "cut down," thus 25n48 reads "Or 'the abomination (which) I cut down.'" See Brown et al., *The Enhanced Brown-Driver-Briggs Hebrew and English Lexicon*, 503.

93. Charlesworth et al., *The Dead Sea Scrolls*, 32–33.

94. Nicholas, *The Trickster Revisited*, 78.

begins his story with deception and a lack of knowledge/recognition. He then repeatedly deals with deception and recognition in his later years. At times, his own lack of recognition haunts him. He begins by deceiving Isaac, causing Isaac to fail to recognize him, but shortly thereafter, Jacob fails to realize that his new wife is Leah, not Rachel.[95] In the Joseph story, the reader recognizes Joseph's plight, but Jacob recognizes wrongly.[96] He fails to recognize the true fate of Joseph at the hand of his own sons (Gen 37:33).[97] In the closing story of manipulation, those same sons do not recognize Joseph (42:7–8). The continued usage of the root נכר in these scenes supports a theme: that the key characters, especially those who are known to deceive, do not themselves *recognize* all that is truly transpiring. This is until, as I explain below, they are ironically counter-manipulated and forced to into self-awareness.

The third function of a *Leitwort* involves the root word occurring *within the narrative world and is therefore known to the character*. This can be a word uttered in the dialog or an object or item known to the character in the story. Often this word or object *comes back to haunt the key character in a manner that sometimes evokes a response by that character*. Here the Hebraic manipulation narrative bears a similarity with classical Greek *anagnorisis* in that at the displaying of the token, the character(s) who had been ignorant responds with "awe[,] ... amazement," or "emotion."[98]

An example of this third function is the word "goat." The root for goat, עז, appears repeatedly in the Jacob narratives and ties together the stories of Jacob's deception of Isaac (Gen 27), Jacob's husbandry manipulation with Laban (Gen 30–32), Judah's deception regarding Joseph's fate, with the blood of a goat on the robe (Gen 37), and finally, where the goat is meant to be the payment from Judah to Tamar. Other livestock do appear frequently in Genesis, such as donkeys (e.g., 12:16; 32:15; 45:23; 49:11), and camels (e.g., 12:16; 24:10–64; 30:43; 31:17, 34; 32:7, 15; 37:25). We could list these other animals and their locations in Genesis, but all of these are typically featured in large groups of property or gifts (12:16; 32:13–15). Only "goat" appears with such regularity at the moment of deception in the Jacob and

---

95. Note the deception and wives theme that began with his grandfather continues to follow this family, Gen 12, 20, 26.

96. But see Sacks who believes that Jacob is in fact aware, at least in part, of his sons' deception: "The father will not be comforted because he believes that his comforters are also the murderers." Sacks, *A Commentary on the Book of Genesis*, 360.

97. "The heretofore shrewd Jacob on his part is just as blind—and will remain so two decades later—as his old father Isaac was before him." Alter, *The Art of Biblical Narrative*, 159.

98. Larsen, *Recognizing the Stranger*, 69.

Judah narratives. The Midrash *Bereishit Rabbah* notes the connection that "goat" establishes between two scenes in Judah's life: "The Holy One, blessed be He, said to Judah: 'Thou didst deceive thy father with a kid of goats; by thy life! Tamar will deceive thee with a kid of goats.'"[99] Although Jewish tradition interprets it this way, what is unclear is just how much the characters themselves are aware of the irony. There is no evocative response from Judah on the mention of the goat, but the reader is aware that again, Judah attempts to manipulate with a goat, this time unsuccessfully. Jacob begins his deception with goats while in league with his mother, "Go to the flock and bring me two good young goats" (27:9). In this usage there is a blending of functions. It ties together these units, and is, moreover, in the narrative world of the characters. The careful reader sees in these scenes the theme of deception underscored, because over and again the manipulators make use of a goat in these scenes.[100] However, there is no indication (found to date) that the meaning of "goat" supports any story themes as the word "recognize" does.[101]

Returning now to the first root mentioned above, notice that the word "recognize" performs different functions. As we observed in Jacob's deception of Isaac and Joseph's deception of his brothers, the word does not occur in the narrative world. However, in two stories between these, it does form part of the narrative world and is used to evoke a response by Judah. When Judah deceives Jacob as to Joseph's fate in 37:32, he says, הַכֶּר־נָא, "please *identify* (recognize) whether it is your son's robe or not." Later, when Tamar produces the signet, cord, and staff, she states, הַכֶּר־נָא, "Please *identify* (recognize) whose these are" (Gen 38:25). I have already noted Judah's immediate response to these items. However, we can now comprehend that when Judah hears his own deceptive *words* repeated back to him, this phrase "please identify" ties this scene of Tamar's deceptive manipulation, back to his moment of deceptively manipulating his father. The memory only increases the pressure on Judah to concede her position.[102]

99. Freedman and Simon, *Midrash Rabbah*, 85:9. This ancient rabbinical document was likely post-Johannine, yet the interpretive insight it provides in all probability reflects Jewish traditions that had been passed down for some time. For a similar perspective on early Jewish literature and the FG, see Menken, "Genesis in John's Gospel and 1 John," 88. Kaiser also identifies "goat" as a *Leitwort*. Kaiser, *Preaching and Teaching the Last Things*, 73.

100. "This example of punishment fitting the crime is further underlined by the slaughtered goat used in both acts of deception (27:9, 16; 37:31)." Mays, *Harper's Bible Commentary*, s.v. Gen 37:21. See also Alter, *Genesis*, 220.

101. Except that a goat is one of the animals most often associated with bearing sin, i.e., the scapegoat, Lev 16:10.

102. Recognition also appears with the story of Jacob, Rachel, Laban, and the

Other examples of *Leitwörter* in these stories, pertinent to our task, are pledge and silver. "Pledge" is present in the narrative world, and it supports a theme. When Judah provides his signet, cord, and staff to Tamar, they are in *pledge* for the goat that was to come later. He says, "What pledge shall I give to you?" (Gen 38:18). The word here is הָעֵרָבוֹן, from the root ערבון ('rbn). With no money in his pocket, he pledges to send payment later.[103] He promises to deliver, and it is a promise that the text later implies is not necessarily based on moral fiber, but just what is needed to satisfy the business transaction (38:17–18, 23).[104] Later, in the Joseph story, the root ערבון appears again when the family's provisions run out. Jacob entreats his sons to, "Go again, buy us a little food" (43:2). Judah quickly steps up and reiterates the conditions that the Egyptian vizier had laid out for their return trip. He then asks Jacob "Send the boy with me . . . I will be a *pledge* of his safety. From my hand you shall require him" (Gen 43:8–9). Here, the word is in its verbal form, אֶעֶרְבֶנּוּ "I will be his pledge."[105] Note here the wordplay. With the beginning of Reuben's plan in 42:37, the text reads, "Then Reuben said," "*vayomer rᵉûben*," וַיֹּאמֶר רְאוּבֵן. But shortly thereafter, in 43:9, Judah offers his plan. The text sounds similarly to the ear: "I will be a pledge," " *'anokhi eérbennu,*" אָנֹכִי אֶעֶרְבֶנּוּ.[106] Note also the "I" is emphatic. In effect, Judah says, "*I* will *Reuben* him. *I* will assume the role of firstborn, *Reuben*, in the family, to protect Benjamin, '*eérbennu,' as Reuben should have done, rather than offering his sons instead.*"[107] Judah is taking the responsibility for the family that a firstborn son should. Moreover, looking back in the stories of Jacob's sons, we see that Reuben, Simeon, and Levi, the first, second, and third born sons, had each tainted themselves for this role. Reuben disqualified himself

---

teraphim: "'Anyone with whom you find your gods shall not live. In the presence of our kinsmen *point out* what I have that is yours, and take it.' Now Jacob did not know that Rachel had stolen them" (Gen 31:32). Here the word is in the narrative world of the characters, but the main character—Jacob, the manipulator of knowledge—is ironically ignorant.

103. In 38:18, the LXX preserves not only the meaning but the sound with this direct Semitic loan word "ἀρραβῶνά." Logos Research Systems, *Septuaginta*; Kittel et al., *TDNT*, 1:475.

104. As indicated by his willingness to drop the matter of payment as soon as a little resistance and potential shame is involved, and his quick condemnation of Tamar for playing the harlot, while he has in fact employed the harlot without paying her. On the brevity of the narrative, indicating a business like transaction, see Alter, *Genesis*, 221.

105. This is Alter's translation. Ibid., 253.

106. Sarna also notices some of this but does not discuss the emphatic "I." Sarna, *Genesis* בראשית: *The Traditional Hebrew Text with New JPS Translation*, 263–64.

107. But here the LXX does not continue the use of ἀρραβῶνά, and instead supplies ἐγὼ δὲ ἐκδέχομαι αὐτόν, "I engage for him." Logos Research Systems, *Septuaginta*.

by sleeping with Bilhah (35:22). The *Genesis Florilegium*, or *Commentary on Genesis*, from Qumran (4Q252), regarding Reuben's blessing from Jacob, reads: "The blessings of Jacob: 'Reuben . . . you shall not be preeminent. You mounted your father's marriage couch, thereby defiling it because he lay on it.' Interpreted this means that he reproved him, because he (Reuben) slept with Bilhah his (father's) concubine. When it says 'You are my first born,' it means . . . Reuben was . . . the first in theory."[108] Ackerman points out that in previous events, Simeon and Levi, the second and third born sons of Leah next in line after Reuben, had disqualified themselves at Shechem to act as the firstborn.[109] The next son in order is Judah, the fourth-born son of Leah. Though he too may have disqualified himself with Tamar,[110] he redeems himself with this act, offering to sacrifice himself for Benjamin. Thus, Judah has reversed the course of previous actions. This behavior is unlike the first time he dealt with a pledge, where the vow would only cost him a goat. The initial plan to save Benjamin, *offered by Reuben*, involved no threat, or cost to Reuben. In fact, Reuben had so far come up with two plans to save the lives of Rachel's sons, both of which threatened not a hair on Reuben's own head. Reuben, though the firstborn, so far shows little or no character development according to the values in Genesis. Nevertheless, Judah, the manipulator has. He has *turned*, reversed the course of both his and Reuben's pledges. Robert Sacks notes the uncharacteristic fashion in which Judah offers his very self as a pledge: "Insofar as the verse is directed to himself, his private thoughts go back to the time he spent with Tamar. When he *pledges* himself in this verse he becomes a replacement for the *bracelet, staff and signet ring* which he gave to Tamar as a *pledge*."[111] The *Leitmotiv* moves the reader. The offer moves Jacob—it works—and Jacob relents.

Then in Egypt, Judah repeats this terminology ("For your servant became a *pledge* of safety for the boy" [Gen 44:32]), and it evokes a highly

---

108. Or *Pesher Genesis*. 4QCommGen A IV, 3. Eisenman and Wise, *The Dead Sea Scrolls Uncovered*, 89. For further analysis of themes shared by both the FG and the Qumran literature, see Thomas, *Meaning of the Terms Life and Death*, 200; Coetzee, "Life (Eternal Life) in St John's Writings and the Qumran Scrolls," 48; Charlesworth, "Qumran, John and the Odes of Solomon," 107–36; Charlesworth, *John and the Dead Sea Scrolls*; Charlesworth, "A Critical Comparison of the Dualism," 76–106. But see also Bauckham, *The Testimony of the Beloved Disciple*, 125–36.

109. Ackerman, "Joseph, Judah, and Jacob," 100.

110. Contra Ackerman further below who asserts that Judah *gained* firstborn status in chapter 37, and still retains it, given that Reuben, Simeon, and Levi have disqualified themselves. Ackerman, "Joseph, Judah, and Jacob," 105.

111. Sacks, *A Commentary on the Book of Genesis*, 372. Ackerman notes the beginning "change" in all the brothers by the manner they deal with their father's grief in chapter 42. Ackerman, "Joseph, Judah, and Jacob," 92.

emotional response from Joseph.[112] The person who sent Joseph to be a slave in Egypt for *profit* is now willing to give himself up to save the life of Benjamin. So here, too, the repeated root word is in the world of the text. It *evokes a response* from someone, the manipulator, and it supports a theme of self-sacrifice. Ackerman notes the parallel pledges and the reversal in Judah: "Whereas he left personal items in pledge (*'rbn*) to Tamar until the kid be brought, he now pledges himself (*'rbn*) to Jacob until Benjamin be returned home safely. If not, says Judah, he (not his sons, the next generation) will bear the guilt all his days."[113] Therefore "pledge," as a *Leitwort*, is both present in the narrative world and it supports a theme—a theme of self-sacrifice rather than sexual or material gain.

The final *Leitwort* I examine is the word silver that the story repeats throughout the selling of Joseph to Egypt, the famine, and the brothers' return.[114] We would do well at this point to remind ourselves again that Alter's categories of *Leitwörter* or *Leitmotiv*, include not only root words but also "a concrete image, sensory quality, action, or object [which] recurs through a particular narrative."[115] The root for silver is כסף. It shows up throughout Genesis. Translators render it variously as silver, money, price, etc. It appears once in Genesis 13, four times in chapter 17, once in chapter 20. It appears again seven times in chapters 23 and 24 to refer to the price of land Abraham bought and the dowry for Rebekah. Then silver virtually disappears, occurring only one more time in twelve chapters: in chapter 31 where Rachel complains that her father has taken all of their silver (Gen 31:15). Then it shows up again suddenly in chapter 37, in the selling price of "twenty shekels of silver" for Joseph to the Midianites (37:28). This virtual twelve chapter hiatus serves as a break before כסף begins to serve as a motif in the Joseph story.[116] The readers hear nothing of silver for several

---

112. And here, the LXX continues with ἐκδέδεκται. Logos Research Systems, *Septuaginta*.

113. Ackerman, "Joseph, Judah, and Jacob," 105.

114. One could obviously examine more, such as "pit" or "prison."

115. Alter, *The Art of Biblical Narrative*, 95. I have blended *Leitwörter* and *Leitmotiv* together in my treatment, as they have blended functions. Buber, whom Alter draws upon, writes, "Dynamisch nenne ich sie, weil sich zwischen den so aufeinander bezogenen Lautgefügen gleichsam eine Bewegung vollzieht: wem das Ganze gegenwärtig ist, der fühlt die Wellen hinüber und herüber schlagen" (I call it "dynamic" because between combinations of sounds related to one another in this manner a kind of movement takes place: if one imagines the entire text deployed before him, one can sense waves moving back and forth between the words). Buber, *Werke 2, Schriften zur Bibel*, 1131. Alter's translation, Alter, *The Art of Biblical Narrative*, 93.

116. Silver is a *Leitwort* tying together various scenes of the entire Joseph story, not a *Leitwort* tying all the manipulation narratives in Gen. See Alter, *Genesis*, 248n25

chapters, but then it appears at Joseph's demise. Then, it appears five times in chapter 42, nine times in 43, five times in 44 and once in 45—a cluster of occurrences.

The first time the reader hears of silver after Joseph's capture in chapter 37 is upon the brothers' first encounter with him as vizier of Egypt, when he returns their money to their sacks (Gen 42:25). The last time they were together, silver changed hands and the brothers profited at Joseph's expense. Here they are presented with the idea that one of them has again made a profit of silver by corrupt means. However, this time it appears to be by stealing from the powerful vizier, much to their chagrin: "Their hearts sank and they turned to each other trembling and said, 'What is this that God has done to us?'" (42:28). The reader hears their statement that God is the cause of the bad fortune, but may not yet be aware whether the silver is linked to the sale of Joseph years earlier.[117] When the brothers arrive in Canaan, they recount the story to their father of finding silver in only *one* pouch. The reader then hears silver repeated again, *in a more troubling situation*, because the brothers now find their silver in all nine pouches. The text marks the growing and agonizing sign of trouble, "When they and their father saw their money bundles, they were afraid" (42:35).

In the next chapter, Jacob, having finally relented, instructs his sons to take "double the amount of silver" to Egypt. Thus, they are now returning the money plus, ironically, enough money to pay back, symbolically, their profit from the sale of Joseph decades earlier. Ackerman ponders their expression of growing guilt, which may have begun with their imprisonment: "Surely part of the reason is a growing sense of *déjà vu* among the brothers." Later he states, "But the silver gained in the context of losing another brother also *echoes* their grim plan to sell Joseph into slavery for silver."[118] This echo then is the haunting effect named above. Something in the story comes back to haunt the manipulator, bringing to mind his previous deed, working him toward a state of remorse. However, upon returning, and before the brothers can explain that they have returned with double the missing money, Joseph

---

where he states that the silver "repeats their receiving of silver from the Ishmaelites for the sale of Joseph as a slave."

117. "But the more recent sequence fillips as well as gratifies our curiosity about Joseph. Did he mean the money to serve a double purpose—a temptation for the brothers and an eye or gap-opener for the father—or is it God that put the test to another use? The cause remains permanently ambiguous—as with Deborah's oracle—to suggest anew the blurring of the borderline between the agent and the lord of history. Yet the plot effect is one of a beneficial chain reaction that shakes the entire family." Sternberg, *The Poetics of Biblical Narrative*, 299.

118. Ackerman, "Joseph, Judah, and Jacob," 91–92; Lambe, "Judah's Development," 62.

summons them to his own house. Notice the brothers' words as they speculate about their fate. In terminology ominously similar to their abduction of Joseph they observe, "We were brought here because of the silver that was put back into our sacks the first time. He wants to *attack us and overpower us and seize us as slaves*" (Gen 43:18). Further on they are told, "*Your God and the God of your father*" (the very same father they deceived twenty years prior) is responsible for the silver returned in their sacks after the first journey (43:23). Here, the reader encounters the textual indeterminacy Sternberg describes: should the brothers feel relieved because the vizier has been paid or should they tremble because God is toying with them because of their past?[119] The reader does not know, and neither do the brothers. The story draws the reader into the narrative world of the unknown.

In the following chapter, Joseph repeats his scheme. Each man's silver is put back into their sacks for their return journey. He, moreover, requires that his *silver* cup be placed into Benjamin's sack. When the steward overtakes the brothers on their journey, they make a terrible vow. In language recalling Jacob's vow to Laban (Gen 31:32), they state, "Whichever of your servants is found with it shall die, and we also will be my lord's servants" (44:9). The brothers, just like Jacob, do not know—they are ignorant of the fact that they are speaking of the relative they least want implicated. The steward's discovery of the silver cup creates such emotion that the brothers rend their garments (44:13). Once again, is silver going to result in the loss of Rachel and Jacob's favored son who was entrusted to the sons of Leah?[120] The eerie feeling of divinely ordered retribution intensifies with the fact that there is no mention of the silver money in the others' bags; only the silver cup has brought consequences. Likely, the brothers wonder why the steward is only concerned with the cup. They have offered that they should all be slaves, but for this powerful vizier, it is not enough. Joseph and the steward ignore this offer (44:10, 17) and prepare to send the sons of Leah home without Benjamin to face their father alone, again. Silver haunts them. This theme, within the narrative world, appears to have been intended by Joseph. Alter observed the resourceful usage of this theme: "The choice of a silver divining goblet for this false accusation of Benjamin is an ingenious fusion of the motif of silver—illicitly received, surreptitiously restored, and ultimately linked with the brothers' guilt toward Joseph—with the central theme of knowledge."[121] The effect is complete: Judah states in verse 16, "God has found out the guilt of your servants." The reader, along with the

---

119. Sternberg, *The Poetics of Biblical Narrative*, 177.
120. Alter, *Genesis*, 263.
121. Alter, *The Art of Biblical Narrative*, 173.

brothers, knows that in this instance, the brothers have done nothing wrong. The admission of guilt, therefore, refers to actions two decades removed.[122]

I have identified three functions of *Leitwörter*, and the resultant haunting *déjà vu* motif. As to the first function, the words are not *within the narrative world*, but only known to the reader. They function as signs of connective tissue, simply joining narratives. In the second function, the *Leitwort* also strengthens the *substantive intent* of the story's content, its moral tale. Such was the case with "recognize" and "pledge." In the examples cited, these words are at times known to the characters and at other times only to the reader. The third function occurs when the root word is *in the narrative world, but is also known to the character*, often an item in the story line, which *comes back to haunt the key character in a manner that sometimes evokes an emotive response*. This haunting effect can even work the character toward remorse, as was the case with the brothers and their silver, or it may mark a point of turning, as the word "pledge" did for Judah. Understanding *Leitwörter* in Genesis, therefore, is a key tool for reading the narratives as part of an overall story. *Leitwörter* are all the more important for seeing the function of each narrative in the manipulation series of each character. They may therefore be important to the reading of John 21.

From Manipulator to Manipulable: The Effect of Counter-Manipulation

The final pattern in Genesis manipulation narratives is the *pattern of moving from manipulator to manipulable and the transformative effect of counter-manipulation*. As discussed earlier, Williams questions whether deceivers in Genesis are evaluated in a positive or negative light. He argues that the text evaluates deception positively when it restores shalom to a situation, thus righting a wrong.[123] I agree that a "one size fits all" approach does not satisfy this debate.[124] The critic's assessment of how the text evaluates manipulators

---

122. Ackerman, "Joseph, Judah, and Jacob," 89; Alter, *The Art of Biblical Narrative*, 173; Sternberg, *The Poetics of Biblical Narrative*, 306.

123. Williams, *Deception in Genesis*, 151, 221–23.

124. Fuchs reasons that the text censures males for their deception but not females. Any implicit judgment of the trickster tactics by the females is left ambiguous. This, she proposes, is due to the patriarchal/androcentric viewpoint of the text and its given assumption of the "moral inferiority" of women. Thus, "if deceptiveness is inherent in female nature, there is no more point in challenging it than there is in challenging the menstrual cycle." Fuchs, "For I Have the Way of Women," 80. But see Otwell, *And Sarah Laughed*, 109, who opposes the hypothesis "that cunning was a female trait in ancient Israel." See below the further discussion of Tamar and Rebekah.

should not be uniform. The text's implicit evaluation of each manipulator usually depends on whether or not he or she is what I now term an *initial manipulator*, or whether the actions are carrying out what the reader anticipates—measure for measure retribution for earlier deception in the story—thus what I am calling *counter-manipulation*. Counter-manipulation occurs when someone, often the first victim, manipulates the initial manipulator in a way that mimics the original wrong behavior.

When Jacob out-maneuvers Laban through breeding and escape, the text implies that Jacob's actions are justified, whereas Laban's are not. It demonstrates this by means of Jacob's protracted verbal defense (Gen 31:36–42), the dream in which God warned Laban (31:24), and Jacob's characterization of that dream (31:42).[125] In retracing the behavior of the initial manipulator, we see that *counter-manipulation* often results in an *undoing* of the original wrong.[126] Thus, Jacob departs from Laban but blessed with wealth (31:18, 43), which stands in contrast with the labor wrestled from Jacob by Laban, and the livestock which Laban attempted to keep from Jacob (31:7–9). Joseph, in counter-manipulating his brothers with a play on "recognition," similar to that which the brothers used on their father, restores family unity, thereby undoing the separation and reconciling his family. André Wénin notes this reconciliation, arguing that the aim of enumerating Jacob and Joseph's families together in Egypt as "the house of Jacob" in Genesis 46:6–28, is to point out "the solemn reunion of the family after the reconciliation of the brothers."[127] Joseph brings about this significant reconciliation by artfully forcing the brothers to recognize their own wrongdoing. He retraces their behavior with silver and a favored son. He counter-manipulates them by retracing, tit for tat, their wrong actions. He *reverses* the family split and makes the brothers manipulable, pliable, even to the point that Judah is willing to sacrifice himself (44:33).[128] Thus, the evaluation is often dependent on whether the episode is an initial manipulation or a counter-manipulation,

---

125. The reader may not expect Laban to dupe Jacob when he switches Rachel and Leah (Gen 29). This act restores no wrong and Laban was not Jacob's previous victim. Thus, in that instance though Laban is a counter-manipulator and the sanctions are ironic and perhaps fitting, no implication of moral justification is present as it is in Gen 31 when Jacob counter-manipulates Laban.

126. A position similar to Williams, *Deception in Genesis*, 121, 151, 221–23. Williams, though, does not bring to light the aspect of a *series* of scenes focused on a key character. The aspect of narrative flow is important to highlight how counter-manipulation works.

127. Wénin, "La gestion narrative de l'espace dans l'histoire de Joseph."

128. Note also that in Gen 43:4 in his plea to their father, Judah, finally, for the first time, refers to Benjamin as "our brother" as opposed to "your son," as he did with Joseph in the beginning of this story. Sternberg, *The Poetics of Biblical Narrative*, 300.

the latter of which are often found at the end of a series of manipulation episodes focusing on a key character.[129] Therefore, there are *initial* or *simple manipulators*, those who initiate deceptive manipulation upon others; and there are *counter-manipulators*, those who return tit for tat and counter-manipulate the manipulator.

Tamar fits into the category of counter-manipulator. We have previously observed that Judah's actions with Tamar as well as with Joseph and Jacob were wrong.[130] In addition, Judah deceives his father with a goat, a garment, and the use of the root *recognize* in the phrase "please identify" (Gen 37:32). The story of Tamar's corrective actions retraces some of those key behaviors, for it involves a goat, garments and the word *recognize*. She responds to him measure for measure, tit for tat. The writer of Genesis is careful to record Judah's words when Tamar counter-manipulates him: "She is more righteous than I, since I did not give her to my son Shelah" (38:26). In one sentence, he indicts his actions.[131] Thus, the text censures the initial manipulator Judah, and Judah calls the counter-manipulator, Tamar, *more righteous*.[132] The following diagram illustrates the convergence of the initial and counter-manipulators.[133]

---

129. "Often" is the operative word here, because this characteristic is not always present. The stories are what they are, but they are remarkable and story-worthy, to both the writer and reader, because of the ironic and interesting pattern of measure for measure justice that frequently appears in these manipulation texts. I propose that the writer/redactor(s) felt no compulsion to force the text into neat and clean Western/Aristotelian motif categories, outlines, or watertight compartments. Thus, the reader can engage a messy human story without the need to explain any "weak points" in the story line—places where the pattern does not completely fit. Note again, the footnote and reference above to Judg: "Everyone did what was right in their own eyes" (Judg 17:6; 21:25). Neither Judg nor Gen by any means entirely exonerates many of the characters who demonstrate *some* model behavior, the passion driven Nazarite, Samson being one such example.

130. Ackerman, "Joseph, Judah, and Jacob," 111; Lambe, "Judah's Development," 55–57; Wenham, *Genesis 16–50*, 365.

131. Lambe, "Judah's Development," 59.

132. Williams, *Deception in Genesis*. As the one who in the end is counter-manipulated, Judah's low moral character and ignorance are highlighted. This is similar to Lied's analysis in 2 Bar 50–51, for she argues that the theme, "the righteous—'those who know,'"—and the wicked—the ignorant, "is an important issue in the entire episode." Lied, "Recognizing the Righteous Remnant?," 333.

133. I have altered the phrases from Gen in the diagram from the ESV translation. I have used the word "recognize" to emphasize its repetition in the Hebrew.

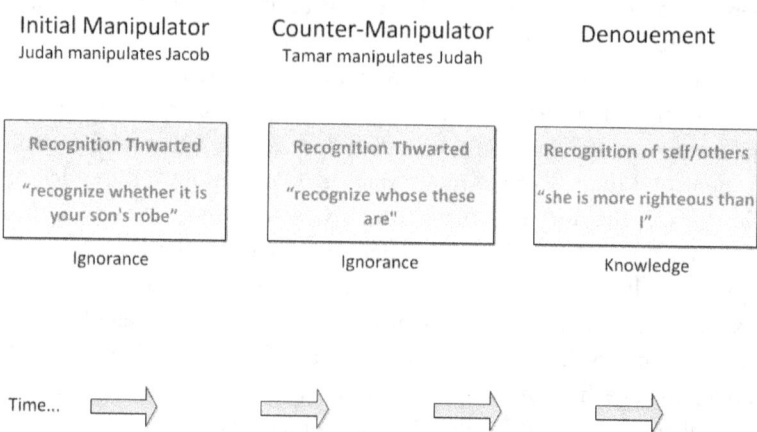

A careful look at these characters shows that Rebekah, Laban, Jacob, Judah and his brothers, Tamar, and finally Joseph, at some point in the narrative, serve as counter-manipulators. At least six individual characters (plus the remainder of the sons of Jacob—minus Joseph—acting as a character group) bring some type of counter-manipulation upon a manipulator. Of those, I argue that four have *some type* of identifiable justification noted or implied in the text: Rebekah, Jacob, Tamar, and Joseph.[134]

In his catalog of deception scenes, Williams begins his assessment of Rebekah ambivalently, discussing Jacob and Rebekah jointly: "The immediate context provides no clear indication of how this entire event is to be regarded." However, he ends the treatment of Jacob's conduct on the negative: "[T]hat deception is implicitly condemned is supported by the difficulties that characterized his life from that point forward."[135] Even so, in a footnote he leaves open the possibility of Rebekah's exoneration, saying, "[F]avoritism for a son and manipulation of a husband can only be regarded as certainly negative if one presumes that there is never an occasion when these may be appropriate."[136] Nicholas likewise opens that door very wide, pointing

---

134. The others enact a reprisal that was at least expected, if not somewhat justified. See "Measure for Measure" and *lex talionis* below. Even Rachel's stealing of the gods, in my view, is implied as retributive after Laban's theft of wages, though this is contra Williams, *Deception in Genesis*, 23.

135. Ibid., 18–19.

136. Ibid., 32n10.

out that in 25:23, when Rebekah hears from YHWH the promise that the older will serve the younger, the direct object is unclear: "The object is left unmarked (ורב יעקב צעיר). Who would serve whom? Rebekah's favoritism clarifies how she interpreted the utterance. Only when the final ruse succeeds do we know how the original oracle was to be understood."[137] *Jubilees* 19:15–31 contributes to this perspective, because early in that story, Abraham blesses a young Jacob with Rebekah present. Thus for the author of *Jubilees*, the assignment of the blessing to Jacob, rather than Esau, was set even earlier.[138] Rebekah's actions may therefore be correcting the direction of the intended blessing, bringing the blessing to bear on the son of God's choice. Gordon Wenham also points to Isaac's culpability in the affair: "[Isaac] is quite deliberately prepared to overlook Esau's misdemeanors and the God-given oracle. Isaac's will is pitted against God's and Rebekah's. The stakes are high. Will Isaac and Esau triumph or Rebekah and Jacob, as the LORD had promised?"[139] Esau may be censured in the description of him as a hunter and a man of the wild, as opposed to Jacob as a peaceful tent dweller (Gen 25:27; 26:34–35; 28:6–9).[140] Wenham also points out that typical deathbed blessing scenes involved the calling of *all* sons and that Isaac may have deliberately avoided Jacob and Rebekah.[141] Finally, the reader is painfully aware of the exchange in 25:29–34 and Jacob's open manipulation of Esau's debased nature, allowing hunger to control him. This manipulation, as we have noted, required no deception. The audience is also told that Esau "despised his birthright," a rare moment of explicit commentary for the Genesis narrative (25:34). Thus, the reader cannot avoid the impression that according to a combination of the oracle given to Rebekah and the deal

---

137. Nicholas, *The Trickster Revisited*, 75n49. The LXX appears to preserve some of the ambiguity. Rather than stating the elder shall serve the younger, it instead reads that the greater will serve the lesser or smaller one, "ὁ μείζων δουλεύσει τῷ ἐλάσσονι." See the note in Brenton, *The Septuagint Version of the Old Testament and Apocrypha*, 31. The same term for Esau, μείζωνι, stands in parallel when used for Leah in 29:16, "μείζονι." See also Syren, *Forsaken Firstborn*, 81–84; Sacks, *A Commentary on the Book of Genesis*, 216–17. On "the wisdom of Rebekah," Sacks states, "Her care and love for Isaac lead her to believe that to deceive him would be better than to make him face his own failure to understand his sons." Ibid., 217.

138. Charlesworth, *The Old Testament Pseudepigrapha*, 92.

139. Wenham, *Genesis 16–50*, 206.

140. Ibid., 215; Ackerman, "Joseph, Judah, and Jacob," 102; Alter, *Genesis*, 136; Sacks, *A Commentary on the Book of Genesis*, 209–10. See also *Jub.* 19:13–14, which reads: "Jacob was smooth and upright, but Esau was a fierce man and rustic and hairy. And Jacob used to dwell in tents. And the youths grew up, and Jacob learned writing; but Esau did not learn, for he was a rustic man and a hunter. And he learnt war, and all of his deeds were fierce." Charlesworth, *The Old Testament Pseudepigrapha*, 92.

141. Wenham, *Genesis 16–50*, 206, 208, 215.

made with Jacob over a bowl of stew, the blessing *should have* belonged to Jacob. In the end however, readers must still wrestle with Rebekah and Jacob's deceit and the consequences that follow them.[142] Thus, the reader may interpret the act of manipulating Isaac into blessing Jacob positively to a measured degree. However, the reader may view the favoritism of both parents and the continued problems in Jacob's life serving as censure of his continuing habit of deceiving others.[143] Notwithstanding, the text does restrict the story morally polar categories.[144] As is clear in Tamar's case, Genesis does not whitewash *en masse* the actions of characters. Judah's words were "She is *more* righteous than I." He does not state that her behavior is completely justified, but rather better than his. Such may be the case with Isaac and Rebekah. Rebekah's behavior may not be exemplary, but given the specific circumstances, it may be viewed as better than Isaac's. Furthermore, the oracle to Rebekah comes at *her request* (25:22). In this way, the text portrays her in a positive light in accordance with the values of the story, over and against Isaac who sets up the blessing *without* any mention of him seeking YHWH and without the presence of Jacob. Additionally, Rebekah was the victim of Isaac's earlier manipulation, when he lied and placed her in a vulnerable position with Abimelech and other men of Gerar (26:6–11). Therefore, she manipulates Isaac the manipulator.

We have already established that Jacob's counter-manipulation of Laban, breeding the sheep to his gain and later escaping, is justified. He is correcting the wrongs that Laban has committed by repeatedly cheating Jacob out of his wages. The text indicates this with Jacob's recounting of the dream regarding the sheep (Gen 31:9–13), Jacob's lengthy response to Laban at Gilead (31:36–42), God warning Laban in a dream (31:24), and Jacob's characterization of that dream (31:42).

Tamar's conduct, as well, needs little further comment. The text clearly evaluates her actions in a positive light. In counter-manipulating Judah, she corrects the injustice he created when he withheld Shelah from her (Gen 38:14).

Before proceeding to the final counter-manipulating narrative of Joseph and his brothers, we need to explore two remaining aspects of the counter-manipulation pattern. The first is the principle of *lex talionis* and *measure for measure* counter-play by the counter-manipulator. The second is the resultant *turning* of the simple manipulator back toward the desired

---

142. As Wenham points out, Rebekah "never sees her son again." Ibid., 216.

143. Alter too speaks of "*some sort* of justification" of the taking of the blessing. Alter, *Genesis*, 136.

144. Wenham, *Genesis 16–50*, 215.

position or path, in accordance with the values of the story world. This desired path is a position that, from the point of view of the narrator and implied author, is the correct one.[145]

Measure for Measure and the *Lex Talionis*

Counter-manipulation, as it functions in Genesis, usually includes an element of reciprocal retribution. Although the measure for measure connection between Rebekah's manipulation of Isaac's and his prior lying to Abimelech is not as clear as in other episodes, it is still present.[146] Rebekah was the one put in danger, at least morally, by Isaac's cowardly lying, and she is the very one who counter-manipulates him, by lying.

This interwoven pattern of measure for measure counter-manipulation is held in place by the system of *retributive justice* focused around the Pentateuch passages of Exodus 21:23–25, Deuteronomy 19:21, and Leviticus 24:17–21, and later termed *lex talionis*.[147] I reproduce them entirely here because reading them against the backdrop of the preceding material discussed emphasizes an important perspective:

> If men who are fighting hit a pregnant woman and she gives birth prematurely but there is no serious injury, the offender must be fined whatever the woman's husband demands and the court allows. But if there is serious injury, you are to take life for life, eye for eye, tooth for tooth, hand for hand, foot for foot, burn for burn, wound for wound, bruise for bruise (Exod 21:23–25).

---

145. Though some stories imply no justification of the counter-manipulator, there is often still an "element of divine justice," as with Laban deceiving Jacob into marrying the sibling, in a manner similar to Jacob deceiving his sibling. This *omniscient dual causality*, whereby Gen portrays God as having a second purpose in mind for the result of the story in addition to the purpose that the human forces had in mind when they caused the events, is evident in many episodes. Alter calls this "a double system of causation and divine." Alter, *Genesis*, 249. The brothers had one plan in mind when they caused Joseph to end up in Egypt, yet God had a second thing in mind and thus was an additional, yet primary cause agent (Gen 50:20). Laban too had one plan, which in the end assisted in the fulfillment of the blessing God gave to Abraham in 12:2: "And I will make of you a great nation . . ." This is reiterated to Jacob in 28:14, "Your offspring shall be like the dust of the earth." See also Ackerman, "Joseph, Judah, and Jacob," 108; Wenham, *Genesis 16–50*, 238, 364; Lambe, "Judah's Development," 66; Sailhamer, *Pentateuch as Narrative*, 3.

146. Jacob does play a role here, but it is apparent that the primary manipulator is Rebekah.

147. Nel, "The Talion Principle in Old Testament Narratives," 21–22.

> Show no pity: life for life, eye for eye, tooth for tooth, hand for hand, foot for foot (Deut 19:21).

> If anyone takes the life of a human being, he must be put to death. Anyone who takes the life of someone's animal must make restitution—life for life. If anyone injures his neighbor, *whatever he has done must be done to him*: fracture for fracture, eye for eye, tooth for tooth. As he has injured the other, so he is to be injured. Whoever kills an animal must make restitution, but whoever kills a man must be put to death. You are to have the same law for the alien and the native-born. I am the LORD your God (Lev 24:17–21).

Even though our text of comparison is Genesis, these passages from outside Genesis still have a bearing on our understanding of manipulation narratives. Sailhamer argues that scholars should interpret the entire Pentateuch as one coherent collection.[148] Earlier, Thomas Mann had argued for a "Pentateuchal Narrative," and observed that scholars from varied backgrounds were beginning to treat the Pentateuch synchronically in its final form.[149] This does not discount that these five writings are still a compilation, regardless of how scholars view their sources, whether theologically disparate or similar.[150] Yet at some point in time, the compilation took place, shaping these five books into their present form. Approaching the Pentateuch in its final form forces the interpreter to ask what impact the presence of the later legal codes had on the shaping of the earlier narratives. Thus, if one approaches the manipulation narratives while interpreting the Pentateuch as one composite unit, the measure for measure actions of these counter-manipulators appear in a new light. In fact, we can interpret much of their behavior, not merely as justified, but rather as *expected* by the implied reader.[151] Even when not justified, readers still expect much of this behavior, because the system of retribution pervades the narrative world of the Pen-

---

148. Sailhamer, *Pentateuch as Narrative*, 1–2.

149. Mann, *The Book of the Torah*, 6–7.

150. Alter characterizes the Documentary Hypothesis as having "reached a point of diminishing returns." Alter, *The Five Books of Moses*, 11. Elsewhere he also states: "I have no quarrel with the courage of conjecture of those engaged in what Sir Edmund Leach has shrewdly called 'unscrambling the omelet,' but the essential point of the validity of the literary perspective is that we have in the Bible, with far fewer exceptions than the historical critics would allow, a very well made omelet indeed." Alter, *The World of Biblical Literature*, 69.

151. But note the *lex talionis* also was probably designed to "limit" the amount of punishment exacted in the community. Davis, *Lex Talionis in Early Judaism and the Exhortation of Jesus in Matthew 5.38–42*, 33.

tateuch. Determining if the behavior is justified is, in some ways, the wrong question, especially if the analysis stops there.

Scholars wrestle with Tamar's adultery and Judah's proclamation of her justification, but actually she responds measure for measure, seed for seed, in conjunction with *lex talionis*. This principle may also explain why Jacob condemns the behavior of Simeon and Levi in Genesis 34. Though Shechem had wronged Dinah, he had taken no life to justify that level of response. The implied reader would consider the Tamar story a "seed for seed" act of retribution. Judah withheld the seed; Tamar took the seed. Phillip Nel argues that the principle of *lex talionis* was an underlying influence for multiple narratives in the Hebrew Bible. He surveys this line of thought through the lives of Tamar, Ruth, and Samson.[152] Nel evinces that the understanding of *talionis* in the Pentateuch should not be limited to the "narrow sense" of the "juridical texts" but should rather be seen as "a *principle* of Yahweh's jurisprudence."[153] He adds, "It is possible to assume that the Biblical authors perceived the *talio* as the underlying principle of a requital pattern of events influencing Israel's history, and therefore, as a part of a supreme Providence."[154] This "requital pattern of events" explains why I have focused my examination on following characters through a series of narratives. These characters, in their first manipulation narrative, demonstrate their own moral deficiencies and therefore set the stage for the later reciprocal acts of justice carried out against them. Thus, when others counter-manipulate, the behavior and scene both function within this system of reciprocal jurisprudence. The first kernel of the counter-manipulation, *the desired benefit*, is the *lex talionis* correction of the original injustice for which the initial manipulator was responsible. Genesis 38:14 reads, "For she saw that Shelah was grown up, and she had not been given to him in marriage." Judah had originally manipulated Tamar to distance her from his seed by omission, ambiguous language, and withholding Shelah, but Tamar counter-manipulates in order to obtain his seed.[155]

The scenes come to resolution by means of fulfillment of the principle of *lex talionis*. The informed implied reader is not surprised that Isaac's *wife* manipulated him into giving the blessing to the correct son via

152. Nel, "The Talion Principle in Old Testament Narratives," 21–29.
153. Ibid., 23.
154. Ibid.
155. She does this using the following devices: masking her face, masking her identity by engaging him a distance from where he would normally find her, approaching him during the distracted time of sheep shearing, and positioning herself as an object of desire, manipulating him in a way similar to Jacob's manipulation of Esau's desire (Gen 38:13–15).

deception—only uninformed readers find this surprising.[156] We should also not be surprised to find that Jacob's own counter-manipulation follows this pattern remarkably. He practices deception by switching places with his *sibling*. Shortly thereafter, Laban counter-manipulates him using deception and a *sibling* switch.[157] Sarna notes the irony with Jacob: "The perpetrator of deception was now the victim, hoist with his own petard."[158] Thus, Sarna understands the sense of counter-manipulation and its irony—the initial manipulator is treated in a manner *strikingly similar* to his or her own devices or plan. The reader groans with the text as Jacob suffers the logical outcome of his repeated manipulations, as others continually manipulate him, over and again, sibling for sibling, kid for kid, garment for garment, and favorite for favorite.[159] The reader groans, yes, but senses this is coming. It is *lex talionis*. It is expected.

This is true also for the episodes beginning with Laban's counter-manipulation of Jacob, continuing through the manipulation enacted by Judah and his brothers when they deceive Jacob with Joseph's robe. These episodes are an extended story *of cheating, circumvention, and con artistry.* Williams evaluates nearly all of these ensuing instances negatively.[160] Their role in the text is to show the *logical outcome* of a life characterized by deceit, but we must ask if the characters of Laban and the sons of Jacob are justified as counter-manipulators. Unlike Rebekah, Tamar, and Joseph, they were probably not as justified in their actions. Nevertheless, the implied reader understood this as expected, and therein lies the story's value for Israel. The logical outcome of deception is exhibited in the life of Jacob, a leader but

---

156. Regarding the "*informed* implied reader," I propose that the readers originally implied by the text were expected to see this because they lived in a world much closer to the narrative world of the text and understood this "basic norm of the Yahwistic community." Nel, "The Talion Principle in Old Testament Narratives," 22. For a similar approach to John's Gospel and the implied reader who is "expected" to understand, see Culpepper, "Symbolism and History in John's Account of Jesus' Death," 48; Pfitzner, "They Knew It Was the Lord," 72.

157. However, there is little in Gen that applauds Laban's behavior.

158. Sarna, *Understanding Genesis*, 184. A petard is a small explosive device. "Dictionary.com Unabridged."

159. Sarna wrote, "The biographical details of Jacob's life read like a catalogue of misfortunes," and "all the foregoing makes quite clear Scripture's condemnation of Jacob's moral lapse in his treatment of his brother and father. In fact, an explicit denunciation could hardly have been more effective or more scathing than this unhappy biography." Sarna, *Understanding Genesis*, 183–84.

160. With the exception of Jacob manipulating Laban by animal breeding, which Williams does not examine, and the secret manner of Jacob's departure in Gen 31. Williams, *Deception in Genesis*, 21–22.

also a habitual deceiver, progressing, albeit slowly, through the character development process.[161]

John Anderson observes the prominence of eye for eye reprisal in the Jacob-Laban narratives: "One learns almost immediately in 29:21–27 that Laban is also a deceptive figure, able to trick the trickster Jacob by giving him Leah instead of Rachel."[162] Victor Matthews and Frances Mims observe the same at the hands of Rachel and her deception of her father Genesis: "Laban had broken many pledges with Jacob and his daughters. Now, when he loses the symbols of his family's success, the story makes a point of tying this directly to his failure to provide Rachel and Leah with a dowry, which would have helped assure their family's success (Gen 31:14). In this way, *the trickster becomes the victim of his own schemes.*"[163] This is after Laban attempts to gather all the material advantages he can, culminating in Jacob's speech to his wives (31:6–16). Laban is accused of "cheating" and "devouring" Jacob and his family of their money, whereas Rachel, in eye for eye fashion, "steals" the gods (31:7, 15, 19, 30, 32).

Parental favoritism plays a significant role in Jacob's participation with Rebekah's deception of Isaac (Gen 25:28). Later in life, Judah and his brothers counter-manipulate Jacob in a situation charged with parental favoritism.[164] In addition to the favoritism, the kid and the clothing serve as uncanny reminders of the kids and garments used by Jacob to deceive his father. To the reader, they are a *measure for measure* turnabout upon Jacob, a "punishment fitting the crime" (27:9, 15; 37:31).[165] Nicholas makes clear the similarity in Judah's actions toward Jacob: "The trickster had again been tricked by a device that previously he had used himself."[166]

Tamar's measure for measure reprisal is one of the most obvious. Judah refuses to give her his *seed*, so she turns the tables and counter-manipulates

---

161. Readers do not, however, see that final outcome in Laban's life because, as demonstrated above, he is not a key character in the narrative but, rather, a supporting one.

162. Anderson, "Jacob, Laban, and a Divine Trickster?," 10. See also Niditch, *Underdogs and Tricksters*, 107.

163. Matthews and Mims, "Jacob the Trickster and Heir of the Covenant," 189.

164 Lambe, "Judah's Development," 62. Jacob heads down a path of forbidden favoritism. See Lev 18:18 and Deut 21:15–17. He may have been intending to pass his inheritance on to Joseph before this misfortune came.

165. Ackerman, "Joseph, Judah, and Jacob," 96. The brothers here appear to have no justification for their actions. Joseph did, however, play a role as he "stirs up opposition" by "insisting on talking about" his dreams. Alter, *Genesis*, 210, 214; Wenham, *Genesis 16–50*, 352; Mays, *Harper's Bible Commentary*, 37:21.

166. Nicholas, *The Trickster Revisited*, 59. See also Wenham, *Genesis 16–50*, 350, 352.

the manipulator into giving her his *seed* directly.[167] And, she does it in a manner that recalls his manipulation of Jacob, by using tools (a kid and garments) and terminology ("identify" or recognize) Judah and the reader cannot mistake (Gen 37:31–32; 38:17,25).[168] Alter sums up the retributive manipulation: "Like a trap suddenly springing closed, the connection with the preceding story of the deception of Jacob is now fully realized. In precise correspondence to Judah and his brothers, Tamar 'sends' evidence—in this case, true evidence—to argue her case. Like them, she confronts the father figure with the imperative, 'Recognize, pray' (*haker-na*)."[169] Therefore, even in the manner of notifying the victim, there is an element of measure for measure justice.

Nel also argues that the system of *lex talionis* holds and ties the narratives together. This characteristic of tying stories together underscores that manipulation narratives occur in a series, and build sequentially: "It is evident that the talion principle not only appears in juridical texts of the Old Testament, but can be traced as part of the context of narrative texts. Its recognition in narratives is *necessary* to comprehend the sequence of events and the plot structure. The talion principle functions as a mechanism of the narrator to create textual coherence within the sequence of events."[170] Jacob reverses Esau's anticipated blessing with a sibling switch, and Laban reverses the circumstances of Jacob's anticipated marriage with a sibling switch. Judah and his brothers reverse Joseph's future by kidnapping him, the favored son of Jacob and Rachel. Later, Joseph reverses Judah and his brothers' situation by threatening to take from the family the other favored son of Jacob and Rachel. Thus, *lex talionis* serves as the juridical basis for the reversal, and the reversal constitutes a major development in the plot. The plot moves toward the transformation of manipulators.

This plot culminates with Joseph as the master of eye for eye countermanipulation. He artfully crafts his deception and manipulation of his brothers so that they are required to "relive the crime."[171] Beginning with concealing his identity, he strings together a long chain of eye for eye misfortunes for his brothers: speaking harshly to them, falsely accusing them,

---

167. Ackerman, "Joseph, Judah, and Jacob," 111. Lied sees a similar reversal of fortunes in the recognition judgment episode of 2 Bar: "The transformation process that follows judgment does not only serve to intensify the appearances of the wicked and the righteous, it also ensures that the *tables are turned*." Lied, "Recognizing the Righteous Remnant?," 328; emphasis Lied.

168. Sacks, *A Commentary on the Book of Genesis*, 363–64; Alter, *Genesis*, 220.

169. Alter, *Genesis*, 222.

170. Nel, "The Talion Principle in Old Testament Narratives," 27.

171. Ackerman, "Joseph, Judah, and Jacob," 93.

placing them in prison, retaining Simeon in prison, providing payment to them similar to what they received for selling him, and finally offering them the chance to repeat the entire moral travesty.[172] Regarding Joseph disguising his identity, Ackerman describes the moral reinforcing pattern, which the *Leitwort* "recognize" establishes:

> [T]he significant pun, in a technique characteristic of the whole story, *reinforcing the moral pattern of measure for measure*. Joseph's dissembling echoes the brothers' conspiring. In 37:4 "they were not able to speak peaceably to him." Now Joseph "speaks harshly to them" (42:7). *Those who had duped their father into "recognition" are now recognized*. The deceivers are now deceived. The ones who had seen Joseph and conspired against him are now on the receiving end, and the key to the deception is Joseph "acting unrecognizably."[173]

This artful counter-manipulation of the brothers culminates in the realization that they are being required to live a "reenactment of the crime" they ruthlessly carried out earlier on Joseph.[174] Probably the most striking instance of this is in 43:11–13. Here, apart from Joseph's knowing and in addition to the steps Joseph has already required, the narrator describes the brothers' preparation and return trip to Egypt with Benjamin as a possible future slave:

> Then their father Israel said to them, "If it must be so, then do this: take some of the choice fruits of the land in your bags, and carry a present down to the man, a little balm and a little honey, gum, myrrh, pistachio nuts, and almonds. Take double the money with you. Carry back with you the money that was returned in the mouth of your sacks. Perhaps it was an oversight. Take also your brother, and arise, go again to the man."

The brothers reenact the sale of Joseph, carrying gifts, three of which—balm, gum and myrrh—were present on the journey forced upon Joseph, the journey into slavery (Gen 37:25).[175] Other clues to the reliving of the crime are

---

172. Ibid., 90–96; Alter, *Genesis*, 248–62; Lambe, "Judah's Development," 62–65; Sacks, *A Commentary on the Book of Genesis*, 379; Sternberg, *The Poetics of Biblical Narrative*, 288–93; Wenham, *Genesis 16–50*, 406–12.

173. Ackerman, "Joseph, Judah, and Jacob," 90.

174. Ibid., 93.

175. Ibid., 90–93; Alter, *Genesis*, 253; Sternberg, *The Poetics of Biblical Narrative*, 293; Wenham, *Genesis 16–50*, 421; Lambe, "Judah's Development," 21. Alter states, "As with the silver sent back and forth, the brothers are thus drawn unwittingly into a process of repetition and restitution for their fraternal crime." Ackerman explains that

the accusation of being spies, keeping the brothers three days in jail for his three years (a "symbolic measure for measure"),[176] the exchange/payment of silver,[177] and finally an opportunity—though never taken—to once again sell off and rid themselves of one of Rachel's favorite sons. Joseph, therefore, is manipulating them toward the crowning intersection of ignorance versus knowledge and recognition versus lack of recognition. The reader is caught in suspense, wondering in indeterminacy what will happen next.[178] Will the brothers fail? Will they recognize their own guilt first and give Joseph the key sign that they are ready to know who he is? Or will Joseph follow to the end the *talionic* principle and keep one or all of them in prison or worse? Must they first abandon their twenty-year avoidance of guilt, pass from ignorance to self-acknowledgment of their attempt at fratricide, before they can be allowed to recognize Joseph?[179] The reader does not yet know but expects something dramatic.[180]

"Turning" the Manipulator

With regard to Judah's turning, Wenham aptly observes the dramatic change from the Judah who kidnapped and sold Joseph, to the Judah who rescued Benjamin:

> Judah seems to be a hard and callous man ... Yet what a different Judah we meet in 44:18–34. Here he appeals for Benjamin's release with great warmth and tenderness, describing with great love his father's suffering since Joseph's disappearance and foreseeing his sorrowful death if Benjamin is not allowed to return to Canaan. He concludes by offering to stay as a slave in place of

---

what "the brothers' experience is the chronological reverse of the earlier plot: first they suffer what had happened to Joseph during and after the crime; then they relive the crime. Chapter 43, verse 26 describes the literal fulfilling of Joseph's dream and initiates the final doubling that must precede the great climax and denouement of the story. In Aristotle's terms, this is the major reversal and a one-sided recognition episode. Yet to come are the full recognition scene ('I am Joseph') and the final working out of the plot."

176. Sternberg, *The Poetics of Biblical Narrative*, 288–90.

177. Ackerman, "Joseph, Judah, and Jacob," 91–92.

178. Recalling the brief discussion above of Sternberg's "plot intermediacy and plot indeterminacy." Sternberg, *The Poetics of Biblical Narrative*, 117–18, 285, 303–4.

179. "Often, different characters attain to knowledge by different routes ... or even in regard to different objects (Jacob finds out the truth about Joseph, the brothers about themselves)." Ibid., 176; Lambe, "Judah's Development," 63.

180. Sternberg asks, "Will they now opt for the brother or for the money?" Sternberg, *The Poetics of Biblical Narrative*, 293.

Benjamin. Clearly, Judah is a *changed* man, and this story shows the *beginning of the transformation* when he admits 'She is in the right, not I' (38:26). *Without this account of Tamar putting her father-in-law to shame, we would be hard pressed to explain the change in his character.* And in its biographical sketches, *character change is what Genesis is all about.*[181]

We cannot overlook that in many of these counter-manipulation narratives, the turning of the initial manipulator is what is at stake. Judah begins by selfishly attempting to protect his own youngest son from Tamar but concludes with a profound admission of guilt (Gen 38:26).[182] Later, Joseph's counter-manipulation brings not only Judah but also the remaining brothers to a penitent state (39:28; 44:14–16). These counter-manipulations deliver adversity to the initial manipulators in an unsettling way that initial manipulators often *cannot* mistake.[183] The result is that Judah is now willing to sacrifice himself for Jacob's youngest. Sternberg describes the powerful effect of measure for measure retribution as "nothing short of a *transformation*" of the brothers, "in Egypt, where the *reenactment* of the false charge leading to imprisonment *elicits the first words of self-reproach*. On the road, subsequently, the discovery of the money *occasions the first reference to God.*"[184]

When dealing with the saga of Joseph and his brothers, we must also not forget Joseph's transformation. Joseph starts out "strutting like a peacock."[185] However, the unfortunate events of his life are *transformative* as well, making him a suitable vizier for Pharaoh.[186] By the end of Genesis, he weeps when the same brothers struggle to accept his forgiveness (Gen 50:17). Victor Turner's work is applicable to Joseph as well. Turner discusses the "liminality vs. status system" that individuals pass through as they transition from one rite of passage/ritual in life to another. In that state of liminality, when the "neophyte" experiences marginalization, he experiences certain characteristics opposite to what he exhibited while in the "status quo." Of the more than twenty sets of characteristics Turner lists, five speak to the turning of the manipulator to manipulable. These are "Humility/just pride of position," "Unselfishness/selfishness," "Silence/speech," "Total obedience/

---

181. Wenham, *Genesis 16–50*, 364; emphasis added.

182. Ackerman, "Joseph, Judah, and Jacob," 104.

183. Ibid., 91. I will note later in further detail that only in the FG is Peter's grieving delayed after the denial.

184. Sternberg, *The Poetics of Biblical Narrative*, 297, 308; emphasis added.

185. Bialik et. al., *The Book of Legends = Sefer Ha-Aggadah*, 51:90.

186. Sternberg, *The Poetics of Biblical Narrative*, 289, 318.

obedience only to superior rank," and "Acceptance of pain and suffering/avoidance of pain and suffering."[187] Nicholas, in discussing Turner's work, speaks of a "status reversal," which may in fact bring about these changed characteristics.[188]

Moreover, the counter-manipulation is often against the initial manipulator's will. Alter, commenting on Judah's reckoning with Tamar, states that Judah is "*compelled* to acknowledge" the items Tamar presents.[189] Concerning Joseph's brothers' consternation over past wrongs and turning back to a position of appropriate familial relationship, Alter believes that, "Events, or rather events *aided by Joseph's manipulation, force them to knowledge and self-knowledge*, this *arduous transition* providing the final resolution of the whole story."[190] Moreover, Sternberg reminds us that "some (like Joseph) seek knowledge, others (like his brothers) have it forced on them, others still (like Jacob) abruptly gain or stumble on it."[191] Do the manipulators experience misfortune and adversity at the hands of their counter-manipulators, often in an unnerving measure for measure way, in order to produce new attitudes and behaviors heretofore lacking? Surely they do.

Judah's turn is so significant that his speech to Joseph in chapter 44 reveals his own deep desire to reverse the past. By offering himself for Benjamin, he can symbolically or retributively reverse the past. Alter characterizes Judah's speech as "a point-for-point undoing, morally and psychologically, of the brothers' earlier violation of fraternal and filial bonds."[192] In the end, careful readers are left with a dramatic saga of personal transformation and familial reconciliation, which ultimately has a lasting significance in the He-

---

187. Nicholas, *The Trickster Revisited*, 38–39; Turner, *The Ritual Process*, 106–7. Turner's work is a cross-cultural study of the trickster character. Granted, I earlier propose caution regarding cross-cultural analysis of trickster characters, but this phenomenon is still worth noting.

188. Nicholas, *The Trickster Revisited*, 36–39.

189. Alter, *Genesis*, 222; emphasis added.

190. Alter, *The Art of Biblical Narrative*, 159; emphasis added. Niditch alludes to this turning as well, although the result she observes is a turn toward establishment and status quo: "[T]he trickster Jacob himself is portrayed as growing into a more establishmentarian elder. So do we all." Niditch, *Underdogs and Tricksters*, 150. Sacks remarks, "[T]he brothers are forced to remember whom they had placed into the pit." Sacks, *A Commentary on the Book of Genesis*, 365.

191. Sternberg, *The Poetics of Biblical Narrative*, 176. In regards to Judah's turning, he notes: "[A] shift from their collective to his personal responsibility... Judah so feels for his father that he begs to sacrifice himself for a brother more loved than himself. Nothing could do more to establish the depth and genuineness of this feeling than the abrupt loss of control reflected in the switch (verse 34) from ceremonial language to a cry from the heart: he cannot bear to see his father stricken." Ibid., 308.

192. Alter, *The Art of Biblical Narrative*, 174.

brew Bible for the establishment of Israel as a nation, since Judah and Joseph serve as key leaders. Joseph repeatedly says that God chose him to preserve the family (Gen 45:5, 7, 8; 50:20). He goes on to lead the family while in Egypt (49:13–26; 50:1–21), including his vow to "provide for you and your little ones" (50:21). He encourages his brothers that God will deliver them from Egypt (50:24–25). Jacob clarifies both Judah and Joseph's leadership roles in their respective blessings (49: 8–12, 22–26). Finally, 1 Chronicles later attests to how the nation viewed them (1 Chr 5:1–2).

Lambe centers almost his entire article, "Judah's Development: The Pattern of Departure-Transition-Return," on the significance of Judah's turning. He believes that Judah's transformation began with Tamar and was a prerequisite for his role in Egypt, where he was willing to pledge for Benjamin.[193] Lambe recognizes that the stage is set for this turn when, in the opening verses of Genesis 38, the text describes Judah's "alienation from his family, past and heritage" as he "sever[s] ties with his family, and furthers the rupture that was evident in Genesis 37."[194] Not only has Judah walked away from his brothers but, as mentioned above, his lack of mourning underscores that he was callous to his son's death.[195] The text is silent concerning any contemplation by Judah that without Tamar and Shelah coming together, he has no future seed. Ultimately, his "alienation is consummated at the point when he gives up his insignia."[196] Indeed a turn is needed. However, when Tamar presents him with his items of identification, Judah begins his *transition*. His recognition was *not* merely that of his seal, cord, and staff. The recognition was one of self, of wrong, of departure from familial ties, including his obligation to Tamar, and possibly "a realization of his deception of and injustice to his father and Joseph."[197]

In counter-manipulation therefore, recognition also becomes the *dénouement*, whereby the manipulator sees into the mirror. The irony is that thwarting recognition is a device of the initial manipulator and counter-manipulator, but true recognition, of oneself and others, is later the mark of the transformed manipulator. The enhanced diagram below of Judah's manipulation and counter-manipulation demonstrates the irony of *lex talionis* and its effect of turning the manipulator.

---

193. Lambe, "Judah's Development," 55.
194. Ibid.
195. Ibid.
196. Ibid., 56, 58. He is just like Esau, who despised his birthright.
197. Ibid., 57–59.

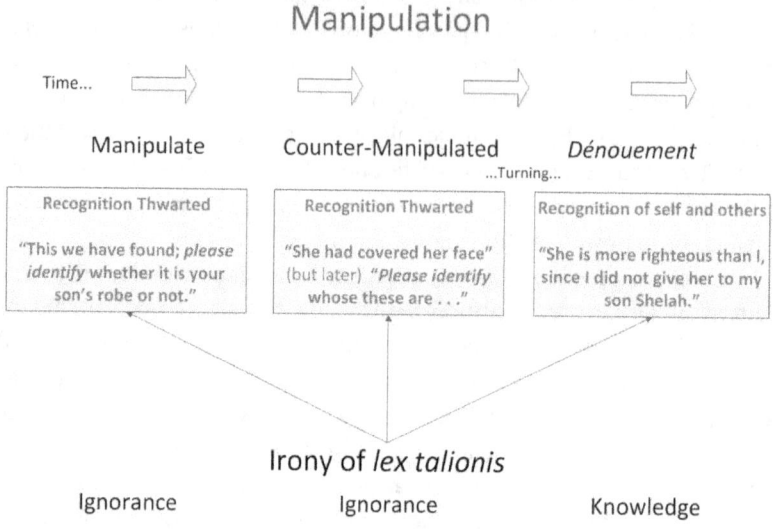

Summary

Thus, when looking back at the key characters, we see that Jacob was a chosen manipulator as evident in the oracle to Rebekah (Gen 25). His character is in much need of development, as revealed by a life of continuing deceptive manipulation. His episodes are littered with *Leitwörter*, especially the term *recognize*—the favorite manipulation device used by Jacob and his family. Evocative words and symbols haunt him in a *déjà vu* like fashion, forcing him to link the past to the present. He disempowers Laban by relieving him of much of his material wealth in a tit for tat chain of retributive acts of manipulation. In the end, Jacob is the one counter-manipulated, not only by Laban and Judah and his brothers, but also unknowingly by his favorite son. In the end, he is forcibly transformed from the supreme manipulator into pliable, elderly Israel who is willing to be manipulable for the sake of the preservation of his family and nation: "If it must be so . . . May God Almighty grant you mercy before the man, and may he send back your other brother and Benjamin. And as for me, if I am bereaved of my children, I am bereaved" (43:11, 14).

Jacob's manipulation series overlaps and culminates in the Judah series. Judah is a character who begins his journey perhaps more deeply mired in the character development process than any other of the chosen manipulators in Genesis. However, in order to be a key leader in Israel's history, he must taste his own medicne and change. The centrality of Judah's character is especially significant in the manipulation narratives. Genesis verifies his importance and place in Israel's history by virtue of his blessing in chapter 49:9–12, where Jacob says that Judah will rule over his enemies and receive the praises of his brothers. Judah's role in the line of David, through the son of Tamar, was also not lost on the nation of Israel (1 Chr 2; Ruth 4). Thus, in a sense, Judah's series becomes the culminating set of manipulation narratives with this fourth son as the prime example of an evil initial manipulator. He begins his schemes by causing his father to recognize incorrectly. Tamar and Joseph forcefully turn him by counter-manipulation, measure for measure via thwarted recognition. These manipulations transform him into a character that is manipulable in the Genesis plot line of God's story. After a life of disempowering Joseph, Jacob, and Tamar, the same type of evocative motifs that haunted Judah's father now haunt him. The disempowerment and counter-manipulation via thwarted recognition by Tamar as well as Joseph forced him to reckon with his past. These episodes transform him from ignorance to knowledge of himself and his obligations to his family. Simply said, he is strikingly different. He is now ready to be the leader of the nation of Israel for which antiquity goes on to celebrate him (1 Chr 5:1–2; Ruth 4:12).

The manipulation narratives in Genesis bear a resemblance to some of the narratives of manipulation and *anagnorisis* in the FG. As such, they have an important bearing for understanding the manipulation series centered on Peter in John 21. Having surveyed these manipulation narratives and developed tools with which to proceed, I will now turn to the Fourth Gospel.

6

Applying a Manipulation Perspective to John 21:1–14

Introductory Matters

Reading Intertextually between Genesis and John

Our question now becomes, "Does any of this have an impact on a reading of John 21?" In his important study, *Reading John in Ephesus*, Sjef van Tilborg writes:

> In my own vision the Gospel of John, or at least the final version of this Gospel, originated in a Jewish quarter of a Hellenistic city... Yet in this study I am not going to try and *prove* that the Johannine Gospel belongs in Ephesus. To avoid the danger of circular argumentation it is necessary to find a way in between. I believe I have found it in the supposition that—notwithstanding the existence of many different opinions—it is important to study how John's text was read or *could have been read* in first century Ephesus.[1]

Tilborg argues for an understanding of how the FG "could have been read" if authored from or read in Ephesus. This gives him a starting point for examining the relevance of Ephesian inscriptions.[2] Tilborg is not intending to prove necessarily an Ephesian origin, and neither am I arguing for an original Johannine readership that was well versed in the Genesis material,[3]

---

1. Tilborg, *Reading John in Ephesus*, 3; emphasis added.
2. Ibid.
3. Though I do believe it nearly impossible to imagine a Johannine author who did not expect at least some of the intended readers to be aquainted with Genesis.

nor that the readers consciously or actively thought of the Genesis manipulation stories or form when reading John 21. This study is asking how John 21 "could have been read" by Johannine readers who were significantly influenced by the Genesis manipulation narratives.[4] How would such readers *understand* (whether or not they actively pondered or realized this) manipulative behavior in Peter and subsequently integrate this into their reading of Jesus' actions with him? Such an audience would be informed not only by the *content* of Genesis but by ancient Hebrew narrative *form* as well.

By its very nature, this method of reading is based in intertextuality. Jean Zumstein reminds us that intertextuality is all about connections, as "every text triggers connections to other texts within its reader's memory."[5] This study is therefore reading John with the heuristic assumption that the FG has triggered its readers' memories of literary content and form from Genesis, whether or not they were *aware* it had triggered them, for narratives can trigger ideas without names, places, or specific stories in history.[6] Some readers could have been aware of such a connection, and others simply subliminally allowed facets of the larger literary world of the time to color their reading of the text, with many other readers scattered along a continuum in between. This then constitutes a spectrum of intertextual reading influence:

---

4. Brooke, in his attempt to shed light on the 153 fish phenomenon, uses a somewhat similar method with the texts of 4Q252 and John 21:11, using the former text to "illuminate" the latter. Brooke, "4Q252 and the 153 Fish of John 21:11," 253.

5. "The Gospel of John . . . is a networked text, that is, an intertext. Although it is usually read and interpreted as an autonomous literary unit, it presumes the existence of other writings, some of which possess canonical status, the Hebrew Bible being a paradigmatic example." Zumstein, "Intratextuality and Intertextuality in the Gospel of John," 121.

6. Such as one might recognize a rags to riches story in a romance film without consciously thinking of *Cinderella* or *Pride and Prejudice*, both of which may have an intertextual element with the modern film, *Maid in Manhattan*.

Orality and "Reading"

Also important to address here are the issues of orality and aurality in the ancient world. Reccent research has greatly informed our understanding of how the ancients handled information, namely, how they composed, delivered, and received texts in their original communities. Anthony LeDonne and Tom Thatcher's 2011 collection of essays, *The Fourth Gospel in First-Century Media Culture*, serves as a prime example of this perspective.[7] However, scholars as far back as the 1950s had wrestled with how an understanding of oral culture influenced the interpretation of ancient texts.[8] In more recent decades, research has steadily increased with key works such as Birger Gerhardsson's *The Origins of the Gospel Traditions* (1979), Walter Ong's monumental *Orality and Literacy: The Technologizing of the Word* (1982), and Werner Kelber's *The Oral and the Written Gospel: The Hermeneutics of Speaking and Writing in the Synoptic Tradition, Mark, Paul, and Q* (1983).[9] More recent is Catherine Hezser's *Jewish Literacy in Roman Palestine* (2001).[10] This entire body of literature takes seriously that literacy was rare in the ancient world—and this affects nearly *everything* when handling biblical texts. Indeed, some scholars have proposed that as little as five percent of the population could read.[11]

Most ancients had to rely on a public reading by a lector.[12] Even private reading was typically accomplished aloud.[13] This causes us to realize that modern researchers, including this one, have "uncritically" read literacy, as well as silent reading, "back into the ancient world."[14] Subsequently, then, we must realize that ancient authors wrote with the oral performance in mind, possibly framing the work while keeping in mind that the lector might perform the text "in character," speaking directly to the audience, as each given character in the narrative.[15] Thus, a lector of the FG at times

---

7. Le Donne and Thatcher, *The Fourth Gospel in First-Century Media Culture*.

8. Hadas, *Ancilla to Classical Reading*.

9. Gerhardsson, *The Origins of the Gospel Traditions*; Ong, *Orality and Literacy*; Kelber, *The Oral and the Written Gospel*.

10. Hezser, *Jewish Literacy in Roman Palestine*.

11. Rhoads and Michie, *Mark as Story*, xii. Some however, argue for literacy rates as high as twenty-five percent. See also Boomershine, "The Medium and Message in John," 99n12; Thatcher, "John's Memory Theatre," 75.

12. Note Neh 8:3, 18.

13. Those who could read rarely read in silence. Boomershine, "The Medium and Message in John," 92. Note the wealth and position of the eunuch who was able to read and the fact that Phillip "heard" him reading from Isaiah (Acts 8:27–30).

14. Boomershine, "The Medium and Message in John," 99.

15. Ibid.

would act—"in character"—talking for instance, as Jesus, then switching to speaking as the narrator, or any other voice in the text, as that character might speak.[16] Fittingly, we can therefore label the "reader" alternatively as "listener" or as a member of the audience. This understanding of orality and aurality has many implications.

A spoken delivery of a text lent itself to varied nuances, which the lector interpreted, and then delivered through gestures, inflections, pauses, and pace.[17] Realizing that lectors read with such inflection has a profound impact on how one interprets texts today.

While scholars have tended to treat oral history as "inferior" to written history, or a "dispensable medium on the way to a written refinement," these ideas are now being challenged.[18] No doubt this mistaken notion is a result of living in a post-enlightenment world in which printed media has become normative. The understanding of the oral transmission of texts has also resulted in new questions with regard to textual criticism. The notion of a fixed original manuscript has been re-opened, and scholars are examining how we approach variants with a new and even "fluid" lens.[19]

Another aspect of orality is its effect on what one might call the "capture" of allusions, *Leitwörter*, and other literary devices such as *inclusio*.[20] Since a Gospel was often performed or recited in one sitting, listeners may have been more apt to catch such ploys of literary artistry. Since the FG takes approximately three hours to recite,[21] a single event of listening to the entire story may not have been uncommon.[22] In such a setting, members of the audience may have been much quicker to recognize the repetition of, for example, *charcoal*, separated by three chapters, than a modern reader may be (John 18:18; 21:9).[23] In modern ecclesiastical circles, where one is often urged to read perhaps a chapter (or less) from the Bible each day, a reader is less likely to catch the connection when three days or more between readings separate the two instances of charcoal. This assumes, of course, that the

---

16. Ibid., 92–93. Envisioning such a performance sharpens the intensity of John 20:29: "Jesus said to him, 'Have you believed because you have seen me? Blessed are those who have not seen and yet have believed.'"

17. Le Donne and Thatcher, *The Fourth Gospel in First-Century Media Culture*, 5.

18. Ibid., 2; O'Day, "Introducing Media Culture to Johannine Studies," 241.

19. See Keith, "A Performance of the Text," 49–72, for his analysis of how orality affects an understanding of the Pericope Adulterae.

20. Spencer, "Narrative Echoes in John 21," 55.

21. Boomershine, "The Medium and Message," 100.

22. Note again Neh 8:3–18, where an audience listened from first light until midday.

23. Although, a trained modern reader might at least note "a purely 'factual' bond between the two passages." Burke, *Terms for Order*, 149.

reader reads every day and continues reading the same book of the Bible, a practice that may be rare. Allusions, repetitions, and the like were probably more a part of active reading in the ancient world than they are today.

Orality affects intertextuality as well, for readers may have quite commonly known of texts from recitations they themselves had heard, as well as from word of mouth. This may affect our understanding of whether the author of the FG, or its implied readers, were aware of any Synoptic traditions. Indeed, the relationship between the Synoptics and the FG is a long and storied one. Many scholars have debated whether the FE knew of, used, or relied on the Synoptics. What scholarship has produced in the last several decades regarding orality may bring more clarity to the issue of the relationship between the Synoptics and the FG.

James Dunn uses an understanding of ancient oral storytelling to show structural parallels in all four Gospels and argued that "[t]here can be little doubt that all four Evangelists were drawing on the same tradition."[24] Zumstein argues that to a degree, regardless of whether or not the FE relies on the Synoptics, the church named it "The Gospel according to John," and thus it was received and read as a part of the *Gospels* collection. How early this happened of course we do not know, but he argued that the FG was then "in a relationship with already extant narratives. From this point on the Johannine *vita Jesu* would be read as a 'Gospel.'" Zumstein also argues that the prepositional phrase "according to John . . . suggests that the work does not articulate just any gospel but *the* gospel itself. The Gospel of John is introduced as a legitimate expression of the one gospel."[25]

Bultmann argues strongly for reliance upon the Synoptic material, though this is now "widely regarded as unproved."[26] Dodd emphatically opposes this type of argument, seeing John's independence from Synoptic influence. In his second commentary on John, he expends quite an amount of energy comparing passages to the Synoptics. He concludes that "in no case is there the remotest likelihood of derivation from Synoptic sources." Dodd believes the FE drew from "an ancient tradition independent of the other gospels."[27] Brown calls Dodd's work "an exhaustive defense of Johannine independence" and himself saw little reliance upon the Synoptics.[28] Over four decades ago, he proposed a staged history of composition that has

---

24. Dunn, "John's Gospel and the Oral Gospel Tradition," 163. No doubt, some will challenge Dunn's conclusion.

25. Zumstein, "Intratextuality and Intertextuality in the Gospel of John," 129.

26. Bultmann, *The Gospel of John*, 6–7; Keener, *The Gospel of John*, 1:37; Sloyan, *What Are They Saying about John?*, 8–23.

27. Dodd, *Historical Tradition in the Fourth Gospel*, 423.

28. Brown, *The Gospel according to John (I–XII)*, xliv.

earned a following for much time. Stage one (of five) was a collection stage, oral and independent of the Synoptics. He does however, voice the possibility of "minor cross-influence from the Synoptic tradition" in the later stages of his proposed compositional history.[29] Concerning chapter 21 and the knowledge that the disciples were fishermen, he writes, "However, it is rash to assume that the evangelist did not know this; he sometimes assumes a general Christian knowledge of details."[30] Timothy Wiarda too examines John 21 from both perspectives, arguing in the end that the FE intended for Peter, as well as the readers, to see the "connection between the symbolism attached to the catch of fish in Luke 5 and its relevance in John 21."[31]

Literary dependence on the Synoptic material is, of course, not the same as awareness of it. Rudolf Schnackenburg, who also argues that the FE did not rely on the Synoptics, points out that awareness and dependence are two different issues.[32] Robert Fortna too argues that in the end one cannot say for certain that John is dependent on the Synoptics or an unknown source but, similar to Schnackenburg, believes that at the same time one must keep a watchful eye for redactive editing. He called this approach, where interpretation takes place while watching with an eye to both angles, a "Steroptic" approach.[33] Earlier, Barrett had demonstrated that the Johannine/Synoptic argument was indeed, by necessity, moving from a simple issue of dependence to include awareness apart from dependence. He posited that "John did not use any of the synoptic gospels as, for example, Matthew used Mark" but that he "had read Mark, and was influenced both positively and negatively by its contents" and that "a few of John's statements may be most satisfactorily explained if he was familiar with matter peculiar to Luke."[34] Even over two decades before that, Edwyn Hoskyns posited a similar position, saying, "The readers of the gospel are presumed to be familiar with the earlier tradition."[35] More recently, Ben Witherington argues that the FE did not rely on the Synoptics but agrees that whether he knew of them is a *different* argument.[36] And most recently, Richard Bauckham reasons that the FG was intended for a broader audience that was in fact

---

29. Ibid., xxxiv, xliv–xlv.
30. Brown, *The Gospel according to John (XIII–XXI)*, 1069.
31. Wiarda, "John 21.1–23," 57–59, 71.
32. Schnackenburg, *The Gospel according to John*, 3:37, 41.
33. Fortna, "Diachronic/Synchronic," 387–99.
34. Barrett, *The Gospel according to St. John*, 34.
35. Hoskyns and Davey, *The Fourth Gospel*, 432.
36. Witherington III, *John's Wisdom*, 35.

diverse, anticipating some readers who were aware of such materials and others who were not.[37]

An example of such awareness is the FE's sudden introduction of John the Baptist as "John" in 1:6 and 1:19 without further explanation.[38] Two chapters later then, the FE offers the *prolepsis* of the imprisonment of that same character in 3:24 without additional details. This parenthetical aside suggests the possibility that the FE expected implied readers to have some familiarity with this tradition.[39] Another instance is in John 11:2, where the narrator refers readers to Mary anointing Jesus' feet with oil, an event the narrator does not explain until 12:3. The FE may assume readers will be aware enough of this story to refer to it before it is narrated. Patrick Spencer argues for such a position: "[T]here is evidence in the earlier version of the Gospel that the authorial reader possesses information regarding certain characters based upon outside traditions that the narrator invites the reader to draw upon in order to interpret the narrative (e.g., Mary and Martha in John 11.1–2)."[40] Nevertheless, even with this myriad of positions, Keener aptly concludes that the FE "goes his own way," regardless of what we think of his sources.[41]

Therefore, given scholarship on this issue, and considering the oral and aural nature of the first century world, I have chosen to read the FG from the perspective that the FE was aware and believed some of his intended readers were also aware of at least some portions of the Synoptic tradition. Moreover, one cannot overstate the oral nature of the New Testament world: when we surmise that a reader was aware of Synoptic material, this by no means implies that she had read the other Gospels, or even heard one of them in its entirety. Accordingly, the reality of an ancient oral culture implies that one could be aware of parts or units of the Synoptics without knowing an entire Gospel or Gospels. Some may have heard parts repeated from what others had heard in entirety. Therefore, the reading of the FG that best brings the pieces of the puzzle together includes deducing that the Johannine intended readers were aware of portions of the Synoptic traditions, rather than a readership completely unexposed to it.

37. Bauckham, *Jesus and the Eyewitnesses*, 122.
38. Brown, *The Gospel according to John (XIII–XXI)*, 1069.
39. But less certain is Borchert, *John 1–11*, 190.
40. Spencer, "Narrative Echoes in John 21," 58.
41. Keener, *The Gospel of John*, 1:37–42. For a thorough history of scholarly positions on the relationship of the FG with the Synoptics, see Smith, *John among the Gospels*. See also Culpepper, *The Gospel and Letters of John*, 245; Pfitzner, "They Knew It Was the Lord," 64–74; Culpepper, "Designs for the Church in the Imagery of John 21:1–14," 64–68.

Overview of John 21

A short summary of the passage follows in order to reacquaint my readers with it. In the preceding chapters, Jesus twice appears to his disciples as a group since the resurrection. Chapter 20 concludes with the well-known statement of purpose for the preceding chapters. The reader then hears, "After this" Jesus revealed himself to his disciples again, this time "by the sea of Tiberias" (John 21:1). Immediately the story informs readers about some of those on this fishing expedition. The evangelilst names Peter, Thomas, and Nathanael and refers to the two sons of Zebedee as such, but does not name them. Two other disciples are noted as well, though unidentified. Readers learn later that one of these seven is "That disciple whom Jesus loved" (21:7). Peter then announces his intentions to go fishing and the others decide to accompany him. They venture out in the boat, fish all night, and catch nothing. As day breaks, Jesus stands on the shore unrecognized by the seven. He asks them, "Children, do you have any to eat?," to which they respond in the negative. He then instructs them to cast the net again, but this time on the right hand side of the boat, and the result is an abundant catch—too abundant to pull aboard. The BD then informs Peter, "It is the Lord!" Responding, Peter dresses himself and "threw himself into the sea" (21:7). The remaining six follow in the boat, dragging the net. The reader learns the disciples are not far away, but only two hundred cubits from shore. When they reach land, they see a charcoal fire with fish and bread. Jesus instructs them to bring some of their catch, and Peter alone returns to the boat, hauling the net ashore to retrieve the fish—153 of them.[42] Despite so large a catch, the

---

42. On the topic of the 153 fish, and whether this number is symbolic, Carson aptly states, "Large quantities of ink have gone into explaining why there should be 153 fish." Carson, *The Gospel according to John*, 672. Wiarda counters, "it is sufficient to note that the text offers the reader no hint concerning any symbolism in the miraculous catch of fish." Wiarda, "John 21.1–23," 60. Limitations of space and purpose do not avail here for us to debate which argument is best, whether the 153 is an instance only of historical vividness or whether it is symbolic, and if the latter, which explanation of the symbol is the better choice. Ibid., 15. Keener believes the number "could simply stem from an accurate memory of a careful count on the occasion, because fish had to be counted to be divided among fisherman; 153 is too exact for a round number (such as 150)." Keener, *The Gospel of John*, 2:1233. However, I am not opposed to seeing some symbolic significance in the number, as well as a historical meaning. Brown argues well that one should examine the possibility of symbolism carefully. "On the principle that where there is smoke there is fire, we would concede to the above-mentioned interpretations the likelihood that the number may be meant to symbolize the breadth or even the universality of the Christian mission." Brown, *The Gospel according to John (XIII–XXI)*, 1075. But Pfitzner disagrees, "No need to speculate on the precise meaning of the 153 fish," noting that these arguments are "never quite convincing." Pfitzner, "They Knew It Was the Lord," 73. The arguments for a symbolic meaning usually see an ecclesiastical

net is not torn. Jesus invites the disciples to join him and eat their morning meal. Finally, now knowing the identity of Jesus, the disciples are silent and do not "dare to ask him 'Who are you?'" (21:12). Jesus takes the bread, gives it to them, and does the same with the fish. The unit is book-ended (*inclusio*) with the statement "This was now the third time that Jesus was revealed to the disciples after he was raised from the dead" (21:14).

Moving on, the FE takes listeners to the conclusion of the meal with "When they had finished breakfast, Jesus said to Simon." Jesus asks Peter, "Do you love me?" three times. Jesus couples the first question with the comparative phrase πλέον τούτων, "more than these." Though the response

---

meaning, such as Jerome's argument that the 153 represents all the species of fish mentioned by Oppian's in his *Halieutica* and thus pointing symbolically to the universality of Peter's mission. However, Jerome was working with a secondary source and the best count of actual fish species comes to only 149. Grant, "'One Hundred Fifty-Three Large Fish' (John 21:11)," 273–75. Much reflection has also gone into the assertion that the number seventeen is a triangular number behind the number 153. In this theory, each of the descending numbers beginning with seventeen, then continuing with sixteen, fifteen, fourteen, thirteen, and so forth, is represented by a row of dots, and when each row is stacked upon each other, the resulting image is a triangle in which the total number of dots is 153. Speculation then proceeds on the significance of the number seventeen. The table of seventeen nations at the Day of Pentecost in Acts 2 is one instance, thus signifying the totality and inclusivity of Peter's catch. Culpepper, "Designs for the Church in the Imagery of John 21:1–14," 21. Gematria accounts for much of the remaining speculation. In gematria, letters in a word each have a corresponding number and the word therefore has a total value. This numerical value has significance that scholars often relate to other texts or themes. Ibid. A well-known instance of gematria, even among non-scholars, is the 666 in Rev 13:18, where some thought 666 corresponded to the Hebrew of the name *Nero Caesar*. Sanders, "The Number of the Beast in Revelation," 97. The connection between gematria and 153 lies in a connection with the eschatological text of Ezek 47:10 "Fishermen will stand beside the sea. From Engedi to Eneglaim it will be a place for the spreading of nets. Its fish will be of very many kinds, like the fish of the Great Sea." The Hebrew numerical value of Gedi is seventeen and that of Eglaim is 153, but some, by working with variants, have also seen the total numerical sum of the two as 153. Brown, *The Gospel according to John (XIII-XXI)*, 1075. On the Hebrew gematria, Culpepper writes, "The numbers not only correspond, but the context does too, as Ezekiel looks to the future, refers to casting the nets, and the ingathering of fish of many kinds." He also, among others, notes the connection with Matt 13:47, "The kingdom of heaven is like a net that was thrown into the sea and caught fish of every kind." Culpepper, "Designs for the Church in the Imagery of John 21:1–14," 6, 23, 26; Shaw, "Breakfast by the Shore," 16; Hoskyns and Davey, *The Fourth Gospel*, 554. Bauckham argues that the FE extensively used numbers not only in gematria, but also in an astounding feat of syllable counting and word counting for thematic as well as stylistic reasons. He combines the triangular number argument with gematria to argue that 153 refers to the messianic texts of Ezek 47, Zech 14:8, and Ps 78:16. Bauckham, *The Testimony of the Beloved Disciple*, 271–84. Although not necessary for my argument, the possibility exists that the FE used the number for both historical vividness and ecclesiastical symbolism.

of feed/tend my lambs/sheep changes each time, the basic question remains the same, until the change in the third occurrence to the verb φιλέω, which Peter has used the previous two times to affirm his love. To this final question, Peter, grievingly, affirms, κύριε, πάντα σὺ οἶδας, σὺ γινώσκεις ὅτι φιλῶ σε, "Lord, all things you know, you know that I love you." To each answer, Jesus replies with a command to feed/tend his sheep/lambs, but varies both the verb and the direct object in each instance. Jesus then predicts the method of Peter's glorifying death, in which he will "stretch out" his hands, be dressed by others, and led where he does not want to go (John 21:18). This prophetic statement is likely an allusion to Peter's death by crucifixion.[43] Jesus then commands Peter to follow him. In the final five verses of the chapter, Peter turns and sees the BD following, as the narrator reminds the audience of chapter 13 where the BD reclined on Jesus' breast and Peter asked about the betrayer (13:25). Jesus, mildly or not, rebukes Peter: Jesus' plans for the BD are not Peter's concern. Instead, Jesus repeats his command to Peter, "Follow me." This time the command is prefaced with the emphatic "σύ." The narrator then dispels the rumor that the BD would not die. The narrator affirms the authoritative source of the BD and then concludes that the world could not contain all the books if all that Jesus did were recorded.

For the purposes of this analysis, I will limit my discussion almost entirely to the first nineteen verses, and in this chapter, to the first fourteen. I concede both that this is a rather large body of material, and that the Genesis material I discussed in previoius chapters was even larger still. However, in some cases, to shorten an already lengthy study, I will only refer to or footnote the work of others on significant issues, such as the debate of the 153 fish. My overall goal is to strengthen the interpretation of John 21 by gleaning what we can from Genesis manipulation narratives. I will also, of necessity, examine other sections of the FG, such as Peter's denial in John 18. Turning now to the text, I will examine the possible nuances gained from reading the *anagnorisis* of John 21 through the lens of the motif of Genesis manipulation.

Manipulation Kernels

In applying the theory of manipulation to the interactions between Jesus and Peter at the close of the FG, I should point out at this juncture that I am by no means asserting that the six kernels of manipulation are present in and will yield identical results with all the remaining Johannine recognition narratives. For instance, no apparent manipulation exists leading to John

43. Morris, *The Gospel according to John*, 876. Michaels, *The Gospel of John*, 1048.

the Baptist saying, "I myself did not know him" (John 1:31). The purpose of examining Genesis manipulation was to see if it can shed light on recognition in John 21. This theory of manipulation is a tool, which may also yield interpretive insight on other narratives in the FG. Such research will have to be conducted beyond this work. Nevertheless, I have here asked what the nature of Genesis recognition is, and how it may affect an understanding of John 21. As I argued in chapter 4, Genesis encapsulates recognition, as a narrative kernel, within narratives of manipulation. The same is true of Peter's recognition of Jesus at the close of the FG.

To analyze the recognition in John 21 using this taxonomy of manipulation, we must first examine Peter's manipulation of his accusers in John 18:15–27. In this scene, Peter acts as an initial manipulator. We first ask what is the *desired benefit* (kernel number one) Peter seeks to gain by lying about his association with Jesus. Though Peter was willing to fight in the previous scene, once the odds have turned and Jesus' arrest is complete, the possibility of arrest and danger may have increased in Peter's mind. This indicates a round character, who, as Chatman reminds us, can change suddenly, and surprise the reader: round characters "possess a variety of traits, some of them conflicting or even contradictory."[44] The location has changed too, and Peter is now in the courtyard of the high priest (John 18:15). Peter's denials imply that he now denies Jesus to avoid further association and possible arrest and harm to himself. When looking at the *manipulation* kernel (number two), we see that Peter is not as shrewd as Laban in his manipulation. Peter simply lies, boldfaced, three times. When asked if he is one of Jesus' disciples, he replies, "I am not." Two of these are communicated by direct character statement (18:17, 25), and the third is reported by the narrator: "Peter again denied it" (18:27). The narrator does not state that Peter avoids arrest or harm (*the benefit achieved*, kernel number three). Nevertheless, the course of the story implies that Peter circumvents these negative consequences because, though the characters in the courtyard believe they have recognized him as a disciple, Peter is free to move about and travel after the crucifixion (20:3). As in the story of Jacob's sons and Shechem, no true confirmation of *recognition* (kernel number four) occurs in the text. Though we can deduce that in the story world of the murder of Shechem, the men of the city likely recognized the truth of the deception, those in the courtyard may not have ever recognized that Peter had deceived them. Furthermore, though the Synoptics record Peter's weeping (Matt. 26:75; Mark. 14:72; Luke 22:62), the FE does not portrays such self-recognition by Peter

---

44. They "may inspire a stronger sense of intimacy, despite the fact that they do not 'add up.'" Chatman, *Story and Discourse*, 132.

at this moment. Like the previous kernel, there is no *statement or challenge in response to the realization* (kernel number five). Yet, the narrator, by stating that a rooster crows (John 18:27), provides a denunciation of Peter's behavior as that which was foretold by Jesus earlier (13:38). Peter is a deceiver as well as a deserter. We can also see the *effect of the manipulation on the plot as well as the characterization* (kernel number six). A degree of reversal occurs as Peter moves from being an outspoken leader of Jesus' disciples (6:68; 13:37), one who is willing to fight for Jesus with the sword (18:10), to one who denies any association with Jesus at all. The story characterizes Peter, by his own words, as unpredictable and *not* a disciple of Jesus (18:17, 25, 27). The fulfillment of the prophecy, which Jesus stated as a response to Peter's boast (13:37, 38), strengthens the negative characterization of Peter: though he boasted he would die for Jesus, he had been *ignorant* of his own self and his future actions. Furthermore, he associates with those who arrest Jesus, his enemies (18:18). I will return to this point later, but by the principle of economy of detail, we see that the FE has intentionally elaborated this characterization, using three statements to direct the reader's attention to Peter's actions (18:18, 25).[45] Jesus however, by Peter's actions, is characterized positively as *knowing* what lies ahead; all the while, his sacrificial trial is intercalated with alternating scenes of Peter's denial.[46]

We can now see how walking through each of the six kernels of manipulation itemizes Peter's behavior. Peter's actions are deceptive and manipulative for a certain desired end—his own well-being. While he demonstrated either bravery or bravado in the garden, the story now characterizes him as a deceptive defector. Though his accusers rightly suspect they recognize him as Jesus' disciple, his denials effectively prevent their full recognition, and they never actually confirm their suspicions. Although Peter safely eludes any negative repercussions, a rooster, as predicted, crows, narratively responding to and notifying Peter, as well as the reader, of the deception. This sets the stage for the episode in John 21, where Jesus, I propose, counter-manipulates Peter.

In chapter 21, the benefit Jesus desires to achieve by the manipulation of the disciples is also not stated, and we must look for implications and statements by the characters and narrator that allude to this. I believe the text implies that the goal is to turn the disciples, especially Peter, back to a proper relationship to Jesus as a follower, disciple, and shepherd. We can

---

45. 1. "Now the servants and officers had made a charcoal fire, because it was cold, and they were standing and warming themselves" (18:18a). 2. "Peter also was with them, standing and warming himself" (18:18b). 3. "Now Simon Peter was standing and warming himself" (18:25).

46. Quast, *Peter and the Beloved Disciple*, 85.

infer these things by how Jesus concludes his time with Peter, commanding Peter to follow him, and feed his sheep in verses 15–19. The narrator also marks the BD's following of Jesus in verse 20, who sets the standard for the others. The continuation of the story from chapter 18 implies that Jesus' manipulation in the opening verses of chapter 21 serves as a correction and restoration regarding Peter's lying in chapter 18. As I discuss below, scholarship has debated whether these disciples are somehow off track in following Jesus. If this is the case, then the manipulation also serves to correct the aimless fishing. I shall also discuss below that the *Leitwort* "charcoal" ties this scene to Peter's denial and that Jesus' threefold questioning of Peter serves as a *lex talionis* mirror of Peter's denial.

Jesus carries out his *manipulation* through masking by space, ambiguous language, and omission. He is located on the shore and the disciples are away from shore in the boat. Later, however, the narrator says, "they were not far from the land, but about a hundred yards off" (John 21:8).[47] Jesus uses ambiguous language when, after appearing on the shore, he calls the disciples "children," rather than by any of their names or an appellation such as "my disciples." If he had, they would have realized he was someone they knew, if not Jesus himself. The reader knows both parties, but by calling the disciples "children," Jesus prolongs their ignorance until after the miraculous catch. We are beginning to see here that Jesus has intentionally delayed the disciples' recognition of him. And he has recently done the same, when, rather than at first calling Mary by name, he referred to her ambiguously as "woman" (20:15). Moments later, she demonstrates that she does not understand his resurrection with the words, "tell me where you have laid him, and I will take him away" (20:15). Resurrected bodies do not need to be placed or taken away by others. Mary supposes Jesus is still dead and his body had to be physically moved: "where you have *laid* him and I will *take* him away" (20:15). After this, he responds with "Mary" (20:16). By calling Mary "woman" and the disciples "children," Jesus' ambiguity delays their recognition of him even further and sharpens for the reader, the lack of recognition. In John 21, Jesus' manipulation is also emphasized by his omission of a useful piece of information—Jesus never gives his name anywhere in the narrative, though readers are told.[48] Again, Jesus related to Mary in the same way in chapter 20. Moreover, Johannine readers also know that Jesus could have simply walked out on the water to speak to them (John 6:19).

---

47. The distance alone may not be significant enough for a failed identification of Jesus, since this phrase serves to explain how the disciples could get to shore dragging the net (21:8), thus indicating it was not far.

48. Johannine readers also know that Jesus could have simply walked out on the water to speak to them (John 6:19).

APPLYING A MANIPULATION PERSPECTIVE TO JOHN 21:1–14

These manipulation devices, including the spatial distance, the ambivalent address, and the withholding of his name, as well as the statement that "Jesus revealed himself" (21:1), indicate, I argue, that Jesus' withholding of his identity was intentional.

In this episode, both the *recognition* and the *response* occur before the narrative signals any *benefit achieved* from Jesus' manipulation. Upon seeing the token of a miraculous netting of fish, the BD exclaims, "It is the Lord" (John 21:7), which informs the reader of the recognition as well as the response. This is not a challenge to the manipulation, but it is a verbal response. Not all responses to manipulations are challenges (Judah responded, with "She is more righteous than I," which was not a challenge, Gen 38:26). Peter also responds by casting himself into the sea (21:7). When the disciples arrive on shore, they are confronted with the presence of bread and fish, which is reminiscent of Jesus' miraculous feeding in chapter 6.[49] Recalling this miracle further verifies Jesus' identity. The disciples respond to this in silence. Later, an additional recognition occurs: Peter concedes that Jesus knows all things, which, by implication, is a self-recognition that in contrast to Jesus, he himself does not know (21:17). This is a reversal of Peter's statement in 6:69 that "we have come to know," and his later statement, claiming he would lay down his life for Jesus (13:37). The logic of such a statement is that Peter thought he *knew* that he would never deny Jesus, which, of course, proved false.

To determine if the *benefit was achieved*, we look to a number of locations in the text. First, the disciples are silenced by Jesus' presence and the miraculous catch. The description of the disciples' reluctance was followed by the narrator's statement, "They knew it was the Lord" (John 21:12). By choosing the title "the Lord," the narrator implies that they recognize his resurrected state. This is needed for a proper relationship to Jesus in terms of believing and following (20:31). When Peter responds in verse 17 that *Jesus* knows all things, his implied self-recognition of ignorance, also indicates that Jesus is achieving his goal of correcting Peter. Finally, the narrator's statement, "This he said to show by what kind of death he was to glorify God" is a *prolepsis*, indicating that at some point beyond the narrative world of the FG, Peter's relationship to Jesus, his following as a disciple at least at the end of his life, aligns with Jesus' intended goals for Peter's counter-manipulation. Rather than deny Jesus, he follows Jesus, glorifying God in his death.

There are multiple *effects of Jesus' counter-manipulation on the plot and characterization*. First, regarding plot, when Jesus forecasts Peter's death as

---

49. I will discuss this further below.

against Peter's own will and in a manner that glorifies God, careful readers will observe that this is a complete reversal of Peter's actions in the courtyard. In that scene, Peter asserts his own will over his fate. By reporting Peter's denials as "I am not," the FE casts Peter disgracefully as the opposite of Jesus, thus *not* glorifying God. Second, by marking the reunion with a meal and with the command to follow, Jesus signified reconciliation to Peter and demonstrated to him the threefold peace offered earlier in John 20:19, 21, 26. This, too, reverses the denials and the distance Peter created between himself and Jesus. By virtue of telling the reader that the BD recognizes Jesus, the narrator has further characterized Peter and the other five disciples as imperceptive. John Painter argues that perception and "seeing" are identified with belief in the FG, an important value in the narrative.[50] The narrator states, "When Peter *heard* that it was the Lord," not "when Peter *recognized or realized* it was Jesus" (John 21:7). Even though the BD himself needed a miracle to recognize Jesus, in contrast, Peter and his five companions are still slow to recognize Jesus. Nevertheless, the characterization of Peter transforms to a more positive one through the course of these nineteen verses. Rather than "I am not" a disciple, Peter now repeatedly responds with the positive, "Yes Lord, you know that I love you" (21:15–18). Rather than "We have come to know," Peter now responds emphatically, "*You* know all things. *You* know that I love you." Finally, the narrator's statement about Peter's death glorifying God is of course, a positive characterization, even if it is not where Peter wants to go.[51]

Thus, while I am not arguing that the FE planned for these scenes to resemble Genesis manipulation narratives, we see that one can analyze them with benefit using this taxonomy. Having now summarized and applied these kernels of manipulation, I now turn to a closer examination of subjects related to manipulation that arise in the text.

---

50. Painter, *John: Witness and Theologian*, 71–72. Or "dull" as evidenced by those moments that demonstrate the need for the characters' development in keeping with the writer's intended plot line and progression for them and according to the values of the text. See also Barrett who used the term "dull disciple" to describe Thomas. Barrett, *The Gospel according to St. John*, 382. But see Harstine who argues against such a characterization of Thomas. Harstine, "Un-Doubting Thomas," 435.

51. The text does not say that he is led unwillingly, but that it is where he does not *want* to go (21:18).

The Disciples Go Fishing (John 21:1–5)

Active Manifestation

In verses 1 and 14, the narrator states three times that this was a manifestation of Jesus.[52] This may be called an active manifestation of himself to his disciples. Pfitzner argues that Jesus' revealing of himself was necessary because he was divine—"all the signs, [are] revelations of divine glory"[53]—"there is no natural perception of his person."[54] However, I contend that Jesus also actively manifested himself to his disciples at a certain point, because until that moment, he was withholding his identity for a purpose.

Pfitzner noted that the word ἐφανέρωσεν occurs only six times in chapters 1–20, one of which is the miracle at Cana (John 2:11).[55] Coupled with the naming of Nathanael in 21:2, this term indicates that "there is a strong reminiscence of this sign," which followed directly after Nathanael's identification of Jesus as "the Son of God" and "the King of Israel" (1:49).[56] Earlier I discussed the significance of Nathanael's appearance in the opening and closing chapters of the FG, and also the connection between the LXX's version of Genesis 41:55 and John 2:5 where Mary says, similar to Pharaoh's command: "ὅ τι ἂν λέγῃ ὑμῖν ποιήσατε." The FE concludes that episode with "This, the first of his signs, Jesus did at Cana in Galilee, and *manifested* his glory" (2:11). Regarding "manifest" in John 21, Brown writes: "The verb *phanēroun*, which is used nine times in the Gospel, occurs twice in this verse and once in vs. 14. It has the general connotation of *emergence from obscurity*, and for John involves a concrete revelation of the heavenly upon earth. The only other example of this verb used to describe a post-resurrectional appearance is the Marcan Appendix (xvi 12, 14)."[57]

This idea of "emergence from obscurity" is in keeping with aspects of manipulation and recognition that we have learned from Genesis. Manipulators, or the persons or objects they have obscured from view, need to transition from obscurity to visibility so that their victims can recognize them. Leah (whom Laban the manipulator had put in Rachel's place), transitions from the darkness of night to the light of morning, and then Jacob recognized her (Gen 29:25), but Laban never recognizes his gods because Rachel keeps them hidden (31:33). Tamar transitions from obscurity as the

---

52. "Revealed" in the ESV.
53. Pfitzner, "They Knew It Was the Lord," 71.
54. Ibid., 72.
55. Ibid., 70.
56. Ibid.
57. Brown, *The Gospel according to John (XIII–XXI)*, 1067; emphasis Brown.

prostitute by actively revealing herself when she calls Judah's attention to his items of identification (38:25), and Joseph actively reveals himself to his brothers (45:1).[58]

Moreover, sometimes in Genesis the obscurity, as well as the manifestation needed for recognition, was thought to be caused by God. Philo attributed the brother's lack of recognition of Joseph to divine intervention:

> And he, when he beheld those who had sold him, immediately recognised them all, though he was not in the least recognised by any one of them himself, since God was not yet willing to reveal the truth on account of some necessary causes which at that time it was better should be buried in silence; and therefore he either altered the countenance of their brother who governed the country, so as to give him a more dignified appearance, or else he perverted the accurate judgment of the mind of those who beheld him."[59]

However, Philo also credits Joseph, in addition to God, as actively engaged in obscuring his identity.[60]

The author of *Jubilees* attributes Isaac's lack of recognition to divine intervention: "'The voice is the voice of Jacob, but the hands are the hands of Esau,' and he did not know him, because the change was from heaven in order to distract his mind" (Jub. 26:17).[61] Earlier, I discussed Joseph's active role in disguising himself, noting the wordplay on the Hebrew root for recognize (*hkr*), and Alter's use of the phrase "makes himself a stranger" to his brothers.[62] Both represent an active role on the part of the one unrecognized, the manipulator. In the manipulation narratives in Genesis, this is the implied norm: the manipulators actively disguise themselves, as Jacob does before Isaac, and at times, the counter-manipulators do as well, as in the cases of Tamar and Joseph. Pfitzner's opinion on John 21 is that Jesus was obscure to observers and needed to reveal himself: "Christ *must* manifest himself in order to be known."[63] Note the FE does not state, "After this,

---

58. "The recognition once again involves God: 'God has found out the crime of your servants,' Judah proclaims in his great speech. Lastly—and this is the real key to the narrative's anagnorisis—agnition is impossible without revelation, and vice versa. The brothers cannot recognize Joseph until he is ready to reveal himself." Boitani, *The Bible and Its Rewritings*, 30.

59. Philo, *The Works of Philo*, 449.

60. Ibid.

61. Charlesworth, *The Old Testament Pseudepigrapha*, 106.

62. Alter, *The Art of Biblical Narrative*, 163.

63. Pfitzner, "They Knew It Was the Lord," 72; emphasis added. But contra Segovia: "[S]uch failure to recognize Jesus at this point is apparently due to the distance of the

the disciples recognized Jesus" in verse 1, nor in verse 14, "This was now the third time that the disciples recognized Jesus after he was raised from the dead." Rather the text states instead "Jesus revealed himself" in verse 1, and "Jesus was revealed" in verse 14. The action, especially in verse 1, is by the manipulator who is recognized, not the victim, who is the recognizer.[64] In addition to using ambivalent language when addressing the disciples in verse 5, Jesus in his resurrected state *must* reveal himself.[65] This is no insignificant detail in the narrative. Just as Alter argues the case for the Hebrew Bible, I assert that in the New Testament as well, "There are virtually no 'free motifs' in biblical narrative."[66]

This necessity for Jesus, as a divine being to reveal himself, is also strongly implied earlier in the FG: "And he who loves me will be loved by my Father, and I will love him and manifest myself to him" (John 14:21).[67] Jesus here characterizes himself as somehow hidden but as someone who

---

boat from the shore." Segovia, "The Final Farewell of Jesus," 178.

64. As I noted above, this was Pfitzner's point too, that Jesus must reveal himself in order to be seen. See also Hoskyns and Davey, *The Fourth Gospel*, 438. Hoskyns also attributes to Peter "active ignorance." When I began my research, I did not discount that the FE may have been aiming at verisimilitude. In the beginning stages of my research, before I came to this conclusion of *active* manifestation by Jesus, I experimented with the stated distance in verse 8, that of two hundred cubits or about one hundred yards. I used a couple of individuals with whom I was acquainted. My observation was that unless they were purposely wearing strange clothing that concealed their features, such as a hooded sweatshirt or a low-pulled hat, I readily recognized them without their speaking. Granted, I knew the experiment was occurring and was purposely looking to see if I could recognize them. However, this was without hearing a voice calling to me. Even though it is plausible, it would seem to me unlikely, if I had six other companions, that all of us would fail to recognize a friend under normal conditions.

65. This may have been the case in Luke 24:16 ("but they were kept from recognizing him"), about which Carson points out, "Whether this is an instance when disciples are kept from recognizing the resurrected Christ . . . is unclear." Carson, *The Gospel according to John*, 670, 674. Nonetheless, verse 31 also states, "Then their eyes *were opened* and they recognized him." So this too supports the idea that an active manifestation on behalf of Jesus, or God the Father, *was necessary*, rather than a simple "*They* opened *their* eyes." The observers were passive in the activity.

66. Alter, *The Art of Biblical Narrative*, 79.

67. John 1:1: "[A]nd the Word was God"; 20:28: "Thomas answered him, 'My Lord and my God!'" Brown writes regarding the translation of 1:1 and its connection to Thomas' proclamation, "'The Word was divine' . . . seems too weak . . . 'The Word was God' is quite correct. This reading is reinforced when one remembers that in the Gospel as it now stands, the affirmation of i 1 is almost certainly meant to form an inclusion with xx 28, where at the end of the Gospel Thomas confesses Jesus as 'My God' (*ho theos mou*). These statements represent the Johannine affirmative answer to the charge made against Jesus in the Gospel that he was wrongly making himself God (x 33, v 18)." Brown, *The Gospel according to John (I–XII)*, 5.

will reveal himself to those who love him. Stibbe states that the disciples must deal with this hiddenness even after the resurrection: "This time they must recognize the risen Jesus. Even here, with his own disciples, Jesus is elusive!"[68]

We may conclude, therefore, that an understanding of Genesis manipulation narratives, as well as the characterization of Jesus earlier in the FG, supports Pfitzner's view, as well as Brown's, that the term "manifested" or "revealed" in John 21, indicates a necessity for Jesus to reveal himself.[69] The lack of recognition in verse 4, is no minor accident due naturally to distance or early morning low light.[70] Moreover, I argue that this manifestation by Jesus was *necessary*, because he has been in the process of *withholding* his identity for a purpose.[71] The use of the ambiguous title "children" also supports this. Purposely providing the catch of abundant fish was therefore necessary and becomes the token of the disciples' recognition.[72] However, though Jesus presents the token to all seven disciples, only the BD, the ideal disciple, is quick to recognize it. Peter, who is characterized as not yet an ideal disciple of Jesus, requires a prompting to recognize Jesus.

---

68. Stibbe, *John's Gospel*, 30. See also Stibbe, "The Elusive Christ: A New Reading of the Fourth Gospel," 37, where he states, "[I]n chs. 18–19, Jesus gives himself up to those who have found him elusive since 5.16–18. Finally, in chs. 20–21, the theme returns in the context of the resurrection. Now it is the risen Jesus who proves elusive (see 13.33, 36; 16.16; then 20.2, 14; 21.4)."

69. See also Carson, *The Gospel according to John*, 675, who states: "As in v. 1, the emphasis is on Jesus' self-disclosure. The verb is stronger than the more common *ōphthē* ('he appeared'), used more commonly in the New Testament (e.g. Luke. 24:34; 1 Cor. 15:5–8)."

70. "Jesus' sudden appearance on the shore is probably meant to be mysterious, for in several of the post-resurrectional narratives he materializes suddenly." Brown, *The Gospel according to John (XIII–XXI)*, 1070. Moreover, the transition from darkness to light may have been intended to symbolize a coming transition in the characters. Burke, *The Philosophy of Literary Form*, 59.

71. Witherington notes that the recognition only comes after obedience. Witherington III, *John's Wisdom*, 355. We noted earlier that Joseph only reveals himself after giving his brothers a chance to pass the test as to whether or not they will betray Benjamin. Thus, I ask here, was the revealing contingent upon obedience? From a logical standpoint, the disciples certainly would not have caught 153 fish if they had not passed the test and let down the net as commanded. Yet Peter has a further examination ahead. *Pace* Claussen, "The Role of John 21," 55–68.

72. As discussed above, Larsen and others have shown that the displaying of a token is a common element in ancient recognition scenes. Culpepper, "Cognition in John," 252–58; Harstine, "Un-Doubting Thomas," 441; Larsen, *Recognizing the Stranger*, 66–68, 212; Wiarda, "John 21.1–23," 59. Spencer however interprets the meal and the "receiving of the bread and fish" as the moment of recognition for the disciples in general. Spencer, "Narrative Echoes in John 21," 64. I believe both serve as tokens in the chapter.

Key Characters and their Characterization

The naming of certain disciples in the second verse and the omission of names of the others also appears to have been intentional. Berlin notes that biblical authors sometimes name characters intentionally to demonstrate relationships and point of view.[73] Bar-Efrat also argues that the choice of names in biblical narrative can indicate the narrator's viewpoint.[74] I argue that in like manner the FE shows intentionality with the choice of each word in this narrative. The FE could have left more of them, or all of them perhaps, unnamed. Consider the wording that could have been used: "Simon Peter, Thomas (called the Twin), the sons of Zebedee, and *three* others of his disciples were together" (skipping Nathanael), or simply "There were seven of his disciples together." The naming of these particular disciples not only points the reader back to chapters 1 and 19, but also presents them, from the narrator's point of view, as key characters in the story. The names of the two sons of Zebedee are not central to the scenes in the chapter. Their identities, other than being the sons of Zebedee, are also not as central to the scene as that of the other characters discussed above, unless of course, one is the BD.[75]

So then Jesus, Peter, Thomas, Nathanael, the sons of Zebedee and two other disciples (and one of these seven is the BD) are respectively the key characters in John 21. They are key characters in that order.[76] The opening sentence of the chapter names Jesus first. The reader knows by this point that Jesus is the central character of the FG. The text names "Simon Peter" next. The FG refers to Peter thirty-four times in all.[77]

---

73. Berlin, *Poetics and Interpretation of Biblical Narrative*, 59.

74. Bar-Efrat, *Narrative Art in the Bible*, 36–37, 118.

75. Some argue the number seven to be symbolic and/or significant. Carson, *The Gospel according to John*, 669; Schnackenburg, *The Gospel according to John*, 3:352; Culpepper, "Designs for the Church in the Imagery of John 21:1–14," 369–402; Zumstein, *L'Evangile selon Saint-Jean (13–21)*, 305. Reinhartz's work shows that unnamed characters can sometimes play key roles in narratives, such as Abraham's servant in the selection of Isaac's wife. Reinhartz, *Why Ask My Name?*, 43. She has also shown that intentional anonymity sometimes is a motif indicating divine beings in the Hebrew Bible. Ibid., 165–67.

76. With the exception that the BD should perhaps be listed somewhere second only to Jesus and Peter, but in the end, we do not know for certain which of the other five he is, though of course, many have argued that it is one of the sons of Zebedee, in particular John. See Keener, *The Gospel of John*, 1:81–139. Contra Brown who asserts, "yet Nathanael's role here is minimal," Brown, *The Gospel according to John (XIII - XXI)*, 1072.

77. Based on a search of Aland et al., *The Greek New Testament*, using *Logos Bible Software*. When referred to either as Peter or Cephas, he is found 165 times (only nine are κηφᾶς) in the New Testament. By contrast, the title "Jesus" alone occurs 244 times

By contrast, Thomas is found only six times in John's Gospel (four times elsewhere in the New Testament), and three of those in John 20. The New Testament names Nathanael only six times, but all in the FG, five of which are in the opening chapter. The last reference is here in chapter 21.[78] The FE refers to BD only twice in the chapter, names Thomas and Nathanael only once, but names Peter seven times. Thus, by naming them, the FE has *noted* these characters in this chapter, and second only to Jesus, Peter is the key figure in question.[79]

But what is their significance and what does the text indicate about possible character development—both as regards the plot line as well as their development as ideal Johannine disciples in the story? Earlier I noted that in John 1, Nathanael is contrasted with Jacob in that he has no deceit. Immediately thereafter, Nathanael *recognizes* Jesus—at least partially and to a degree greater than others—by titles, though he may not yet have understood what "Son of God" implied, including divinity.[80] We should again remember that today we read this text in a post-enlightenment worldview and tend to put characters and themes in neat categories, but this is not the method of the biblical writer. Sometimes the categories have rough edges, as do the characters. In the category of ignorance versus knowledge, Jacob understood just enough at Bethel to decide that YHWH would now be his

---

in John and 917 times in the New Testament. When contrasting Peter in the FG to the Synoptics, one finds that he is named thirty-four times in John, twenty-three times in Matthew, twenty times in Mark and only nineteen times in Luke. Peter is quite an important figure in this Gospel, second only to Jesus.

78. Brown notes the *inclusio:* "The reminder that Nathanael came from Cana in Galilee (21:2) takes us back to chapter 1 (strictly speaking, 1:45–2:1), and provides us with another example of the familiar Johannine inclusion." Brown, *The Gospel according to John (XIII–XXI)*, 1079–80; Pfitzner, "They Knew It Was the Lord," 65–70; Blaine, *Peter in the Gospel of John*, 145. The title for Peter "Σίμων Ἰωάννου," also serves an *inclusio* purpose, hearkening back to John 1:42. Culpepper, "Peter as Exemplary Disciple in John 21:15–19," 171. See also Connick, "The Dramatic Character of the Fourth Gospel," 165; Zumstein, "Intratextuality and Intertextuality in the Gospel of John," 123.

79. "Though seven disciples are mentioned, it is Peter who heads the list (v. 2) and he who decides to go fishing (v. 3)." Wiarda, "John 21.1–23," 57. Carson states, "Of the seven disciples, Simon Peter . . . appears first probably because he was the unofficial leader, as suggested by his initiative in the next verse." Carson, *The Gospel according to John*, 668. See also Spencer, who says Peter "represents the disciples as a character group in ch. 21." Spencer, "Narrative Echoes in John 21," 58, 60. Regarding the unnamed two disciples, anonymity does not render them invisible. However, had the FE focused on their anonymity, it would also signal readers that the anonymity had an additional function. See Reinhartz, "Samson's Mother," 25–37; Reinhartz, *Why Ask My Name?*, 5, 43.

80. A title Jews later regarded as blasphemous (19:7). See my earlier footnote regarding Brown's comments on John 1:1 and 20:28.

Elohim (יְהוָה לִי לֵאלֹהִים Gen 28:20–21). Upon initial reading, one would think that Jacob is very perceptive here; but the astute reader realizes that Jacob still has lessons to learn, moving from ignorance to knowledge in the character development process, and does not *recognize* the full import of all that comes his way (37:32–33). Culpepper notes the limited nature of Nathanael's recognition (1:49).[81] However, the declaration is significant, and Breck argues that it was intended to function with Thomas' recognition in 20:28.[82] Nathanael's recurrence in chapter 21 therefore is no accident. The evangelist takes the trouble to inform the reader of his identity, unlike the "two other disciples" as a matter not only of *inclusio*, but also to bring the reader back to the issue of deceit, knowing, and recognition. Nathanael is one "in whom there is no deceit" (John 1:47). This is in strong contrast to Peter, who just three chapters ago had deceived concerning his relationship to Jesus (John 18). Thus Nathanael's name and presence actually serve as a *Leitwort*, indicating literary continuity; "this story goes with that one," which was the first function I discussed regarding *Leitwörter*.[83] The naming of Nathanael also is employed in the second function as well, in that it *reinforces the substantive intent of the story's content—its moral tale*. Nathanael had no deceit and had recognized Jesus—at least partially—earlier in the narrative.

These patterns are often implied or described without explicit use of terms such as ἀναγνωρίζω.[84] The FE does this, for example, with Nathanael's words, "Rabbi, you are the Son of God! You are the King of Israel!" (John 1:49).[85] With this information, then, we note that Nathanael is now side-by-side in a boat with Peter. By virtue of the appellation, "an Israelite indeed, in whom there is no deceit" (δόλος, the LXX word for deceit, 1:47), and his partial recognition (1:49), Nathanael represents an opposite characterization compared to Peter, who claimed to "know" (6:69), boasted (13:37), then deceived (18:15–27), and refused to be recognized as Jesus' disciple (18:15–27). Peter is a round and complex character who recently manipulated his accusers. He is still developing in accordance with the values of the FG. To this point, Peter has not yet completely recognized or come to realize

---

81. Culpepper, "The Johannine Hypodeigma," 138–39; emphasis added.

82. Breck, "John 21," 37.

83. The mention of Cana may serve this function well since Nathanael's introduction occurs in Galilee, the day before the miracle at Cana. However, this is the first the reader is told that Nathanael is from Cana. Carson, *The Gospel according to John*, 669; Brown, *The Gospel according to John (XIII–XXI)*, 1068.

84. Or ἀναγνωρίζομαι.

85. Which Neyrey notes in Nathanael, and contrasted with Peter in this episode in chapter 1. Neyrey, *The Gospel of John in Cultural and Rhetorical Perspective*, 273–79.

the depth of who Jesus is (21:4).[86] *The fact that in all of the New Testament, Nathanael only shows up in John 1:43–51 and 21:2 is important when coupled with the allusion in John 1 to Jacob and deceit, and the upcoming connection to Peter in John 21.*[87] The repetition of Nathanael implies that true perception and recognition are at stake here. Diana Culbertson observes the importance of all the disciples' future belief and recognition of Jesus: "It is clear from the entire passage (1:35–51) that 'belief' implies a relationship with Jesus that the disciples have entered into *but still do not fully comprehend.* The final verb is future tense: 'You will see' (1:51)."[88]

This brings the discussion to the third function of a *Leitwort*, namely, where the root word occurs *within the narrative world and is therefore known to the character*, in this case, Peter. Despite the fact that Nathanael exists *in the narrative world and is also known to the character* (Peter is no doubt aware of Nathanael's presence in both chapter 1 and 21), there is no indication in the text that Nathanael's presence serves to haunt the key character. Nathanael does not elicit a response from Peter analogous to the response of guilt that the silver in the Joseph story elicits from his brothers (Gen 42:28; 44:13).[89]

Thomas was also present in the narratives leading up to this chapter. Readers find Thomas in the FG on three separate occasions (John 11:16; 14:5; 20:24–27) prior to his appearance here in John 21. He, too, is named and functions in this chapter in relationship to recognition. He does not perceive Jesus' divine ability to restore life; thus, he misunderstands Jesus' plan and purpose for a visit to Lazarus and defaults to the idea of an impending death upon returning to Judea and the Jewish authorities: "Let us also go, that we may die with him" (11:6). In chapter 14, he admits his ignorance, "Lord, we do not know where you are going. How can we know the way?"(14:5). Finally, in chapter 20, he is unwilling to accept Jesus' ability to rise from the dead, based solely on the word of his companions.[90] He

---

86. Claussen states that "all sorts of people simply do not recognize Jesus' true identity," and this starts from the beginning of the Gospel in John 1:26. Claussen, "The Role of John 21," 62. The FE omits Peter's statement in Matt 16:16, "You are the Christ, the Son of the living God." Lied sees a similar aspect to recognition, saying, "The observer must have the ability to understand the true meaning of what he or she observes, in order to establish the identity or the type of the observed object." Lied, "Recognizing the Righteous Remnant?," 313.

87. Contra Keener, *The Gospel of John*, 2:1225n3.

88. Culbertson, *Poetics of Revelation*, 158; emphasis added.

89. Unless Nathanael is the BD, of whom Peter asks, "Lord, what about this man?" (21:21). This would be a further *inclusio*, with Nathanael partially recognizing Jesus in chapter 1, and then fully recognizing the risen Lord in chapter 21.

90. "Thomas does not understand the resurrection." Culpepper, "The Johannine

must *see* and *touch* in order to *believe*, i.e. "*recognize and know the truth, and subsequently believe*" (20:24–29).[91] When Thomas finally sees and thus recognizes Jesus, he utters a response not unlike Nathanael in chapter 1 ("My Lord and my God!"). Jesus' response indicates that those who believe without requiring sight better fit the description of an ideal Johannine disciple and are thus "blessed." The author's decision to name Thomas fits the understanding of a *Leitwort*, as well. It tells the reader that these aforementioned stories are connected. Recalling them informs the reading of the upcoming story and reinforces the substantive intent of the narrative—that the disciples should recognize the risen Jesus. Yet none of the disciples will initially recognize Jesus in 21:4 until they *see* the miracle token of the catch of fish. Therefore, Thomas is characterized similar to his unperceptive self in the previous chapter and fits in well with his fellow disciples and their failure to recognize the risen Jesus. Naming him thus enables the reader to better perceive what is at work in the following verses.

This brings the analysis to Peter.[92] In addition the frequency with which we find him in the FG, when Jesus gives him a new name, this also clues the reader to the fact that he would be an important character (John 1:40–42).[93] Peter, though a round character who progresses, is nevertheless characterized somewhat negatively throughout the Gospel when compared to the likes of the BD, Nathanael, and Martha (1:49; 11:24; 13:23–24; 18:15–18, 25–26; 20:1–10; 21:7, 20–21).[94] In many ways, he represents the typical character that misunderstands. As the story unfolds, Peter is quite willing and vocal about his understanding of Jesus and at times makes important Johannine assertions: "Lord, to whom shall we go? You have the words of eternal life" (6:68), "You are the Holy One of God"(6:69). Even so, he states more than he can live up to: "Lord, why can I not follow you now? I will lay down my life for you" (13:37).

The narrator does not name Peter from chapter 7 through chapter 12, though almost all of the disciples remain unnamed in this segment. When

---

Hypodeigma," 139.

91. Brown notes, "To a certain extent 'knowing' and 'believing' are interchangeable in John." Brown, *The Gospel according to John (I–XII)*, 513.

92. Space and purpose, of course, limit the treatment of Peter's character. For a recent and thorough treatment of Peter in the Gospel of John, see Blaine, *Peter in the Gospel of John*.

93. A motif also found in Genesis, with Abraham, Sarah, and Jacob.

94. Spencer sees this in the first twenty chapters of the FG but does not comment on it in the final chapter: "[T]he characterization of Peter in ch. 21 differs from his characterization in chs. 1–20; namely, his portrayal in chs. 1–20 is negative (anti-Petrine), while his portrait in ch. 21 is positive." Spencer, "Narrative Echoes in John 21," 53, 60.

readers come to chapter 13, the story portrays Peter wrestling with a proper understanding of the mission of Jesus. Culpepper links *love, knowledge,* and *ignorance* in John 13, where Peter fails to understand and to comply initially with Jesus' attempt to wash his feet.[95] This is highly significant because all three of these will come to the fore in 21:17.

Chapter 13 opens by reminding the reader of two essential aspects of Jesus. The first is that Jesus *knows*, and the second is what he had already done, i.e., "having loved," contrasted with what the devil had already done, i.e., "having already put into the heart of Judas Iscariot."[96] This *knowing* forms the basis of Jesus' following actions and sets the stage for the whole of chapter 13:[97]

> Now before the Feast of the Passover, Jesus *knowing* that His hour had come that He would depart out of this world to the Father, having loved His own who were in the world, He loved them to the end. During supper, the devil having already put into the heart of Judas Iscariot, the son of Simon, to betray Him, Jesus, *knowing* that the Father had given all things into His hands, and that He had come forth from God and was going back to God, got up from supper, and laid aside His garments; and taking a towel, He girded Himself (13:1–4).[98]

Culpepper notes that Jesus' knowing in verse one "sets the agenda for the foot washing and the farewell discourse which will follow."[99] He also points out the "extended participles" in the knowing in verse one is carried through and repeated in verse 3, and is in contrast to the devil who "had already put it

---

95. Culpepper, "The Johannine Hypodeigma," 133–52.

96. Ibid., 136.

97. "Indeed, Jesus' knowledge as the incarnate logos has been a vital part of John's characterization of Jesus from the beginning of the Gospel:
Jesus knows Nathanael before Philip called him (1:48);
he knows all things, even what is in the hearts of others (2:24–25);
he knows that the testimony about him is true (5:32);
he knows what he is about to do (6:6);
he knows when his disciples grumble about him (6:61);
he knows those who do not believe in him and he knows who his betrayer will be (6:64);
he knows the one who sent him (7:29; 8:55);
he knows from whence he came and where he was going (8:14);
he knows that the Father always hears him (11:42);
he knows that the Father's command is eternal life (12:50)." Ibid., 135.

98. I have here used the *New American Standard Bible* because of its employment of "knowing," twice, as parallel participles, whereas the ESV translates the first occurrence, in verse 1, as "knew." Lockman Foundation, *New American Standard Bible*.

99. Culpepper, "The Johannine Hypodeigma," 136.

into the heart of Judas Iscariot, Simon's son, to betray him."[100] Additionally, the twice repeated knowing in verses 1 and 3, as well as the devil's *having put*, βεβληκότος, in verse 2, are all perfect active participles, thus cueing the reader to their parallel construction. Verses 1–3 then, are all together one opening sentence "setting the agenda" (Culpepper's phrase) for the action that begins in verse 4 with the vivid historical present ἐγείρεται, and continuing through the rest of the Gospel. This parallel construction, along with the contrast to the "mind of the devil," sets the mental stage, not just for the following verses and discourse, but for the remainder of the Gospel: Jesus knows—and thus he acts, initiating a sequence of events taking him to the cross.[101] We will see the opposite in Peter: he misunderstands—and thus he acts, over and again.

In verse 7, in response to Peter's question, "Lord, do you wash my feet?" Jesus answers, "What I am doing you do not *understand* now, but afterward you will *understand*." Culpepper notes that this response "asserts Peter's ignorance" and that set against the backdrop of the first few verses, "the contrast between Jesus and Peter could not be put any more sharply."[102] Thus, Culpepper argues that chapter 13 "highlights the recurring theme of knowledge and ignorance."[103] This is in agreement with Painter's argument that knowing is tied to believing in the FG, both of which are markers for the progression of character development in this Gospel.[104]

Chapter 13 details what Jesus knew and the actions that proceeded from that knowledge. Peter and Judas in particular misunderstand and their actions result from this ignorance.[105] In verse 8 of chapter 13, Peter boldly refuses Jesus' act of service: "You shall never wash my feet." Culpepper explains that Peter's refusal of Jesus' loving act demonstrates a misguided reaction, "one that grows out of ignorance."[106] When we traced the series of manipulation narratives in Genesis, we saw that they often involve a ma-

---

100. Ibid., 137.

101. Culpepper, "The Johannine Hypodeigma," 136–37.

102. Ibid., 138. Here Culpepper also pointed out that this is the first of "three statements by Peter and three responses from Jesus." Note that this threefold pattern between the two is resumed in 21:15.

103. Ibid., 133.

104. Painter, *John: Witness and Theologian*, 86–100.

105. Culpepper, "The Johannine Hypodeigma," 133–34.

106. Ibid., 139; emphasis added. Culpepper notes as well, that foot washing occurs in Gen 43:24. Note the verse: "And when the man had brought the men into Joseph's house and given them water, and they had washed their feet . . ." Ibid., 137, 148n8. In both the Johannine recognition/ignorance story and the narrative with Joseph and his brothers, the ones who fail to recognize get their feet washed or have the water for the washing provided by the one whose identity they are unable to recognize.

nipulator involved in the character development process. Since knowledge, as opposed to ignorance, is an important value according to the FG, Peter, as a character, here demonstrates his need to progress in accordance with the values of the FG.[107] Notice Culpepper's explanation of John 13:8: "What is its impact or effect on the reader? Peter does not respond by asking what it is that he does not understand. Instead, he adamantly persists in refusing to let Jesus wash his feet. Peter is stubbornly pursuing a response that grows out of ignorance."[108] Chapter 13 is therefore a clear portrayal of Peter as a character *early* in that development process—he is still in need of transformation. Furthermore, this characterization stands, to some degree, in contrast to that of Nathanael. Gerald Janzen argues regarding Nathanael: "He is not a Jacob who will *force the coming of the promise* by cunning, *deceit* or *revolutionary force*. Nathaniel [sic] is to the people of his day as the deeply-hidden and not-yet-named Israel to the wily Jacob prior to Jabbok."[109] At the foot washing Peter misunderstands and merely responds inappropriately, but his character will continue to develop, and his responses will become more pronounced. Janzen's words describing the younger manipulative Jacob are vividly appropriate for the Peter whom readers find in chapter 18, where he manipulates by outright lie. Until that point, the reader passes through more than four chapters without mention of Peter.

The next time one hears of Peter he has a sword in his hand.[110] Culpepper argues that Peter is "characterized as one who does not understand Jesus' death . . . [n]ow he cannot understand Jesus' departure. The *irony of Peter's pledge of loyalty is pointed*. He cannot follow—that is, he cannot discharge his duty as a disciple—because he does not understand the meaning of Jesus' death."[111] Culpepper again points out the sharp contrast between the characters of Peter and Jesus: "Jesus confronts Peter with reality: that very night he would deny Jesus three times. The contrast between knowledge and ignorance of the revelation conveyed by Jesus' death is complete."[112] The reader well versed in the Genesis manipulation narratives may note the *serial* nature of scenes where Peter is characterized as dull or imperceptive

---

107. Painter, *John: Witness and Theologian*, 86–100.

108. Culpepper, "The Johannine Hypodeigma," 139.

109. Janzen, "How Can a Man Be Born When He Is Old?," 335–36; emphasis added.

110. "Peter does not understand the need for Jesus to die (13:36–38; 18:10–11)." Culpepper, "The Johannine Hypodeigma," 139. But see Blaine, *Peter in the Gospel of John*, 128, who says, "As we have seen, Peter fares quite well in the first twenty chapters of the Gospel."

111. Culpepper, "The Johannine Hypodeigma," 147; emphasis added.

112. Ibid.

and still early in the character development process.¹¹³ He did not want Jesus to wash his feet, he did not want Jesus to be taken by the Roman soldiers, and he will now manipulate in order not to be identified as Jesus' disciple. In the end, all of these behaviors begin with his misunderstanding of Jesus' identity. And, if a reader has been influenced significantly by Genesis manipulation narratives, that reader may also sense that Peter's ignorance means he does not recognize his own need to change.

Thus coming to chapter 21, the reader has been prepared to see that in these opening verses the disciples, *most importantly Peter*, are still imperceptive. They must still see in order to believe, and this seeing is not just seeing Jesus in the flesh, but also seeing the revealing power of the risen Jesus in the miraculous catch.¹¹⁴ Only then do they see and believe, and even then, this must be prompted by the BD. The reader, the narrator hopes (John 20:29–31), will believe despite the disadvantage of not witnessing these manifestations firsthand.

Fruitless Fishing

Resuming with verse 3, we read that Peter states that he will go fishing. Scholarship has carefully debated the tenor of this statement and what the FE intends by it. The opinions range from apostasy to the idea that the disciples at least need to provide sustenance and a means of living.¹¹⁵ Others see fishing in symbolic ecclesiastical and salvific terms, representing the rescuing of fish from the "wicked" or "malevolent waters below."¹¹⁶ John Pritchard believes that Peter "restlessly announces that he is going fishing."¹¹⁷

---

113. Wiarda notes the "series of events" focused around Peter in John 21. Wiarda, "John 21.1–23," 53.

114. One may counter that it has also been noted that the manifestation by Jesus was necessary on his part, and ask how, in a manner of speaking, can my research hold the disciples accountable for not recognizing Jesus and being dull or out of step if at the same time Jesus has not chosen to reveal himself until the moment the swollen net breaks the surface of the water. One need not completely separate these two causes. Thinking back, the manipulators in Gen were often in similar situations. I established that Judah was clearly out of step, but Tamar actively disguised and later revealed herself as well. Her action was prompted by his lack in character. The brothers were certainly off course and very dull (especially Reuben), but Joseph also choose to conceal, and reveal himself—when he was ready. Thus, both causative reasons are at work here.

115. Brown, *The Gospel according to John (XIII–XXI)*, 1069, 1096; Wiarda, "John 21.1–23," 58; Hoskyns and Davey, *The Fourth Gospel*, 552.

116. Culpepper, "Designs for the Church in the Imagery of John 21:1–14," 12; but contra Wiarda, "John 21.1–23," 67.

117. Pritchard, *A Literary Approach to the New Testament*, 206.

Wiarda argues that the statement could hardly be considered neutral and should therefore be regarded as an intentional juxtaposition between fishing and discipleship, which sets up the reader to question just what the disciples were up to in the scene.[118] According to Wiarda, the fact that so many scholars wrestle with this statement made by Peter suggests that something in fact is going on here; the FE appears to intend for the reader to feel indeterminacy. Neither readers nor scholars, therefore, have been able to ignore this implied tension. Taken in conjunction with the previous series of scenes in which Peter still appears in the character development process, the question about the fishing adventure gains clarity. There appears to be a degree of *aimlessness*, especially on the part of Peter. He has gone home, back to some degree of normalcy, rather than to the focused "on-task" mission stated in 20:26, implied in 20:23, and demonstrated later in the canon (Acts 2).[119] Recalling Culpepper's words referred to above, Peter "cannot follow—that is, he cannot discharge his duty as a disciple—because he does not understand the meaning of Jesus' death."[120] The FE's implied readers may also recall that Peter has deviated from Jesus' plan before, by refusing a foot washing, responding with a sword in hand, and manipulating by completely denying Jesus in the courtyard.

An astute listener might also note the absence of Peter's name in the two resurrection appearances to the disciples in the previous chapter and start to wonder. He may wonder if Peter did not comprehend who Jesus was in his resurrected state, if he understood Jesus' threefold offer of peace in 20:19, 21, 26, or if Peter was present at all.[121] We cannot know with any certainty the answer to these questions, but this indeterminacy does contribute to the tension in the text. Nonetheless, the implication in 21:3 is ambiguity regarding Peter, his understanding, and his actions. He, along with at least five of his companions (the BD is the one possible exception, since he recognized Jesus before the others), do not have a full recognition of who Jesus is. This has resulted in his decision to go fishing, rather than proclaim the message of 20:23. In this way, the counter-manipulation in chapter 21 serves as a culminating episode in the characterization of Peter

---

118. Wiarda, "John 21.1–23," 57–8. "Yet suddenly we find some disciples back at their old vocation (at least for a few of them), fishing in Galilee." Pfitzner, "They Knew It Was the Lord," 64.

119. "[T]his fishing expedition and the dialogue that ensues do not read like the lives of men on a Spirit-empowered mission. It is impossible to imagine any of this taking place in Acts, *after Pentecost*." Carson, *The Gospel according to John*, 669; emphasis Carson.

120. Culpepper, "The Johannine Hypodeigma," 147.

121. Crosby, *Do You Love Me?*, 188.

in the FG, much as the brothers' final visit to Egypt and counter-manipulation functions as a culminating episode for the characterization of Judah in Genesis.[122] In both Genesis and John, the themes of manipulation, lack of recognition, and character development play out in the lives of these characters until the dramatic resolution in the final recognition episode. In Genesis, this occurs with Judah and his brothers. In the FG, it is brought to a zenith in the life of Peter.

Michael Crosby writes following about Peter in the beginning of chapter 21: "He appears to have no other option but to return to the trade by which he made his living previous to meeting Jesus. *Without resurrection faith, what else is there to do?*"[123] Jerome Murphy-O'Connor surmises that this recourse might not have been one of necessity due to limited means and opportunities. As a fisherman Peter may have been "a man of substance in control of his life."[124] Archeological evidence of dwellings also indicates that the fishing trade was very profitable in Galilee.[125] Note that according to Mark 1:20 this trade often included hired employees, as was the case for the sons of Zebedee.[126] If one examines Peter through the manipulator lens, one sees that when he resorts to fishing, he turns "to something he could manage and control."[127] He empowers himself and put Jesus' plan to the perimeter. Below I shall argue that Jesus' actions disempower Peter and bring him to true knowledge, just as Tamar did to Judah and as Joseph did to Judah and his brothers. Jesus predicts that Peter will in the future become manipulable. He will yield to Jesus' plan for him and move to a position of relinquishing control and therefore surrendering to the leading of another.[128]

Turning to the following verses, we see that the results of the fishing expedition become interesting. The next thing the reader learns is that under *their control, the disciples were powerless and unable to succeed*; "they caught nothing" (John 21:3). In addition to having employees, Galilean fishermen knew their trade, its ins and outs, and this body of water.[129] Fishing was an established trade. Murphy-O'Connor adds that they had to deal with taxes, take their fish to the fish factory to be salted and prepared: "Against

---

122. Stibbe also sees a culminating aspect in a series of recognition scenes, but believes Thomas in chapter 20 serves this function. Stibbe, *John's Gospel*, 36.

123. Crosby, *Do You Love Me?*, 188; emphasis added.

124. Murphy-O'Connor, "Fishers of Fish, Fishers of Men," 25.

125. "[T]he prosperity of at least one fisher family in Bethsaida is attested by a spacious 1750 square-foot house." Ibid., 26.

126. Ibid., 27.

127. Wright, personal discussions.

128. Wiarda, "John 21.1–23," 65.

129. Murphy-O'Connor, "Fishers of Fish, Fishers of Men," 25.

this background of a relatively well-off family, it becomes possible to understand how Simon Peter and Andrew were financially able to become, first, disciples of John the Baptist (1:40–42) and then the disciples of Jesus."[130] Percy Ainsworth argues any fishing failure would have been obvious to the first or second century reader:

> Mind you, these men were no novices. They knew their business. They had known the Galilean sea from their boyhood—all its moods and tempers, its dangers and its possibilities. Their story as breadwinners had been told upon the waters—they were experts, yet their boat was empty. They had worked hard and wisely and the sea had beaten them. In spite of their instincts and a lifetime on its waters, the sea sent them ashore with an empty boat.[131]

Furthermore, from *the readers' perspective*, Jesus *knows* and is the divine master over the Johannine world, thus he can easily provide this catch.[132] He has turned water to wine (John 2); he himself can provide for sustenance—in abundance (John 6), he has power over the waters of the very lake in question (6:16–21).[133]

The *power* of Jesus underscores the *powerlessness* of the disciples. Blaine describes the values of honor, shame, and power that are at work in this *anagnorisis*: "[T]he reader is meant to take notice of the changing fortunes of the disciples, who are transformed from empowered to powerless."[134] Blaine

---

130. Ibid., 27. See also Bailey, *Jesus through Middle Eastern Eyes*, 141.

131. Ainsworth, "The Miraculous Draught of Fishes," 26–27. This is an excerpted edited reprint from Ainsworth's 1909 collection of sermons in a periodical.

132. Noting that the implied readers were *expected* (John 20:30–31) to believe in the world of supernatural knowledge, events, and miracles on the part of Jesus, unlike an un-implied readership in ancient or modern times that might include ambivalence or opposition to this idea. There is no reason to supply a *natural* reason for Jesus knowing where to fish, such as his seeing a school of fish that the disciples did not. See Brown, *The Gospel according to John (XIII–XXI)*, 1070–71. Pfitzner writes, "There is no need to posit some natural reason for the failure of the disciples to recognize Jesus—tiredness and frustration after a bad night's fishing, morning mists or swirling fog, or the distance from the shore. There is no explanation, so the reader must be expected to understand the point being made, to make the appropriate explanation." Pfitzner, "They Knew It Was the Lord," 72.

133. See also Segovia who writes, "First of all, if the 'fishing' is taken as literal, then the section ironically portrays the disciples as being in the safety of Galilee and as going fishing on their own, ignoring thereby Jesus' command of mission in and to the world. Secondly, if the 'fishing' is taken as metaphorical, with reference to the mission itself, then the section also shows that the disciples can have no success whatever aside from Jesus." Segovia, "The Final Farewell of Jesus," 167–90.

134. Blaine, *Peter in the Gospel of John*, 136n28.

spots the same motif, in that the fishing scene (John 21:3) was at night, with the darkness symbolizing powerlessness, even in fishing.[135] Thus, when the disciples come to shore, they are speechless. They are powerless at fishing and are now in a position to receive and be transformed. Jesus is in control and is providing the sustenance, and in doing so, he has revealed who he really is. Joseph's manipulation of his brothers offers interpretive insight. Joseph was in complete control and provided for his brothers both before and after his revealing. As noted earlier, initial manipulators put themselves in a place of power, of control, in order to change the outcome of events. Later, they are often counter-manipulated and disempowered by others. Thus, Peter who manipulates and lies to gain power over his own fate, is now, along with his companions, powerless to catch fish. When he and the other disciples realize who Jesus is, their disempowerment will be complete.[136] The miraculous provision of the catch by the risen Lord emphasizes who is empowered and who is not.

John 21 may offer another clue to the empowered state of the resurrected Jesus and the disempowered state of those who do not recognize him. In verse 3b the FE informs us: "but that night they caught nothing." "Caught," πιάζω, occurs twelve times in the New Testament.[137] Eight of these are here in the FG. The *New American Standard Bible* frequently translates this term as "seize." No other Gospel writer uses this terminology. The other four occurrences are outside the Gospels and there, too, the term stands for "seize" or even "arrest," as the *English Standard Version* frequently translates it.[138] Note, as well, the Johannine usage leading up to chapter 21: "So they were seeking *to arrest* him, but no one laid a hand on him, because his hour had not yet come"(John 7:30); "The Pharisees heard the crowd muttering these things about him, and the chief priests and Pharisees sent officers *to*

---

135. Ibid., 146–47. In regard to those, such as Bailey, who point out that fishing on Galilee *normally* took place at night, this emphasis is not at odds with the fact that at night, alone, they catch nothing. In the day, with Jesus, they have a miraculous catch. The FE still has to *choose* to include this detail in his narrative. Since the FE has made the choice, the reader must ask why. Additionally, Bailey, regarding the call of Peter in Luke 5, states: "The very idea that a landlubber from the highlands of Nazareth, who has never wet a line should presume to tell a seasoned fishing captain what to do is preposterous. The fish can see and avoid the nets during the day, but they feed at night." Bailey, *Jesus through Middle Eastern Eyes*, 137–41, 204; emphasis added.

136. Wiarda speaks of "upsetting [Peter's] equilibrium." Wiarda, "John 21.1–23," 53.

137. Once in the LXX, insignificant perhaps for purposes here, in Songs 2:15 of catching foxes.

138. Acts 3:7; 12:4; 2 Cor 11:32; Rev 19:20. *Seized* or *arrested* nine times, *caught* twice here in John 21, and *captured* in Revelation. See also Brown, *The Gospel according to John (XIII-XXI)*, 1069.

arrest him"(John 7:32); "Some of them wanted to *arrest* him, but no one laid hands on him" (7:44); "These words he spoke in the treasury, as he taught in the temple; but no one *arrested* him, because his hour had not yet come" (8:20); "Again they sought *to arrest* him, but he escaped from their hands"(10:39); "Now the chief priests and the Pharisees had given orders that if anyone knew where he was, he should let them know, so that they might *arrest* him"(11:57).[139]

However, in 21:3, the FE uses πιάζω for catching fish. The author of Luke uses λαμβάνω and συγκλείω for the same purpose (Luke 5:5–6).[140] Thus, should a reader note that in the previous seven Johannine instances, the ones *attempting* the catching catch nothing? In verse 10, Jesus tells the disciples to bring in the fish that they had "*caught.*" Seven of the eight times in the FG, those attempting to seize, get nothing. Important to note here is that six of those are the religious elite—those who notoriously do not know who Jesus is and therefore misunderstand his mission (John 9).[141] The seventh occurrence of πιάζω is the disciples' fishing in John 21:3, led by Peter. Only in 21:10 is this verb used in the FG in the sense of a successful venture.

---

139. But in describing the arrest when the soldiers do take Jesus, after they "drew back and fell to the ground" (18:6), the narrator switches to συλλαμβάνω (18:12) which can mean "to take along," "to assemble," "to take prisoner," as well as "to arrest." Delling, "συλλαμβάνω," in Kittel and Friedrich, eds., *TDNT*, 7:759–62.

140. The disciples are called ἁλιεῖς in Luke 5, Matt 4, and Mark 1. Additionally, Louw and Nida do *not* list πιάζω for the semantic domain of "Animal Husbandry, Fishing," though "ἅλωσις εως" is listed for the "capture or catching of animals." Louw and Nida, *Greek-English Lexicon of the New Testament*. Concerning whether or not this episode is referring to the same event as Luke 5, Pfitzner writes, "The non-recognition of Jesus (v 4) is a key factor in the argument for taking the two stories in Luke and John as pointing to a common event . . . How could Peter have failed to recall a similar prior event, and how could the disciples fail to recognize Jesus after he had already appeared to them in Jerusalem? Only John has the motif of non-recognition, and of Peter swimming to shore." Pfitzner, "They Knew It Was the Lord," 69. This is a valid question from a source critical perspective, but from a narrative approach, this is what makes the episode *story worthy* and *remark-able*. If a reader is aware of the Synoptic material, such a reader would ask, "How *could* Peter fail to recognize Jesus? Is this really happening? Something must be amiss with these disciples!" Further still, "How could Jesus restore him after three denials added to the fact that Peter still doesn't recognize him?" This is surprising for the reader, and something an author puts to ink and paper. Sternberg writes, "Both suspense and curiosity are active interests, generated and sustained by felt discontinuities that interpretation does its best to repair. We know that we do not know, and behave accordingly. In contrast, the production of surprise depends on the reader's being lured into a false certitude of knowledge." Sternberg, *The Poetics of Biblical Narrative*, 309. Brown, *The Gospel according to John (XIII–XXI)*, 1070.

141. Even in 18:12 when the FE switches to συλλαμβάνω and Jesus is taken away, there is irony in that Jesus is powerful enough that his verbal response results in their falling to the ground. They do not "catch" him; instead, he gives himself to them.

Only after Jesus tells them where to fish do they seize fish. This becomes the point of their recognition. The seizers seize nothing seven times and, ironically, Jesus, whom others wanted to seize, facilitates the catch by telling the disciples where to fish, and they seize 153 fish.[142] Thus, readers would have had the freedom to see in this verse the *power* of the manipulator, Jesus, emphasized and the powerlessness of the disciples magnified. More specifically, Peter is counter-manipulated here. He who manipulated and deceived in chapter 18 in order to protect his own fate—successfully at first I add—now experiences reversal. This is similar to Laban, who successfully manipulates at first, but is out-manipulated by Jacob (Gen 31), and Joseph's brothers who successfully manipulate Joseph and their father, only to be counter-manipulated later (Gen 37–45). Peter is characterized as powerless when he moves out on his own in chapter 21. This occurs in conjunction with Jesus counter-manipulating him with thwarted recognition. Peter is still out of step as a chosen leader. He demonstrates "aimless activity."[143] He may not be characterized as in apostasy, but he certainly is not the type of leader that we see later in the canon. But will transformation occur? The reader wonders.

We next read, "Jesus stood on the shore, yet the disciples did not know that it was Jesus" (John 21:4). Using manipulation theory as an analytical tool, notice how Jesus begins his counter-manipulation in the next verse, using the ambiguous language noted earlier: "Children, do you have any fish?" He counter-manipulates the disciples; by using language that intentionally prolongs their lack of recognition. This is especially relevant for Peter, the named key leader who earlier manipulated by outright lie and denied any recognition of Jesus, as illustrated below.

---

142. Brown also notes irony in verse 5, stating, "the writer may well have intended an ironical hint that Jesus knew the helplessness of the disciples when left on their own. It is notable that never in the Gospels do the disciples catch a fish without Jesus' help." Ibid., 1071.

143. Brown, *The Gospel according to John (XIII–XXI)*, 1096.

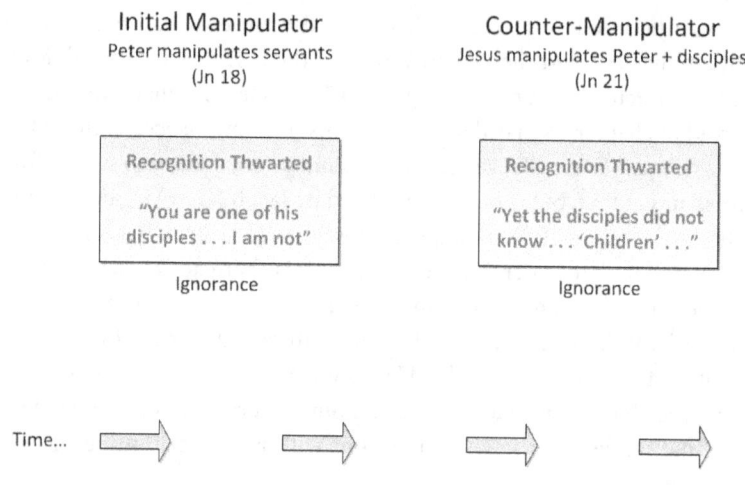

This theory of manipulation augments the classical Greco-Roman understanding of *anagnorisis* that Larsen carefully sets forth and applies to the first twenty chapters of John.[144] The implied reader would see Peter's misunderstanding and manipulative actions in chapter 18 and thus consider Jesus justified, via the system of *lex talionis*, when he ironically counter-manipulated Peter in the same manner as Peter, who thwarted others from recognizing him as Jesus' disciple. Instead of Peter's manipulative lying propelling himself to a position of power, he is ironically counter-manipulated by Jesus who withholds his own identity on the shoreline. Jesus turns the tables further on Peter by questioning Peter's love three times. Malina notes the justification for this: "Peter denied Jesus, not once, but a number of times. Such disloyalty normally required satisfaction on the part of the one dishonored."[145] Jesus questions Peter in an "eye for eye, tooth for tooth" fashion. I am not implying that Jesus considers revenge. I believe that the FE intends Jesus' threefold questioning to mirror Peter's threefold denials in order to force Peter to connect the incidents and in response, reverse course and follow Jesus without future denials. I concede that to the Western mind, this might be seen as spite, but if we see these actions as having the end goal of transforming the accused, they take on a different look.

144. Larsen, *Recognizing the Stranger*.
145. Malina and Rohrbaugh, *Social Science Commentary on the Gospel of John*, 290.

Feeding the Manipulated

Notice also that both Joseph in Genesis and Jesus in the FG treat their counterparts with ambiguity, as strangers, yet provide food for these hungry unrecognizing manipulators.[146] They also eventually reconcile them. Yes, Jesus feeds them on shore after they recognize him, but his first (and abundant) provision comes before the recognition. Is this how Joseph and Jesus turn the heart of traitors, by feeding the very people who have abandoned them? Feeding, then, may be a tool of agonistic manipulation.[147] By feeding one's adversary, *giving* to them, at the very moment when in a position to be *taking* from them in revenge, the counter-manipulator demonstrates ironic benevolence despite power over their opponents. This humbles the opponents. This may suggest one reason why Jesus did not use the typical word for fish when he called out, "Children, have ye any meat?" (John 21:5), as the *Authorized Version* translated it. This might not be simply a Johannine "penchant for synonyms," but rather προσφάγιον may have been chosen, partly because it carried the nuance of "fish for a meal," or simply "something to eat."[148] I will return to this further below, but for now, we note that the reader may see the power/shame dynamic in the irony of Jesus abundantly feeding (just as he did in John 2 and 6) the traitor Peter—the one who had betrayed him—and his companions, who are yet in the character development process.[149]

Many note possible connections to John 6, but quite often these connections are made on the basis of "the sea of Tiberias" in verse 1 or in verse 9 with the mention of the meal of bread and fish.[150] Malina states, "This first part of chapter 21 is clearly reminiscent of chapter 6, the story of the loaves

---

146. One finds this theme of counter-manipulation and feeding elsewhere too. Elisha feeds his enemies who ironically do not recognize him as the man they sought (2 Kgs 6:19, 23).

147. So too Esther feeds Haman in an elaborate feast and sets the stage for exposing to the king Haman's plans to murder Mordecai and the rest of the Jews (Esth 5:4–5). Esther's actions however, do not result in Haman's correction, but rather his death.

148. Carson, *The Gospel according to John*, 665; Bultmann, *The Gospel of John*, 707. See also Louw and Nida, *Greek-English Lexicon of the New Testament*, 50–51, which reads, "In literature outside the NT, προσφάγιον normally refers to some type of relish eaten with bread, but in Jn 21:5 (the only occurrence in the NT) the reference is to the flesh of fish." Swanson put it in his list of "non-diminutives." Swanson, "Diminutives in the Greek New Testament," 139. See further below.

149. Though "traitor" and "betrayal" may be a strong words for Peter's actions, the irony was probably not lost on the Fourth Evangelist when he wrote that it was Peter who prompted the question of who would betray him (13:24–25). See further below on Peter's actions in chapter 18.

150. Spencer, "Narrative Echoes in John 21," 59.

and fishes that led the Galilean crowd to *recognize* Jesus as a prophet."[151] Note also how the crowd responds to the miracle in 6:14, "This is indeed the Prophet who is to come into the world!" This is similar to Nathanael's statement in 1:49, "Rabbi, you are the Son of God! You are the King of Israel!" However, 21:5 offers another allusion that may be intended to direct the reader to connect this story with the miracle of abundant feeding in chapter 6. Many scholars point out the unusual occurrence of παιδία in chapter 21.[152] This term has intratextual significance with John 6:9, when the lad, παιδάριον, brought five loaves and two fish.[153] Both terms are diminutives of παῖς, referring to young persons or slaves, but παιδία can also carry the connotation of "undeveloped understanding, like νήπιος."[154] It might even refer to "little boy" as opposed to fading simply to lad or boy. Yet how does an interpreter determine this? Since the FE repeatedly uses diminutives in chapter 21, this brings the larger topic of diminutives and faded diminutives into the picture and requires a bit of an excursus.[155] Though the following section is lengthy, I believe it is important for showing how these diminutive nuances sharpen our understanding of Jesus' dialogue with Peter and the disciples. In particular, when we consider the force of the diminutives in the passage, we will see that the dialogue displays Jesus' power and the disciples' lack thereof (and at times emphasizes this with irony). Since this is a feature of manipulation and counter-manipulation, a careful examination is warranted.

Faded Diminutives? . . . An Excursus

David Schaps offers us a good introduction to diminutives:

> A diminutive may be disparaging ('kinglet'), friendly ('Joey'), pleonastic ('Katyushka'), ironic (Robin Hood's Little John), or

---

151. Malina and Rohrbaugh, *Social Science Commentary on the Gospel of John*, 288. Emphasis added.

152. Ibid., 288; Bultmann, "záō, zōḗ (*bióō, bíos*)," 290; Brown, *The Gospel according to John (XIII–XXI)*, 1070; Carson, *The Gospel according to John*, 665.

153. Brown notes its usage also in 16:21. Brown, *The Gospel according to John (XIII–XXI)*, 1070.

154. Which is found in Heb 5:13, "For everyone who lives on milk is unskilled in the word of righteousness, since he is a child." Oepke, "παῖς," in Kittel and Friedrich, eds., *TDNT*, 5:638; Preisker "νεφρός," Ibid., 4:911; Brown, *The Gospel according to John (XIII–XXI)*, 1070.

155. Interestingly, Petersen points out that Homer's poems contain no diminutives. This may have been due to the poet's distaste for them, or to a dialect that did not have or use them. Petersen, *Greek Diminutives in -ION*, 199.

simply a regular part of a word ('Mädchen') or a name (Theodor Herzl). A diminutive may refer to a difference of importance ('baronet') or sex ('majorette') rather than size, and may even refer to something larger that [sic] of the simple form: it is by a quirk of historical linguistics that a hamlet is larger than a home, but it is a fact of the synchronic language.[156]

Diminutives often fade in their meaning. Donald Swanson asks the following question about παιδίον: "When does it cease to mean 'little boy' and become simply 'boy'?"[157] An interpreter might ask, "Has it indeed ceased to mean little boy?" In either refinement of meaning, the reader may ask why the disciples did not recognize the risen Christ on the shore and recall his ability to provide fish for them to eat on the shore, as he did with the παιδάριον in 6:9. But the diminutive question does not stop here. There are several other diminutives in John 21. In addition to παιδίον, there is ὀψάριον, πλοιάριον, ἀρνίον, and προβάτιον.[158] If these are faded diminutives as Brown uses the term,[159] we must ask not only why the FE uses them, but also whether they were chosen intentionally. To make matters more complex, Walter Petersen points out that even the ancients disagreed on whether such terms retained their diminutive nuance: "The Greek grammarians, however, erred not only in their theories, but their facts are often quite untrustworthy, partly because they were *often describing phenomena which antedated themselves by centuries*, and of which they could have no more empirical knowledge than we have, partly because *pre-conceived notions obscured their view*."[160] Since the FE uses five different diminutives in nineteen verses, this warrants further examination.

To work through this problem, one must first consider the basic sense of diminutives and then their resultant nuances of meaning. Much of the following discussion is from the work of Walter Petersen and Donald Swanson and addresses what factors can and should color interpretation.[161] From that point, I will address each particular diminutive as it arises in the text to

---

156. Schaps, "When is a Piglet Not a Piglet?," 208.

157. Swanson, "Diminutives in the Greek New Testament," 135; Brown, *The Gospel according to John (XIII–XXI)*, 1069.

158. Despite its -ιον suffix, προσφάγιον is not a diminutive. The -ιον suffix does not always indicate a diminutive, and I can find no lexicon that identifies it as such. See Petersen, *Greek Diminutives in -ION*, 155; Swanson, "Diminutives in the Greek New Testament," 139. Contra Brodie, *The Gospel according to John*, 583.

159. Brown, *The Gospel according to John (XIII–XXI)*, 1069.

160. Petersen, *Greek Diminutives in -ION*, 1–2.

161. Ibid.; Swanson, "Diminutives in the Greek New Testament," 134–51.

see whether there is evidence to suggest that we should regard these terms as having any diminutive nuances in John 21.

Diminutive Meanings: Smallness

The original sense of a diminutive had to do with smallness or diminished size.[162] Petersen prefers this semantic definition: "a word which either originally or in the consciousness of the person using it, designated a small object or a closely associated or related idea like youth, elegance, nicety, and the like."[163] An example from classical literature is the primitive δέλφαξ–pig, and its diminutive δελφάκιον - piglet.[164] The most common example of a diminutive in the New Testament is the one first encountered in John 21—παιδίον.[165] In this instance, the idea of being smaller or younger begins with the primitive "child," when παῖς was "used for baby," for instance by Homer, without the need for a diminutive form.[166] But language changes—drastically. Thus, the understanding of Greek diminutives is complicated by the fact that the literature that must be analyzed ranges over nearly a millennium.[167] Some diminutives are then further complicated when the diminished sense has been added to a primitive lexical form that already denoted something smaller or younger than something else did. Thus, παιδίον (and παιδάριον) probably had the broadest range of meaning of any single diminutive in the New Testament. Its sense can refer to not only small physical size, but also fewer in years, or even "immature."[168] From this original diminished sense arise a very wide range of meanings.

These lead to great lexical utility, but at the risk of over simplification, my discussion will narrow to some generally recognized categories. However, what follows are not completely separate categories unanimously

---

162. Though Petersen notes this is not true of all diminutives, it is generally the root concept from which the phenomena of diminutives arises, and this appears to be true in multiple languages. Ibid., 1–2.

163. Ibid., 4.

164. Schaps, "When is a Piglet Not a Piglet?," 208.

165. Petersen, *Greek Diminutives in -ION*, 171; Swanson, "Diminutives in the Greek New Testament," 143.

166. Before the usage of -ιον diminutives had begun. Petersen, *Greek Diminutives in -ION*, 11, 53, 102.

167. Amundsen, "Some Remarks on Greek Diminutives," 14; Petersen, *Greek Diminutives in -ION*, 112, 135–36, 164–66, 182, 204; Robertson, *A Grammar of the Greek New Testament*, 66.

168. Petersen, *Greek Diminutives in -ION*, 103; Schaps, "*When is a Piglet Not a Piglet?*," 208.

agreed upon by scholars, nor even of one scholar.[169] We must allow for overlap since language grows and usage as well as interpretation is fluid. Thus, for the purposes of this research, I summarize four separate but overlapping categories.

Deteriorative Nuance

Perhaps better known than smallness is the deteriorative nuance and its frequent usage in Greek comedy and plays.[170] In this usage, the idea of smallness indicates a negative sense. This usage is also a common idiom in modern English, such as when two men are joking, or even insulting one another; one may refer to the other as "little man." As Petersen affirms, size and strength are often considered positive male traits whereas smallness can be subject to ridicule and associated with weakness. These nuances may occur together, when a person is actually small but also looked upon pejoratively because of this trait. This is not only used to refer to persons but to objects as well, and such is common in the Greek comedies.[171] Here one may also add Schaps' ironic category where he cites the more modern example of Robin Hood's "Little John."[172]

The idea of "less than" is also a diminutive nuance in this class, implying that something is less than its true essence. Thus, an illegitimate child, instead of being referred to as a παῖς, may be instead called a παιδίον . . . a son, yes, "but no real son."[173] Likewise, illegitimate children whose mothers were foreigners may be called νόθοι, bastards, or παιδία, "in contrast to the full citizens and foreigners."[174] The deteriorative sense is the frequently translated nuance of γυναικάριον found in 2 Timothy 3:6.[175]

---

169. See for instance Petersen's elaborate table of contents where he has nine chapters alone for possible nuances of the suffix of –ιον, not including the longer suffixes containing –ιον, such as –αιον, –υιον, etc. Petersen, *Greek Diminutives in -ION*, 9–11.

170. "[N]o branch of literature displays a richer selection of diminutives than the comedy." Amundsen, "Some Remarks on Greek Diminutives," esp. 5. See also Swanson, "Diminutives in the Greek New Testament," 134–51.

171. Amundsen, "Some Remarks on Greek Diminutives," 8; Petersen, *Greek Diminutives in -ION*, 112–14.

172. Schaps, "When is a Piglet Not a Piglet?," 208.

173. Petersen, *Greek Diminutives in -ION*, 112.

174. Ibid., 112–13.

175. E.g., "silly women" (KJV). Swanson, "Diminutives in the Greek New Testament," 146–47. But Bassler counters: "Taken by itself this term is not as pejorative as the NRSV translation, 'silly women,' suggests." Bassler, *1 Timothy, 2 Timothy, Titus*, 160.

Hypocoristic Nuance

Diminutives can also be used hypocoristically, or endearingly.[176] This is when the object, person, or animal is spoken of with affection. A prime example is the usage of the suffix "y" in English. Thus, when readers "hear the sound at the end of Johnny we immediately recognize it as an expression of endearment."[177] Children do this when they call a small dog "doggy" or a cat "kitty," even when the animal may not be small. Therefore, large dogs might not normally be referred to with a diminutive ending, yet a "pet dog" or "house dog" can be called a κύων.[178] So too, παιδίον can be used with these two senses to mean "dear little son."[179] This is the usage in Matthew 18:2–4 with three occurrences of παιδίον, "Whoever humbles himself like this child is the greatest in the kingdom of heaven." Donald Hagner renders this "little child," though it probably should be "dear little child."[180] Additionally, the endearing nuance is often used in the second person and with the vocative case. This is frequently so with παιδίον and in such instances, it usually is a marker of an "endearing expression."[181] Endearment then branches into other nuances. It can be used to denote something as "pretty" and/or to denote the feminine, which may or may not be classed as hypocoristic.[182] Daniel Wallace posits that γύναιον is often used with "derision" but rarely with "endearment."[183] The hypocoristic sense can also imply pity, as Leiv Amundsen believes was likely the case when Luke, switching to the diminutive, "lets Jesus heal the ὠτίον, the poor damaged ear of the servant who was perhaps only ordered to the garden by his master" (Luke 22:51).[184]

Nuances Related to Food

A distant cousin of the hypocoristic (endearment) nuance has to do with animals, especially those that are small; and when spoken of as an article of food, this will overlap with the category of appurtenance (meaning "to

---

176. Swanson, "Diminutives in the Greek New Testament," 135.
177. Petersen, *Greek Diminutives in -ION*, 128, 174.
178. Swanson, "Diminutives in the Greek New Testament," 146–47.
179. Petersen, *Greek Diminutives in -ION*, 171.
180. Hagner, *Matthew. 14-28*, 515–17; Decker, *Koine Greek Reader*, 46.
181. Petersen, *Greek Diminutives in -ION*, 174, 219.
182. Ibid., 11; Swanson, "Diminutives in the Greek New Testament," 135.
183. Wallace, *Greek Grammar beyond the Basics*, 333n50.
184. Amundsen, "Some Remarks on Greek Diminutives," 14.

pertain to") below.¹⁸⁵ When animals are spoken of as food, the diminutive can also mean the item is not only palatable but also "delicious," and the smallness itself can connote "daintiness" or "delicacy." It can also be difficult to separate these two meanings. At times they are both present; other times only the tastiness is intended.¹⁸⁶ Though eating a delicious lamb does not fit the context of John 21, the Greek comics used the term ἀρνίον frequently in this way, and this connotation will be a consideration when examining the occurrence of ὀψάριον in the text.¹⁸⁷

Appurtenance Nuances

The last, and perhaps broadest, category is that of appurtenance.¹⁸⁸ Petersen defines appurtenance as "belonging to" or "connected with."¹⁸⁹ When explaining this usage, we might use the phrases "pertaining to," "made of," "belonging to the category of," "a kind of," or even "that which is like."¹⁹⁰ Often the meaning has no apparent connection to small size or youth, and Petersen regards this diminutive nuance as a "substantivized secondary adjective and the word 'diminutive' means nothing."¹⁹¹ A good example is "συναγώγιον as 'that connected with the assembling.'"¹⁹² This is done in modern English, with many suffixes that often have no relation to size. Someone might say, for example, that a gathering had a "churchy" feel to it, or members of a group agree to meet at "noon-ish"; a work of literature is called "Kafkaesque," or one may remark that a food item tastes "fishy." This last example brings to the fore Greek diminutives where animals classed as food items *overlap* with the hypocoristic. In English, "veal," although not a diminutive, is an animal that is younger and preferred in taste because of its younger age but is also a *type of* beef. More commonly in English, when speaking of an animal as a class of food, instead of using a diminutive suffix, one says *pork* for *pig* and *beef* for *cattle*. A diminutive of appurtenance

---

185. Swanson, "Diminutives in the Greek New Testament," 141.

186. Petersen, *Greek Diminutives in -ION*, 141, 171–73. However, Petersen does not classify this meaning as a part of the hypocoristic.

187. Ibid., 157.

188. Here what Petersen elaborately explains I have especially condensed.

189. Ibid., 39.

190. Ibid., 11, 53, 102, 136, 206.

191. Ibid., 12.

192. Ibid., 39. Petersen classifies this term under "Place names." Petersen also cites diminutives of the subclass "Like, but not equivalent to the primitive" as late as the second or third century C.E. See also ibid., 11–12, 112, 229.

achieves this without changing morphemes. Thus in Greek, ἀρνίον can carry the connotations of both size and food, or either by itself.[193]

Faded Diminutives or Interpretable Nuances?

But what of so-called "faded diminutives," and what factors should color interpretation of these possibilities? First, observe that even the terms "diminutive" and "faded diminutives" do not seem to carry consensus among scholars. Note Swanson's narrow definition: "The inclusion of a word in the deminutive [sic] list must hinge on a demonstration that the word has a meaning of smallness (or related meaning)."[194] This would arguably exclude appurtenance terms as true diminutives and quickly broaden what we deem faded. Petersen, however, classifies faded diminutives as when the new term ceases to modify or be associated with its primitive. This can begin subtly.[195] For instance, "fading of the idea of small size may take place in words like σφυρίον, 'a small kind of hammer,' . . . for the carpenter may think of the larger and smaller kinds of the same instruments as quite distinct from each other, just as a musician thinks of a flute and piccolo as different."[196] Here note that hammer is a technical term for the carpenter, and that different words for fish may be recognizably technical terms to fisherman, of which any nuances would be most keenly felt by some of the disciples in John 21, even if these nuances are now lost upon the reader.

Therefore, without creating too much complexity, the task is to get at the meanings of these five diminutives: παιδίον, ὀψάριον, πλοιάριον, ἀρνίον, and προβάτιον. Since some argue that these are only synonyms, the working question will be, "Are these terms no longer distinct from their primitive morphemes and instead only stylistic synonyms?" This is the only real interpretive issue at the moment. For if all the diminutive forms in John 21 are faded in this sense, then all the terms in the chapter for fish simply mean fish, and both terms for boat simply mean boat without any shading of meaning, and the same goes for the terms for sheep. This would mean the three forms of παῖς in the entire FG all simply denote "child" and the reader is not expected to detect any shadings.[197] Moreover, this would mean that none of the forms for fish, children, boat, or sheep contribute any

---

193. Ibid., 157.

194. Swanson, "Diminutives in the Greek New Testament," 141.

195. Thus, Petersen and Swanson are difficult to reconcile as to what are diminutives and faded diminutives.

196. Ibid., 165.

197. Though only one is used in chapter 21.

diminutive nuances indicative of smallness of size, youthfulness, endearment, disparagement, or even appurtenance. I will argue that this is not the case, and the following are the interpretive guidelines that have proven helpful in working through the text:

1. That a term ends in -ιον is no guarantee it is a diminutive of any kind. Petersen asserts, "[I]t is manifestly unsafe to classify all possible cases as diminutives, and when there does not seem to be a difference in usage between primitive and derivative, the burden of proof rests upon him who claims diminutive origin."[198]

2. The opposite is also true: Amundsen states of Jens Hanssen's work on Latin diminutives that he has "proved that *one should hesitate to discard the specific meaning of a diminutive form too early*, and the same warning may prove valid as regards Greek."[199] Thus, interpreters are on unsafe ground if they assume that authors never intended all or most diminutive nuances.

3. Textual criticism preferences may too often discard the diminutive form and thus its meaning. Keith Elliott proposes that the "intimate language" of Koine had worked its way into the higher Attic, raising the ire of some writers: "It is therefore not surprising to find that Atticist stylists like Phrynichus objected to the proliferation of -ιον -αριον endings in Greek and sought to eliminate these forms."[200] Petersen notes similarly, "While there can be no doubt that language in its higher forms can not revel in diminutives like some popular dialects, it does not necessarily follow that it must avoid them altogether."[201] Working with variants and the belief that the diminutive was distasteful to copyists, Elliott concludes, "Given our general rule, the diminutive form is more likely to be eliminated by stylistically conscious scribes than that the diminutive forms were written in for no obvious purpose."[202] The variant in Galatians 4:19 of τέκνα in "my little children" is an example.

---

198. Petersen, *Greek Diminutives in -ION*, 155.

199. Amundsen, "Some Remarks on Greek Diminutives," 12; emphasis added. On the other hand, he tempers this with, "In this connection it is interesting to review the language of the *New Testament*, which to a certain degree represents popular speech, on different levels. The topics of the Biblical writings naturally call for only a very limited number of diminutives." Ibid. But see Wallace, *Greek Grammar beyond the Basics*, 19n17, "[T]he meaning is often unaltered from the normal form." Thus there is a need for guidelines.

200. Elliott, "Nouns with Diminutive Endings in the New Testament," 391.

201. Petersen, *Greek Diminutives in -ION*, 199.

202. Elliott, "Nouns with Diminutive Endings in the New Testament," 391, 396.

Amundsen points out that the diminutive is very often the *lectio difficilior*, noting that Eberhard Nestle omits τεκνία and "in accordance with his textual principles—puts τέκνα in his text; the diminutive is obviously preferable."[203]

4. We must use caution so that tradition and reverence for the text do not lead to flat characters that have no texture, and narrative dialogues that have no contours.[204] Chatman, drawing upon Bradley's method of character analysis, generally urges a "careful re-scanning of text, especially in places where *tradition may have blinded us by simplistic attitudes.*"[205] The character of Jesus in the Gospels was certainly round and had texture. Rather than portraying composure, he acted violently in zealous anger (John 2:17) and wept at sorrow (11:35). He even used the deteriorative of "dog" with refusal language, *accismus*,[206] which sounded like the "pride of a Jew"[207] to maneuver a conversation into a vivid demonstration of great gentile faith for his disciples (Matt 15:26).[208] Thus when interpreters read a diminutive form, they must *work through* possible readings with the categories of smallness, hypocoristic, deteriorative, or appurtenance in mind. Allowing for such texture in characters would in no way weaken the authority of the text, since Genesis readers are familiar with such acts as the command for Abraham to sacrifice Isaac (Gen 22), in which God, as a character, is certainly complex and not lacking in texture.

5. The more often a word is used, the more likely it is to have faded in its original diminutive force. Petersen argues, "On the whole it may be said that the oftener a word is used, the less likely will it be to suffer analysis, and words like παιδίον, which were in daily or hourly use,

---

203. Amundsen, "Some Remarks on Greek Diminutives," 13. Thus below, one must ask, as Amundsen believes, if προβάτια is preferred.

204. Nathan Maxwell, personal interview, Palm Beach, Florida, October 21, 2010; Forster, *Aspects of the Novel*, 103–4. This warning is an especially important for those who, like me, are evangelicals. I argue that evangelicals have tended to overlook or minimize the difficult behavior of biblical characters, such as Peter's racist behavior in Gal, which was confronted by Paul.

205. Chatman, *Story and Discourse*, 134; emphasis added.

206. Bullinger, *Figures of Speech used in the Bible*.

207. Amundsen, "Some Remarks on Greek Diminutives," 12.

208. Contrast the diminutive κυναρίος here with Jesus' using non-diminutive κυσὶν in Matt 7:6. Although the Vulgate preserves the diminutive in the woman's response of *catelli* in Matt 15:27, it has been laundered from Jesus' lips in verse 26 and replaced with *canibus*. Ibid., 12.

would be analyzed most rarely and fade most easily."[209] These five diminutives occur at this frequency: παιδίον occurs fifty-two times in the New Testament, and thirteen times in the FG;[210] ὀψάριον occurs five times, all in John's Gospel; πλοιάριον has four appearances in the New Testament, all but one penned by the FE;[211] ἀρνίον is found thirty times in the New Testament,[212] all but the occurrence in John 21:15 are found in Revelation. Finally, προβάτιον is only found as two variants in John 21:16–17 and is not a preferred reading either by Metzger,[213] the Nestle-Aland 28th edition,[214] or the SBL edition.[215]

6. Hard and fast rules or rigid categories about how any particular diminutive should *always* be interpreted may be hazardous to the interpreter's task. Frequently Petersen advises that simply because at a certain point in time, a diminutive has faded in regards to its nuance of small size, does not mean that all users of the diminutive form from that point forward would use the term without regard for its diminutive nuance:[216] "One individual might still be in touch with an obsolete meaning of a word while another had no longer any idea of it."[217] With

---

209. Petersen, *Greek Diminutives in -ION*, 165. Aelius Theon, in *Exercises*, spoke of the multiple meanings of παῖς alone—child, son, slave—without even mentioning its diminutive possibilities. See Kennedy, *Progymnasmata*, 63.

210. Omitting παῖς, which occurs twenty-four times in the New Testament and twice in the FG, and παιδάριον, which occurs only once—in John 6:9. Swanson counted forty-nine occurrences of παιδίον and remarked that "it is interesting to note that John uses all three derivatives of pais." Swanson, "Diminutives in the Greek New Testament," 143–45. These searches were performed in Aland et al., *The Greek New Testament*, using Logos Bible Software. This was the 27th edition. Variants mentioned herein were also checked against the 28th edition.

211. Swanson counted six. The Textus Receptus has the diminutive form in Mark 4:36, having also the same count of three diminutive boats in John 6 as the UBS4/NA27 and the NA28, but uses the diminutive form in different points in the dialogue. Logos Research System, *Stephen's 1550 Textus Receptus*; Aland et al., *The Greek-English New Testament*, 28th ed., 624.

212. Swanson counts twenty-nine. Swanson, "Diminutives in the Greek New Testament," 143.

213. Metzger et al., *A Textual Commentary on the Greek New Testament: A Companion Volume*, 4th ed., 220.

214. Though the 23rd edition prefers προβάτια in both verses 16 and 17. Aland et al., *Novum Testamentum Graece*, 23rd ed., 296.

215. Holmes and Society of Biblical Literature, *Greek New Testament: SBL Edition*.

216. Petersen, *Greek Diminutives in -ION*, 165.

217. "The hearer, however, and still more the reader, will often not be able to follow what was in the mind of the speaker or writer, and consequently the two classes of diminutives can not always be sharply distinguished in actual interpretation . . . We can

different locations and times of speakers, diminutives might be used "*ad libitum*," and could therefore be "coined" and used variously from speaker to speaker.[218] Swanson agrees: "It is difficult to distinguish completely the true from the faded meanings, even in context; it is possible that even as new words were being coined with diminutive suffixes, older words with the same suffix(es) were losing their diminutive meaning."[219] And again, Petersen, in addressing the evolution of double diminutives,[220] speaks not only of the formation of additional suffixes, but explains the sender-receiver communication problems that gave rise to them. One speaker may have used the diminutive form of a primitive, which itself had already carried a "diminutive force." Then, the hearer of the new diminutive form might still regard the diminutive nuance in the primitive, which the speaker did not. The result is that an additional new diminutive is eventually created.[221] Consequently, even the first intended recipient of the communication had hurdles to overcome in ascertaining meaning. This is especially true when one author uses different meanings for the same word.[222] Is this speaker referring simply to smallness, or implying contempt, or showing endearment, etc.? Or is the opposite true? Is the usage carrying no diminutive force at all but is now equivalent to its primitive? Certainly, with listeners and even readers of a text who lived in the same cultural time and space as the author, there were clues that aided in the process. Petersen proposes that ideally, "[t]o judge correctly all of the different words would require a most intimate knowledge of the mental habits of the ordinary Greek people."[223] Unfortunately, these clues may no longer be apparent to modern readers, giving occasion for an overly flat reading. But the query must forge ahead, for certainly

---

not always tell whether the speaker had in mind a particularly small calf when using μοσχίον or a particularly small child when using παιδίον." Ibid., 102.

218. Ibid., 139.

219. Swanson, "Diminutives in the Greek New Testament," 146–47.

220. Two combined diminutive suffixes attached to one primitive.

221. Petersen, *Greek Diminutives in -ION*, 206. Swanson appears to be in the same camp: "It is also possible that the rise of double and triple diminutives is due to the process of fading." Swanson, "Diminutives in the Greek New Testament," 146–47.

222. Herodotus used παιδίον when referring to a "baby" as well as to four and nine year olds. *Herod.* 1.111; 4. 187; 5.51. One can certainly envision a mother, in English at least, calling her grown child "my baby," thus we experience this lexical flexibility in English as well. Petersen, *Greek Diminutives in -ION*, 136, 140; Herodotus, *The Histories* (Greek).

223. Petersen, *Greek Diminutives in -ION*, 128, 154.

an *en masse* dismissal of diminutive force is just as egregious to the text as an overzealous application thereof.

7. The emotive tenor in the text is a significant factor, for, as Petersen says, "in the case of diminutives, so much depends on the emotional tone of the passage or the particular flavor of a word."[224] An excellent example of this would be the two diminutives in John 6. The tone of the dialogue is one of unbelief and doubt as to whether so little of an amount of food (John 6:9) is enough for so large a crowd (6:2): "There is a boy (παιδάριον) here who has five barley loaves and two fish (ὀψαρίων), but what are they for so many?" The smallness of size is likely laced into both terms, and though we cannot say for certain, given the frequent theme of unbelief on the part of the disciples, a reading with the following deteriorative meanings is arguable: "Well, there is this little boy here who has five barley loaves and two puny fish but how are we going to feed a huge crowd with this?"

8. Plausibility of the nuance must be demonstrated. As stated earlier, Petersen believes the burden of proof lies with the one who argues diminutive meaning: "he must be able at least to suggest a *plausible* association between a comparatively large and small object."[225] Though Petersen is speaking here generally of identifying diminutives, the same is true for a given pericope and the application of specific nuances. Diminutive meanings must certainly fit with the overall scheme of meaning in a unit, and if such cannot be reasonably argued, the application of any of the diminutive connotations may then be abandoned. Thus in John 6:9, the contrast between the large size of the crowd and the small amount of food is certainly present, and the interpretation of Andrew's statement to Jesus as emphasizing the boy's small size in a negative way, and belittling his two fish as insufficient, is *plausible,* if not probable.

9. Finally, when encountering diminutives in the FG, Zumstein's method of understanding a text via *relecture* is helpful:

> The relecture model of composition takes account of a typical phenomenon of the Gospel of John: certain parts of the narrative are supplemented by texts of various lengths and orientations. It must be stressed from the outset that these additions are not intended to fill holes in the plot but to extend theological reflection of the text as it exists. Hence there is

---

224. Ibid., 4. Note the mention of γύναιον above.
225. Ibid., 155; emphasis added.

a meaningful relationship between the original text (the so-called "reference text") and its supplementation (the so-called "reception text"). The relecture model tries to determine the nature of this relationship more precisely. The reference text and the reception text are not simply strung together but refer closely to one another, since the reference text leads to the emergence of the reception text.²²⁶

The relecture may not speak directly to whether or not a diminutive force is intended, but it does clarify the overall meaning of a passage. In the example of John 6, the opening fifteen verses offer the account of the feeding of the five thousand. Immediately after the intervening six verses, where Jesus walks on the water, the FE offers the reader an additional thirty-seven verses adding theological import to the multiplication of the bread and relating it to Jesus and also, intertextually, with Moses and manna from heaven.²²⁷ When the reader carefully examines the manna narrative in Exodus, she finds that this too was a test (Exod 16:4), presented in the context of grumbling over what little food God had provided (16:2–12). Moses was therefore angry with the people for their lack of trust in divine provision for enough food and, in the end, they learned that the manna was, in fact, enough (16:18–21). Hence, the method of relecture elucidates and sharpens the nuances associated with the *little* boy, the loaves, and *just two* fish, all considered too insignificant to feed five thousand. Relecture will also assist in examining this and other diminutives in chapter 21 further below.

Restated briefly, these nine guidelines are as follows: 1) Not all –ιον endings indicate diminutives; 2) Interpreters should not be too quick to assume diminutive meaning, nor to dismiss it; 3) Scribal practices, as well as those of textual criticism, have tended to minimize diminutives in the text; 4) Reverence for the text may lead to overly flat characters and simplistic narratives; 5) Frequently used diminutives are more likely to have lost their diminutive effect; 6) Any particular diminutive generally cannot be restricted to the same meaning, even with the same author; 7) The emotional tenor of a passage is a key tool for picking up on the diminutive nuance; 8) Plausibility of a diminutive nuance must be demonstrated and the burden

---

226. Zumstein, "Intratextuality and Intertextuality in the Gospel of John," 126.

227. See also Hoskyns and Davey, *The Fourth Gospel*, 368–70: "The author of the Fourth Gospel adds an interpretation to the parable of the Good Shepherd, just as previously he had added an interpretation to the miracle of the Feeding of the Five Thousand."

of proof lies with the one who argues for it; 9) Relecture is a known device in the FG which may be helpful in determining the meaning of diminutives.

Given these recommendations, one can see that it is *equally* precarious either to assume that most diminutives have become only synonyms of their primitive root or to look for a diminutive nuance with every diminutive suffix that occurs in the text. Some Johannine scholars tend toward the former.[228] Thus these principles need application throughout the text, to which the work now returns, examining each diminutive as it arises.

Little Ones Wrestle with a Great Catch (John 21:5–9)

Little Ones?

Retracing our steps, we recall that the FE uses the diminutive παιδία when Jesus inquired if the disciples had anything to eat. The available translation options are "children," "slaves," "little children," "dear little children" or some type of negative meaning. There are a number of issues with this term. It is the most frequent diminutive in the New Testament, so it is more likely to have lost diminutive meaning. At the same time, it already indicates smallness of size in its primitive form of παῖς, thus the reading cannot rule out size or youth as a distinction. Second, the FE has already used this term, but in the double diminutive form παιδάριον, in chapter 6 for a small boy. There the FE used the term in conjunction with both a lack of food to eat and with negative associations with what the little boy had supplied to eat. Still, this was on the lips of Andrew (John 6: 8), not Jesus, as in 21:5. Do these points minimize the sense of youthfulness in παιδίον, used by Jesus, over against παιδάριον, used by Andrew? Perhaps not, and the LXX offers further support, for παιδίον and παιδία in Genesis are consistently translated "child," "lad," "children," "youngster," "babe," or "little ones," including in some locations in the Joseph novella.[229] Moreover, I have already established that the

---

228. In that they note the FE's frequent use of synonyms, the difficulty of faded diminutives, or that a diminutive is interchangeable with other terms. *John (XIII–XXI)*, 1069; Bultmann, *The Gospel of John*, 700–707; Pfitzner, "They Knew It Was the Lord," 65; Keener, *The Gospel of John*, 2:1228.

229. Such as Gen 33:2, 5, 13; 44:20, 22, 32, 33, 34; 45:19. This analysis was completed in both the Brenton LXX as well as the *New English Translation*. Additionally, the diminutive form is never translated as "servant," "slave," or "bondservant" in Gen, and almost never in the entire LXX. It is translated "servants" in 2 Macc 8:28 in Brenton's translation, but "children" in the *New English Translation*. The double diminutive form παιδάριον, is translated "servant" roughly one-fifth of the time in the LXX, forty-five out of 233 instances in the Brenton LXX. None of the instances of παιδάριον in Gen is

FE is not bound to use the term or meaning in the same category in both chapters.

Since I argue that these seven disciples are "aimless fishermen," Jesus, with his usage of the vocative, may be using "little" in the hypocoristic subcategory of pity.[230] Petersen notes that with παιδίον, smallness of size and youth can be combined with the hypocoristic nuance. He also notes the usage of pity with this term.[231] Furthermore, since the meaning of the primitive παῖς already includes youth, an author may use these two meanings in combination with the nuance of immaturity in comparison to adults. Petersen's work supports this meaning too and notes that it could even refer to "below the adult in intelligence" or "stupidity" in comparison to adults, though a singular pejorative sense is not what is in play here.[232] Adding the tool of relecture, note that Jesus later commands Peter to feed the sheep, and makes the prophetic statement of "when you were young . . . but when you are old" in verse 18. I do not think that Jesus is referring here literally to a young Peter, but figuratively to a younger Peter, whom Jesus has just fed.[233] This Peter is younger comparatively, the text implies, than the older, more mature Peter—in accordance with the values of the FG—whom Jesus predicts will later follow Jesus by glorifying God in his death (John 21:19). This present, younger Peter gird himself and left the other disciples, going where he wanted. Moreover, Jesus has just fed this younger Peter. If this interpretation is correct, then Jesus, in referring to the disciples as "children," may have felt pity for their immature state: a state in which they go fishing under their own power and were powerless to feed themselves.[234] All three nuances then—youth, immaturity and pity—are plausible in παιδία. This is based on the relecture, found in verse 18, of the shoreline call to the disciples as "children," and Jesus' subsequent feeding of these young, immature disciples. They do not yet seem to understand that "apart from me you

---

translated "servant." Brenton, *The Septuagint Version of the Old Testament and Apocrypha*; Pietersma and Wright, *A New English Translation of the Septuagint*.

230. "Thus the sense of nothingness, which was first expressed by the nightlong failure to achieve anything, is now compounded by the fact that they are little children who have not a bite." Brodie, *The Gospel according to John*, 583.

231. Petersen, *Greek Diminutives in -ION*, 173, 178.

232. Ibid., 114, 174.

233. Bultmann is certain Jesus was using a proverb in John 21:18. Bultmann, *The Gospel of John*, 713. Carson, *The Gospel according to John*, 679. Jesus may also be alluding to Psalm 37:25. Köstenberger, *John*, 598. Regardless, Jesus likely is not referring to mere chronological youth.

234. As to possible intertextuality, here the "little ones," in "So do not fear; I will provide for you and your little ones" (Gen 50:21), טַף, is not translated as παῖς in the LXX but rather τὰς οἰκίας ὑμῶν.

can do nothing" (15:5).²³⁵ This evokes Jesus' pity. His active manifestation through the miracle of the catch, in light of the entire tone of the passage, may be regarded as a gentle rebuke to the entire group and a complete rebuke and implied eventual restoration of Peter who leads the fishing trip.²³⁶ In that scenario, which of the disciples can dare ask Jesus who he was? The FE may have intended perceptive readers to take note of some or all of these subtleties.

Big Fish Little Fish

Earlier I noted the unusual term προσφάγιον, referring to the fish that the disciples had not caught in verse three. I observed that lexical evidence supports this word referring to fish as food.²³⁷ But if the FE is echoing John 6:9, why is it not the same word for fish, ὀψάρια, on Jesus' lips as it was on Andrew's in John 6:9?²³⁸ Further still, why did the FE use either term when neither was frequently used for fish?²³⁹

---

235. "[T]he episode immediately takes on a highly symbolic dimension: with the break of light and the appearance of Jesus, the failure of the night before is radically reversed—from no fish at all to an enormous catch. In other words, the section pointedly teaches that it is only with Jesus that the disciples can prosper and succeed (cf. 15:4–5)." Segovia, "The Final Farewell of Jesus," 178. When considering that the two miracles (catching fish and providing breakfast) in John 21 are miracles of sustenance, this comment from Witherington on John 6 is relevant to the understanding of παιδίον: "[I]n Wisd.Sol. 16:20–26 the author discusses how 'without their toil you supplied them from heaven with bread ready to eat.' This in itself appears on the surface to be just another discussion of the Exod wonders, until one arrives at v. 26 and hears, 'so that your *children* whom you loved, O Lord, might learn that it is *not the production of crops* that feeds humankind but that *your word* sustains those who trust in you.' This is the same sort of point the Fourth Evangelist is driving at in the discourse in John 6—'Do not work for the food that perishes, but for the food that endures for eternal life, which the Son of Man will give you'(6:27)." Witherington III, *John's Wisdom*, 24; emphasis added.

236. Peter's leading role in the narrative was argued above.

237. Louw and Nida, *Greek-English Lexicon of the New Testament*, 50–51. I earlier stated that Swanson put it in his list of "non-diminutives." Swanson, "Diminutives in the Greek New Testament," 139.

238. Both terms carry the idea of smallness: προσφάγιον in the idea of a relish, and ὀψάρια sometimes rendered "tidbit" (in antiquity). Louw and Nida, *Greek-English Lexicon of the New Testament*, 1:50. On προσφάγιον in 21:5, "[T]he narrative context contrasts the disciples' lack of success in providing a meal with the Lord's role as chef, vss. 9–13." Danker et al., *A Greek-English Lexicon*, 6th ed., 746, 886. Shaw's position represents those who see the ecclesiastical symbolism beginning here: "[B]ut the προσφάγιον which they catch in response to his directions is a full complement of the whole church." Shaw, "Breakfast by the Shore," 18.

239. Louw and Nida, *Greek-English Lexicon of the New Testament*, 50.

Perhaps προσφάγιον was chosen to emphasize food, and the simple matter of its lack. This nuance may have been intended more so than indicating that the food was fish. From a lexical standpoint, this is certainly possible.[240] But προσφάγιον also has an intratextual allusion to chapter 6 and the feeding of the five thousand. Recalling that the New Testament authors often wrote with an aural audience in mind, I argue that in John 21, προσφάγιον may refer the reader back to a previous episode in the FG. In the Gospels, the word ἐσθίω, meaning "to eat," is used frequently: twenty-four times in Matthew, twenty-seven times in Mark, thirty-three times in Luke, and fifteen times in John. In the aorist and future though, it shifts to ἔφαγον and φάγομαι, respectively.[241] προσφάγιον is thought to be related to or a derivative of φαγεῖν, "to eat," an infinitive form.[242] Interestingly, Matthew uses the morpheme ἐσθι- rather than the φαγ- form eleven out of twenty-four times; Mark uses it eleven out of twenty-seven times; and Luke uses it in twelve of thirty-three occurrences. But the FE *never* draws on the morpheme ἐσθι- but adheres exclusively to φαγ-. The FE frequently uses it of Jesus speaking about consuming spiritual food, which of course, others frequently misunderstand. In 4:32 Jesus says, "I have food *to eat* that you do not know about," and in 6:50, "This is the bread that comes down from heaven, so that one *may eat* of it and not die." The chapter distribution of its usage is also significant:[243]

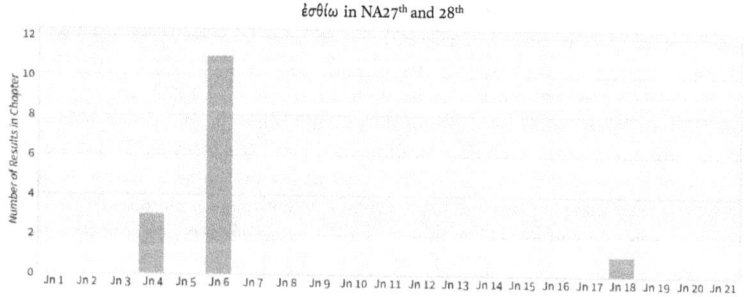

ἐσθίω in NA27th and 28th

240. Arndt et al., *A Greek-English Lexicon of the New Testament and Other Early Christian Literature*, 719. But see "fish," in Newman and Logos Research Systems, *A Concise Greek-English Dictionary of the New Testament*, 155.

241. Scott, *Reading New Testament Greek*, 8. See also Danker et al., *A Greek-English Lexicon*, 6th ed., 318, 853, where "φαγεῖν" is listed as a separate lexical entry, the "inf. of ἔφαγον . . . used as aor. 2 of ἐσθίω."

242. Or φαγῶ. Liddell, *A Lexicon: Abridged from Liddell and Scott's Greek-English Lexicon*, 699, 853; Hartman, "An Attempt at a Text-Centered Exegesis of John 21," 34.

243. John 4:31, 32, 33; 6:5, 23, 26, 31 (twice), 49, 50, 51, 52, 53; 18:28.

Προσφάγιον in 21:5 may have been a calculated word choice which could doubly mean food and fish, but which intratextually invoked the last episode at the Sea of Tiberias. With this word choice, there is a probable allusion to the *feeding* of the five thousand in chapter 6, in that an aural audience may have heard the similarity. But later the choice of ὀψάριον also builds the connection to John 6 with another layer, increasing the intratextuality of the narrative by giving the reader a second clue. I will discuss ὀψάριον in greater detail below, when our discussion moves to verse 10.

Recalling from 6:6 that Jesus was prone to "test" his disciples while knowing he would miraculously provide abundant sustenance, Jesus' words here in 21:5 recall that examination and hint that this too is a test: "Dear children, you don't have anything to eat, do you?"[244] Based on the syntax, we see that Jesus expects a negative answer.[245] This supports the idea of a test. Here the disciples are powerless to catch their breakfast if not for the merciful Lord.[246] In the feeding of the five thousand, the disciples were unaware— *ignorant of* Jesus' ability to provide abundantly—and they therefore stood in *unbelief* that Jesus would feed them from such a small store of bread and fish (John 6:9).[247] Therefore, προσφάγιον might have been chosen in John 21 to further link to the lessons of that feeding.

Verse 6 reads: "He said to them, 'Cast the net on the right side of the boat, and you will find some.'[248] So they cast it, and now they were not able

244. Boitani's observation is noteworthy. In commenting on Thomas Mann's *Joseph and his Brothers*, Boitani noted the German *Kinder*, "children," in Joseph's mouth where he reveals to his brothers, "Children, here I am, I am your brother Joseph!" Boitani argues that Mann's portrayal of Joseph "is alluding to its figural fulfillment in the New Testament. *Kinder* is the word Jesus uses, in the Lutheran Bible, in addressing the disciples when he appears to them, after the Resurrection, on Lake Tiberiad, and *es* is the pronoun with which his beloved disciple recognizes him immediately afterwards . . . in chapter 21 of John's Gospel: *Es ist der Herr*, 'It is the Lord.'" Boitani, *The Bible and Its Rewritings*, 45.

245. See Danker et al., *A Greek-English Lexicon*, 6th ed., 886, which suggests translating it "*you have no fish to eat, have you?*" See also ibid., 649, where under μήτι it reads, "though, the best rdg. is not μήτι but μή τι"(two words separated by a space, rather than μήτι), and ibid., 722, under οὐ, where the lexicon therefore, based on this syntax, argues for an expected negative answer from the disciples.

246. John 21:10, 12: "Bring some of the fish that you have just caught . . . Come and have breakfast."

247. Once again, Jesus' knowing is emphasized in 6:15: "Perceiving (γνοὺς) then that they were about to come and take him by force to make him king, Jesus withdrew again to the mountain by himself." Though Peter is not named in the chapter 6 feeding (as being present, that is), nor any of the other five named in chapter 21, it nonetheless has been recalled to the listener's mind by Jesus' words.

248. Scholars have also discussed whether the right side of the boat could demonstrate some intertextuality with Matthew: "Jesus' right side is the auspicious side, for it

to haul it in, because of the quantity of fish."[249] For the first time in chapter 21, the narrator has uttered ἰχθύων, "fish." Not once in this entire chapter does the Johannine Jesus use this term. I will return to the significance of this in a moment, but the enormous catch returns the reader to the themes of empowerment and disempowerment. The disciples had no power to catch fish, but Jesus has ample power to catch a large quantity of fish. In the theme of empowerment and disempowerment, those who know and recognize are empowered, and those who are ignorant, deceived, or who do not recognize are disempowered. The disciples' inability to catch fish all night long emphasizes their lack of power when working apart from Jesus. When they are immensely successful upon following the directions from Jesus, they recognize Jesus; their powerlessness by themselves is once again underscored while the power of Jesus is featured. Here one is reminded to some extent of Joseph, who counter-manipulated and held power over his once powerful brothers. He did so by withholding his identity from them who had withheld his true fate from their father. By withholding his identity until the end of Judah's speech (Gen 44:35), Joseph manipulates his brothers and his power is dramatized for the audience. When he reveals his identity, the brothers are "dismayed at his presence" (45:3). In John 21, Jesus withholds his identity and has positioned his manipulators where they too can only be humbled. They have been reminded that without him they are powerless. They are indebted to the one who has knowledge and power, and Peter in particular has been *positioned for reconciliation by means of his own devices*. Just like Joseph in Genesis 45, Jesus does not follow this opportunity for revenge to its logical *lex talionis* outcome; rather, he will eventually act compassionately toward Peter and his co-fishermen.

---

is there that the elect 'sheep' are gathered; the 'goats' gather ignominiously on his left. Augustine (*Homilies on John's Gospel*, 122.7) maintains that the fish caught on the right side of the boat represent people worthy of eternal life." Blaine, *Peter in the Gospel of John*, 148–49. See also Brown, *The Gospel according to John (XIII–XXI)*, 1071.

249. "The simplest explanation of course, is that the Johannine Jesus possesses supernatural knowledge!" Blaine, *Peter in the Gospel of John*, 149. This also aligns with a singular aspect of the Joseph story, namely, Joseph's ability to divine. *The TDOT*, in dealing with cognate languages under discussion of ידא, notes that in the magical realm of surrounding cultures, the gods, or diviners and magicians were the keepers of knowledge. See Botterweck and Ringgren, *TDOT*, 5:448–52. Thus Joseph says "don't you know that I practice divination?" (Gen 44:15). Joseph not only makes himself as a god to them but, emphasizing his knowledge and their ignorance, asserts that this is from a supernatural ability. This is in keeping with the overall theme of the story that Joseph was given such divine favor that he was entrusted with all of Egypt. Jacob too, in counter-manipulating Laban, is blessed with divine direction that disempowers Laban (Gen 31).

Why "Girding"?

At verse 7, one hears that the beloved disciple is the one who recognizes Jesus first, and this is no surprise.[250] As I noted earlier and as Segovia has written, "Recognition now takes place on the basis of a miraculous deed (cf. 2:1–11), and such recognition is formulated specifically in terms of the first part of Thomas' confession in 20:26–29: It is the Lord!"[251] These details of verse 7 are fairly trodden ground among scholars.[252] What is of interest for this study are the actions of Peter and the next detail of him "girding" himself. Scholars wrestle with the inclusion of this action in the passage. Brown declares that even if we determine why or to what degree Peter was disrobed, "one is still faced with the absurdity of adding clothes before swimming."[253] The FE also includes the detail that Peter throws himself into the sea and leaves his companions in the boat to get to Jesus on their own.[254] The emotion of recognizing Jesus brought the impetuous Peter to a sudden dramatic action.[255] In fact, Peter's behavior here is set in almost comical terms.[256] The word for Peter's leap is ἔβαλεν (βάλλω), the same word for casting the net into the sea. The narrator repeats the term three times. However, translations and smoothing miss the repetition in the Greek: "He said to them, '*Cast* (βάλετε) the net on the right side of the boat, and you will find some.' So they *cast* (ἔβαλον) it, and now they were not able to haul it in, because of the quantity of fish. That disciple whom Jesus loved therefore

---

250. Brooke, "4Q252 and the 153 Fish of John 21:11," 264.

251. Segovia, "The Final Farewell of Jesus," 178. Others, discussed above, see the miraculous catch as the sign or token which reveals Jesus to the BD. Shaw as well notes this. Shaw, "Breakfast by the Shore," 13.

252. For instance, Shaw states "This recognizably redactional verse may well have been introduced to raise the status of the apostle John in the view of his readers by comparison with Peter." Ibid., 17.

253. Brown, *The Gospel according to John (XIII–XXI)*, 1072.

254. "Literally, 'threw himself.'" Brown, The Gospel according to John (XIII–XXI), 1072. "There is not even a faint implication in the text that he swims away from Jesus ... To believe that his first act upon hearing BD's confessional cry is to swim away from Jesus is also to believe that subsequent to that maneuver he changes his mind and swims back toward Jesus, but that the Redactor lets the change in course (and thinking) go unreported." Blaine, *Peter in the Gospel of John*, 153.

255. Larsen comes to similar conclusions about emotion and recognition in general: "Aristotle gave a possible explanation for the popularity of anagnorisis by characterizing it as one of the strongest means of bringing about emotional affect in tragedy ... 1450a31–34." Larsen, *Recognizing the Stranger*, 25.

256. Stibbe argues for comedy and satire in the FG. Stibbe, *John's Gospel*, 107–29. Spencer also notes comical aspects in John 21. Spencer, "Narrative Echoes in John 21," 57, 59.

said to Peter, 'It is the Lord!' When Simon Peter heard that it was the Lord, he put on his outer garment, for he was stripped for work, and *cast* (ἔβαλεν) himself into the sea!"[257]

But why tell the reader that Peter had to gird himself and how does this fit into the story? Much has been made of this, but would not a Genesis reader assume that such details are necessary to the story?[258] The FE does not tell about the details of gathering equipment before setting off in the boat or about the weather; therefore, why include this detail? When trying to make sense of an apparently superfluous detail in the text, especially when approaching the text narratively, one must ask why the author *chose* to include this detail here. Economy in writing dictates choices. This was true not only of Hebrew narrative, as "conciseness" was espoused by rhetoric as well.[259] Alter reminds us that each detail is very important to the story.[260] Therefore, we must assume that the detail of Peter's girding himself is significant, even if at first we do not know what that significance is. Perhaps Alter would call it a "strategically introduced specification."[261] Including such a detail seems so abnormal to the story line that the phrase "for he was stripped for work" becomes an explanatory parenthetical phrase, because "he put on his outer garment" *does* seem out of place. I propose there are other reasons why these details are included that do not depend on how naked Peter was, nor his shame, though shame is a factor in Peter's reconciliation.[262] Truly, shame may have caused Peter to clothe himself, but this may not tell why the FE chose to inform the reader of that part of the story. If Peter was disrobed for working, some of the other six were likely disrobed as well. *Why tell the reader of Peter's behavior?*

The verb διαζώννυμι, "girding" in this passage, is the identical word used when Jesus girded himself with a towel in 13:4.[263] The lemma, ζώννυμι

---

257. This is simply the *English Standard Version* translation, with the exception of the last "cast." Contra Brodie, *The Gospel according to John*, 585, who views Peter's actions as symbolic and that the "distance is spiritual but Peter helped to close that distance."

258. Again, reading from the perspective of a Gen reader accustomed to reading, or hearing, Hebrew Bible *form*: "When a detail of dress, or physical appearance, or cuisine, or agency and action, is introduced in ancient Hebrew narrative, one can reasonably assume that it is there for a special purpose of thematic assertion of concatenation of plot, though this is not always evidently so." Alter, *The World of Biblical Literature*, 93.

259. Kennedy, *Progymnasmata*, 32.

260 Alter, *The Art of Biblical Narrative*, 79–80.

261. Alter, *The World of Biblical Literature*, 106.

262. See Blaine, *Peter in the Gospel of John*, 151–52.

263. Brown notes the occurrence in chapter 13 as well. Ibid., 1072. The word for "garment" in John 13 is ἱμάτια, while the word for garment in John 21:7 is ἐπενδύτην,

with δια prefixed to it, is found *nowhere* else in the New Testament or the LXX, other than these two places: twice in John 13:4-5, and once in John 21:7. Moreover, if scholars note the similar parallel occurrence of charcoal in only two Johannine passages and speculated about an intended allusion between the two (John 18:18; 21:9), why not here with this term?[264] In chapter 13, Jesus, too, had "laid aside his garments," and girded himself with a towel to serve those around him. He thus portrayed for them how, even as master and lord, a true servant washes the feet of others (13:14). The first time one hears of Peter girding himself is on this fishing expedition, which I have previously argued was aimless. Upon making the catch, Peter jumps from the boat, leaving the others in the boat to deal with the catch. Segovia notes that this implies "a certain disregard for the other disciples."[265] Observe also the adversative δὲ which begins this statement, οἱ δὲ ἄλλοι μαθηταὶ τῷ πλοιαρίῳ ἦλθον. Peter is contrasted with his companions. He has left them alone. Has the FE compared Peter's behavior, which follows after he girds himself in chapter 21, with Jesus' behavior after he girds himself in chapter 13? The FE may be portraying Peter's girding and following action as somewhat selfish, compared to Jesus girding and following action that was selfless. At the least, Peter's behavior, leaving his companions behind, cannot be a selfless act. If one remembers Jesus' words, "a servant is not greater than his master" (13:16), one may see a budding contrast growing between Peter's girding scene and the girding of Jesus. To see if this will blossom, I will return to the issue of girding below, where the FE returns to it, and further explore its purpose in the text.

Little Boat?

Regarding the boat that Peter abandons, the *New American Standard Bible* translates the FE's switch to πλοιαρίῳ, the dative of the diminutive form πλοιάριον: "But the other disciples came in the little boat, for they were not far from the land, but about one hundred yards away, dragging the net full of fish" (John 21:8).[266] This sets a contrast between the full net and the boat

---

and occurs only this once in the New Testament. Ἱμάτιον however occurs several times in all four Gospels. Thus there appears to be no immediate parallels between the actual garments of John 13 and those of chapter 21. The parallel lies in the girding.

264. Carson, *The Gospel according to John*, 671; Gaventa, "The Archive of Excess," 243–47; Quast, *Peter and the Beloved Disciple*, 84; Keener, *The Gospel of John*, 2:1092.

265. Segovia, "The Final Farewell of Jesus" 177, 179.

266. The Lockman Foundation, *New American Standard Bible*. The diminutive form is also preserved in the KJV, NKJV, and a few others. See also Alter, *The Art of Biblical Narrative*, 96, 182–83, on dialog between characters, and also Schaps, "When Is

size.²⁶⁷ In verses 3 and 6, the FE used πλοῖον. Brown discusses both forms and states, "Although some of the older commentators took the diminutive seriously, from it we can tell nothing of the size of the boat."²⁶⁸ Here he refers to Swanson's previously discussed position that "faded diminutives" no longer carry the diminutive connotation. A.T. Robertson also joins this group.²⁶⁹ Earlier, we explained Elliott's concerns regarding the textual elimination of diminutives. Yet, though Elliott asserts πλοιάρον to have been original in John 6:22, he believes "[t]here is no difference in the meaning in the context and unless it can be proved that John deliberately varies his language for stylistic purposes the diminutive should be maintained throughout this passage."²⁷⁰ However, Petersen's explanation supports a diminutive meaning, because the suffix of the diminutive here is -αριον. He explained that this ending may add the nuance of "merely, nothing but, etc." and cited the use of πλοιάριον.²⁷¹ Reading John 6:22 therefore as "there had been *only a small boat*," "*a mere boat*," or "*nothing but a little boat*" hints at the paucity of available sailing vessels and underscores that there were not many ways in which Jesus could have crossed the lake, especially given the previous night's storm. Moreover, when the diminutive form is used in chapter 21, it is contrasted in size to another object, the net, which was already described as so full that it could not be pulled aboard (21:6). The contrast supports the position that the use of the diminutive was intentional. Alter argues ef-

---

a Piglet Not a Piglet?," 208–9.

267. Though the word "full" is not in the Greek, Wallace asserts τὸ δίκτυον τῶν ἰχθύων to be a genitive of content rendered "the net full of fish." Wallace, *Greek Grammar beyond the Basics*, 93.

268. Brown, *The Gospel according to John (XIII-XXI)*, 1069.

269. Robertson, *A Grammar of the Greek New Testament*, 82; Swanson, "Diminutives in the Greek New Testament," 138–40; Brown, *The Gospel according to John (I-XII)*, 257.

270. Elliott, "Nouns with Diminutive Endings in the New Testament," 391, 396–98. See also Elliott, "The Third Edition of the United Bible Societies' Greek New Testament," 261, where he says, "John vi 23: The diminutive form πλοιάρια ought to stand firm. The v.l. reading the basic form is likely to be a stylistic alteration by scribes who objected to the overuse of faded diminutives in Koine Greek."

271. Petersen, *Greek Diminutives in -ION*, 269. Verses 23 and 24 also stay with the diminutive πλοιάριον, whereas the three occurrences of boat in verses 17–21 are not diminutive. I believe the FE stays with the diminutive in 23 and 24 to show the crowd's determination to get to Jesus. They are willing to get into "other little boats from Tiberias" just to get to Jesus. With the awareness of the previous night's storm, this move by the crowd can be seen as a risk. The switch between forms is consistent and marked, with all three instances in the first paragraph (6:17–21) using the primitive form, whereas the second paragraph (6:22–25), are all in the diminutive. If these were stylistic synonyms, one would expect the mixing of the forms to be more random.

fectively that in the narrative of the Hebrew Bible, "repetition tends to be at least partly camouflaged, and we are expected to *detect* it, to pick it out as a *subtle* thread of recurrence in a *variegated* pattern, a flash of suggestive likeness in seeming differences,"[272] adding later that "it behooves us to watch for the *small differences*."[273] Verses 3 and 6 of John 21 use πλοῖον, the primitive morpheme, but in the repeated reference to the fishing vessel in verse 8, the narrator *switches* to the diminutive πλοιαρίῳ, describing the "little" boat, behind which a full net of fish is being dragged without our main character. Moreover, the diminutive form is rare and occurs only five times in the New Testament (Mark 3:9; John 6:22, 23, 24; 21:8). It is never used in the LXX, but the primitive form occurs forty times. Additionally, if the diminutive form was present in John 21 because this was a regional dialectic's term for boat, and therefore faded, we might expect that the narrator would use it consistently. However, this is not so. Only at this moment has the boat diminished in size for narrative effect. In reality, the boat has not gotten smaller, but figuratively speaking, Peter may have. Alter is again insightful: "[T]he biblical writers like to lead their readers to inferences through *oblique hints* rather than insisting on explicit statement."[274] Daniel Wallace also renders the term, in this verse, as, "in a small boat."[275]

In this method of reading, the phrase "for they were not far from the land, but about a hundred yards off" (John 21:8) also serves parenthetically to explain how they were able to manage this "net full of fish" despite being abandoned by the disciple-turned-fisherman Peter, who, ironically, initiated the adventure. If a reader was aware of some Synoptic traditions, he or she may have recalled the Lukan catch. In that scene, the disciples' full nets almost swamped two boats, even when the fishermen spread the catch between at least two nets in two boats (Luke 5:7). Accordingly, juxtaposed against this large catch, the boat in John 21 also seemed too small for the task. The diminutive πλοιαρίῳ, little boat, becomes the rhetorical device of deliberate understatement, *meiosis*, which magnifies the size of the catch.[276] Ethelbert Bullinger explains this device: "By this figure one thing

---

272. Alter, *The Art of Biblical Narrative*, 96; emphasis added.

273. Ibid., 183; emphasis added. However, Alter's main emphasis in this quote is on repeated dialogue or speech.

274. Ibid., 183; emphasis added. And in a whimsical way as well, "[B]iblical literature, like its counterparts elsewhere, repeatedly offers us insights and pleasures that exceed the strict limits of ideological intention." Alter, *The World of Biblical Literature*, 45.

275. Wallace, *Greek Grammar beyond the Basics*, 155. Although Michaels in his recent commentary says, "[B]ut the words are used interchangeably (as in 6:17, 19, 23)." Michaels, *The Gospel of John*, 1034.

276. Though he does not use the term *meiosis*, Cicero speaks of deliberate

is diminished in order to increase another thing ... In Meiosis there is an omission therefore, not of words, but of sense. One thing is lowered in order to magnify and intensify something else by way of contrast. It is used for the purpose of emphasis; to call our attention, not to the smallness of the thing thus lessened, but to the importance of that which is put in contrast with it."[277] In lessening the sense of the boat's size, the reader's attention is drawn to the great catch—which Jesus has powerfully provided—but which Peter has left the others to drag to shore.[278]

Breakfast by a Charcoal Fire
(John 21:9–14)

At verse 9 the FE tells the reader that the disciples see a charcoal fire.[279] Carson explains the implied significance of this term's appearance: "Since this is the second of only two places where *anthrakia* is mentioned, and the other is the setting for Peter's disowning of Jesus, some have suggested that this mention of *anthrakia* is John's subtle pointer to that earlier failure, since at this charcoal fire restoration takes place. If so, the connection is very subtle indeed."[280] Though subtle to the modern Western reader, the reader acquainted with ancient Hebraic narrative would be quite accustomed to listening for such markers, such as *silver, pledge, recognize*, or even "*gum, balm and myrrh ... down to Egypt*" in the Joseph narrative.[281] Though perhaps ἀνθρακιά may not iteratively haunt Peter as silver did Joseph's brothers, its appearance is significant enough. Because of the linkages between the threefold denial and threefold question of "Do you love me" between the same two lead characters (Jesus and Peter), Peter's boasting, and Jesus'

---

understatement. "Then again are those intentional understatements or overstatements which are exaggerated to a degree of the astonishing that passes belief" (*De Or.* 2.66.267); "[T]hen exaggeration designed to overstate *or understate* the facts" (3.53.203); emphasis added.

277. Bullinger, *Figures of Speech used in the Bible*, 155. Quintilian advises his readers to "avoid" this device, but concedes that it could be used purposefully. "We must also avoid μείωσις a term applied to meagreness and inadequacy of expression, although it is a fault which characterises an obscure style rather than one which lacks ornament. But meiosis may be deliberately employed, and is then called a figure." Quint. *Inst.* 8 3.50.

278. But see also Rowe who classifies *meiosis* with "barbarisms:" Rowe, "Style," 155.

279. Hoskyns and Hasitschka both view Peter as reaching the shore only after the other disciples in the boat. Hasitschka, "The Significance of the Resurrection Appearance in John 21," 317; Hoskyns and Davey, *The Fourth Gospel*, 553.

280. Carson, *The Gospel according to John*, 671.

281. Found both on Joseph's journey as well as Benjamin's journey to Egypt in Gen 37:25 and 43:11, 15.

prediction of denial, I have become increasingly doubtful that "charcoal" would be missed by such a reader. At the least, the FE may have purposefully positioned the reader to experience tension at its occurrence.[282] The disciples may have felt that tension as well for, ultimately, the reader hears that none of them "dared ask" him a question.

Thus the charcoal may remind the reader, as it has scholars, of Peter's denials in 18:15–27. Though Peter does not flee, his denials accomplish the same effect—his own self-protection. In this manner, the charcoal, once coupled with the three questions to come, obliquely reminded Peter of his past, that he is more like a young, little sheep in the eyes of his shepherd Jesus than a mature shepherd ready to feed sheep. This sets the context for Jesus' following words to humble Peter, who will eventually die in a manner that the narrator says glorified God.

Next, the reader learns that the disciples also see fish and bread (John 21:9). Jesus has now provided food (προσφάγιον) in two ways—the miraculous catch, as well as the fish and bread on the shore. The narrator, up to this point, has only used ἰχθύων (twice, 21:6, 8), but now switches to the term ὀψάριον, which is the aforementioned diminutive form of ὄψον. In the New Testament, the diminutive form only occurs in John 6:9, 11 and 21:9, 10, 13. It occurs once in the LXX in the alternate text of Tobit 2:2. In that passage the variation between the standard and alternate texts is the difference between the diminutive and non-diminutive ὄψα, yet the *New English Translation* (NET) renders this term as "fine foods" and "foods," without the mention of fish in either reading.[283] In John 21:10 the reader hears Jesus also: "Bring some of the fish that you have just caught." Here, Jesus likewise uses ὀψαρίων. Earlier, I explained that lexical definitions include the connotation of fish as food. Eugene Louw and Johannes Nida state that in earlier antiquity ὀψάριον was rendered "a tidbit of food eaten with bread," but that "it occurs in later Greek in the meaning of fish."[284] However, Brown believes that in this passage, "it is used to describe freshly caught fish."[285] Generally as diminutive, this would put it in the very broad appurtenance category, of "*pertaining to*" food. It may also be faded as Swanson and others point out,

---

282. Sternberg, *The Poetics of Biblical Narrative*, 118, 177, 285, 303–4.

283. The Brenton LXX translates it "meat." Brenton, *The Septuagint Version of the Old Testament and Apocrypha*; Pietersma and Wright, *A New English Translation of the Septuagint*.

284. Louw and Nida state, "in the NT this meaning occurs only in the fourth Gospel (compare the usage in Jn 6:9 with ἰχθύς in parallel passages)." Louw and Nida, *Greek-English Lexicon of the New Testament*, 5.16.

285. Brown, *The Gospel according to John (XIII–XXI)*, 1073.

with no further diminutive force of meaning.²⁸⁶ Part of the confusion over ὀψάριον is due to its messy evolution from a strictly hypocoristic diminutive to become simply "fish" at times. Petersen addresses its conglutination (the joining of two suffixes over time):

> ὀψάριον originally a hypocoristic form for ὄψον, became the ordinary word for 'fish' as food, and consequently, when the diminutive ὀψαρίδιον was formed from it, the -αρι- necessarily remained intimately connected with the root ὀψ- as part of one and the same idea, and there is no necessity of the diminutive force being sought in -αριδιον and the consequent abstraction of such a suffix. When, however, the "diminutive" force of a certain primitive was felt by some and not by others, the transmission of its "diminutive" derivative from a speaker to whom the primitive had no "diminutive" force to a hearer who did feel it in that way, could cause the latter to abstract a complex conglutinate from a word like ὀψαρίδιον.²⁸⁷

For Petersen, the loss of "diminutive force" occurs when the new term ceases to modify or be associated with its primitive but has its own object of reference. Petersen's second point is that a term could be perceived as having a type of diminutive nuance by some speakers or hearers and not by others. Thus, a new conglutinated double diminutive could be formed, such as ὀψαρίδιον, while the original diminutive ὀψάριον, which is in John 21, may or may not continue to carry diminutive connotation when spoken or heard by others.

So, this renders plausible the argument that this term could have had some diminutive nuance in the FG. I already established that the FE used it for the small quantity of only two fish in John 6.²⁸⁸ But in 21:9 the text is indicating an extremely large amount when referring to the catch of 153. Yet in both chapters, there is reference to consuming fish. Does the FE have some double intention, not only of fish to eat, but also referring back to the miracle of abundance with a small amount of ὀψάρια in chapter 6? And if so, how?

Context, as well as caution about flat characters and simplistic narrative dialogues, demands a second look. The voice of the narrator resumes in verse 11 saying, "So Simon Peter went aboard and hauled the net ashore, full

---

286. Swanson, "Diminutives in the Greek New Testament," 134–51; Elliott, "Nouns with Diminutive Endings in the New Testament," 391–98.

287. Petersen, *Greek Diminutives in -ION*, 206.

288. The idea that the choice of term seems purposeful is strengthened when one observes that the other evangelists use ἰχθύας. Matt 14:17, 19; Mark 6:38, 41; Luke 9:13, 16. Danker et al., *A Greek-English Lexicon*, 6th ed., 746.

of large fish, 153 of them." The terms for large fish are ἰχθύων μεγάλων. In this verse, Jesus calls the fish in the net ὀψαρίων but the narrator calls them ἰχθύων μεγάλων. The immediate switch in terms by the narrator back to ἰχθύων μεγάλων and the contrasting connotations were likely not lost upon an aural audience. Nor would a reader, if accustomed to the narrative device of repetition with variation, likely have missed the variation. This also, I believe, lessens the likelihood that the diminutive form was due to a dialect, for in that case we would expect consistency, but instead, the narrator changes terms.[289] Noting this switch in terminology, we see that the narrator's point of view is elucidated by the intentional addition of μεγάλων. In fact, in *both* instances of the narrator's usage of ἰχθύων, the characteristic of small size is carefully *juxtaposed* against it—πλοιαρίῳ in the first instance, and ὀψαρίων in the second.[290] Accordingly, we could translate Jesus' command and the narration of Peter's response as, "Bring some of those little fish that you have just caught. So Simon Peter went aboard and hauled the net ashore, full of lunkers, 153 [of them]." The use of ὀψαρίων is no mere synonym. Rather, this is a purposeful diminutive of irony, *understatement for contrastive purposes*. It is a rhetorical device, *tapeinosis*, a form of *litotes*. Bullinger describes this device as follows: "This differs from *Meiosis* in that in *Meiosis* one thing is diminished in order, by contrast, to increase the greatness of another, or something else. However, in *Tapeinosis* the thing that is lessened is the same thing which is increased and intensified."[291] English speakers do this, for example, when saying of a mansion, "Nice little house you have here!" The understatement playfully nods at the large size of the home. Stibbe argues that in John 8, Jesus used strong, "biting" satire in his exchange with the Jews in the closing verses. Yet, in his discussion, Stibbe also describes the lighter Horatian, or "smiling satire."[292] In this higher form, the speaker aims

---

289. Noting that the narrator uses the term as well in verse 9, it is not likely a dialect limited to only Jesus and the disciples. There is a clear switching of terms in certain strategic locations in the dialog. Petersen addresses the development of diminutives throughout the Indo-European languages, and includes in his analysis the consideration of various dialects in Greek. See Petersen, *Greek Diminutives in -ION*, 3, 13n2, 46n2, 60, 64, 95, 180, 199, 201, 202, 206, 216, 221, 252, 276.

290. Brown states, "The suggestion that there were other, smaller fish besides the 153 larger ones is unlikely." Brown also sees these terms as "interchangeable" but notes this as contra Blass, Debrunner, and Funk's grammar, which also identifies it as a diminutive as "the names for various dishes: ὀψάριον 'fish (as a food).'" Brown, *The Gospel according to John (XIII–XXI)*, 1073–74; Blass et al., *A Greek Grammar of the New Testament and Other Early Christian Literature*, 61. Swanson also concludes that "ὀψάριον can mean 'tidbit' in general as food eaten with bread." Swanson, "Diminutives in the Greek New Testament," 146.

291. Bullinger, *Figures of Speech used in the Bible*.

292. Stibbe, *John's Gospel*, 114.

artfully but spiritedly, to correct the listener.[293] Hence, this rhetorical device, on the lips of Jesus, may have contributed to the silence of the disciples, in that Jesus' deliberate and satirical understatement emphasizes just how huge the catch was.[294] It also underscores the irony of the phrase "you have just caught" in that they were *not* responsible for the catch—Jesus was.

This effect also strengthens the allusion to the feeding miracle in John 6 and the connotation of fish as caught for food, since this term could carry both the idea of small size as well as a food item. The term is first used by the narrator's voice to describe what the disciples saw at the fire: "ὀψάριον ἐπικείμενον καὶ ἄρτον"(John 21:9). The immediate connection of this term to bread brings the reader back to John 6:9: "πέντε ἄρτους κριθίνους καὶ δύο ὀψάρια" ("five barley loaves and fish"). Scholarship often notes the "sacral meal" connection with John 6, but there is a clear testing and paucity/

---

293. Ibid.

294. Aristotle notes this effect, and urges caution: "Further, the use of diminutives amounts to the same. It is the diminutive which makes the good and the bad appear less, as Aristophanes in the Babylonians jestingly uses 'goldlet, cloaklet, affrontlet, diseaselet' instead of 'gold, cloak, affront, disease.' But one must be careful to observe the due mean in their use as well as in that of epithets." *Rhet.* 3.2.14–15. Quintilian again considers this a base form of rhetoric: "Next to indecency of expression comes meanness, styled ταπείνωσις, when the grandeur or dignity of anything is diminished by the words used." *Quint. Inst. 8 3.48*. But the FE would not be the only writer to have departed from rhetorical rule, as Anderson notes Paul to have done in Rom 1. Anderson, *Ancient Rhetorical Theory and Paul*, 212. Additionally, note the aforementioned distaste of Koine by the Atticists and such might not be considered a poor form of speech in Koine. Elliott, "Nouns with Diminutive Endings in the New Testament," 391, 396. Amundsen notes this back and forth use of diminutives with obvious "lessening effect" in the dialogue between Jesus and the Canaanite woman in Matt 15:24–27: "Jesus first remarks, with the pride of a Jew: it is not right to take the children's bread and βαλεῖν τοῖς κυναρίοις (xv.26)—to which she humbly remarks that τὰ κυνάρια ἐσθίει ἀπὸ τῶν ψιχίων τῶν πιπτόντων, . . . the diminutives denoting contempt, then modesty. Mark vii.27 similarly κυνάρια and τῶν ψιχίων τῶν παιδίων." Amundsen, "Some Remarks on Greek Diminutives," 12. See also Bullinger, *Figures of Speech used in the Bible*, 814, where he sees *meiosis* coupled with irony in this story for the purpose of a test or trial. For the Gen reader, note a similar device on the lips of Abraham, understatement for humility's sake in the presence of deity. He understates his own offer to the messengers of God who visit his tent in the heat of the day: "Let a little water be brought, and wash your feet, and rest yourselves under the tree, while I bring a morsel of bread, that you may refresh yourselves, and after that you may pass on" (Gen 18:4–5). Afterward, Abraham proceeds to supply them with a feast of an enormous amount of bread and beef for five persons, garnished with curds and milk. Abraham deliberately tones down the amount of food he provides, and then the narrative immediately contrasts it with the *specific description of the amount*. Perhaps Jacob too: "Carry a present down to the man, a *little* balm and a *little* honey, gum, myrrh, pistachio nuts, and almonds. Take double the money with you." Gen 43:11b–12. No chances were going to be taken with Rachel's second son. Thus, a Gen reader would be accustomed to these devices as well.

abundance motif as well.²⁹⁵ Both narratives indicate food, testing, doubt, and a scarcity of items to eat, with a subsequent abundant feeding. The contrast between the lack of food and the later abundant supply would appear intentional and the turn from paucity to abundance hinges upon the irony of a lack of faith and/or dullness on the part of the disciples. If in fact the FE, in John 6, only used δύο ὀψάρια as fish as a food item without reference to size or amount, this would be a different argument. However, since Andrew in chapter 6 remarks, "There is a boy here who has five barley loaves and two fish, *but what are they for so many?*" one should be cautious about ignoring the contrast in size and lack of perceptiveness in both feeding stories. Therefore, I argue that the diminutive ὀψάριον carries the nuance of small size as well as that of food.²⁹⁶ A new reading, then, would run as follows:

> When Simon Peter heard that it was the Lord, he put on his outer garment (for he was stripped for work) and cast himself into the sea. The other disciples came in the little boat, dragging the net full of fish (for they were not far from the land, but about a hundred yards off). When they got out on land, they saw a charcoal fire in place, with (a) small fish laid out on it, and bread.²⁹⁷ Jesus said to them, "Bring some of the little fish to eat that you have just caught." So Simon Peter went aboard and hauled the net ashore, full of large fish—153 of them! And although there were so many, the net was not torn.²⁹⁸

When read in this manner, the understanding of "little boat" and "little fish" reveals the texture of the dialogue and narration. This was the *manifestation* coming as the culmination of a long narration of σημείων. Manifestations of the Divine are σημείων and are shocking. The contrast is between the disciples' lack of perception and powerlessness, and the huge catch that occurred because of Jesus' powerfully effective command—and it jars the disciples into silence. This is also another instance of a *Leitwort*, namely

---

295. Beasley-Murray, *John*, 401; Brown, *The Gospel according to John (XIII–XXI)*, 1073; Lincoln, *The Gospel according to Saint John*, 512.

296. "Daintiness" as a food item category almost covers both, but that often indicates greater desirability of the food related to the small size, which is not indicated by context in either story. If one can imagine Jesus saying it with a slight smile, the term "sardines" almost fits. They are edible and small, and also can carry a satirical effect, as they are often considered common or low food.

297. On the issue of "fish," "a fish," or "one fish" on the fire, see Brown, *The Gospel according to John (XIII–XXI)*, 1073.

298. Often, the un-torn net is seen symbolically, in conjunction with the 153 fish and the universality of the catch. Hoskyns and Davey, *The Fourth Gospel*, 554; Spencer, "Narrative Echoes in John 21," 67.

ὀψάριον. This *Leitwort* serves in all three functions discussed above. By reading the repeated use of the term ὀψάριον, the reader is reminded that John 21 is tied to John 6. The connection to abundance/paucity, the lack of faith, and "apart from me you can do nothing" theme aids in the realization that it functions in the second manner—it reinforces the didactic content of the story. In fact, we should here keep in mind that ἄρτος, "bread," another *Leitwort*, occurs twenty-four times in the Gospel.[299] Twenty-one of these are in John 6, and two of them are here in these five verses (John 21:9–13). A careful reader would perhaps see that the FE had been *very* intentional about not only connecting these verses to John 6, but also that Jesus is here reminding the disciples of his previous track record of supplying their need when they lacked food and the odds of supplying those needs were against them.[300] Finally, hearing that ὀψαρίων is on the lips of Jesus means that it exists in the narrative world of the disciples and not only in the reader's mind, as with ἰχθύων when the narrator speaks. This further explains the silence. Like the silence of Joseph's brothers (Gen 45:3), the silence of Jacob upon hearing Laban's response to the sibling switch (Gen 29:28), or even the very brief response of Judah upon hearing "recognize these" (Gen 38:26), Jesus' disciples cannot speak. Upon seeing and hearing the evocative items from the previous miracle of abundance, they experience a similar *déjà vu*. As they sit down to a meal provided by their counter-manipulator, their dullness, disempowerment, and on-going character development process are once again underscored. They are humbled into silence.

"Come and have breakfast" in verse 12 may also be an intentional reference back to the Good Shepherd metaphor of chapter 10. Kenneth Bailey points out that Western farms have barns with hay for the winter, but Middle Eastern sheep must go out, led by the shepherd to eat by grazing *every morning*, "each and every day, winter and summer."[301] This adds a nuance to Jesus' words in the morning, "Children, do you have anything to eat," in verse 4, and now also here in verse 10, "Come and have breakfast." The narrator eventually concludes the meal in verse 15 with the phrase, "when they had finished their breakfast." Consequently, just like the shepherd referred to in Bailey's work, Jesus has called them and fed them breakfast. Since this is when these sheep most assuredly *should* have known the identity of their Shepherd, this also contributes to the awkward silence. This is the moment of surprise in narrative, when characters move from the stable past to a

---

299. The diminutive of bread, ἀρτίδιον, is not found in either the New Testament or the LXX. It *may* have developed later. Petersen refers to one usage of it, in *Diog. Laert* 7. 18 (third century CE), in which he translated it "merely," or "nothing but . . . a loaf of bread." Petersen, *Greek Diminutives in -ION*, 237.

300. The other occurrence of ἄρτος is in 13:18.

301. Bailey, "The Shepherd Poems of John 10," 7. Hoskyns's work precedes Bailey's. Hoskyns and Davey, *The Fourth Gospel*, 371–72.

recognition of the troubling present.³⁰² In this moment the catch and the breakfast trouble the disciples by reminding them of their lack of perceptiveness—*this is the risen Jesus*. They are therefore silent, surprised, and transitioning from ignorance to knowing.³⁰³ They should have recognized the risen Jesus, if not earlier, at least at the same time as the BD. The result may imply silent shame and a cautious dumfounded-ness akin to the silence of Joseph's brothers or Judah's terse reply to Tamar. The surprise at the unveiling of the unrecognized one is disempowering.

In verse 13, the narrator again uses wording reminiscent of John 6: "Jesus came and took the bread and gave it to them, *and so with the fish* (καὶ λαμβάνει τὸν ἄρτον καὶ δίδωσιν αὐτοῖς καὶ τὸ ὀψάριον ὁμοίως)."³⁰⁴ John 6:11 reads, "Jesus then took the loaves, and when he had given thanks, he distributed them to those who were seated. *So also the fish* (ἔλαβεν οὖν τοὺς ἄρτους ὁ Ἰησοῦς καὶ εὐχαριστήσας διέδωκεν . . . ὁμοίως καὶ ἐκ τῶν ὀψαρίων)."³⁰⁵ Why *does* Jesus feed them? This may be interpreted as an act of reconciliation and restoration. Joachim Jeremias, explaining what it implied when Jesus ate with sinners, clarifies that "sharing a table meant sharing life":

> To understand what Jesus was doing in eating with 'sinners', it is important to realize that in the east, even today, to invite a man to a meal was an honour. It was an offer of peace, trust, brotherhood and forgiveness; in short, sharing a table meant sharing life. The report in II Kings 25.27–30 (par. Jer. 52.31–34) that Jehoiachin was brought by the king of Babylon from prison to the royal *table* is a public proclamation of his rehabilitation. In a similar way, king Agrippa I had the supreme commander

---

302. Sternberg, *The Poetics of Biblical Narrative*, 309.

303. Larsen points to the moment of recognition when the observer undergoes a "chaos of emotions and an inability to find words" and mentions the "need for physical contact . . . falling at each other's feet, and embracing." Larsen, *Recognizing the Stranger*, 69–70. This may further explain Peter's sudden swim to shore. See also Cave, *Recognitions*, 44.

304. Some manuscripts conclude the phrase here with ἄρτον ευχαριστησας εδωκεν, which was likely an addition to strengthen the tie to John 6 as well as the eucharistic significance of the meal. Aland and Aland, *Greek-English New Testament*, 218. "The addition of εὐχαριστήσας (xxi. 13) in Codex Bezae suffices to show how normal Christians at a somewhat later date read the verse; and if the story is not to be allowed any Eucharistic significance it is up to those who hold that view to demonstrate what alternative symbolism or connotation a meal of fish and bread would have held for original readers of the Fourth Gospel." Shaw, "Breakfast by the Shore," 12. "Although the latter lacks the participle εὐχαριστήσας, the echo is distinct, evoking the meal in John 6 with all its Christological and Eucharistic significance. Jesus is the bread from heaven (6:31–33, 41, 50, 58), the bread of life (6:35, 48, 51, 58), and the risen Lord." Culpepper, "Designs for the Church in the Imagery of John 21:1–14," 8.

305. Pfitzner, "They Knew It Was the Lord," 73; Spencer, "Narrative Echoes in John 21," 59; Brown, *The Gospel according to John (XIII–XXI)*, 1099.

Silas, who had fallen out of favour, invited to his table as a sign that he had forgiven him.[306]

The meal implies fellowship with the life (and death) of Jesus and the certainty of restoration. Thus, Jesus does here what he will command Peter to do in just moments—he feeds the sheep, which is an act of reconciliation. Joseph did the same with his brothers, sharing portions from his table with them and drinking with them (Gen 43:34).[307] Without Jesus, there were no fish and no meal in the early morning. Now that they share the meal, they recognize in awe. Implicitly, Peter's reversal has commenced and restoration, in keeping with the peace Jesus offered in 20:19, 21, 26, has begun.

The theory of manipulation with its six kernels of manipulation narratives, when applied to John 21:1-14, clarifies Jesus' actions. Jesus, by counter-manipulating Peter with thwarted recognition, has mirrored Peter's manipulative behavior in chapter 18 where he prevented others from recognizing him as Jesus' disciple. By providing the disciples with an abundant catch of fish and feeding them a meal, Jesus has also emphasized his power over and against their powerlessness—apart from him they can do nothing. Moreover, the FE's use of diminutives throughout these verses carefully underscores this aspect of manipulation and counter-manipulation in the dialog between these two parties. The disciples are little children, needing to be fed by a powerful master. Turning to the threefold questioning of Peter, the narrator closes the window on this section with the reaffirmation that Jesus had just *manifested* himself to the disciples for the third time.[308]

---

306. Jeremias, *New Testament Theology*, 115. The account of Agrippa and Silas, which Jeremias references, is found in Josephus, *Ant.* 19.317-25, esp. 321. Josephus and Whiston, *The Works of Josephus*. Also, "In the ancient Near East, table fellowship was one of the main signs, if not the main sign, of human intimacy and sharing, for an ordinary person seldom had other things that she or he could give to or share with friends." Witherington III, *John's Wisdom*, 359. Finally, see also Bailey, *Poet and Peasant and through Peasant Eyes*, sect. 2:92, where the excuse "We ate and drank in your presence" in Luke 13:26 is a claim to intimate relationship with the master.

307. Although in Joseph's case, he was sharing life with his brothers and they did not yet know whom he was. In fact, Joseph was not done with his brothers. With Jesus, the disciples know with whom they are sharing life, but Jesus is not done with Peter—he has yet to question him.

308. On the significance of τοῦτο ἤδη τρίτον, "this [was] now the third [time]," Segovia proposes that this count does not include the appearance to Mary Magdalene. Segovia, "The Final Farewell of Jesus," 176. Lincoln however, posits that the count omits appearances to the "*individual* woman." Lincoln, *The Gospel according to Saint John*, 514; emphasis added. This perspective reminds one of the FE's use of the plural μαθηταῖς, and that this may point to three appearances to a *group* of disciples.

7

One Little Sheep Becomes a Shepherd: John 21:15–19

If we look at verses 15-18 with an understanding of the principle of *lex talionis* as a background, we realize that Jesus could have counter-manipulated Peter with three denials. Jesus, however, does not do this. Instead, similar to Joseph, he reverses the full force of *lex talionis* with three questions. These challenge Peter's love, recalling his boastful past and previous failures. I propose also, that the presence of near synonymous terms in the dialogue underscore Jesus' challenge to Peter the manipulator. Like the sheep he will feed, Peter is immature, powerless, and has a childlike need to grow. Peter must transform and become a shepherd willing to feed other little sheep.

An implied Genesis reader would, I argue, interpret all of this together as a part of Jesus' artful counter-manipulation of Peter, even if only with Chatman's "unconscious felicity."[1] By adding the ambiguous "more than these" to the questioning, Jesus not only ironically mirrors Peter's three denials, but ties them to Peter's previous behavior, including his earlier boast and his aimless fishing. This strengthens the character contrast between Jesus, for whom Peter claimed he would lay down his life (John 13), and this same disciple whom the reader finds in the courtyard (John 18). This counter-manipulation brings the past to the fore, as it did for manipulators like Jacob, Judah, and his brothers who were counter-manipulated by the likes of Laban, Tamar, and Joseph. They were forced to face their past, and now Peter must face his. This results in humbled terse answers to Jesus' questions because Peter, the initial manipulator now realizes what has transpired. Reading with this perspective, we see that Peter's grief and admission that Jesus knows and understands all things constitutes the *dénouement*, and the strongest indication within the narrative world of Peter's reversal.

---

1. Chatman, *Story and Discourse*, 55.

It emphasizes the humbling disempowerment of this bold manipulator and his recognition that he himself does not know all things—only Jesus does. Moreover, the presence of charcoal at the breakfast just moments before has set the stage for the reader to realize that this is no minor reversal. Peter is moving from the opposite of an ideal example—a shameful traitor standing with Jesus' enemies—to one who will be girded by others and die. Jesus' prediction indicates that Peter will eventually, outside the bounds of the narrative, move even more toward an honored disciple willing to follow Jesus in death, and thus concludes Peter's developmental characterization beyond the story world. To these issues I now turn.

The Significance of *Lex Talionis*

According to the principle of *lex talionis*, when Peter responds to Jesus' three questions, our constructed implied reader of Genesis might not have been surprised if Jesus were to respond along the lines of "an eye for an eye;" that is, if Jesus were to respond in a way that more sharply mirrored Peter's three denials. Although the implied readers of the FG may have been aware of some Synoptic material, we should not assume that Jesus' reversal of *lex talionis* in Matthew 5:38–42 had pervaded and transformed their culture. The very way that Jesus phrased this saying indicated that retributive justice had not been forgotten and that he was challenging contemporary thinking: "You *have heard* it said . . . *But* (δὲ) I say to you . . ." (Matt 5:38–39).

Indeed, implied readers may have detected a similar opportunity for Jesus to reply retributively to the woman at the well in John 4. When she says to Jesus, "our father Jacob . . . gave us the well" (John 4:12), by calling Jacob "our father" she includes herself in Israel's descendants, something which may have been offensive to a Jew in the FG's setting (4:9). Kenneth Bailey argues that her remark could have generated a retributive reply: "[T]he average Jew of the times would have replied, 'You Cuthite, what right have you to claim Jacob as your father? We know that you are the descendants of Gentile tribes brought in to take our place when we were in captivity! You have no right to claim Jacob as your ancestor!'"[2] Hence, although I do not argue that readers expected Jesus to do so, first-century Mediterranean readers would know that Jesus *could* have replied thus: "You cowardly disciple, what right have you to claim that you love me, much less love me more than these? Everyone here knows of your boasting and then your cowardly lying, standing, and warming yourself around a charcoal fire with my enemies! You have no right to claim that you love me!" He could

---

2. Bailey, *Jesus through Middle Eastern Eyes*, 206.

have also replied tersely to each of Peter's answers with, "You do not." This would even more closely mirror Peter's terse "I am not" replies to his accusers in the courtyard. Moreover, a Genesis reader would especially be aware of this tension and therefore, also notice that Jesus, just like Joseph, puts an end to the drama of *lex talionis*. He simply says, "Feed my lambs . . . tend my sheep . . . feed my sheep." Ironically, he does mirror the threefold nature of the denials—in order, I argue, to facilitate Peter's recognition of his prior behavior—but reverses the retributive aspect of *lex talionis*, thereby implying trust and forgiveness in commissioning Peter to become a true disciple, a shepherd, and to lay down his life for the brethren.

With the opening words of the address, Jesus refers to Peter by his previous name. The account switches from Simon Peter (same title as in John 21:2) in the narrator's voice to "Simon son of John" in Jesus' voice, omitting "Peter." Jesus himself had given Simon this name in 1:42. The double name "Simon son of John" is directly juxtaposed by the narrator's use of the double name "Simon Peter," separated only by ὁ Ἰησοῦς. Janzen reminds us that in the life of Jacob, a model deceiver, "radical change [is] memorialized in the change of his name."[3] But why does Jesus not wait and rename Simon in John 21:18, instead of chapter 1? Just like Jacob at the ford of Jabbok in Genesis 32, Peter, at the Sea of Tiberias in John 21, begins to undergo a radical change. This may be because similar to Jacob, Peter, even after his name change in chapter 1, "displays characteristics of both" titles.[4] Abraham also underwent a name change (Gen 17:5), but continued his pattern of lying (Gen 20). Jacob undergoes a name change (32:28), but again lies to Esau about where he plans to travel (33:14–17). Indeed these are chosen leaders still in the character development process, despite their new names. James Hastings also invokes Genesis for understanding this change in title. He argues that Jesus uses this title as "a gentle reminder to him of the weakness which had led to his denial; and it would recall to him the Master's words before his fall, when he purposely abstained from giving him the name that implied firmness and strength, but used instead the old name, 'Simon,' which bore to 'Peter' the same relation as 'Jacob' (the 'supplanter') bore to 'Israel' (the 'prince of God')."[5] Similarly, Spencer states, "Jesus' referral to Peter as 'Simon, son of John' in vv. 15ff. forms an inclusio with the initial calling of Peter (cf. 1.2), thus suggesting to the implied reader that Peter, who represents the disciples as a character group in ch. 21, is depicted as

---

3. Janzen, *"How can a Man be Born when He is Old?,"* 324.
4. Ibid., 330.
5. Hastings, *The Great Texts of the Bible: St. John*, 420.

undergoing *a reversion in discipleship*."[6] Jesus begins his questions by recalling Simon to his status prior to becoming one of Jesus' disciples. All of the interpretive conclusions of this research thus far confirm Spencer's assertion. The aimless Peter is still dull and not following as he should.

The Synonyms for Love, Feed, and Sheep

A great deal of scholarship has focused upon the synonyms found in John 21:15–17. The words for love, feed, tend, sheep, and lambs have indeed caused scholars to explore whether the variations in vocabulary have any impact on the intent of the unit.[7] With what has been discussed about the value of variation within repetition,[8] combined with what I have argued regarding the synonyms for fish and boat, I also believe these are more than stylistic variations.[9] While there is no reason to exhaust the literature on both sides of the debate, I will summarize recent arguments before offering some additional options.

ἀγαπάω and φιλέω

Regarding these two terms, I believe that the variation may underscore Jesus' rebuke. However, scholars have rigorously considered the significance between these two words for love and have not yet reached a conclusion.[10] Brown concedes that "most scholars have reverted to the older idea that the variations are meaningless stylistic peculiarities."[11] Bultmann holds the same position,[12] and recently, Blaine has agreed with Brown.[13] Keener also notes that good rhetorical writers used variety, citing the *Rhetorica ad Herennium*

---

6. Spencer, "Narrative Echoes in John 21," 58, 61; emphasis added.

7. Brown, on the different words for love, points out, "With the partial exception of Origen, the great Greek commentators of old, like Chrysostom and Cyril of Alexandria, and the scholars of the Reformation period, like Erasmus and Grotius, saw no real difference of meaning in this variation of vocabulary." Brown, *The Gospel according to John (XIII–XXI)*, 1102. See also Keener, *The Gospel of John*, 2:1235–37.

8. To this can be added Segovia, "The Final Farewell of Jesus," 170.

9. Thomas Brodie remarks similarly, "A do-you-love-me situation is not the time for meaningless variations. In such a discussion every syllable tends to be important." Brodie, *The Gospel according to John*, 591.

10. McKay, "Style and Significance in the Language of John 21:15–17," 319.

11. Brown, *The Gospel according to John (XIII–XXI)*, 1102.

12. Stating clearly that the change between the terms "cannot be significant," because of Jesus' switch in terms in the third question. Bultmann, *The Gospel of John*, 711.

13. Blaine, *Peter in the Gospel of John*, 166.

and Aulus Gellius to support his argument.[14] Most recently, Culpepper notes that "even if the verbs for love in verses 15–17 have different nuances, that difference is not central to the meaning of this dialogue."[15] Culpepper also inventories how often βόσκω, ποιμαίνω, πρόβατα, and ἀρνία all occur in the rest of the Johannine writings.[16] Many have, however, argued that ἀγαπάω is a more "noble form" of love while φιλέω is the "lower form."[17] McKay, after dealing extensively with synonyms in the FG, concedes, "When one bears all this in mind it is difficult to avoid the conclusion that the pattern of variation of forms of ἀγαπάω and φιλέω in this passage are not pointless, but constitute a contextual distinction which is not blatant, but gently significant."[18] I, too, lean in this direction and turn to the LXX for further exploration of this idea.

The verb ἀγαπάω is found over 270 times in the LXX, but only eleven times in Genesis. Consistently in Genesis it is translated as "love," in both the Brenton LXX and the NET. Moreover, these often occur in narratives where the love referred to is of either an intensive or comparative nature between individuals: Abraham *loving* his *beloved* son (Gen 22:2), Isaac *loved* Esau but Rebecca *loved* Jacob (25:28), Jacob *loved* Rachel more than Leah (29:18, 20, 30), Jacob *loved* Joseph more than all the brothers (37:3), and Judah explaining to Joseph that his father *loves* Benjamin so much that the loss of the son would be the death of Jacob (44:20).[19] However, we cannot argue for such intensity for φιλέω, found only thirty-two times in the entire LXX, and only eleven times in Genesis. In Genesis it is translated "kiss" seven times (equally in Brenton and NET), "like" or "cherish" three times (equally in Brenton and NET), and "love" (once each in Brenton and NET).[20] The story of Jacob and Esau serves as an example of the different nuances. Isaac and Rebecca each *loved* (ἀγαπάω) Esau and Jacob respectively (25:28), but Isaac requests Esau to prepare game the way he *likes* it (φιλέω, 27:4). Re-

---

14. *Rhet. Her.* 4.28.38; *Noct. att.* 1.4; 2.5.1. Keener, *The Gospel of John*, 2:1236. But note Theon's distaste for the overuse of synonyms. *Exercises* (Spengel's page number 84), in Kennedy, *Progymnasmata*, 33. For Kennedy's discussion of dating *Excersises* "almost any time in the first century after Christ," see ibid., 1.

15. Culpepper, "Peter as Exemplary Disciple in John 21:15–19," 165–67.

16. Ibid., 165. ἀρνία occurs twenty-nine times in Revelation.

17. Brown, *The Gospel according to John (XIII–XXI)*, 1103.

18. McKay, "Style and Significance in the Language of John 21:15–17," 333.

19. There are however, instances where the love is either ignoble (34:3), or not significantly intense (24:67).

20. The only divergences between the Brenton LXX and the NET are in 27:14 where the Brenton LXX has "liked" and the NET has "loved," and in 37:4 where the Brenton translation has "loved" and the NET has "cherishing."

becca goes on to make the meal the way her husband *likes* it (φιλέω, 27:9). This does not mean that there is a stark difference in these verbs, for they can be used together of the same relationships: Jacob indeed loved (ἀγαπάω) Joseph more than his brothers (37:3), but the brothers notice this—that their dad loved (φιλέω, 37:4) Joseph more.[21] Therefore, the difference, though present, is subtle. Nevertheless, ἀγαπάω is the term which is consistently used in the LXX translation of Genesis for more intensive love, or greater love when compared with that of another.

One option then is to consider whether Peter is responding to each question with a less than bold answer. He might not be willing to proclaim the most intense type of love for Jesus, after proclaiming what he would do (John 13:37), and then denying Jesus later (John 18). Does the memory of his denial prevent him from affirming that he loves Jesus most intently? This also suggests the possibility that Jesus' switch to "φιλεῖς με" in the third inquiry (21:17), may be for the purpose of questioning even this slightly milder form of love to which Peter is willing to admit. This would also punctuate the rebuke implied by Jesus' threefold questioning mirroring the threefold denial. No doubt this is overstating it, but for the purpose of illustration, could this be something akin to asking, "Do you love me? Do you love me? Do you even like me?" Or else, perhaps this is closer, "Do you love me? Do you love me? Are we even friends?"[22] To consider this reading, I should underscore that a Genesis reader would understand this entire counter-manipulation narrative as oriented toward Peter's character development. This is not rebuke for rebuke's sake, but a rebuke for transformation's sake.

βόσκω and ποιμαίνω

Scholars also debated the significance of the two synonyms βόσκω and ποιμαίνω. I believe that together they allude to shepherding imagery in Israel's history. Regarding their similar meanings, some have maintained that βόσκω refers primarily to feeding, while ποιμαίνω "moves from just feeding towards totally tending the lambs."[23] Brown, citing Philo, demonstrates the historical precedence of this argument: "A sentence from Philo, *Quod deterius VIII #25*, catches the nuance of the two verbs: 'Those who feed [*boskein*] supply nourishment . . . but those who tend [*poimainein*] have the power of

---

21. This is the Brenton LXX. The NET reads "was cherishing."
22. I am grateful to Dr. Jo-Ann Brant, of my doctoral committee, who pointed out this possible reading to me.
23. Keener, *The Gospel of John*, 2:1236.

rulers and governors.' When combined, the two verbs express the fullness of the pastoral task assigned to Peter."[24]

For our purposes, we should also note the intertextuality with what Culpepper called a "rich web of texts."[25] This web supports the imagery of shepherds as overseers over Israel, the flock. The imagery is found throughout the Hebrew Bible.[26] To further explore this imagery, we turn again to the Septuagint. The LXX uses βόσκω twenty-seven times, and the term is usually translated as some form of "feed." It occurs three times in Genesis (Gen 29:7; 37:12; 41:2). The Brenton LXX translates it in Genesis consistently as "feed," but the NET twice translates as "pasture" (29:7; 37:12) and once as "grazing" (41:2). The only other variation from "feed" is found in Isaiah 34:17, where the Brenton LXX translates the infinitive form as "pasture," whereas the NET translated it "food . . . to eat." Other than these instances, translators render the term consistently as "feed" or "graze." Additionally, the LXX translation of Ezekiel 34 has three shepherding terms in common with John 21: βόσκω, ποιμαίνω, and πρόβατα.[27] Granted, my text of comparison is Genesis, and I do not wish to expand my scope. Yet the confrontational nature of the Ezekiel 34 prophesy against Israel's selfish shepherds warrants examination, especially given the proposed context of counter-manipulation in John 21. The chapter opens with "Son of man, prophesy against the shepherds (ποιμήν) of Israel" (Ezek 34:2). In 2b, the reader learns one of the reasons for the chastisement. The shepherds have been feeding, βόσκουσιν, themselves. Verse 3 reiterates that these shepherds "slaughter the fat ones, but you do not feed (βόσκετε) the sheep (πρόβατά)."

The imagery continues in the New Testament,[28] but especially in the FG. In chapter 10 Jesus states that the Good Shepherd lays down his life for the sheep, whereas the hired hand flees (John 10:11-15). Culpepper observes that the FE alluded to this imagery when Jesus questioned Peter and commands him to feed and tend his sheep.[29] An allusion to Ezekiel

24. Brown, *The Gospel according to John (XIII-XXI)*, 1105. Bultmann does not address the problem in his commentary. Bultmann, *The Gospel of John*, 711-12.

25. Culpepper, "Peter as Exemplary Disciple in John 21:15-19," 168.

26. Num 27:17; 2 Chr 18:16; Jdt 11:19; 2 Sam 5:2; Ps 77:20; 78:52; 100:3; Ezek 34; Jer 48:4; 49:20; 50:45; Isa 53:6; 63:11. For a treatment of the FE's frequent use of the Hebrew Bible, see Hanson, *The Prophetic Gospel*.

27. Blaine points out that in Ezek 34:14, βόσκω "describes the administration of spiritual sustenance, as it does in our passage, with God's scattered elect (πρόβατα)." Blaine, *Peter in the Gospel of John*, 167-68. The FG is so replete with Old Testament imagery that in Ball's words it 'requires' a knowledge of the Old Testament. Ball, *"I Am" in John's Gospel*, 270-76.

28. Matt 9:36; Mark 6:34; Luke 12:32; 1 Pet 2:25; 5:4; Acts 20:28-29; Eph 4:11.

29. Culpepper, "Peter as Exemplary Disciple in John 21:15-19," 168. This is also,

34, therefore provides a context for readers' understanding of Jesus' command for Peter to tend and feed the sheep.[30] If the FE were alluding to the shepherds in Ezekiel, either in chapter 10 or 21, this would, at the least, not weaken the idea that in this last chapter, Jesus is counter-manipulating the not yet fully mature Peter, transforming him into a selfless shepherd. Typical shepherds in Israel had been confronted for selfishly failing to shepherd in time past. So too Peter, as future shepherd, has not yet stepped into that role. He will learn shortly that he is to feed others and surrender his life for the glory of God.

πρόβατά and ἀρνία

Apart from their diminutive form and the possibility that Jesus used emphatic variation to further emphasize and complete his rebuke, I offer no new insights regarding why the FE switches between πρόβατά and ἀρνία. Brown is in a similar position.[31] He returns to the FE's unusual pattern in the employment of synonyms: "Why the variation is not consistently introduced elsewhere remains a puzzle; for instance, in ch. x John uses the same word for sheep fifteen times."[32] Yet here in chapter 21, the evangelist uses πρόβατά twice and ἀρνία once.

What I offer instead, is that the feeding of sheep in verses 15–17 is intended to stand in parallel to the feeding of the disciples by the risen Jesus in the opening verses, as a relecture of verses 1–14.[33] Thus, the FE's reason for choosing προσφάγιον in verse 5 would appear even clearer: Jesus *feeds*

---

where scholars note the ecclesiastical implications of Peter's commissioning. Zumstein, "Intratextuality and Intertextuality in the Gospel of John," 125.

30. See Hanson, *The Prophetic Gospel*, 96–115. At the same time, though, the FE may have used the writing as a tool to educate less informed readers. The variation between direct quotations and implicit allusions *may* suggest an implied audience with different levels of knowledge of the Hebrew Scriptures. Thus a reader, real or implied, could be significantly less versed in Ezek or Gen.

31. Brown, *The Gospel according to John (XIII–XXI)*, 1105.

32. Ibid., 1102. Brown makes a similar observation about the FE's use of terms for love: "[I]n xiii 34 and xiv 21 John uses the same verb 'to love' (agapan) three and four times respectively." Ibid.

33. As mentioned earlier, the concept of relecture has been established by Zumstein, "Intratextuality and Intertextuality in the Gospel of John," 126. In the context of the Good Shepherd in chapter 10, Hoskyns writes, "In similar fashion the significance of the Feeding of the Five Thousand is not exhausted until the bread is expounded as the flesh which Jesus will give for the life of the world." Further on he observes, "The author of the Fourth Gospel adds an interpretation to the parable of the Good Shepherd, just as previously he had added an interpretation to the miracle of the Feeding of the Five Thousand." Hoskyns and Davey, *The Fourth Gospel*, 368.

his sheep in verses 5-14; Peter is commanded to feed Jesus' sheep in verses 15-17. This is in addition to the earlier argument that the FE intended προσφάγιον to indicate intratextuality with chapter 6 and consequently a strong emphasis on something to eat.[34] The diminutives of προβάτιον and ἀρνίον assist in this understanding, for they stand in *parallel* with the diminutive παιδία in verse 4. Jesus asks the *little children* if they have anything to *eat* and then feeds them. Later, Jesus tells Peter to *feed* Jesus' *little sheep*. However, the two instances of the diminutive form προβάτια are textual variants in verses 16 and 17.[35] As mentioned earlier, Elliott argues that many diminutives should be considered the original reading, because scribes were prone to stylistic preferences. As time went on, they shunned "nursery" language. However, Elliott does not think that there was a "special indication of endearment" here.[36] Amundsen however, not only agrees with the variant readings, but also included the "loving character" of the word: "In John xxi.16 and 17, after the resurrection, Jesus says to Peter: ποίμαινε τὰ προβάτια μου, βόσκε τὰ προβάτια μου, the only place where this diminutive occurs in the New Testament. Cod. Sinaiticus and several other mss. read πρόβατα, but the diminutive is clearly the *lectio difficilior* and we should not like to dispense with the loving character of the word. Both Itala and Vulgate render: *pasce agnos meos.*"[37] Additionally, if the diminutive readings are allowed to stand in verses 16-17, this constitutes an instance of assonance in verses 15-17, ἀρνία, προβάτια, and προβάτια (*probatia* is repeated).

Petersen defines the diminutive nuance of προβάτιον as "lazy sheep."[38] He also adds, under the topic of faded diminutives, that at times it might also only carry the meaning of its primitive morpheme, "προβάτιον: πρόβατον, 'sheep.'"[39] However, he also clarifies this by saying that "most easily those

---

34. Moreover, with less of an emphasis on fish specifically. This is evidenced by some translations, e.g., King James Version, "[H]ave ye any meat?"; Common English Bible, "[A]nything to eat?"; New King James Version, "[A]ny food?"

35. Aland et al., *The Greek-English New Testament: Novum Testamentum Graece, English Standard Version*, 752. In verse 16 προβάτα is supported in ℵ A D K N W Δ Θ Ψ 𝔐; the variant is προβάτιά, and found in B C 565 b. In verse 17 προβάτα is supported in ℵ D K N W Γ Δ Θ Ψ 𝔐, whereas the variant is again προβάτιά, found in A B C 565. But see Schnackenburg, *The Gospel according to John*, 3:364.

36. Elliott, "Nouns with Diminutive Endings in the New Testament," 391-94. So too Michaels, "There is no difference in meaning in any case." Michaels, *The Gospel of John*, 1044.

37. Latin "feed my *lambs.*" Amundsen, "Some Remarks on Greek Diminutives," 13.

38. Petersen, *Greek Diminutives in -ION*, 125. Emphasis Petersen.

39. Ibid., 166.

words become equivalent to their primitive, of which the root already carried with it the idea of small size or youth as compared to something else."[40]

Even if we do not choose the variant readings, the diminutive term, ἀρνίον, in verse 15, clearly stands in parallel to the sheep in verses 16–17. Petersen explains that the sense of smallness as well as the deteriorative nuance (smallness in a negative or inferior sense) is emphasized by the diminutive form of ἀρνίον:

> For Greek -ιον I may mention the following examples in which the contempt which is associated with the suffix is directed against an object because of its small size, youth, and the like. The quality of sheepishness is considered as still greater in a little lamb than in a full grown sheep, and this has led to the diminutive ἀρνίον 'little lamb' getting the additional implication of cowardice ... Since a child is both little and below the adult in intelligence, the diminutive παιδίον 'little child' could get the accessory idea of stupidity, and so become deteriorative.[41]

Therefore, if we allow for the diminutive force of ἀρνία, we see that these are not called little sheep simply because they are young but because of the characteristics that come with immaturity. They are timid, somehow cowardly even, unable to feed themselves, and in need of leadership.

Feeding Little Children and Feeding Little Sheep

Given Petersen's explanation of the deteriorative nuance of sheep in ἀρνίον, as well as his pointing to the cowardice nuance in *both* ἀρνία and παιδίον, the parallel now becomes plausible: feeding and tending *little sheep* in verses 15–17 stands in parallel with feeding *little children* in verses 5–14. In both verse 5 as well as verses 15–17, the ones referred to as getting fed—the disciples and Jesus' sheep—are referred to with diminutives that indicate immaturity and fear. The latter, ἀρνία, also carries a negative sense. Since I have argued that a reader well acquainted with Genesis would not only be accustomed (even if unconsciously) to the content of Genesis but also to its form, Alter's following words are relevant to the potential of such a listener recalling the miraculous catch of fish and the subsequent feeding of the disciples in verses 1–12:

---

40. Ibid.

41. Ibid., 113–14. Petersen also informs his readers that προβάτιον and ἀρνίον could also carry the sense of delicateness in the sense of food (ibid., 142, 157), but this is of course not the context of the Johannine shepherding metaphor.

> Again and again, a revelation or a shift in attitude, perspective, or situation is introduced through the alteration of a single word, the deletion of a phrase, the addition of a word, a switch in the order of items, as statements are repeated; it is a technique *with a power and subtlety* that could have worked only on an *audience accustomed to retain minute textual details as it listened* and thus to recognize the small but crucial changes introduced in repetition. A listener who could in this way detect close recurrence and difference within the frame of a single episode *might reasonably have been expected to pick up a good many verbal echoes* and situational correspondences between far-flung episodes.[42]

If indeed παιδίον and ἀρνίον were intended to stand in parallel, then the second term, "little sheep," may illuminate the former "children," as *deficient and fearful in the skills of leading and feeding oneself and therefore in need of guidance*.[43] The hypocoristic nuance of dearness may be included as well. Earlier, I noted that Petersen affirms the endearing nuance in παιδίον as "dear little son,"[44] and that this is often the sense when authors used it in the second person in the vocative case: a construction that can serve as a marker of an "endearing expression."[45] These characteristics of young sheep—namely vulnerability, dearness, cowardice, etc.—stand parallel with παιδίον, the disciples, in verse 5, and the diminutive nuances of dearness, pity, and an intimation of rebuke in the "apart from me you can do nothing" lesson that was discussed earlier. This may also clarify the failure of Mary (John 20:15), Peter, and his companions, including the BD (21:4), to know Jesus by his voice, as his sheep should know the shepherd's voice (10:16, 27). I have earlier argued that Mary had not yet believed and understood that Jesus was resurrected, as shown by her phrase "where you have laid him and I will take him away" (20:15). Perhaps the FE is trying to indicate that knowing and believing in Jesus is a *process*, which these young sheep have not completed yet, and that failing to recognizing the master's voice is a problem that they need to redress.

---

42. Alter, *The World of Biblical Literature*, 113; emphasis added. Yet herein lies the rub for the scholar. Since this technique is so very implicit and subtle, there likely will never be any method of empirical verification for the presence of such an allusion. Verification of its presence then must lie in the collective voice of peer review.

43. Jer 11:18–19 indicates naiveté or a lack of knowledge in sheep: "The LORD made it known to me and I knew; then you showed me their deeds. But I was like a gentle lamb led to the slaughter. I did not know it was against me."

44. Petersen, *Greek Diminutives in -ION*, 171.

45. Ibid., 174.

If my conclusions concerning this intended parallel are correct, then Jesus' use of βόσκω and ποιμαίνω describes more fully what Jesus himself has been doing in this chapter—feeding and shepherding. Feeding was a separate act in the opening scene(s), but shepherding describes the overall interaction with the disciples, culminating in the third scene. Given what I have explained thus far, following are the parallels that I am arguing for, with verses 15–17 re-lecturing and strengthening the understanding of verses 1–14. Some of these are explicit, and some are implied by the intratextual allusions to chapters 6 and 10:

Verses 1–14	Verses 15–19
Little children (παιδία)	*Little* sheep (ἀρνία, προβάτια,
Jesus, the Good *Shepherd* . . . (John 10:11, ποιμὴν)	Peter commanded to *shepherd*[46] (ποίμαινε)
. . . *feeds* the little children *food*, (φαγ- in John 6, προσφάγιον in 21:5)	Peter commanded to *feed* the little sheep (βόσκε)[47]

---

46. The command to feed comes before the command to shepherd/tend. Thus, I am not arguing for strict ordering, but rather overall parallels. Peter, the little sheep, must grow, and, like Jesus, feed and tend to other little sheep.

47. Brodie also notes the nuance of "little" with sheep and the parallel with the youth of Peter. However, he took the three statements of feed/tend lambs/sheep in these verses to represent "the three main stages of life—when people are young (lambs) and need to be fed; when people are adult (sheep) and need shepherding; and when people are old, yet in some ways are once more like children (little sheep) and once again need to be fed. This meaning finds support from the fact that the text which immediately follows implies three basic states ('When you were young . . .')." Brodie, *The Gospel according to John*, 591. Brodie seems to surmise that Peter's younger years, "when you were young," conform the first stage and with the diminutive in Jesus' first answer, ἀρνίον; and Peter's age at the time of the episode to be the second stage, coinciding with Jesus' second response, but adhering to the primitive/non-diminutive reading, πρόβατά; and finally, the third stage, predicted by Jesus in the words "but when you are old," is represented, apparently, by the diminutive form, προβάτια, in verse 17. However, Brodie does not explain this detail. Brodie connects the allusion to Peter's younger years with the words "little sheep." On this last point I agree but also believe that the younger years are referring to a life that unfolds up to the point just moments ago when Peter gird himself and jumped into the sea. Second, if Brodie has selected the diminutive in verse 17 but not verse 16, he has not given a reason why he chooses one and not the other. Finally, nothing in Jesus' prediction of Peter's future life as an old man has any feeding nuance associated with it in verse 18, nor does Brodie explain why an old man needs to be fed, but not shepherded. The variations are likely purposeful, but we would benefit if we could see further explanation of how these nuances and variations fit together.

Moreover, the diminutive description fits the characterization of Peter we find in chapters 18–21. Although bold in the garden (John 18:10–11), he shrinks back in the courtyard (18:15–27); he cannot catch his own food while fishing (21:3). Moreover, his future sheep, like Peter, will be deficient and fearful in leading and feeding themselves and will therefore need someone to move them from fear to courage. Jesus intends his actions to transform Peter so that he will manifest a brave selflessness in the death that Jesus has predicted (21:18).

More Than These?

Scholars have also debated for some time the exact meaning of the phrase "more than these?" Carson points out that moments earlier, when the disciples concluded their meal, the text reads that "they" had finished eating: this is a group that included Jesus, Peter, and his six fellow disciples. This scene, just like the scene of Peter's denials, was in the context of a group. Moreover, Peter's boast, "I will lay down my life for you" in 13:37, also occurred in public, uttered while the other disciples were present. Such a public boast required a "public" restoration.[48] Carson therefore preferred a reading of "more than these other disciples do?" because in his public boast, Peter had said, "I will lay down my life for you [not 'We' and 'our'!] (13:37)."[49] Brown argues that the FG does not contain the most poignant boast.[50] But Ramsey Michaels has lately called Peter's boast in the FG "a rash promise that no other disciple was willing to make."[51] If so, the boast in 13:37 is an important episode in the ongoing characterization of Peter. It sets the stage for a significant contrast with Peter's refusal *to be recognized* as Jesus' disciple in chapter 18: οὐκ εἰμί! (John 18:17, 25). This adds depth to the understanding

---

48. Carson, *The Gospel according to John*, 675. See also Malina and Rohrbaugh, *Social Science Commentary on the Gospel of John*, 123, 147: "This refers to the state of public loss of honor—negative shame."

49. Carson, *The Gospel according to John*, 676.

50. "It has been proposed that there is irony here: Jesus is testing Peter who boasted at the Last Supper of a love greater than that of the other disciples. However, this particular boast was not made in John, but in the Synoptic accounts (Mark xiv 29; Matt xxvi 33: 'Even though they all fall away, I will not'), unless the fact that only Peter protested his loyalty in John xiii 37 is tantamount to a boast of greater love." Brown, *The Gospel according to John (XIII–XXI)*, 1104. Culpepper agrees: "Against this interpretation . . . Peter's boast, recorded in the Synoptics (Mark 14:29; Matt 26:33), does not appear in John." Culpepper, "Peter as Exemplary Disciple in John 21:15–19," 172. But, earlier, Culpepper affirms 13:37 as a boast. See Culpepper, *Anatomy of the Fourth Gospel*, 175; Keener, *The Gospel of John*, 2:1238.

51. Michaels, *The Gospel of John*, 1043.

of Peter's actions, because in a manner speaking, he is *turning aside from Jesus* in chapter 18, not unlike Judah *turning aside* and *going down* from his brothers (Gen 38:1).

Taking a different position, Wiarda argues that the phrase "more than these" refers to the fishing implements the narrator mentions so frequently in the early verses of the chapter, and which in verses 1–2 especially stand in contrast to discipleship. This would also fit because the phrase "more than these" would be referring to the aimlessness I argued for in the opening verses—loving fishing more than Jesus would fit the earlier proposed purposelessness.[52] Failing to proclaim the forgiveness of sins for others (John 20:23), the disciples choose fishing instead. Jesus therefore challenges Peter to love him more than fishing. According to Wiarda, therefore, Jesus is asking, "You say you love me. If you really mean it, this is what you will do for me."[53]

I argue that regardless of the referent of the pronoun "these," Jesus' question of "more than these" forces Peter to return to and examine his failures, whether they be loving fishing more than Jesus, loving Jesus more than he loves his companions,[54] or claiming to love Jesus more than his fellow disciples do.[55] However, also important for this study is that if Peter did in fact love Jesus more than the other disciples did, if he were a "good sheep," would he not have been the *first* to recognize his shepherd, rather than the BD in 21:7? Jesus' question, then, recalls not only the willful denial in the courtyard of the high priest (John 18:15–27), but also *sharpens the failed recognition in 21:4*. Spencer argues that the ambiguity may be intentional, referring to either the disciples or the fishing implements, and that "more than these" "functions as a double entendre."[56] Marguerat argues similarly for intentional ambiguity by the FE in 19:13 where Pilate sits Jesus on the judgment seat. The implied reader must sense the ambiguity and note the ironic reality, that "it is Jesus who judges the judges."[57] Given the function of textual indeterminacy discussed earlier in Genesis, perhaps the ambiguity in 21:15 is intentional. In such a reading, the question of "more than

---

52. So too Culpepper, "Peter as Exemplary Disciple in John 21:15–19," 172–73.

53. Wiarda, "John 21.1–23," 64.

54. Thus, would Jesus here be challenging Peter to a change in relationships? "When characters recognize Jesus, they must realign their relationships with others." Brant, *Dialogue and Drama*, 51.

55. "Jesus is quite capable of 'testing' his disciples (as he did Philip; see 6:6), and here he seems to be doing just that." Michaels, *The Gospel of John*, 1042.

56. Spencer, "Narrative Echoes in John 21: Intertextual Interpretation and Intratextual Connection," 61–62.

57. Marguerat," *L'exégèse biblique à l'heure du lecteur*," n.p.

these" would certainly force Peter to mentally return to the past and examine his failures, including the failed *anagnorisis* in verse 4.[58] That failed recognition serves therefore, as a contextual background for Jesus' overall counter-manipulating questions here in verses 15–17. Given this, how can Peter answer? He simply states his love—no more. Jesus knows the degree, and Peter has no need to proclaim it.[59]

Finally, the debate over πλέον τούτων must not cloud our view of the position in which the initial manipulator finds himself. When Jesus asks Peter if he loves him, *he indeed can boast again if he wants. He can deny three times again if he wants.* He has a chance to repeat *either crime*—the boasting *or* the denials—*right in front of a charcoal fire*. With textual indeterminacy in the narrative, the reader wonders, "Did Jesus intentionally create the fire for this purpose, just as Joseph planted silver in the sacks of his brothers?" Alternatively, has the FE only mentioned it as a motif? Either way, it haunts the reader, scholars, and possibly Peter as well, moving him toward a state of remorse.

You Know and Understand Everything

Turning now to Peter's response, the expression of grief here in verse 17 is dramatically very important to the development of Peter's character as well as his *peripeteia*. In the Synoptics, Peter grieves immediately after the third denial and the subsequent rooster crow (Matt 26:74–75; Mark 14:72; Luke 22:60–62). However, in John, the FE omits Peter's weeping. The narrator instead moves on after the denial and begins to narrate the crucifixion: "Peter again denied it, and at once a rooster crowed. Then they led Jesus . . . " (John 18:27–28). This accomplishes two things.

First, it paints a picture of Peter as one who has not yet confronted his failures. Scholars often speak of the Johannine Jesus, or the Markan Jesus, and so forth. But to correctly interpret what is happening around the

---

58. Blaine has also adopted a view similar to Spencer: "What the Redactor is *really* doing here, I think, is supplying a referent he means to remain ambiguous. Neither Peter nor the implied reader is supposed to know exactly what πλέον τούτων signifies. No matter how Peter elects to translate the words, his answer must be that his love for Jesus is unsurpassed and unsurpassable." Blaine, *Peter in the Gospel of John*, 164. However, Blaine is incorrect in stating that Peter *must* answer Jesus that his love is "unsurpassed and unsurpassable." Since Peter recognized Jesus only *after* the BD, there is *no possible way* he can claim to love better than these.

59. Concerning the remote possibility of intertextuality with John 15:3, Peter has already responded in the affirmative with the verb φιλέω. The *switch* to this term is done by Jesus alone, and thus Peter is not claiming now to lay down his life for his friend, φίλους.

charcoal fire, one must take full notice of the "Johannine Peter." The Synoptic Peter "broke down" (Mark) and "wept bitterly" (Matthew and Luke), but we are not told this about the Johannine Peter. Hereafter, the only mention of the Johannine Peter before his aimless "I am going fishing" of 21:3, is the footrace to the tomb where that narrative unit concludes with, "Then the other disciple, who had reached the tomb first, also went in, and he saw and believed" (John 20:9). There is no mention of belief on the part of Peter. Thus, when the perceptive reader begins chapter 21, he, along with countless scholars, rightly questions just what is going on with Peter and his companions. Is he focused on the mission of John 20:23? Has he dealt with his past? Although readers only formulate these questions from the text's near silence about Peter in the intervening chapters, his eagerness to come to Jesus in chapter 21 may signal to the reader that Peter now seeks reconciliation. Even so, if Peter's swimming to shore does indicate a desire to reconcile, such does not necessarily also imply that he has dealt with the past—or that he is willing to do so. Like a child, he may wish to reconcile and hope that the past will simply be overlooked.

Second, when the reader hears in 21:17 that Peter was grieved, it creates a dramatic turning point. Peter must now face his failures. He finally admits that Jesus knows and understands everything, including his boasting, his three denials, his lack of belief, and his aimless fishing.[60] Belief and knowledge go hand in hand in the FG, just as ignorance and unbelief go hand in hand. The unbelieving and ignorant disciple-fisherman is cornered. Here, Lied's findings regarding the recognition/judgment episode of 2 Baruch 50:1–51:6 are very similar. She notes the reversal of power between the righteous and the wicked in that recognition scene and the position in which the wicked found themselves as a result of recognizing those rightfully in authority over them: "they are forced to acknowledge their own failure."[61] Just like Judah in response to Tamar, *Peter has no* choice except to admit his failures and that Jesus knows all. Grieving then marks Peter's turning point. It is the culmination of the delayed grief that began at the denials in chapter 18.

After the narrator explains Peter's grief, Peter responds with: "Lord, all things you *know*. You *understand* that I love you," "κύριε, πάντα σὺ οἶδας σὺ γινώσκεις . . ." (John 21:17). As noted earlier, Jesus responds to the first of Peter's three statements with the answer, "What I am doing you do not *understand* now, but afterward you will *understand*." Observe that those two

---

60. Dschulnigg, *Jesus Begegnen: Personen und ihre Bedeutung im Johannesevangelium*, 69.

61. Lied, "Recognizing the Righteous Remnant?," 322, 329, 331.

words for "understand" are οἶδας and γνώσῃ (γινώσκω).⁶² In 21:17, Peter uses the same two verbs to affirm his love for Jesus: "Lord, you know (οἶδας) everything; you know (γινώσκεις) that I love you."⁶³ In "The Johannine Hypodeigma: A Reading of John 13," Culpepper reaffirms his belief that the FG's plot hinged on "the conflict between belief and unbelief as responses to Jesus' central role as the revealer. In a series of repetitive episodes, the Gospel narrative explores various responses to Jesus. It exposes the errors of unbelief and its attendant misunderstandings."⁶⁴ Culpepper here ties unbelief to misunderstanding and ignorance. Knowing, receiving, and believing—and their opposites—are all tied together in John 1:10–12: "He was in the world, and the world was made through him, yet the world *did not know* him. He came to his own, and his own people *did not receive* him. But to all who *did receive* him, who *believed* in his name, he gave the right to become children of God." Thus, if one does not believe the revealer, one responds in both unbelief and ignorance. Some characters begin in ignorance (1:26), some, as the Pharisees in chapter 9, are blind to the truth but think they see, and some willfully choose to take a position of ignorance, as Peter does

---

62. This would almost be a mirror, but in the affirmative, of Peter's denial in Mark 14:68, "I neither know nor understand what you mean," except that the verbs are οἶδα and ἐπίσταμαι.

63. This combination of "know and understand" is somewhat common in the New Testament. In addition to the construction found in Peter's denial in Mark 14:68, similar wording is also found in John 10:38. Here both words in the English, "know" and "understand," are subjunctive forms of γινώσκω, but yet different tenses, the first aorist, the second present. Robertson rendered this "that ye may come to know . . . that ye may keep on knowing." Robertson, *Word Pictures in the New Testament*, 190. However, this was formerly a "C"-rated variant, now with a "B" rating. Manuscripts differ on whether the second occurrence of γινώσκω should read as γινώσκητε, πιστεύητε, "or omitted entirely." See Aland et al., *The Greek New Testament*, 372; Metzger, *A Textual Commentary on the Greek New Testament: A Companion Volume*, 233; Brown, *The Gospel according to John (I–XII)*, 404; Metzger et al., *A Textual Commentary on the Greek New Testament: A Companion Volume*, 4th ed., 198. Brown notes the FE's fondness for γινώσκω (fifty-six times) and οἶδα (eighty-five times) and sums up the arguments that they are virtually synonymous versus that they have different nuances, but sided in the end with the former. Brown, *The Gospel according to John (I–XII)*, 513–4. First John 5:20 also combines them but even adds a third word for know/understand, διάνοια. Carson writes that "oida and ginōskō (both rendered 'you know' in v. 17) . . . have not stirred homiletical imaginations." Carson also states," Incidentally, it is unwarranted to try to resolve this issue by appealing to the underlying Aramaic that was probably spoken on this occasion . . . we have no access to the actual words other than what this text provides." Carson, *The Gospel according to John*, 677. Blaine says that the "alternation" between the two is "probably not important." The FE is not trying to differentiate between two different types of knowing, but is using repetition by Peter to emphasize that *Jesus* knows and understands *everything*. Blaine, *Peter in the Gospel of John*, 168.

64. Culpepper, "The Johannine Hypodeigma," 133.

in chapter 18.[65] Culpepper concludes: "The Gospel of John, therefore, is a dynamic, performative text. It *engages the reader*, elicits responses, and then *critiques deficient responses* as the reader works *through* the episodes of the narrative *sequentially*."[66] Therefore, what we see in Genesis is also true of John's Gospel: "No ignorance, no conflict; and no conflict, no plot."[67] The reader *sequentially* works *through* episodes that serve to characterize Peter: his misunderstanding of the foot washing and Jesus' prediction of his denial in John 13, his sword wielding in John 18, his initial manipulation and choice to deny Jesus—recognition thwarted—in John 18, his aimless choice to go fishing, and finally, Jesus' counter-manipulation and Peter's failed recognition of Jesus on the shore in John 21. This serial characterization of Peter underscores that, in fact, Peter *does not* completely discern who Jesus really is. Therefore, 21:3 and 4 are *implicit commentary*: the response of Peter and the other six disciples—going fishing . . . not recognizing—is a *deficient response* for those having been with Jesus for the previous twenty chapters. Marguerat reminds us of how intently the implied reader of the FG is expected to look past appearances: "The reader constructed by this text is attracted to the unspoken, invited to pierce through appearances to gain a sense of the meaning of the events of the narrative."[68] Here the commentary is implied in the fact that without Jesus (15:5) they caught nothing, thus contrasting them with the success of fishing with Jesus in verse 6. When the disciples did not *know* it was the Lord, this also contrasts them with the risen Christ who *knows* everything (21:17). As Culpepper affirms of chapter 13, "the contrast between Jesus and Peter could not be put any more sharply;" so also here in 21:17.[69]

We also note with Brown that in all three of Peter's responses of "You know . . .," the "you is expressed, and this is a sign of emphasis."[70] It is actually expressed twice: σὺ οἶδας σὺ γινώσκεις. These two instances of "you,"

---

65. John 1:26 is also paradigmatic announcement of the forthcoming behavior of many characters in the Gospel.

66. Culpepper, "The Johannine Hypodeigma," 133.

67. Sternberg, *The Poetics of Biblical Narrative*, 173.

68. "Le lecteur construit par ce texte est attiré du côté du non-dit, invité à percer les apparences pour gagner le sens des événements narrrés." Marguerat, *L'exégèse biblique à l'heure du lecteur*, n.p. Again, I offer my thanks to Dr. Craig Hanson for his assistance.

69. Culpepper, "The Johannine Hypodeigma," 133.

70. Brown, *The Gospel according to John (XIII–XXI)*, 1104. Brown also points out that this statement of Peter, "know and understand," is the "same language" as that of 2:25, "and needed no one to bear witness about man, for he himself knew what was in man." It is also reminiscent of 16:30, "Now we know that you know all things and do not need anyone to question you; this is why we believe that you came from God." Ibid., 1106.

which seem superfluous at first, instead strengthen the contrast Peter is making between himself and Jesus. That two verbs are being used here also intensifies Peter's statement and the contrast with his lack of knowledge and recognition. Patrick Reardon promotes the view that Peter is finally relinquishing his claims to knowledge and boldness: "At this point the chastened Peter, no longer trusting himself, relies completely on the Lord's knowledge of his heart (John 21:17)."[71] Carson characterizes Peter's answer this way: "Despite my bitter failure, he says in effect, I love you—*you know that I love you* ... There is no trace of self-righteousness in Peter's response. He can only appeal to the fact that the Lord knows everything."[72] Thus, John 21:17 is a fulfillment of 13:7: "What I am doing you do not understand now, but afterward you will understand." Therefore, by verse 17, Peter finally recognizes his ignorance and Jesus' knowledge. His statement about Jesus and himself is the *dénouement*:

Peter's Counter-Manipulation

Time... →	→	→	→
Manipulate	**Counter-Manipulated**		**Dénouement**
			...Grieving...
Recognition Thwarted	Recognition Thwarted		Recognition of self & others
"You are one of his disciples... 'I am not'"	"Yet the disciples did not know ... 'Children'..."		"Lord, you know all things, you know that I love you"
		Irony of *lex talionis*	
Ignorance	Ignorance		Knowledge

If we apply the constructed implied reader whose reading has been colored by Genesis, the similarities to aspects of the counter-manipulation narratives in Genesis are noticeable. The brothers, chosen leaders—future tribes of Israel—are speechless in Egypt at the recognition of their lost brother (Gen 45:3). They too cease their bold plots against Rachel's sons. They are moved to humility, loyalty, and service toward Joseph (50:18). Recognition,

---

71. Reardon, "Peter at the Charcoal Fire," 21.
72. Carson, *The Gospel according to John*, 677–78.

within manipulation narratives, tells us as much about characterization as about plot. In addition, counter-manipulation within the narrative world sometimes changes the character. It can transform and humble the bold impetuous manipulator.

Truly, Truly, You Shall Lay Down Your Life

After Peter's humble response, Jesus foretells things to come for Peter, when he will follow the example that Jesus has set forth (John 13:15): "For I have given you an *example* that you also should do just as I have done to you." In 21:18, Jesus announces, "Truly, truly, I say to you, when you were young, you used to dress yourself and walk wherever you wanted, but when you are old, you will stretch out your hands, and another will dress you and carry you where you do not want to go." Jesus has stated that in the future, Peter will finally glorify God, similar to the example of Jesus. The FE has artfully tied Peter's future death, intratextually, not only to the example put in place by Jesus, but also to Peter's previous failures.

Charcoal Revisited—The Example of a Martyr

To demonstrate this connection, it is necessary to refer back to the issue of seeing the charcoal fire (βλέπουσιν ἀνθρακιὰν), for it increases the dramatic effect of Jesus' upcoming prediction. Jean-Marie Sevrin states, "Repetitions and variations in the narrative are functional."[73] By repetition, the word charcoal is a *Leitwort* and a marker that this manipulation episode is in a series. When the disciples see the charcoal fire, textual indeterminacy causes the reader to pause. Here are clear similarities with the Hebrew manipulation narratives. *Pledge, goat, robe,* and *silver* all recur in the Jacob-to-Joseph narratives. In the Joseph finale, silver haunts the brothers—an element that was intended both by Joseph within the narrative world and the Genesis author without. Here in the FG, the reader asks, "Did Jesus intentionally make a charcoal fire? Does only the reader see this, or do the characters also see its significance? And is this an instance of an evocative *déjà vu* motif?"

Quast is one of many scholars who observe the connection to chapter 18: "We will see that the description in ch. 21 is probably intended to strengthen the ties between Peter's experiences here in ch. 18 with his

---

73. "Répétitions et variations dans le récit sont fonctionnelles." J. Sevrin, "'EGW EIMI/OUK EIMI,'" 354. I am again indebted to colleague Dr. Craig Hanson for his assistance with the French.

three-fold 'interrogation' in ch. 21."[74] Wiarda however, sees "no need to look further back to Peter's threefold denial at the time of Jesus' arrest."[75] But Alter reminds interpreters that a *Leitwort* or *Leitmotiv* may be an "object [that] recurs through a particular narrative."[76] Hence, the use of charcoal fire in John 18 and 21 is, in fact, similar to that of the silver in the Joseph story. I argue, therefore, that asking about the function of charcoal in Peter's story is a valid inquiry.

Culpepper notes that in the denial scene, the οὐκ εἰμί from Peter is a phrase standing in opposition to Jesus' ἐγώ εἰμι.[77] Quast argues that the denial of Peter is woven around the interrogation of Jesus and serves to contrast Peter and Jesus, rather than Peter and the BD.[78] He also notes the FE's artful switching between settings and scenes of Jesus, then Peter, then Jesus again in 18:12–27. The FE focuses on Jesus in verses 12–14, Peter in verses 15–18, Jesus in verses 19–24, and finally, Peter's final two denials in verses 25–27, before Jesus is sent to Pilate in verse 28. He maintains, "This construction alone should be enough of a clue to lead to the conclusion that the Beloved Disciple is not the primary counterpart of Peter in the narrative. Rather, Jesus and Peter make up the main contrast."[79] He further pointed out that in verse 25, Peter's "standing and warming himself is explicitly reminiscent of v. 18," where the servants and officers had done the same.[80] Moreover, when one looks back and examines closer, one will find that this "standing and warming" construction is a *threefold repetition*, emphasizing Peter's subtle alignment with them. In verse 18a, the slaves and officers first are standing and warming themselves, and then Peter in 18b. Again, Peter is re-emphasized, standing and warming in verse 25, before his final denials. Sevrin points out this alarming similarity between Judas, who "*was standing with them*" (John 18:5), that is, with "a band of soldiers and some officers" (18:3), and Peter who "*was standing with them*" (18:18b), with "servants

---

74. Quast, *Peter and the Beloved Disciple*, 84, "All that can be said regarding the use of ἀνθρακιάν can also be said regarding the explanatory phrase ὅτι ψῦχος ἦν [Lowdermilk—it was cold] that immediately follows the mention of the fire. That is, it may very well be based on first-hand experience . . . for it adds to the graphic picture being painted of a cold dark spring night. A fire has drawn servants and officers together to warm themselves while the prisoner inside is being interrogated."

75. Wiarda, "John 21.1–23," 65.

76. Alter, *The Art of Biblical Narrative*, 95.

77. Culpepper, *The Gospel and Letters of John*, 222. See also Larsen, *Recognizing the Stranger*, 149, 172.

78. Quast, *Peter and the Beloved Disciple*, 85. Peter is also contrasted with John the Baptist. See also Sevrin, "'EGW EIMI/OUK EIMI," 353–55.

79. Quast, *Peter and the Beloved Disciple*, 85.

80. Ibid.

and officers" (18:18a): "While in the courtyard scene (the place at which [we] also find Jesus and Peter), Peter stands *with* the servants and guard (ἦν μετ'αὐτῶν ἑστώς), just as Judas [had] in the garden. Peter in his act of denial, has changed sides."[81] The triple repetition demonstrates Peter siding with Jesus' enemies and contrasts him with Jesus. Peter has fully, and *shamefully*, denied Jesus completely and acted the part of the traitor.[82] Therefore, when we realize in John 21 that his admission of love and his restoration are tied to John 18 by the common setting at a charcoal fire, we can better trace his character as it transforms. Similar to transformed manipulators in Genesis, he progresses from the opposite of an ideal character—a traitor—toward the ideal: toward someone who, in Peter's case by his death, will glorify God.[83]

Returning to the scene of the second charcoal fire, using what we now know of power and counter-manipulation in Genesis, we must ask if a reader well acquainted with this pattern would sense the tension related to possible retribution afforded to Jesus, as the betrayed one, by the principle of *lex talionis*. Moreover, will that same reader, accustomed not only to betrayal, but also to reconciliation in Genesis manipulation, expect Jesus to *reverse* the law of *lex talionis* and embrace Peter? This would be similar to the gracious reconciliation Joseph offered to his brothers, or even that which Esau extended to Jacob (Gen 33). Culpepper argues that Jesus' death eventually caused the disciples "to *revolutionize their understanding of status, honor*

---

81. "Tandis que dans la scène de la cour (lieu dans lequel se trouvent en même temps Jésus et Pierre), Pierre se tient *avec* les serviteurs et les gardes ἦν μετ'αὐτῶν ἑστώς, tout comme Judas dans le jardin. Pierre, qui se nie, a changé de côté." Sevrin, "'EGW EIMI/OUK EIMI,'" 351; Translation Dr. Craig Hanson. Sevrin has collapsed the Greek phrase in verse 18. Note though that Judas was standing with "soldiers and officers," whereas Peter stood with "servants and officers."

82. Keener writes, "Given the values of honor toward one's teacher, the view may have been widespread that the honor of a person's teacher or disciple should be as dear to one as one's own." And, "Whereas Jesus proves bold, Peter's denials (18:25–27) appear shameful. In Jewish martyr stories, the protagonists refuse to renounce their ancestral faith even under the most terrible tortures and executions." Thus, Peter's denial would have been seen as very shameful. Keener, *The Gospel of John*, 2:1092, 1096. "Among these warming themselves is another suspect, Peter." Quast, *Peter and the Beloved Disciple*, 85.

83. I will address the tradition of Peter's martyrdom below. Culpepper notes these intratextual connections: "Greater love has no man than this, that a man lay down his life for his friends (15:13). Indeed, the hour is coming when whoever kills you will think he is offering service to God (16:2). This he said to show by what death he [Peter] was to glorify God (21:19)," Culpepper, "The Johannine Hypodeigma," 142. In John 13, drawing from Schnackenburg, Culpepper argues the following parallel as well: "'If I then ... you also ought to ...' (v. 14).'For I have ... that you also should ...' (*hina kathōs*, v. 15)." Ibid., 143.

and shame, and their calling as apostles."[84] Perhaps the cause of that revolution includes Jesus' graceful commissioning of Peter here as well. The reader might have sensed a tension, in that Jesus could have shamed Peter by denying Peter three times. The mention of charcoal set up that tension. From the implied Johannine reader's perspective, Jesus knows all things, and so he knows about the first charcoal fire at the trial. I hold to the possibility that an implied reader may have interpreted that Jesus intentionally creates the second charcoal fire in chapter 21 to recall Peter's mind to the first fire and his three denials. Regardless, the FE assists the reader and describes both fires with the term "charcoal," causing the reader to see the reversal of shame and *lex talionis* and the import of Jesus' restoration and commissioning of Peter. Jesus does this even though Peter displayed a complete abandonment of Jesus at the first charcoal fire. The repetition of the charcoal fire prepares the implied reader. The entire episode of counter-manipulation appears artfully staged to force Peter to face his past. He may be expecting shame and denial, but Jesus offers restoration in the form of a meal. Then Jesus predicts Peter's death, which the narrator characterizes as glorifying God.

When You Were Young . . . When You Are Old

The phrase "when you were young," ὅτε ἦς νεώτερος, is also important. After the extensive discussion of diminutives earlier, the intended referent for "young" becomes clearer. Using the diminutive παιδία, Jesus speaks with fondness toward these, his young sheep, for whom he has already laid down his life. But the term also included pity and an intimation of rebuke. The diminutive form adds these nuances, but παῖς, the primitive form by itself, can indicate youth. Here then, νεώτερος is in parallel with and refers to the culminating point of Peter's youthful abandonment of his fellow disciples in the boat when Jesus calls them παιδία (John 21:5). With Hoskyns, I believe Jesus is recalling Peter's self-driven return to Galilean fishing, accentuated by his behavior on the boat: "The boisterous and irresponsible freedom of youth is now at an end. He can no longer act as he had just acted when he girded himself, and left the fish half caught, and swam alone to the shore."[85] Chapters 13 and 18 also demonstrate Peter acting and speaking in a manner that protected what *he* wanted, in contrast to what Jesus wanted. One such example is "you shall never wash my feet" (13:8). Thus, Spencer notes in chapter 21, "Peter's actions in v. 7 contrast with those of Jesus in 13.3–5:

---

84. Ibid., 144; emphasis added.
85. Hoskyns and Davey, *The Fourth Gospel*, 557. But see Schnackenburg, *The Gospel according to John*, 3:364.

whereas Jesus takes off his clothing and girds a towel around his waist, Peter puts on his clothing by girding his 'outer garment' around himself."[86] On the boat, he demonstrated his youthfulness by abandoning his brothers and going where he wanted. When he is old though, he will change.

The prediction "someone else will gird you" also harkens back to chapter 13.[87] Immediately after Jesus' explanation of the foot washing in chapter 13, Jesus directs their thoughts to his betrayal and death using the typical Johannine double amen statement: "Truly truly, I say to you, one of you will betray me" (John 13:21). In so doing, Jesus initiates the discussion of his death *directly after disrobing and girding*.[88] Now in chapter 21, Jesus speaks directly to Peter of his future death, *shortly after Peter's disrobing and girding*, and Jesus does so with *a double amen* statement.[89] Also very important to note is that this occurs right when Peter has finally come to terms with his past and recognizes κύριε, πάντα σὺ οἶδας, σὺ γινώσκεις. Now, Jesus recalls what has happened all of Peter's life but was even more pronounced on this fishing trip: "you used to *gird* yourself and walk wherever you wanted, but when you are old, you will stretch out your hands, and another will *gird* you and carry you where you do not want to go." I have replaced "dress" from the *English Standard Version* with "gird" to emphasize the connection to other passages in the FG. The words for dress/gird here in 21:18 are of the same word group and derivation as that found in the girding in 21:7 and 13:4-5: ζωννύω, ζώννυμι, διαζώννυμι.[90] In 13:4-5 and 21:7, the FE uses

---

86. "Peter's mode of discipleship is explicated by the implied author with the echo created by the dual use of the verb ζώννυμι in v. 18, which invokes imagery of 13.3-5 for a second time in the discourse of ch. 21." Spencer, "Narrative Echoes in John 21," 62-63.

87. Ibid.

88. Culpepper argues for the intratextuality between laying aside of garments, foot washing, and Jesus' predicted death in John 13: "The connection between the foot washing and Jesus' death raises the alternative possibility that Jesus was exhorting his disciples to be ready to die for one another. This interpretation receives further support from statements later in the Gospel: Greater love has no man than this, that a man lay down his life for his friends (15:13). Indeed, the hour is coming when whoever kills you will think he is offering service to God (16:2). This he said to show by what death he [Peter] was to glorify God (21:19)." He also argued that this was the position of the Johannine community as represented in the epistles: "By this we know love: that he laid down his life for us; and we ought to lay down our lives for the brethren" (1 John 3:16). Culpepper, "The Johannine Hypodeigma," 137, 141-44.

89. "The words verily, verily in the gospel mark the movement of an argument . . . They are not used to introduce a wholly new episode." Hoskyns and Davey, *The Fourth Gospel*, 366. But Schnackenburg sees these words as a marker that "the editor presumably sees a close connection between the two sayings." Schnackenburg, *The Gospel according to John*, 3:366.

90. Oepke, "ζώννυμι," in Kittel and Friedrich, eds., *TDNT*, 5:303-7.

ONE LITTLE SHEEP BECOMES A SHEPHERD: JOHN 21:15-19   261

διαζώννυμι. In 21:18 there are two occurrences from this word group. The first is ἐζώννυες, from ζωννύω, and the second is ζώσει, from ζώννυμι. The first is simply a different lexical type for ζώννυμι.[91] Together, these instances of the term without the prefix δια, are only found here, with the exception that ζώννυμι is also found in Acts 12:8.[92] Therefore, here the reader has an additional *Leitwort*. The narrative units of Jesus' girding in chapter 13, Peter's girding on the boat early in chapter 21, and his future girding at death—all are tied together. In the spirit of the Genesis episodes, one learns now that "this story goes with that one," and not only the two previous stories, but also the third one: Peter's future death. The scarcity of the term in the New Testament, and the connections already noted between John 13 and 21 render this likely. The connections Culpepper has argued between Jesus' girding/foot washing and death in chapter 13 have now been transferred to Peter.

Brown believes that perhaps this prediction by Jesus indicates that the FE was aware of the tradition that Peter was crucified on Vatican Hill.[93] Other scholars note not only the allusion to crucifixion, but also the preparation by girding, the stretching out of the hands, as well as the sequence of these actions in crucifixion.[94] The allusion to the tradition of Peter's

---

91. Swanson and Logos Research Systems, *Dictionary of Biblical Languages with Semantic Domains: Greek (New Testament)*.

92. When miraculously freed from prison, Peter is told by the angel "*Dress* (gird) yourself and put on your sandals." ζώννυμι is found only twice in the LXX (Ezek 9:11; 16:10). ζωννύω is found fourteen times (Exod 29:9; Lev 8:7, 13; 16:4, 1 Kgdms 17:39; 25:13; 1 Macc 6:37; 2 Macc 10:25; Job 38:3; 40:7; Isa 11:5; Ezek 23:15). They are consistently translated as "gird," or to "fasten" or "tie" a belt or other article of clothing about the waist.

93. Brown, *The Gospel according to John (XIII–XXI)*, 1118.

94. "It was widely assumed in the ancient world that Peter died by crucifixion," and "The description of a person 'stretching out hands' was used by many ancient writers as shorthand for the Roman practice of crucifixion." Blaine, *Peter in the Gospel of John*, 173–76. As to the concern that binding or girding, as in capture or imprisonment, would come before one is stretched on a cross, whereas Jesus predicts stretching first then girding, Brown believes that the stretching is listed first purposefully because it is a *hysteron proteron*, a rhetorical device, where the components of a subject or idea are reversed in order to put a greater emphasis on a particular aspect of it: "It is better to suggest that by a type of hysteron proteron the Johannine writer placed the stretching out of the hands first in order to call attention to it, precisely because it was the key to the whole interpretation." Brown, *The Gospel according to John (XIII–XXI)*, 1108, 1121. See also Carson, *The Gospel according to John*, 678–79; Hoskyns and Davey, *The Fourth Gospel*, 557; Keener, *The Gospel of John*, 2:1237–38; Schnackenburg, *The Gospel according to John*, 3:366–67. Most recently, Michaels states, "[T]here is no reason to suppose that Jesus is predicting literal crucifixion in Peter's case." Michaels, *The Gospel of John*, 1048.

leadership as well as his martyrdom is important. In the canonical books of Acts, Galatians, and 1 Corinthians, Peter is reported to have acted as a shepherd in various ways: leading (Acts 1:15; 15:7), preaching (Acts 2; 4; 10), performing miracles (3:1–11; 5:1–16; 9:32–43), and once narrowly escaping martyrdom (Acts 12). The apostle Paul references Peter's ministry leadership in both Galatians and 1 Corinthians (Gal 2:7–8; 1 Cor 3:22; 9:5; 15:5), as well as his own rebuke of Peter for withdrawing from Gentiles in the presence of Jews (Gal 2:11–14). Outside the canon, 1 Clement 5 refers to Peter's martyrdom: "Through envy and jealousy, the greatest and most righteous pillars [of the church] have been persecuted and put to death. Let us set before our eyes the illustrious apostles. Peter, through unrighteous envy, endured not one or two, but numerous labours; and when he had at length suffered martyrdom, departed to the place of glory due to him" (1 Clem. 5:2–4).[95] Ignatius of Antioch refers to those who had "touched and believed" Jesus after the resurrection, and "[t]herefore they despised even death and were found to be above death."[96] Bauckham contends that we cannot infer the location of Peter's death from 1 Clement, and therefore argued that the *Apocalypse of Peter* offers the earliest "unequivocal indication" of the location of Peter's death as Rome (Apoc. Pet. 14:4–6).[97] Tertullian reports that Peter died in Rome a death like Jesus: "How happy is its church, on which apostles poured forth all their doctrine along with their blood! where Peter endures a passion like his Lord's!"[98] He also alludes to John 21:18, by saying that Peter was "girt by another, when he is made fast to the cross."[99] Later traditions that Peter was crucified upside down may have originated from the *Acts of Peter*.[100] Thus, although outside the FG, church

---

95. ANF, 9:230. Some challenge whether this is a direct reference to Peter's martyrdom, but see Bauckham's defense: Bauckham, "The Martyrdom of Peter in Early Christian Literature," 553–62.

96. Ign. *Smyrn*.3:2–3 (trans. Bauckham). Bauckham argues that since Peter is the only named apostle in the passage, it must be a reference to his martyrdom. Ibid., 563.

97. "And go to a city which rules over the west, and drink the cup which I have promised you at the hands of the son who is in Hades." This is Bauckham's translation of the Greek text. The "son" is, Bauckham argues, a reference to Nero, and "drink the cup" is the same "martyrological expression" found in Matt 20:22–23 and Mark 10:38–39. Ibid., 572–73.

98. *Praescr.* 36 (*ANF*, 3:260).

99. *Scorp.* 15. Ibid., 260.

100. *Acts Pet.* 37. Bauckham, "The Martyrdom of Peter in Early Christian Literature," 578–79. See also Eusebius, *Hist. Eccl.*3.3.2: "Peter appears to have preached in Pontus, Galatia, Bithynia, Cappadocia, and Asia to the Jews of the dispersion. And at last, having come to Rome, he was crucified head-downwards." Schaff and Wace, *A Select Library of the Nicene and Post-Nicene Fathers of the Christian Church*, 1:132.

tradition affirmed Jesus' prediction that eventually Peter's behavior would resemble that of Jesus.

At the foot washing, Jesus first girded himself, but is later girded by others in crucifixion and lays down his life for the sheep.[101] If the reader views girding oneself *for* one's self as a selfish act, the reader may see a contrast between Peter's girding in chapter 21 with what Jesus did, girding himself to serve others in chapter 13. Additionally, Jesus was later wrapped, περιέβαλον, in a purple robe *by others*: "And the soldiers twisted together a crown of thorns and put it on his head and *arrayed* (περιέβαλον) him in a purple robe" (John 19:2).[102] Then, others lead him to crucifixion: "So they took Jesus, and he went out, bearing his own cross" (19:17). Remembering that motifs need not be limited to word-for-word exactness, we see here that girding/wrapping is a strong and pervasive *Leitmotiv*.[103] Along similar lines, Burke speaks of "operational synonyms," such as "stillness" and "silence," which readers are expected to link.[104] The FE also used thematic parallels and allusions of intratextuality and was not bound by a point-by-point need for identical terminology. When Jesus states "and another will dress you and carry you where you do not want to go" (21:18), the FE has tied this prediction to Jesus' suffering in chapter 19. The reader learns that Peter must no longer be a little child; he must no longer be like the evil shepherds of Israel. He must follow Jesus as the sacrificial shepherd who was girded *by others* and *for others* and who stretched out his hands and was led *by others* where he did not want to go. In this manner, Jesus predicts that Peter will become pliable, *manipulable* to Jesus' command, because, in fact, a true shepherd "lays down his life for the sheep" (10:11-18).

After girding, Peter throws himself into the sea while leaving the others in the boat to deal with the catch.[105] He girds himself, strikes out on his own away from others, and swims to shore. Furthermore, Spencer, commenting on 21:1, states, "The disciples, rather than acting upon their faith

---

101. "The unique feature in the Johannine picture of the shepherd is his willingness to die for sheep." Brown, *The Gospel according to John (I–XII)*, 398. "[A]among all the NT uses of shepherd imagery, only John x specifies that one of the functions of the model shepherd is to lay down his life for his sheep." Brown, *The Gospel according to John (XIII–XXI)*, 1114.

102. This may also be an instance of intertextuality with Ezek 34, for the evil shepherds περιβάλλεσθε (wrap/clothe) themselves with the wool of the sheep (34:3).

103. Alter, *The Art of Biblical Narrative*, 95.

104. Burke, *Terms for Order*, 158. Burke suggests moving from "factional" words to "operational synonyms" for analysis of themes and structures in a literary work.

105. "The boisterous and irresponsible freedom of youth is now at an end. He can no longer act as he had just acted when he girded himself and left the fish half caught, and swam alone to the shore." Hoskyns and Davey, *The Fourth Gospel*, 557.

by following the directions of Jesus, are doing what they themselves want to do ... The reader does not recognize this point until verses 18–19 when Jesus tells Peter that while he was young he would walk wherever he wanted, but when he grew old he would be led where he did not wish to go."[106] Peter announces his fishing plans. They follow. After the catch he girds himself and goes where he wants, abandoning the boat and the catch to others.[107] Thus, Jesus is specifically contrasting Peter's earlier behavior of aimlessly fishing with his future behavior of selfless death.[108] The future Peter will resemble the example of Jesus in chapter 13. Wiarda observes, "There is an emphasis on Peter not being able to do what he wants to do, 'θέλω,' a situation which contrasts with that described in v. 3."[109] Here again, the relecture in verses 15–18 parallels the previous verses, as well as previous episodes in the lives of Jesus and Peter:

---

106. Spencer, "Narrative Echoes in John 21," 58n27.

107. "For the stretching out the old man's hands there is no contrasting action on the part of the youth." Brown, *The Gospel according to John (XIII–XXI)*, 1107. Additionally, there is no hint of stretching of the hands in Jesus' statement looking back to when Peter was young, but only in the future, "older Peter" prediction by Jesus. However, it is interesting that he may have stretched his arms out in the act of swimming. Virtually any form of swimming requires some stretching of the arms. But this can only be inferred, since swimming behavior is not even pointed out to the reader, and there is no other support in the text.

108. "Death for members of John's group is another way of 'glorifying God.'" Malina and Rohrbaugh, *Social Science Commentary on the Gospel of John*, 290. Peter, like other noted ancients, will die nobly. Greco-Roman evaluation of a person's life included how that person died: "I think, too, that the way in which the men died makes manifest a difference in their high excellence." Plutarch, *Comp. Ag. Cleom. cum* 3.1. Contrast Anthony's unwillingness to chance his death for others with that of Peter's foretold sacrifice: "Antony deserted others, for he ran away from those who were risking their lives for him. Demetrius may therefore be blamed for making his soldiers so hostile to him, and Antony for abandoning a goodwill and confidence which was so much in evidence. *As for their deaths, neither is to be commended.*" Plutarch, *Comp. Demetr. Ant.* 6.1–2; emphasis added. Likely, the FE's readers saw Peter's death as unjust under the Roman government. Note then the similarity with the death of Agis: "Agis, then, on his way to the halter, saw one of the officers shedding tears of sympathy for him. 'My man,' said he, 'cease weeping; for even though I am put to death in this lawless and unjust manner, I have the better of my murderers.' And saying these words, he offered his neck to the noose without hesitation." Plutarch, *Ag. Cleom.* 20.1.

109. Wiarda, "John 21.1–23," 65.

21:1–14	21:15–19
Little children (παιδία)	*Little* sheep (ἀρνία, προβάτια, προβάτια)
Jesus, the Good *Shepherd* . . . (10:11, ποιμὴν)	Peter commanded to *shepherd* (ποίμαινε)
. . . *feeds* the little children breakfast (φαγ- in John 6, προσφάγιον in 21:5)	Peter commanded to *feed* the little sheep (βόσκε)

Chapter 13; 18; 19:2,17 & 21:1–7	21:18
Jesus *girded* for others (13:4)	
Jesus *girded* by others (19:2)	
Peter *girded* himself (21:7)	Peter will be *girded* by others
Jesus *stretched* out his hands (implied in crucifixion 19:17–18)	Peter *will stretch* out his hands
Peter went to Galilee, later left the boat (21:1–7)	Peter *will be led* where he does not want to go.

Implied readers would notice this episode as a continuation of the previous Petrine episodes and that Peter's future characterization will come closer to that of Jesus—and starkly contrast his own previous behavior.[110] From the incident of the foot washing, Jesus girds himself as well, but is later bound by others (John 18:12), wrapped (19:2), and taken to the cross, stretching out his hands to be crucified (19:16–18). Although the FE does not mark the stretching of the hands and girding with lexically identical terms, these are tied together as *images*; the activity patterns of Jesus and Peter are intended first to be contrasted and then compared. When in 21:19 the FE narrates that Jesus says this to indicate how Peter would "glorify God" in his death, this phrase is a return to the terminology of chapter 13. In that scene, Jesus concludes by saying, "Now is the Son of Man *glorified*, and God is *glorified* in him. If God is *glorified* in him, God will also *glorify* him in himself, and *glorify* him at once" (13:31–2).[111] The FE also has two other instances of

---

110. "The use of repetition (or redundancy) to evoke narrative echoes occurs frequently in narrative literature . . . Because of the aural nature of literature in antiquity, the authorial audiences of the four Gospels would be more apt to recognize repetition or redundancy and moreover the rhetorical effects of such." Spencer, "Narrative Echoes in John 21," 55.

111. Hoskyns and Davey, *The Fourth Gospel*, 562.

intratextuality with the example of death. Looking back, we find a similar structure along with wording describing "what kind of death" Jesus would die:

John 12:33

τοῦτο δὲ ἔλεγεν <u>σημαίνων ποίῳ θανάτῳ</u>

Verses 32–33 "'And I, when I am lifted up from the earth, will draw all people to myself.' He said this *to show by what kind of death* he was going to die."

John 18:32

ἵνα ὁ λόγος τοῦ Ἰησοῦ πληρωθῇ ὃν εἶπεν <u>σημαίνων ποίῳ θανάτῳ</u>

Verses 31–32 "'It is not lawful for us to put anyone to death.' This was to fulfill the word that Jesus had spoken *to show by what kind of death* he was going to die."

John 21:19:

τοῦτο δὲ εἶπεν <u>σημαίνων ποίῳ θανάτῳ</u> δοξάσει τὸν θεόν. καὶ τοῦτο εἰπὼν λέγει αὐτῷ· ἀκολούθει μοι.

Verses 18b–19 "'... when you are old, you will stretch out your hands, and another will dress you and carry you where you do not want to go.' This he said *to show by what kind of death* he was to glorify God. And after saying this he said to him, 'Follow me.'"

Thus the implied readers, familiar with Roman crucifixion, would have noticed the imagery common in these three passages—lifting up (12:32–33), not carried out by the Jews (18:31–22), and done by the stretching out of hands (21:18b–19)—linked by the phrase "σημαίνων ποίῳ θανάτῳ." If the implied reader is alert to *Leitwörter*, the deduced reading sharpens: Jesus' counter-manipulation of Peter will be effective, and Peter will indeed follow Jesus in the *same kind of death, crucifixion*, by which they both glorify the father.

"A Need for Change Within Peter Himself"

Spencer alerts us to the fact that ἀκολουθέω occurs in all four of the chapters in the FG that were shown to have significant intratextuality with chapter 21: chapters 6, 10, 13, and 18.[112] Wiarda notes the progressive characterization of Peter and concludes that Peter's threefold questioning "might have been intended to communicate something about a need for change within Peter himself."[113] This is a change that Peter has continuously, *iteratively*, wrestled with, much as Jacob's wrestling at Jabbok came even after his radical name change. He, like Jacob, is "a divided soul."[114] Janzen notes Genesis' tendency to keep calling that patriarch by both Jacob and Israel: "Still capable of his old tricks, he is, however, no longer consistently conniving, but *begins* to display capacities for trust and patience."[115] For Jacob and Peter both, there is not a singular moment of total change. Janzen adds, "[W]restling Jacob is being wrestled into a fuller self-knowledge."[116] Just as I noted earlier that Jacob was the prototypical manipulative character of Genesis whose life was defined, as well as haunted, by deception, ignorance, and knowledge, I argue now that Peter may be read as the prototypical manipulative character of John, whose final days with Jesus were haunted by deception, ignorance, and knowledge. If Jacob was being wrestled into fuller self-knowledge, the same is an appropriate description for this growing shepherd as well.

Eventually, Simon son of John will come to a point when he fully lives as Simon Peter. By adding the commentary, "Jesus said this to indicate the kind of death by which Peter would glorify God," the FE tells the reader that this change is not over. Jesus has *reversed* the power and shame perspective that underlies the relationship between Peter and Jesus in the preceding eighteen verses. This comment by the narrator explains that the words of Jesus *eliminate* the shame that Peter held. Carson states, "[T]he indelible shame Peter bore for his public disowning of the Lord Jesus Christ . . . was

---

112. "ἀκολουθέω occurs in the following places in chs. 1–20: 6.2; 8.12; 10.4, 5, 27; 11.31; 12.26; 13.36, 37; 18.15; 20.6." Spencer, "Narrative Echoes in John 21," 62.
113. Wiarda, "John 21.1–23," 68.
114. Janzen, *"How can a Man be Born when He is Old?,"* 330.
115. Ibid.; emphasis added.
116. Ibid., 327.

forgiven by the Lord himself."[117] But the power is reversed as well. Peter no longer does what, or goes where, he wants to go.[118] In effect, when Jesus tells Peter about his future death, he is saying, "You're not in control of that [your death] either!"[119]

In summary, a reader well acquainted with Genesis would read John 21:15–19 as a continuation of Jesus' counter-manipulation of Peter. Having earlier used thwarted recognition of himself, Jesus also had the freedom to bring justice and full reciprocal punishment under a culture of *lex talionis* justice. Like Joseph, he instead *brings reconciliation*. He uses three questions, mirroring three denials, to transform Peter. The transformative effect of this counter-manipulation forces Peter to recall his past. The result is that he can no longer boast about his devotion. Jesus knows all, and Peter, far from arrogant, can only affirm his love (φιλῶ)—nothing more. He is like a little sheep, but must now begin the transformation to maturing shepherd. Accordingly, when Jesus in verses 18–19 predicts Peter's ultimate destiny of a dying shepherd, the Genesis reader learns that Jesus' counter-manipulation will hit its mark.[120] Peter the manipulator will finally turn even more toward a pliable manipulable servant. Finally, church tradition regarding his death affirms that Peter eventually follows Jesus and glorifies God.

---

117. Carson, *The Gospel according to John*, 680.

118. Schnackenburg, *The Gospel according to John*, 3:366.

119. Wright, Personal Discussions, on this Date and Others, about Power and Shame in John 21.

120. Spencer, "Narrative Echoes in John 21," 63, 66.

8

Conclusion

When I began this project, the nexus of two points intrigued me. First, the Gospel of John draws richly from Genesis as a text of reference. Starting with the first verse of the Gospel, Readers can better interpret many passages in John, if they understand Genesis. Second, although Genesis is a book with many recognition scenes, scholars had not yet judiciously examined it for an understanding of Johannine recognition. I have carefully examined several instances of recognition in Genesis and argued for a theory of manipulation narratives that I believe is beneficial for reading Johannine *anagnorisis*.

The Theory of Manipulation in Genesis and John

Manipulation, as an alternative to the trickster terminology, describes the broad array of behaviors and actions carried out by Genesis characters to influence others for a desired goal. Manipulation occurs when person or group "A" carries out certain actions, in an indirect, masked, or camouflaged manner, in order to obtain a desired objective. "B" does not know or recognize that "A" has acted this way. Later however, "B" usually, though not always, recognizes the manipulative behavior. The manipulative behavior ranges widely, from wrongful outright deception to crafty maneuvering, designed to correct a previous injustice. The term "manipulation" contributes greater theoretical specificity than the term "tricking" does.

The taxonomy provided in chapter 4 identifies six kernels frequently occurring in manipulation narratives: 1) The desired benefit the manipulator is pursuing, 2) The actual manipulation, carried out through a variety of devices, 3) The benefit achieved, 4) The moment of recognition, 5) The statement or challenge in response to the manipulation, and 6) The effect the manipulation has on plot and characterization. Not all manipulation narratives include all six kernels, but the analysis demonstrates that this taxonomy can strengthen our understanding of not only Genesis, but also Johannine manipulation and recognition.

The purpose Genesis characters intend when they prevent recognition, goes beyond the testing we see carried out by Odysseus when he returns to Penelope and delays her recognition of him. We can better understand recognition, and more specifically thwarted recognition in Genesis if we view it in light of the overall manipulation type-narratives. Initially, preventing or delaying recognition is not an isolated event, but part of a deceptive scheme designed to gain a selfish goal. Later, the same action may be used by a counter-manipulator to correct this injustice. These actions by the counter-manipulator can rise to excess, as in the case of Jacob's sons counter-manipulating the men of Shechem. Nevertheless, we can better understand recognition in Genesis if we see it as one narrative kernel, that has a functional role in cause and effect manipulation and counter-manipulation narratives.

In the FG, at least two recognition narratives demonstrate characteristics of manipulation narratives (John 18 and 21). Peter lies outright to his accusers in the courtyard. The reader infers that he does this in order to obtain the desired benefit of preserving his well-being. The narrative implies that Peter achieves this goal, because he never suffers arrest or harm and is free to move about and travel after the crucifixion. The victims of Peter's manipulation never come to recognition and no character responds to the manipulation, but a rooster crows, indicating to the reader a censure of Peter's manipulative behavior.[1] The entire manipulation episode serves to characterize Peter negatively. He is unpredictable, unwilling to stand as a disciple of Jesus (contrary to his boast earlier), and he associates with Jesus' enemies. Jesus, however, is characterized positively. Peter later affirms that Jesus indeed knows all things (21:17). He knew Peter would deny him (13:38; 18:27), and he now knows Peter's future. Moreover, Jesus himself was willing to lay down his life for his sheep.

Jesus' dealings with Peter and his companions can be analyzed as a counter-manipulation of Peter's behavior in the courtyard. I have argued that the text implies that Jesus' goal is to turn the disciples, especially Peter, back to a proper relationship to him as followers. We can infer this from the content of Jesus' questions and response to Peter in 21:15–17. Jesus' manipulation of Peter and his companions mirrors Peter's actions in the courtyard. By use of space, the ambivalent appellation "children," and omitting his own

---

1. I noted earlier that the Gen text never indicates the men of Shechem recognizing the manipulative schemes of Jacob's sons. Laban too never recognizes that Rachel has stolen his *teraphim*.

name, Jesus intentionally delays their recognition of him. After the meal, he questions Peter three times, reflecting Peter's threefold denial and failure to recognize Jesus as his master. Therefore, Peter is counter-manipulated in a manner similar to his own devices of manipulation used in the courtyard.

The recognition kernel, as well as the response kernel, both occur before the narrative indicates any benefit achieved by Jesus' actions. The BD affirms, "It is the Lord" (21:7). Upon seeing the bread and fish on shore, the other disciples also respond, but with silence. Moreover, when Peter responds, "*you* know all things, *you* know that I love you," this too serves as a recognition of Jesus by Peter. This statement also serves to show that Jesus has achieved his desired goal. Peter is beginning to acknowledge who Jesus is, and, in contrast to Jesus, that he himself does *not* know all things. The text implies this by the emphatic and repeated σύ. Moreover, the narrator's explanation of Jesus' prediction of Peter's death indicates that in the future, outside the narrative, the end of Peter's life will align with Jesus' intended goals for him: rather than deny Jesus, he will glorify God in his death. The effect of Jesus' counter-manipulation is Peter's reversal and reconciliation. Peter is no longer characterized disgracefully as the opposite of Jesus but as one who is beginning the reconciliation with his master, sharing a meal and sharing life. He moves from a boasting, imperceptive disciple to a humbled, perceptive one. Rather than saying, "I am not" a disciple, Peter now repeatedly responds with the positive, "Yes Lord," and then "*you* know all things, *you* know that I love you."

Assessing the Characteristic Manipulation Patterns in John

To review, the four characteristic patterns of Genesis manipulation identified were as follows: 1) The chosen manipulator in the character development process, 2) The disempowerment of the manipulated and empowerment of the manipulator, 3) The presence of evocative *déjà vu* motifs, and 4) The transforming effect of counter-manipulation. Due to the way these patterns work together, I will discuss disempowerment after evocative *déjà vu* motifs.

The Chosen Manipulator in the Character Development Process

Upon examining the Johannine text, I found that Peter fits the pattern of a chosen leader in the character development process. He is second only to Jesus as a main character. He is one of God's chosen (John 6:70; 13:18; 15:16–19) and is specifically named for the task of feeding and shepherding.

He does not always make the right choices but is nevertheless in the process of knowing Jesus. His characterization is highlighted in the FG with the following scenes: affirmation of Jesus as the bearer of eternal life (6:68), claim to know and believe in Jesus (6:69), confused misunderstanding of Jesus' foot washing (13:6–11), boastful statement of self-sacrificial commitment (13:37), sword wielding (18:10–11), absolute denial (18:15–18, 25–27), delayed belief (20:8–9), aimless fishing and a lack of recognition (21:1–4), final boast-less affirmation of love for Jesus (21:15–17), and a prediction of ultimate sacrificial love and devotion (21:18–19). According to the values of the FG, he does not yet fully *know and understand* Jesus' true significance and thus acts in ways that betray that misunderstanding. Although Peter is indeed chosen to lead, he may also be typified as a manipulator. John 21 is very much about Peter's character development process.

Evocative *Déjà Vu* Motifs

I discussed seven instances of *Leitwörter/Leitmotiv* in the context of John 21: *Nathanael, Thomas, charcoal, girding, fish* (specifically ὀψάριον), *bread,* and the *image of crucifixion*. These strengthen the literary connection of the manipulation episode of John 21:1–19 to previous stories. The presence of Nathanael in chapter 21 reminds the reader of Nathanael's partial recognition in 1:49. The presence of Thomas ties John 21 to his previous doubt but eventual recognition in 20:28. Charcoal ties Peter's threefold restorative questioning by Jesus to his threefold denials of Jesus in the courtyard in 18:18. The girding, at both the beginning and end of chapter 21, ties this narrative to Jesus' girding in 13:4 and also to where he is dressed and led away by others in 19:2, 17. The use of ὀψάριον and ἄρτον recommends to the reader that the story of the great catch and the breakfast by the shore is meant to be read in light of the miraculous feeding in John 6. Finally, the terminology of σημαίνων ποίῳ θανάτῳ, "to show by what kind of death," ties Jesus' words about Peter's death to Jesus' own crucifixion referred to in 12:33 and 18:32.

Some of these instances of *Leitwörter* also serve to support the *moral intent* of the story. The presence of Nathanael and Thomas in John 21 gives the lack of recognition in 21:4 an even stronger ring, thereby reinforcing the implication of John 21—that Jesus' sheep should recognize him, and that these sheep, despite previous recognitions, are similar to little children and need a shepherd. The girding/wrapping *Leitwörter* strengthen the message that Peter will eventually *follow* Jesus and will be girded and led to a death that glorifies God. The ὀψάριον and the bread reinforce the didactic message that Jesus indeed can supply abundance despite strong circumstances of paucity. Together they remind the disciples that they must rely on Jesus' divine power and that without him they can do nothing (John 15:5). Finally, the threefold occurrence of σημαίνων ποίῳ θανάτῳ and the predicted image of crucifixion underscore the relentless message of the FG: "follow me," whether in life or in death.[2]

As in the Genesis narratives, some of these *Leitwörter* occur in the narrative world in such a way that a perceptive reader may suspect that they *haunt* the characters. When the disciples come to shore, they see a *charcoal* fire, with *fish* and *bread*. They respond with silence. Examined in the light of the functions of *Leitwörter*, the reason for the silence of the disciples may be that the full recognition of Jesus has brought them face to face with their aimless fishing. *Charcoal, little fish, and bread* all serve to bring these now humbled disciples hauntingly back to the miraculous feeding in John 6 and Peter's denial in John 18. This *déjà vu* moment and their realization of their out-of-step choice to go fishing provoke an evocative response of silence that the narrator points out to the reader, "Now none of the disciples dared ask him, 'Who are you?'" A few moments later, Peter responds and concedes Jesus' position of knowing all things.

The Disempowerment of the Manipulated and Empowerment of the Manipulator

In the Genesis material, I have shown that often the manipulator walked away in a position of greater power than the manipulated victim. In some cases, the victim ended up in a pit or in prison, or even dead, as was the case with the victims of Simeon and Levi's manipulation.

In the FG, Peter does successfully disempower his accusers in the courtyard: they are unable to recognize who he is, and he therefore preserves his anonymity and freedom. However, the effect of disempowerment is even more prevalent when it comes from the hand of Jesus as the counter-manipulator. He very effectively disempowers Peter in John 21. Just as Judah was humbled to concede Tamar's greater degree of righteousness, Peter is disempowered and humbled to the point that, by the end of chapter 21, he will no longer promote his status with boasts or manipulate with lies. By the

---

2. When asked if he was a disciple of Jesus, Peter responded, "I am not." Inherent in being a μαθητής is the concept of following, and Peter's manipulation narrative in John 21 concludes with "Follow me." This therefore ties chapters 13, 18, and 21 together. "Follow" and "disciple" occur in chapter 13. "Disciple" and "I am not" occur in chapter 18. The manipulation episode in John 21 closes with "Follow me." Thus, these two terms also are tied together on a thematic level.

end of the three questions, Jesus predicts that this future shepherd will heed the plan Jesus has for his life and be led by someone else, laying down his life to glorify God (John 21:18–19). This reversal is not a reversal of fortune, but one of character. Like Jacob, who no longer clings to the life of his favored son, Peter will reach a point in the future when he glorifies God by ceasing to cling to his own life. He becomes manipulable in God's hands, ultimately becoming like Jesus in his death.

The aspect of power is also seen in the case of Jesus, who, as the master of the catch, implicitly reminds the disciples that "apart from me, you can do nothing." No one in the Gospel can "catch" anything, except when Jesus speaks (John 7:30–32, 44; 8:20; 10:39; 11:57; 21:3). Jesus' miraculous feeding here in chapter 21 is an echo of the powerful feeding in chapter 6. He holds sway over the disciples, the fish, and all of nature (6:16–21). The great catch jars the disciples into silence and, much like Joseph's brothers, is evidence of their disempowerment—there is nothing they can say (Gen 45:3; John 21:12). Additionally, the use of the diminutive παιδίον may refer to the disciples' powerlessness as young little ones in pitiful need of a great catch. Jesus, as counter-manipulating master, *holds all the power*. Thus in working through Peter's two manipulation episodes in the FG, it becomes clear that disempowerment executed by the *initial manipulator* is attempted and is temporarily achieved (John 18). Nevertheless, the empowerment of the *counter-manipulator* and disempowerment of the initial manipulator is evident and is a function of the plot to move the initial manipulator from ignorance to knowledge.

The Transforming Effect of Counter-Manipulation

Peter bears a resemblance to the protagonists of Genesis who are frequently portrayed as cowards and/or liars, since, by *the end of* John 18, he is also a coward and liar. This sets the stage for counter-manipulation in chapter 21. A Genesis reader therefore may have seen the turning aspect of counter-manipulation, when Jesus brings Peter and the other disciples face to face with a knowledge of themselves, their own discipleship, and where that discipleship should lead. Jesus causes them to move from ignorance to knowledge, not simply recognizing a figure on a shoreline, but, *especially in the case of Peter*, recognizing that the resurrected Jesus knows and understands all things (John 21:17).

Jesus in John 21 commands Peter to follow him. He predicts Peter's death as well. After lying by saying three times that he was not Jesus' disciple,

Peter will now be transformed from a young, selfish little sheep, to an older shepherd who surrenders his life in a death that glorifies God.

I also argued that, reading from the framework of *lex talionis*, Jesus responds to Peter with actions similar to Peter's own behavior: Jesus thwarts Peter's recognition and then mirrors Peter's three denials with three questions, asking Peter three times to affirm his love, rather than deny his discipleship. I have also argued that a Genesis reader would sense the tension that *lex talionis* creates in the story. Jesus could have issued a threefold denial of Peter, consistent with Peter's denials, but he does not. By feeding his antagonistic counterpart, Jesus the counter-manipulator demonstrates benevolence despite his power over Peter and his fellow disciple-fishermen, thus humbling them (John 21:9–13). After feeding his sheep, Jesus moves a step further and commissions Peter to feed his sheep. Peter's response in verse 17, "κύριε, πάντα σὺ οἶδας σὺ γινώσκεις," serves as evidence that Peter is beginning the transformation process. The phrase "to show what kind of death he would die" in 21:19, indicates by intratextuality with chapters 12 and 18, that the counter-manipulation would continue to transform Peter. Peter's death would be like the death of Jesus. Canonical and non-canonical traditions, moreover, do not contradict this. Beyond the narrative of the FG, Peter will continue the character development process.

The Effect of Understanding Diminutives

I also examined the role of Greek diminutives in John 21, their neglect, and how they add details to the understanding of the dialogue. I considered the diminutives παιδίον, πλοιάριον, ὀψάριον, ἀρνίον, and προβάτιον and set forth nine interpretive guidelines for analyzing diminutive nuances. I argued that interpreters should not assume that diminutive nuances were lost by the time of the New Testament writers, and that textual criticism has too often preferred to abandon the diminutive form and its meaning. Another guideline I proposed is that reverence for the text can lead to reading characters as overly flat and overlooking diminutive nuances and certain aspects of dialogue between characters. Because of the complex ways in which diminutives could be used, I asserted that hard and fast categories of usage and meaning do not serve the exegete well and that the emotive tone of the text plays an important role for the researcher. This also led to the proposition that relecture can be a tool for evaluating diminutive nuances. Finally, I argued that the burden of proof lies with the scholar who argues for diminutive force in translation.

When applying these principles, I proposed that the diminutives παιδίον, πλοιάριον, ὀψάριον, ἀρνίον, and προβάτιον, coupled with rhetorical devices, reinforce Jesus' use of "smiling satire" to extend his manipulation and subtle rebuke to his young, powerless disciple-fishermen. Therefore, the understanding of diminutives served to focus the reading of manipulation and counter-manipulation in John 21.

Conclusions, Implications, and Questions

Using a theory of Genesis manipulation narratives to increase an understanding of recognition in John 21 has been a worthwhile exercise. Seen from the perspective gained from analyzing Genesis, the importance of *anagnorisis* in John 18 and 21 moves beyond the recognition of persons. These two passages concern the *manipulative behavior* of Peter to *deceive and prevent others from recognizing him*, and Jesus' ironic response, in chapter 21, where he *counter-manipulates* Peter, resembling Peter's manipulation of his accusers in chapter 18. The purpose of this counter-manipulation is to turn and reconcile Peter. Preventing or delaying Peter's recognition of him, along with his threefold questioning, is how Jesus manipulates Peter. Consistent in these two scenes and in Genesis is manipulation to gain a desired goal, and a counter-manipulator who responds in a similar manner to transform and create a reversal—not of fortune, but of character—in a deceptive manipulator. In John 21, this particular *dénouement* resolves the plot, restores and reconciles the character of Peter. Peter, like Judah, is manipulated into a fuller self-knowledge and pliability in God's hands.

A research project of this size always raises questions, and this work is no exception. The so-called "trickster" narratives are not limited to Genesis. More work is required to see if this theory and taxonomy of manipulation applies in Exodus, Judges, and other Hebrew Bible texts. One may then ask what manipulation and recognition in other Hebrew Bible texts may tell us about manipulation and recognition in the FG and other New Testament texts.

The theory and taxonomy of manipulation developed here should now be applied to the first twenty chapters of the FG to see what it can yield for the remaining recognition narratives in John.[3] Though, for example, John

---

3. Brant writes, "Modern readers have a tendency to treat recognition in the Fourth Gospel as a function of character rather than plot." Brant, *Dialogue and Drama*, 57. Culbertson writes, "Initially in Greek literature, recognition was a function of plot. Subsequently, it was perceived as an aspect of character." Culbertson, *Poetics of Revelation*, 2. The approach of this study has been to tie the two together. Recognition in the character of Peter is therefore regarded as a function of both plot and character. This aspect too can be applied to the first twenty chapters of the Gospel for further analysis. See also Mleynek, *Knowledge and Mortality*, 11.

the Baptist's recognition in chapter 1 does not include any manipulation, we should ask how an understanding of the recognition narratives in all of the FG would change in light of the Genesis manipulation narratives. How does the understanding of manipulation narratives modify a reading of Jesus and the Samaritan woman in John 4? Will a manipulation perspective change the reading of the Pharisees' lack of recognition in John 9? In that chapter, is Jesus answering (John 9:39–41) the Pharisees' statements of lack of recognition (9:16, 29) in response to some previous behavior of theirs (such as "We know that this man is a sinner," 9:24)? Also, how would one view Mary's recognition episode in John 20, since she is certainly not a deceiver like Peter? Is Jesus somehow countering lack of belief on her part, intending to sharpen *her* (not just the reader's) awareness of her own lack of belief and therefore move her to belief?

Importantly, the FE's understanding of recognition may have been influenced—even if subconsciously—by both Genesis manipulation and the Greco-Roman understanding of recognition. Therefore, if the Genesis manipulation perspective is an important addition to our understanding of Johannine recognition, how can we now *integrate* both literary traditions in our understanding of Johannine *anagnorisis*?

Finally, we need to apply what we have learned of diminutives to the remainder of the Fourth Gospel. There may be other narratives that will read more clearly if we give further consideration to diminutive nuances.

In summary, I have argued that recognition is but one kernel in manipulation narratives, in which a manipulator attempts to wrest a desired benefit from a victim, who at first is unaware of the camouflaged manipulation. Recognition occurs when the ruse unravels, and the victim realizes the manipulation. Understanding recognition in this manner elucidates the reversal of character that often begins as a result of counter-manipulation. Jesus' manipulation of Peter in chapter 21 is understood here as a countering response to Peter's deceptive manipulation of his accusers in the courtyard in John 18. Seeing *anagnorisis* from this perspective assists our understanding of the developmental characterization of Peter, his reversal, and his reconciliation. John 21 is an important early church narrative, encapsulating what Jacob, Judah, and the rest of Joseph's brothers had already learned: attempts to manipulate others may succeed at first, but eventually the initial manipulator's character faults will show through. However, if in the end the manipulator will submit to God's ironic measure for measure counter-manipulation, he or she will learn that there is, in fact, hope for little sheep that are still learning to follow.

Bibliography

Aberbach, Moses, and Bernard Grossfeld, eds. *Targum Onkelos to Genesis: A Critical Analysis Together with an English Translation of the Text*. New York: KTAV, 1982.
Ackerman, James S. "Joseph, Judah, and Jacob." In *Literary Interpretations of Biblical Narratives*, edited by J. S. Ackerman and D. G. Louis, 2:85–113. Nashville: Abingdon, 1982.
Ainsworth, P. C. "The Miraculous Draught of Fishes." *Weavings* (2001) 24–30.
Aland, Barbara, et al. *The Greek New Testament*. 4th ed. Federal Republic of Germany: United Bible Societies, 1993.
Aland, Kurt, et al. Deutsche Bibelgesellschaft, and Universität Münster. Institut für Neutestamentliche Textforschung. *The Greek-English New Testament: Novum Testamentum Graece, English Standard Version*. 28th ed. Stuttgart: Deutsche Bibelgesellschaft, 2012.
Aland, Kurt, et al. *Novum Testamentum Graece*. 23rd ed. Stuttgart: Privilegierte Württembergische Bibelanstalt, 1957.
Aland, Kurt, and Barbara Aland. *Greek-English New Testament: Greek Text Novum Testamentum Graece, in the Tradition of Eberhard Nestle and Erwin Nestle*. Stuttgart: Deutsche Bibelgesellschaft, 2008.
Alter, Robert. *The Art of Biblical Narrative*. New York: Basic, 1981.
———. *The Five Books of Moses*. New York: Norton, 2008.
———. *Genesis*. New York: Norton, 1996.
———. *The World of Biblical Literature*. New York: Basic, 1992.
Alter, Robert, and Frank Kermode. *The Literary Guide to the Bible*. Cambridge, MA: Belknap, 1987.
Amundsen, L. "Some Remarks on Greek Diminutives." *Symbolae Osloenses* 40, no. 1 (1965) 5–16.
Anderson, John E. "Jacob, Laban, and a Divine Trickster? The Covenantal Framework of God's Deception in the Theology of the Jacob Cycle." *Perspectives in Religious Studies* 36, no. 1 (2009) 3–23.
Anderson, Paul N. "From One Dialogue to Another: Johannine Polyvalence from Origins to Receptions." In *Anatomies of Narrative Criticism: The Past, Present, and Futures of the Fourth Gospel as Literature*, edited by Tom Thatcher and Stephen. D. Moore, 93–110. Atlanta: SBL, 2008.
———. *The Riddles of the Fourth Gospel: An Introduction to John*. Minneapolis: Fortress, 2011.

Anderson R. Dean. *Ancient Rhetorical Theory and Paul*. Leuven: Peeters, 1999.
The Ante-Nicene Fathers. Vol. 9. Edited by A. Menzies. Peabody, MA: Hendrickson, 1897.
Aristotle. *Rhetoric*. Translated by John Henry Freese. London: Heinemann, 1926. http://www.perseus.tufts.edu/hopper/text?doc=Perseus:text:1999.01.0060.
Aristotle. *Aristotle in 23 Volumes*. Translated by W. Hamilton Fyfe. Cambridge, MA: Harvard University Press, 1932.
Arndt, William F., et al. *A Greek-English Lexicon of the New Testament and other Early Christian Literature: A Translation and Adaptation of the Fourth Revised and Augmented Edition of Walter Bauer's Griechisch-Deutsches Wörterbuch zu den Schriften des Neuen Testaments und der Übrigen Urchristlichen Literatur*. Chicago: University of Chicago Press, 1979.
Ashton, John. *The Interpretation of John*. Edinburgh: T. & T. Clark, 1997.
Auerbach, Erich. *Mimesis: The Representation of Reality in Western Literature*. Princeton: Princeton University Press, 1953.
Babcock-Abrahams, Barbara. "'A Tolerated Margin of Mess': The Trickster and His Tales Reconsidered." *Journal of the Folklore Institute* 11, no. 3 (1975) 147–86.
Badawi, El-Said. M., and Abdel Haleem. *Arabic-English Dictionary of Qur'anic Usage*. Leiden: Brill, 2007.
Bailey, Kenneth. E. *Jesus through Middle Eastern Eyes: Cultural Studies in the Gospels*. Downers Grove, IL: InterVarsity Academic, 2008.
———. *Poet and Peasant and through Peasant Eyes: A Literary-Cultural Approach to the Parables of Luke*. Grand Rapids: Eerdmans, 1980.
———. "The Shepherd Poems of John 10: Their Culture and Style." *Theological Review* 14, no. 1 (1993) 3–21.
Ball, David. M. *"I Am" in John's Gospel: Literary Function, Background, and Theological Implications*. Sheffield: Sheffield Academic, 1996.
Bar-Efrat, Shimeon. *Narrative Art in the Bible*. Translated by Dorothea Shefer-Vanson. Sheffield: Almond, 1989.
Barrett, C. K. *The Gospel according to St. John*. London: SPCK, 1970.
Bassler, Jouette M. *1 Timothy, 2 Timothy, Titus*. Nashville: Abingdon, 1996.
Bauckham, Richard. *Jesus and the Eyewitnesses: The Gospels as Eyewitness Testimony*. Grand Rapids: Eerdmans, 2006.
———. "The Martyrdom of Peter in Early Christian Literature." In *Vorkonstantinisches Christentum: Neues Testament (Sachthemen)*, edited by W. Haase and H. Temporini, 539–95. ANRW II/26. 1. Berlin: de Gruyter, 1992.
———. *The Testimony of the Beloved Disciple: Narrative, History, and Theology in the Gospel of John*. Grand Rapids: Baker Academic, 2007.
Bauer, Walter. *Das Johannesevangelium*. Tübingen: Mohr/Siebeck, 1925.
Beasley-Murray, George. *John*. WBC. Dallas: Word, 1989.
Bennema, Cornelis. *Encountering Jesus: Character Studies in the Gospel of John*. Colorado Springs: Paternoster, 2009.
———. "A Theory of Character in the Fourth Gospel with Reference to Ancient and Modern Literature." *Biblical Interpretation: A Journal of Contemporary Approaches* 17, no. 4 (2009) 375–421.
———. *A Theory of Character in New Testament Narrative*. Minneapolis: Fortress, 2014.

Berlin, Adele. *Poetics and Interpretation of Biblical Narrative*. Winona Lake, IN: Eisenbrauns, 1994.
Bialik, Hayyim. N., et al. *The Book of Legends = Sefer Ha-Aggadah: Legends from the Talmud and Midrash*. New York: Schocken, 1992.
Black, C. Clifton "The Words That You Gave to Me I Have Given to Them: The Grandeur of Johannine Rhetoric." In *Exploring the Gospel of John*, edited by R. Alan Culpepper and C. Clifton Black, 220–39. Louisville: Westminster John Knox, 1996.
Blaine, Bradford B. *Peter in the Gospel of John: The Making of an Authentic Disciple*. Atlanta: SBL, 2007.
Blass, Friedrich, et al. *A Greek Grammar of the New Testament and Other Early Christian Literature*. Chicago: University of Chicago Press, 1961.
Bockmuehl, Marcus N. A. *The Remembered Peter: In Ancient Reception and Modern Debate*. Tübingen: Mohr/Siebeck, 2010.
Boitani, Piero. *The Bible and Its Rewritings*. Oxford: Oxford University Press, 1999.
———. *The Tragic and the Sublime in Medieval Literature*. Cambridge: Cambridge University Press, 1989.
Boomershine, Thomas E. "The Medium and Message in John: Audience Address and Audience Identity in the Fourth Gospel." In *The Fourth Gospel in First-Century Media Culture*, edited by A. Le Donne and Tom Thatcher, 92–120. London: T. & T. Clark, 2011.
Borchert, Gerald L. *John 1–11*. Nashville: Broadman & Holman, 1996.
Borgman, Paul. *Genesis: The Story We Haven't Heard*. Downers Grove, IL: InterVarsity, 2001.
Botterweck, G. Johannes., and Helmer Ringgren. *TDOT*. Grand Rapids: Eerdmans, 1974.
Bowen, Nancy R. "The Role of YHWH as Deceiver in True and False Prophecy." PhD diss., Princeton Theological Seminary, 1994.
Brant, Jo-Ann. A. *Dialogue and Drama: Elements of Greek Tragedy in the Fourth Gospel*. Peabody, MA: Hendrickson, 2004.
Breck, John. "John 21: Appendix, Epilogue or Conclusion?" *St Vladimir's Theological Quarterly* 36, nos. 1–2 (1992) 27–49.
Brenton, Lancelot C. L. *The Septuagint Version of the Old Testament and Apocrypha: with an English Translation and with various Readings and Critical Notes*. London: Bagster, n.d.
"Britannica Online." Britannica Online. http://www.britannica.com/.
Brodie, Thomas L. *The Gospel according to John: A Literary and Theological Commentary*. New York: Oxford University Press, 1997. http://www.netlibrary.com/ebook_info. asp?product_id=23535.
Brooke, George J. "4Q252 and the 153 Fish of John 21:11." In *Antikes Judentum und Frühes Christentum: Festschrift für Hartmut Stegemann zum 65. Geburtstag*, edited by B. Kollmann and H. Stegemann, 253–65. Berlin: de Gruyter, 1999.
Brouwer, Wayne. "The Testimony of the Beloved Disciple: Narrative, History, and Theology in the Gospel of John." *Calvin Theological Journal* 44, no. 2 (2009) 397–99.
Brown, Francis, et al. *The Enhanced Brown-Driver-Briggs Hebrew and English Lexicon with an Appendix Containing the Biblical Aramaic*. Oak Harbor, WA: Logos Research Systems, 2000.

Brown, Raymond. E. *The Community of the Beloved Disciple*. New York: Paulist, 1979.
———. *The Gospel according to John (I–XII)*. Garden City, NY: Doubleday, 1966.
———. *The Gospel according to John (XIII–XXI)*. Garden City, NY: Doubleday, 1970.
Brown, Raymond. E., et al., eds. *Peter in the New Testament: A Collaborative Assessment by Protestant and Roman Catholic Scholars*. Minneapolis: Augsburg, 1973.
Browne, R. A. "Types of Self-Recognition and Self-Reform in Ancient Drama." *American Journal of Philology* 64, no. 2 (1943) 163–71.
Buber, Martin. *Werke 2, Schriften zur Bibel*. Münich: Kösel, 1964.
Buber, Martin, and Nahu N. Glatzer. *On the Bible: Eighteen Studies*. New York: Schocken, 1968.
Bullinger, E. W. *Figures of Speech used in the Bible, Explained and Illustrated*. London: Eyre & Spottiswoode, 1898. http://www.archive.org/stream/figuresofspeechu00bull#page/n5/mode/2up.
Bultmann, Rudolf. K. "Die Bedeutung der Neuerschlossenen Mandäischen und Manichäischen Quellen für das Verständnis des Johannesevangeliums." *Zeitschrift für die Neutestamentliche Wissen*schaft 24 (1925) 100–146.
———. *The Gospel of John: A Commentary*. Philadelphia: Westminster, 1971.
———. "záō, zōḗ (*bióō, bíos*)." *TDNT: Abridged in One Volume*, 290.
Burke, Kenneth. *The Philosophy of Literary Form: Studies in Symbolic Action*. New York: Vintage, 1957.
———. *Terms for Order*. Edited by S. E. Hyman. Bloomington: Indiana University Press, 1964.
Burridge, Richard A. *What Are the Gospels? A Comparison with Greco-Roman Biography*. Grand Rapids: Eerdmans, 2004.
Carson, D. A. *The Gospel according to John*. Grand Rapids: InterVarsity, 1991.
Cassidy, Richard J. *Four Times Peter: Portrayals of Peter in the Four Gospels and at Philippi*. Collegeville, MN: Liturgical, 2007.
Cassuto, Umberto. *A Commentary on the Book of Genesis 2: From Noah to Abraham*. Jerusalem: Magnes, 1992.
Cave, Terance. *Recognitions: A Study in Poetics*. Oxford: Oxford University Press, 1988.
Charles, R. H., ed. "Testaments of the Twelve Patriarchs." In *Pseudepigrapha of the Old Testament*, 282–367. Public Domain ed. Bellingham, WA: Logos Research Systems, 2004.
Charlesworth, James H. "A Critical Comparison of the Dualism in 1QS 3:13-4:26 and the 'Dualism' Contained in the Gospel of John." In *John and the Dead Sea Scrolls*, edited by James. H. Charlesworth, 76–106. New York: Crossroad, 1990.
———. *John and the Dead Sea Scrolls*. New York: Crossroad, 1990.
———. *The Old Testament Pseudepigrapha*. Vol. 2, *Expansions of the "Old Testament" and Legends, Wisdom and Philosophical Literature, Prayers, Psalms, and Odes, Fragments of Lost Judeo-Hellenistic Works*. Garden City, NY: Doubleday, 1983.
———. "Qumran, John and the Odes of Solomon." In *John and the Dead Sea Scrolls*, edited by James H. Charlesworth, 107–36. New York: Crossroad, 1990.
Charlesworth, James H., et al. *The Dead Sea Scrolls: Hebrew, Aramaic, and Greek Texts with English Translations*. Vol. 4A, *Pseudepigraphic and Non-Masoretic Psalms and Prayers*. Tübingen: Mohr/Siebeck, 1997.
Chatman, Seymour. B. *Story and Discourse: Narrative Structure in Fiction and Film*. Ithaca, NY: Cornell University Press, 1978.

———. "What Novels Can Do That Films Can't (and vice versa)." In *Film Theory and Criticism: Introductory Readings,* edited by Leo Braudy and Marshall Cohen, 435–51. New York: Oxford University Press, 1999.

Chavel, Charles B. *Ramban Commentary on the Torah. Genesis: (Nachmanides).* New York: Shilo, 1971.

Cicero. *De Oratore in Two Volumes: I, Books I, II*. Translated by E. W. Sutton and H. Rackham. London: Heinemann, 1959.

Claussen, Carsten. "The Role of John 21: Discipleship in Retrospect and Redefinition." In *New Currents through John: A Global Perspective,* edited by Francisco Lozada and Tom Thatcher, 55–68. Atlanta: SBL, 2006.

Clines, David J. A. *What Does Eve Do to Help? And other Readerly Questions to the Old Testament.* Sheffield: JSOT, 1990.

Coetzee, J. C. "Life (Eternal Life) in St John's Writings and the Qumran Scrolls." *Neotestamentica* 6 (1972) 48–66.

Coleridge, Samuel T., and J. Shawcross. *Biographia Literaria.* Vol. 2. London: Oxford University Press, 1967.

Collins, Raymond. F. "From John to the Beloved Disciple: An Essay on Johannine Characters." *Interpretation* 49, no. 4 (1995) 359–69.

———. "The Representative Figures of the Fourth Gospel." *Downside Review* 94 (1976) 26–46.

———. *These Things Have Been Written: Studies on the Fourth Gospel.* Louvain: Peeters, 1990.

Combrink, H. J. B. "Multiple Meaning and/or Multiple Interpretation of a Text." *Neotestamentica* 18 (1984) 26–37.

Connick, Charles M. "The Dramatic Character of the Fourth Gospel." *Journal of Biblical Literature* 67, no. 2 (1948) 159–69.

Conway, Colleen M. *Men and Women in the Fourth Gospel: Gender and Johannine Characterization.* Atlanta: SBL, 1999.

———. "The Production of the Johannine Community: A New Historicist Perspective." *Journal of Biblical Literature* 121, no. 3 (2002) 479–95.

———. "Speaking through Ambiguity: Minor Characters in the Fourth Gospel." *Biblical Interpretation: A Journal of Contemporary Approaches* 10, no. 3 (2002) 324–41.

Craffert, Pieter. F. "Did Jesus Rise Bodily from the Dead? Yes and No!" *Religion & Theology/Religie & Teologie* 15, nos. 1–2 (2008) 133–53.

———. "Jesus' Resurrection in a Social-Scientific Perspective: Is There Anything New to Be Said?" *Journal for the Study of the Historical Jesus* 7, no. 1 (2009) 126–51.

Crosby, Michael. *Do You Love Me? Jesus Questions the Church.* Maryknoll, NY: Orbis, 2000.

Culbertson, Diane. *Poetics of Revelation: Recognition and the Narrative Tradition.* Macon, GA: Mercer University Press, 1989.

Cullmann, Oscar. *Peter: Disciple, Apostle, Martyr.* Philadelphia: Westminster, 1962.

Culpepper, R. Alan. *Anatomy of the Fourth Gospel: A Study in Literary Design.* Foundations and Facets: New Testament. Philadelphia: Fortress, 1983.

———. "Cognition in John: The Johannine Signs as Recognition Scenes." *Perspectives in Religious Studies* 35, no. 3 (2008) 251–60.

———. "Designs for the Church in the Imagery of John 21:1–14." In *Imagery in the Gospel of John: Terms, Forms, Themes, and Theology of Johannine Figurative Language (Conference Proceedings: Wissenschaftliche Untersuchungen zum Neuen Testament 2005)*, edited by Jörg Frey et al., 369–402. Tübingen: Mohr/Siebeck, 2006.

———. "The Gospel of John as a Document of Faith in a Pluralistic Culture." In *What is John? Readers and Readings of the Fourth Gospel*, edited by Fernando. F. Segovia, 107–28. Atlanta: Scholars, 1996.

———. *The Gospel and Letters of John*. Interpreting Biblical Texts. Nashville: Abingdon, 1998.

———. "The Johannine Hypodeigma: A Reading of John 13." *Semeia* 53 (1991) 133–52.

———. *John, the Son of Zebedee: The Life of a Legend*. Columbia: University of South Carolina Press, 1994.

———. "Peter as Exemplary Disciple in John 21:15–19." *Perspectives in Religious Studies* 37, no. 2 (2010) 165–78.

———. "The Plot of John's Story of Jesus." *Interpretation* 49, no. 4 (1995) 347–58.

———. "Symbolism and History in John's Account of Jesus' Death." In *Anatomies of Narrative Criticism: The Past, Present, and Futures of the Fourth Gospel as Literature*, edited by Tom Thatcher and Stephen D. Moore, 39–54. Atlanta: SBL, 2008.

Dahl, Nils A. "The Johannine Church and History." In *The Interpretation of John*, edited by J. Ashton, 147–68. Edinburgh: T. & T. Clark, 1997.

Danker, Frederick W., et al. *A Greek-English Lexicon of the New Testament and Other Early Christian Literature*. 6th ed. Chicago: University of Chicago Press, 2000.

Davies, Margaret. *Rhetoric and Reference in the Fourth Gospel*. Sheffield: Sheffield Academic, 1992.

Davis, J. F. *Lex Talionis in Early Judaism and the Exhortation of Jesus in Matthew 5.38–42*. London: T. & T. Clark, 2005.

Davis, J. C. "The Johannine Concept of Eternal Life as a Present Possession." *Restoration Quarterly* 27, no. 3 (1984) 161–69.

De Boer, Martinus C. *Johannine Perspectives on the Death of Jesus*. Kampen: Kok Pharos, 1996.

———. "Narrative Criticism, Historical Criticism, and the Gospel of John." In *The Interpretation of John*, edited by John Ashton, 307–14. Edinburgh: T. & T. Clark, 1997.

———. "Narrative Criticism, Historical Criticism, and the Gospel of John." *JSNT* 47 (1992) 35–48.

Decker, Rodney J. *Koine Greek Reader: Selections from the New Testament, Septuagint, and Early Christian Writers*. Grand Rapids: Kregel, 2007.

"Dictionary.com Unabridged." Random House. http://dictionary.reference.com/browse/.

Dodd, C. H. *Historical Tradition in the Fourth Gospel*. Cambridge: Cambridge University Press, 1965.

———. *The Interpretation of the Fourth Gospel*. Cambridge: Cambridge University Press, 1960.

Donaldson, James, et al. *The Ante-Nicene Fathers*. Vol. 3. Buffalo, NY: Christian Literature, 1885.

Droge, Arthur J. "The Status of Peter in the Fourth Gospel: A Note on John 18:10–11." *Journal of Biblical Literature* 109, no. 2 (1990) 307–11.

Dschulnigg, Peter. *Jesus Begegnen: Personen und ihre Bedeutung im Johannesevangelium.* Münster: Lit, 2002.

Dunn, James D. G. "John's Gospel and the Oral Gospel Tradition." In *The Fourth Gospel in First-Century Media Culture,* edited by Anthony Le Donne and Tom Thatcher, 157–85. London: T. & T. Clark, 2011.

Eisenman, Robert H., and M. O. Wise. *The Dead Sea Scrolls Uncovered: The First Complete Translation and Interpretation of 50 Key Documents Withheld for Over 35 Years.* Shaftesbury, Dorset: Element, 1992.

Elliott, J. Keith. "Nouns with Diminutive Endings in the New Testament." *Novum Testamentum* 12, no. 4 (1970) 391–98.

———. "The Third Edition of the United Bible Societies' Greek New Testament." *Novum Testamentum* 20, no. 4 (1978) 242–77.

Ewen, Joseph. *Character in Narrative.* Tel Aviv: Sifri'at Po'alim, 1980.

———. "The Theory of Character in Narrative Fiction." *Hasifrut* 3 (1971) 1–30.

Fallis, D. "Lying and Deception." *Philosophers' Imprint* 10, no. 11 (2010) 1–22.

Farmer, Kathleen. "The Trickster Genre in the Old Testament." PhD diss., Southern Methodist University, 1978.

Fentress-Williams, Judy. "Location, Location, Location: Tamar in the Joseph Cycle." *Bible and Critical Theory* 3, no. 2 (2011) 20.1–20.8.

Fishbane, Michael A. "Composition and Structure in the Jacob Cycle (Gen 25:19—35:22)." *Journal of Jewish Studies* 26, nos. 1–2 (1975) 15–38.

———. *Text and Texture: Close Readings of Selected Biblical Texts.* New York: Schocken, 1979.

Forster, E. M. *Aspects of the Novel.* New York: Harcourt, Brace & World, 1954.

Fortna, Robert T. "Diachronic/Synchronic: Reading John 21 and Luke 5." In *John and the Synoptics,* edited by Adelbert Denaux, 387–99. Leuven: Leuven University Press, 1992.

Freedman, H., and Maurice Simon. *Midrash Rabbah.* Vol. 2, *Genesis.* London: Soncino, 1983.

Fuchs, Esther. "For I Have the Way of Women: Deception, Gender, and Ideology in Biblical Narrative." *Semeia* 42 (1988) 68–83.

Gadamer, Hans. G. *Truth and Method.* New York: Crossroad, 1989.

Gaventa, Beverly R. "The Archive of Excess: John 21 and the Problem of Narrative Closure." In *Exploring the Gospel of John.* Edited by R. A. Culpepper and C. C. Black, 240–52. Louisville: Westminster John Knox, 1996.

Gerhardsson, Birger. *The Origins of the Gospel Traditions.* Philadelphia: Fortress, 1979.

Grant, Robert. M. "'One Hundred Fifty-Three Large Fish' (John 21:11)." *Harvard Theological Review* 42, no. 4 (1949) 273–75.

Hadas, Moses. *Ancilla to Classical Reading.* New York: Columbia University Press, 1954.

Hagner, Donald A. *Matthew 14–28.* WBC. Dallas: Word, 1995.

Hamilton, Victor P. *The Book of Genesis: Chapters 1–17.* Grand Rapids: Eerdmans, 1990.

Hanson, Anthony T. *The Prophetic Gospel: A Study of John and the Old Testament.* Edinburgh: T. & T. Clark, 1991.

Harstine, Stan. "Un-Doubting Thomas: Recognition Scenes in the Ancient World." *Perspectives in Religious Studies* 33, no. 4 (2006) 435–47.

Hartman, Lars. "An Attempt at a Text-Centered Exegesis of John 21." *Studia Theologica* 38, no. 1 (1984) 29–45.
Harvey, W. J. *Character and the Novel*. Ithaca, NY: Cornell University Press, 1965.
Hasitschka, Martin. "The Significance of the Resurrection Appearance in John 21." In *Resurrection of Jesus in the Gospel of John*, 311–28. Tübingen: Mohr/Siebeck, 2008.
Hastings, James. *The Great Texts of the Bible: St. John*. Grand Rapids: Eerdmans, 1958.
Herodotus. *The Histories (Greek)*. http://www.perseus.tufts.edu/hopper/text?doc=Perseus%3atext%3a1999.01.0125.
Hezser, Catherine. *Jewish Literacy in Roman Palestine*. Tübingen: Mohr/Siebeck, 2001.
Hitchcock, F. R. M. "The Dramatic Development of the Fourth Gospel." *Expositor* 4 (1907) 266–79.
———. *A Fresh Study of the Fourth Gospel*. London: SPCK, 1911.
———. "Is the Fourth Gospel a Drama?" *Theology* 7 (1923) 307–17.
Hochman, B. *Character in Literature*. Ithaca, NY: Cornell University Press, 1985.
Hoffmeier, J. K. "The Wives' Tales of Genesis 12, 20 and 26 and the Covenants at Beer-Sheba." *Tyndale Bulletin* 43 (1992) 81–100.
Holladay, William L., and Ludwig Köhler. *A Concise Hebrew and Aramaic Lexicon of the Old Testament, Based upon the Lexical Work of Ludwig Koehler and Walter Baumgartner*. Grand Rapids: Eerdmans, 1971.
The Holy Bible: English Standard Version. Wheaton, IL: Standard Bible Society, 2001.
The Holy Book. Cairo: Society of the Holy Bible, 1969.
Holmes, Michael W., and SBL. *Greek New Testament: SBL Edition*. Atlanta: SBL, 2010.
Hoskyns, Edwyn C., and F. N. Davey. *The Fourth Gospel*. London: Faber and Faber, 1954.
Hylen, Susan. *Imperfect Believers: Ambiguous Characters in the Gospel of John*. Louisville: Westminster John Knox, 2009.
Janzen, J. G. "How Can a Man Be Born When He Is Old? Jacob/Israel in Genesis and the Gospel of John." *Encounter* 65, no. 4 (2004) 323–43.
Jeremias, Joachim. *New Testament Theology: The Proclamation of Jesus*. New York: Scribner, 1971.
Josephus, Flavius, and W. Whiston. *The Works of Josephus: Complete and Unabridged*. Peabody, MA: Hendrickson, 1987.
Kaiser, Walter C. *Preaching and Teaching the Last Things: Old Testament Eschatology for the Life of the Church*. Grand Rapids: Baker Academic, 2011.
Keener, Craig S. *The Gospel of John: A Commentary*. 2 vols. Peabody, MA: Hendrickson, 2003.
Keith, Chris. "A Performance of the Text: The Adulteress's Entrance into John's Gospel." In *The Fourth Gospel in First-Century Media Culture*, edited by Anthony Le Donne and Tom Thatcher, 49–72. London: T. & T. Clark, 2011.
Kelber, Werner H. "Metaphysics and Marginality in John." In *What Is John? Readers and Readings of the Fourth Gospel*, edited by Fernando F. Segovia, 129–54. Atlanta: Scholars, 1996.
———. *The Oral and the Written Gospel: The Hermeneutics of Speaking and Writing in the Synoptic Tradition, Mark, Paul, and Q*. Philadelphia: Fortress, 1983.
———. "The Quest for the Historical Jesus: From the Perspectives of Medieval, Modern and Post-Enlightenment Readings, and in View of Ancient, Oral Aesthetics." In *The Jesus Controversy: Perspectives in Conflict*, edited by John D. Crossan et al., 75–116. Harrisburg, PA: Trinity, 1999.

Kennedy, George A. *Progymnasmata: Greek Textbooks of Prose Composition and Rhetoric.* Atlanta: SBL, 2003.

Kennedy, Philip F., and Marilyn Lawrence. *Recognition: The Poetics of Narrative: Interdisciplinary Studies on Anagnorisis.* New York: Lang, 2009.

Kittel, Gerhard, and Gerhard Friedrich, eds. *TDNT.* Translated by Geoffrey W. Bromiley. 10 vols. Electronic ed. Grand Rapids: Eerdmans, 1964–1976.

———. *The TDNT: Abridged in One Volume.* Translated by G. W. Bromiley. Electronic ed. Grand Rapids: Eerdmans, 1985.

Koester, Craig R. "The Death of Jesus and the Human Condition: Exploring the Theology of John's Gospel." In *Life in Abundance,* 141–57. Collegeville, MN: Liturgical, 2005

———. "Messianic Exegesis and the Call of Nathanael (John 1:45–51)." *JSNT* 39 (1990) 23–34.

Köhler, Ludwig, et al. *The Hebrew and Aramaic Lexicon of the Old Testament.* Leiden: Brill, 2001.

Köstenberger, Andreas J. *John.* Grand Rapids: Baker Academic, 2004.

———. *A Theology of John's Gospel and Letters: Biblical Theology of the New Testament.* Grand Rapids: Zondervan, 2009.

Lambe, Anthony J. "Judah's Development: The Pattern of Departure-Transition-Return." *JSOT* 83 (1999) 53–68.

Larsen, Kasper B. "Recognizing the Stranger: *Anagnorisis* in the Gospel of John." PhD diss., University of Aarhus, 2006.

———. *Recognizing the Stranger: Recognition Scenes in the Gospel of John.* Leiden: Brill, 2008.

Le Donne, Anthony, and Tom Thatcher. *The Fourth Gospel in First-Century Media Culture.* London: T. & T. Clark, 2011.

Lee, Edwin K. "The Drama of the Fourth Gospel." *Expository Times* 65, no. 6 (1954) 173–76.

Liddell, H. G. *A Lexicon: Abridged from Liddell and Scott's Greek-English Lexicon.* Oak Harbor, WA: Logos, 1996.

Lied, Liv I. "Recognizing the Righteous Remnant? Resurrection, Recognition and Eschatological Reversals in 2 Baruch 47–52." In *Metamorphoses: Resurrection, Body and Transformative Practices in Early Christianity,* edited by Turid K. Seim and Jorunn Økland, 311–36. Berlin: de Gruyter, 2009.

Lincoln, Andrew T. *The Gospel according to Saint John.* Peabody, MA: Hendrickson, 2005.

Lockman Foundation, The. *New American Standard Bible.* Anaheim, CA: Foundation, 1997.

Logos Research Systems. *Logos Bible Software, 2002–2009,* Ver. 4.2. Bellingham, WA: Logos, 2009.

———. *Septuaginta: With Morphology.* Stuttgart: Deutsche Bibelgesellschaft, 1996.

———. *Stephen's 1550 Textus Receptus: With Morphology.* Bellingham, WA: Logos, 2002.

Louw, J. P., and Eugene A. Nida, eds. *Greek-English Lexicon of the New Testament: Based on Semantic Domains.* Electronic ed. of the 2nd ed. New York: United Bible Societies, 1996.

MacFarlane, John. "Aristotle's Definition of Anagnorisis." *American Journal of Philology* 121, no. 3 (2000) 367–83.

Malbon, Elizabeth. S. *In the Company of Jesus: Characters in Mark's Gospel*. Louisville: Westminster John Knox, 2000.

———. *Mark's Jesus: Characterization as Narrative Christology*. Waco, TX: Baylor University Press, 2009.

Malina, Bruce J., and Richard L. Rohrbaugh. *Social Science Commentary on the Gospel of John*. Minneapolis: Fortress, 1998.

Mann, Thomas W. "'All the Families of the Earth': The Theological Unity of Genesis." *Interpretation* 45 (1991) 341–53.

———. *The Book of the Torah: The Narrative Integrity of the Pentateuch*. Atlanta: Knox, 1988.

Marguerat, Daniel. "L'exégèse biblique à l'heure du lecteur." In *la Bible en récits : L'exégèse biblique à l'heure du lecteur: Colloque international d'analyse narrative des textes de la Bible, Lausanne (Mars 2002)*, edited by D. Marguerat, n.p. Geneva: Labor et fides, 2003.

Mathews, K. A. *Genesis*. Nashville: Broadman & Holman, 1996.

Matthews, Victor H., and Frances Mims. "Jacob the Trickster and Heir of the Covenant: A Literary Interpretation." *Perspectives in Religious Studies* 12, no. 3 (1985) 185–95.

Maxwell, Kathy R. "The Role of the Audience in Ancient Roman Theater." Unpublished doctoral research paper, Baylor University, Waco, TX.

Maynard, Arthur H. "The Role of Peter in the Fourth Gospel." *New Testament Studies* 30, no. 4 (1984) 531–48.

Mays, James L., et al. *Harper's Bible Commentary*. San Francisco: Harper & Row, 1996.

McKay, Heather A. "Lying and Deceit in Families: The Duping of Isaac and Tamar." In *The Family in Life and in Death: The Family in Ancient Israel: Sociological and Archaeological Perspectives*, edited by Patricia Dutcher-Walls, 28–41. London: T. & T. Clark, 2009.

McKay, K. L. "Style and Significance in the Language of John 21:15–17." *Novum Testamentum* 27, no. 4 (1985) 319–33.

Meeks, Wayne A. "The Man from Heaven in Johannine Sectarianism." In *The Interpretation of John*, edited by John Ashton, 169–206. Edinburgh: T. & T. Clark, 1997.

Menken, Maarten J. J. "Genesis in John's Gospel and 1 John." In *Genesis in the New Testament*, edited by Maarten J. J. Menken and Steve Moyise, 83–98. London: T. & T. Clark, 2012.

———. *Numerical Literary Techniques in John: The Fourth Evangelist's use of Numbers of Words and Syllables*. Leiden: Brill, 1985.

Merenlahti, Petri. "Characters in the Making." In *Characterization in the Gospels: Reconceiving Narrative Criticism*, edited by David M. Rhoads and Kari Syreeni, 49–72. Sheffield: Sheffield Academic, 1999.

Metzger, Bruce M. *A Textual Commentary on the Greek New Testament: A Companion Volume to the United Bible Societies' Greek New Testament*. London: United Bible Societies, 1975.

Metzger, Bruce M., et al. *A Textual Commentary on the Greek New Testament: A Companion Volume to the United Bible Societies' Greek New Testament*. 4th rev. ed. Stuttgart: Deutsche Bibelgesellschaft: United Bible Societies, 1994.

Meyer, Marvin W., ed. *The Nag Hammadi Scriptures*. New York: HarperOne, 2007.

Meynet, Roland. *Rhetorical Analysis: An Introduction to Biblical Rhetoric*. Sheffield: Sheffield Academic, 1998.

Michaels, J. Ramsey. *The Gospel of John*. Grand Rapids: Eerdmans, 2010.
Miller, Regan. "Social and Political Elevation in Middle Kingdom Egypt: A Socio-Historical Assessment of the Joseph Narrative, A Paper Read at the Annual Meeting of the Evangelical Theological Society." New Orleans, LA, November 18–20, 2009.
Minear, Paul S. "The Original Functions of John 21." *Journal of Biblical Literature* 102, no. 1 (1983) 85.
Mittelstadt, Martin. *Personal Discussions about Narrative Form and Techniques in the New Testament*. Springfield, MO: 2000.
Mleynek, Sherryll S. *Knowledge and Mortality*. Anagnorisis *in Genesis and Narrative Fiction*. New York: Lang, 1999.
Moloney, Francis J. "Who Is 'the Reader' in/of the Fourth Gospel." In *The Interpretation of John*, edited by John Ashton, 219–34. Edinburgh: T. & T. Clark, 1997.
Moore, Stephen. D. "Afterword: Things Not Written in this Book." In *Anatomies of Narrative Criticism: The Past, Present, and Futures of the Fourth Gospel as Literature*, edited by Tom Thatcher and Stephen D. Moore, 253–58. Atlanta: SBL, 2008.
———. *Literary Criticism and the Gospels: The Theoretical Challenge*. New Haven: Yale University Press, 1989.
———. *Post Structural-Ism and the New Testament: Derrida and Foucault at the Foot of the Cross*. Minneapolis: Fortress, 1994.
Morris, Leon. *The Gospel according to John*. Grand Rapids: Eerdmans, 1995.
Mouton, J., A. G. Van Aarde, and W. S. Vorster. *Paradigms and Progress in Theology*. South Africa: Human Sciences Research Council, 1988.
Muecke, D. C. *Irony*. London: Methuen, 1970.
Murphy-O'Connor, Jerome. "Fishers of Fish, Fishers of Men: What We Know of the First Disciples from Their Profession." *Bible Review* 15, no. 3 (1999) 22.
Nel, Philip J. "The Talion Principle in Old Testament Narratives." *Journal of Northwest Semitic Languages* 20, no. 1 (1994) 21–29.
The NET Bible First Edition. Spokane, WA: Biblical Studies, 2006.
Newman, Barclay M., and Logos Research Systems. *A Concise Greek-English Dictionary of the New Testament*. Stuttgart: Deutsche Bibelgesellschaft/United Bible Societies, 1993.
Neyrey, Jerome H. *The Gospel of John in Cultural and Rhetorical Perspective*. Grand Rapids: Eerdmans, 2009.
Nicholas, Dean A. *The Trickster Revisited: Deception as a Motif in the Pentateuch*. New York: Lang, 2009.
Niditch, Susan. *Underdogs and Tricksters: A Prelude to Biblical Folklore*. San Francisco: Harper & Row, 1987.
O'Neill, Barry. "A Formal System for Understanding Lies and Deceit." Unpublished paper. http://citeseerx.ist.psu.edu/viewdoc/download?doi=10.1.1.116.4728&rep=rep1&type=pdf.
O'Day, Gail R. "Introducing Media Culture to Johannine Studies." In *The Fourth Gospel in First-Century Media Culture*, edited by Anthony Le Donne and Tom Thatcher, 239–49. London: T. & T. Clark, 2011.
Ong, Walter J. *Orality and Literacy: The Technologizing of the Word*. London: Methuen, 1982.
Oepke, Albrecht "παῖς," *TDNT*, 5:638.
———. "ζώννυμι," *TDNT*, 5:303–7.

Otwell, John H. *And Sarah Laughed: The Status of Woman in the Old Testament.* Philadelphia: Westminster, 1977.
Painter, John. *John: Witness and Theologian.* London: SPCK, 1975.
Pelton, Robert D. *The Trickster in West Africa: A Study of Mythic Irony and Sacred Delight.* Berkeley: University of California Press, 1980.
Petersen, Walter. *Greek Diminutives in -ION. A Study in Semantics.* Weimar, Germany: R. Wagner Sohn, 1910. http://www.archive.org/details/greekdiminutivesoopeteuoft.
Petersen, David L., and Carolyn Osiek. "Genesis and Family Values." *Journal of Biblical Literature* 124, no. 1 (2005) 5–23.
Pfitzner, Victor C. "They Knew It Was the Lord: The Place and Function of John 21:1–14 in the Gospel of John." *Lutheran Theological Journal* 20, nos. 2–3 (1986) 64–75.
Philo. *The Works of Philo: Complete and Unabridged.* Translated by Charles D. Yonge. Peabody, MA: Hendrickson, 1995.
Pietersma, Albert, and Benjamin G. Wright. *A New English Translation of the Septuagint.* Oxford: Oxford University Press, 2007. http://ccat.sas.upenn.edu/nets/edition/.
Plutarch. *Plutarch's Lives.* Translated by Bernadotte Perrin. n.p.: Heinemann, 1921. http://www.perseus.tufts.edu/hopper.
Porter, Stanley E. *Handbook of Classical Rhetoric in the Hellenistic Period, 330 B.C.–A.D. 400.* Leiden: Brill, 1997.
Potter, Nancy N. "What Is Manipulative Behavior, Anyway?" *Journal of Personality Disorders* 20, no. 2 (2006) 139–56.
Powell, Mark A. *What Is Narrative Criticism?* Minneapolis: Fortress, 1990.
Preisker, Herbert. "νεφρός," *TDNT*, 4:911.
Price, James L. "Light from Qumran upon Some Aspects of Johannine Theology." In *John and the Dead Sea Scrolls*, edited by James H. Charlesworth, 9–37. New York: Crossroad, 1990.
Pritchard, John P. *A Literary Approach to the New Testament.* Norman: University of Oklahoma Press, 1972. http://www.netlibrary.com/ebook_info.asp?product_id=15399.
Quast, Kevin. *Peter and the Beloved Disciple: Figures for a Community in Crisis.* Sheffield: JSOT, 1989.
Quintilian. *The Institutio Oratoria of Quintilian.* Translated by Harold. E. Butler. Cambridge, MA: Harvard University Press, 1920. http://www.perseus.tufts.edu/hopper.
Reardon, Patrick. H. "Peter at the Charcoal Fire." *Touchstone (US)* 14, no. 3 (2001) 21.
Reinhartz, Adele. "Samson's Mother: An Unnamed Protagonist." *JSOT* 55 (1992) 25–37.
———. *Why Ask My Name? Anonymity and Identity in Biblical Narrative.* New York: Oxford University Press, 1998.
Resseguie, James. L. *Narrative Criticism of the New Testament: An Introduction.* Grand Rapids: Baker Academic, 2005.
Rhoads, David M., and Donald Michie. *Mark as Story: An Introduction to the Narrative of a Gospel.* Philadelphia: Fortress, 1982.
Ricoeur, Paul. *The Symbolism of Evil.* New York: Harper & Row, 1967.
Rimmon-Kenan, Shlomith. *Narrative Fiction: Contemporary Poetics.* London: Routledge, 2002.
Robbins, Vernon. K. *The Tapestry of Early Christian Discourse: Rhetoric, Society, and Ideology.* London: Routledge, 1996.

Robertson, A. T. *A Grammar of the Greek New Testament in the Light of Historical Research*. New York: Hodder & Stoughton, 1919.
———. *Word Pictures in the New Testament*. Vol. 4. Nashville: Broadman, 1966.
Robinson, Robert B. "Wife and Sister through the Ages: Textual Determinacy and the History of Interpretation." *Semeia* 62 (1993) 103–28.
Rowe, Galen O. "Style." In *Handbook of Classical Rhetoric in the Hellenistic Period, 330 B.C.-A.D. 400*, edited by Stanley E. Porter, 121–58. Leiden: Brill, 1997.
Rudinow, Joel. "Manipulation." *Ethics* 88, no. 4 (1978) 338–47.
Sacks, Robert D. *A Commentary on the Book of Genesis*. Lewiston, NY: Mellen, 1990.
Sailhamer, John H. *Pentateuch as Narrative*. Grand Rapids: Zondervan, 1992.
Sanders, H. A. "The Number of the Beast in Revelation." *Journal of Biblical Literature* 37, no. 1 (1918) 95–99.
Sarna, Nahum. M. *Genesis* בר־אשית: *The Traditional Hebrew Text with New JPS Translation*. Philadelphia: Jewish Publication Society, 1989.
———. *Understanding Genesis*. New York: Schocken, 1970.
Schaff, Philip, and Henry Wace. *A Select Library of the Nicene and Post-Nicene Fathers of the Christian Church*. Vol. 1, series 2. Grand Rapids: Eerdmans, 1979.
Schaps, David. "When Is a Piglet Not a Piglet?" *Journal of Hellenic Studies* 111 (1991) 208–9.
Schmid, Konrad. "Abraham's Sacrifice: Gerhard von Rad's Interpretation of Genesis 22." *Interpretation: A Journal of Bible & Theology* 62, no. 3 (2008) 268–76.
Schnackenburg, Rudolf. *The Gospel according to John*. Vol. 1. New York: Crossroad, 1982.
———. *The Gospel according to John*. Vol. 3. New York: Crossroad, 1982.
Schneiders, Sandra. M. "John 20:11–18: The Encounter of the Easter Jesus with Mary Magdalene—A Transformative Feminist Reading." In *The Interpretation of John*, eited by John Ashton, 235–60. Edinburgh: T. & T. Clark, 1997.
———. "John 21:1–14." *Interpretation* 43, no. 1 (1989) 70–75.
Scholes, Robert E., and Robert L. Kellogg. *The Nature of Narrative*. New York: Oxford University Press, 1966.
Scodel, Ruth. *Listening to Homer: Tradition, Narrative, and Audience*. Ann Arbor: University of Michigan Press, 2002.
Scott, Bernard B. *Reading New Testament Greek: Complete Word Lists and Reader's Guide*. Peabody, MA: Hendrickson, 1993.
Segovia, Fernando F. "The Final Farewell of Jesus: A Reading of John 20:30—21:25." *Semeia* 53 (1991) 167–90.
Sevrin, Jean-Marie. "'EGW EIMI/OUK EIMI." In *Repetitions and Variations in the Fourth Gospel: Style, Text, Interpretation*, edited by Gilbert v. Belle et al., 347–55. Leuven: Peeters, 2009.
Shaw, Alan. "Breakfast by the Shore and the Mary Magdalene Encounter as Eucharistic Narratives." *Journal of Theological Studies* 25 (1974) 12–26.
Silbermann, A. M. *Chumash with Targum Onkelos, Haphtaroth and Rashi's Commentary*. 5 vols. Jerusalem: Feldheim, 1973.
Sloyan, Gerard S. *What Are They Saying about John?* New York: Paulist, 1991.
Smalley, Stephen . S. "The Sign in John XXI." *New Testament Studies* 20, no. 3 (1974) 275–88.
Smith, D. Moody. *John among the Gospels*. Columbia: University of South Carolina Press, 2001.

Snyder, Graydon F. "John 13:16 and the Anti-Petrinism of the Johannine Tradition." *Biblical Research* 16 (1971) 5–15.
Speiser, E. A. *Genesis*. Garden City, NY: Doubleday, 1964.
Spencer, Patrick E. "Narrative Echoes in John 21: Intertextual Interpretation and Intratextual Connection." *JSNT* 22, no. 75 (1999) 49–68.
Staley, Jeffrey. "Reading Myself, Reading the Text: The Johannine Passion Narrative in Postmodern Perspective." In *What Is John? Readers and Readings of the Fourth Gospel*, edited by Fernando F. Segovia, 59–106. Atlanta: Scholars, 1996.
Steinberg, Naomi. "Israelite Tricksters, Their Analogues, and Cross-Cultural Study." *Semeia* 42 (1988) 1–13.
Sternberg, Meir. *The Poetics of Biblical Narrative: Ideological Literature and the Drama of Reading*. Bloomington: Indiana University Press, 1985.
Stibbe, Mark. W. G. *The Gospel of John as Literature: An Anthology of Twentieth-Century Perspectives*. Leiden: Brill, 1993a.
———. *John*. Sheffield: JSOT, 1993b.
———. *John as Storyteller: Narrative Criticism and the Fourth Gospel*. Cambridge: Cambridge University Press, 1992.
———. *John's Gospel*. London: Routledge, 1994.
Swanson, Donald C. "Diminutives in the Greek New Testament." *Journal of Biblical Literature* 77, no. 2 (1958) 134–51.
Swanson, James, and Logos Research Systems. *Dictionary of Biblical Languages with Semantic Domains: Greek (New Testament)*. Oak Harbor, WA: Logos, 1997a.
———. *Dictionary of Biblical Languages with Semantic Domains: Hebrew (Old Testament)*. Oak Harbor, WA: Logos, 1997b.
Sylva, Dennis. "Dialogue and Drama: Elements of Greek Tragedy in the Fourth Gospel (Review)." *Journal of Biblical Literature* 125, no. 3 (2006) 604–7.
Syren, Roger. *Forsaken Firstborn: A Study of a Recurrent Motif in the Patriarchal Narratives*. Sheffield: Sheffield Academic, 2009.
Tate, W. Randolph. *Biblical Interpretation: An Integrated Approach*. Peabody, MA: Hendrickson, 1991.
Thatcher, Tom. "John's Memory Theatre: A Study of Composition in Performance." In *The Fourth Gospel in First-Century Media Culture*, edited by Anthony Le Donne and Tom Thatcher, 73–91. London: T. & T. Clark, 2011.
Thiselton, Anthony. C. *New Horizons in Hermeneutics*. Grand Rapids: Zondervan, 1992.
Thomas, Richard W. "Meaning of the Terms Life and Death in the Fourth Gospel and in Paul." *Scottish Journal of Theology* 21 (1968) 199–212.
Thompson, Stith. *Motif-Index of Folk-Literature: A Classification of Narrative Elements in Folktales, Ballads, Myths, Fables, Mediaeval Romances, Exempla, Fabliaux, Jest-Books, and Local Legends*. Bloomington: Indiana University Press, 1955.
Tilborg, Sjef v. *Reading John in Ephesus*. Leiden: Brill, 1996.
Tolmie, D. Francois. "The (Not So) Good Shepherd: The Use of Shepherd Imagery in the Characterisation of Peter in the Fourth Gospel." In *Imagery in the Gospel of John: Terms, Forms, Themes, and Theology of Johannine Figurative Language*, edited by Jörg Frey et al., 353–68, Tübingen: Mohr/Siebeck, 2006.
Townsend, John T. *Midrash Tanhuma*. Vol. 1. Hoboken, NJ: KTAV, 1989.
Trudinger, L. Paul. "An Israelite in Whom There Is No Guile." *Evangelical Quarterly* 54 (1982) 117–20.

Turner, Victor. W. *The Ritual Process: Structure and Anti-Structure*. New Brunswick, NJ: Aldine Transaction, 2007.
Vorster, W. S. "The Historical Paradigm-Its Possibilities and Limitations." *Neotestamentica* 18 (1984) 104–23.
———. "Towards a Post-Critical Paradigm: Progress in New Testament Scholarship?" In *Paradigms and Progress in Theology*, edited by J. Mouton et al., 31–48. Pretoria, South Africa: Human Sciences Research Council, 1988.
Waetjen, Herman C. *The Gospel of the Beloved Disciple: A Work in Two Editions*. New York: T. & T. Clark, 2005.
Wallace, Daniel B. *Greek Grammar beyond the Basics: An Exegetical Syntax of the New Testament*. Grand Rapids: Zondervan, 1996.
Walvoord, John F., Roy B. Zuck, Dallas Theological Seminary, and Logos Research Systems. *The Bible Knowledge Commentary: An Exposition of the Scriptures*. Wheaton, IL: Victor, 1983.
Watt, J. G. v. d. *An Introduction to the Johannine Gospel and Letters*. London: T. & T. Clark, 2007.
Wead, David W. *The Literary Devices in John's Gospel*. Basel: Reinhardt, 1970.
Wehr, Hans, and J. Milton Cowan. *A Dictionary of Modern Written Arabic: (Arabic-English)*. Ithaca, NY: Spoken Language Services, 1994.
Weinsheimer, Joel. *Gadamer's Hermeneutics: A Reading of Truth and Method*. New Haven: Yale University Press, 1985.
Wenham, Gordon J. *Genesis 16–50*. WBC 2. Dallas, TX: Word, 1994.
Wénin, André. "La gestion narrative de l'espace dans l'histoire de Joseph." Paper presented at the Symposium du reseau RRENAB, Montpellier/Sète, France, 22–23 March 2003.
Westermann, Claus. *Genesis 1–11: A Commentary*. Translated by John Scullion. Vol. 1. Minneapolis: Augsburg, 1984.
Wiarda, Timothy. "John 21.1–23: Narrative Unity and its Implications." *JSNT* 14, no. 46 (1992) 53.
Williams, Michael J. *Deception in Genesis: An Investigation into the Morality of a Unique Biblical Phenomenon*. New York: Lang, 2001.
Witherington, Ben, III. *John's Wisdom: A Commentary on the Fourth Gospel*. Louisville: Westminster John Knox, 1995.
Wright, Gerald. *Personal Discussions, on This Date and Others, about Power and Shame in John 21*. West Palm Beach, FL: June 25 2010.
Zumstein, Jean. "Intratextuality and Intertextuality in the Gospel of John." Translated by Mark Gray. In *Anatomies of Narrative Criticism: The Past, Present, and Futures of the Fourth Gospel as Literature*, edited by Tom Thatcher and Stephen D. Moore, 121–35. Atlanta: SBL, 2008.
———. *L'Evangile selon Saint-Jean (13–21)*. Geneva: Labor et Fides, 2007.

General Index

ἀναγνώρισις. *See* Anagnorisis.
Abimelech, 5, 49, 103, 121, 154–55
Abraham, Abram, 4, 5, 11, 35, 37, 50, 62, 64, 69, 91, 103, 108, 109, 110, 116, 121–29, 134–35, 146, , 153, 155, 187, 191, 212, 232, 239, 241
Absalom, 83
accismus, 212
Adam, 5, 45–46, 109, 121, 123
Adam, 5, 45–46, 109, 121, 123
agnoia, 42
Amnon, 83
anagnorisis, 3, 4, 5, 6, 9, 11, 14, 17, 29, 31–36, 38–42, 44–47, 51–52, 54, 59, 65, 77, 79, 89, 93, 94, 97, 116–17, 142, 167, 177, 184, 189, 198, 202, 223, 251, 269, 276–77
Andrew, 9, 198, 215, 217, 219, 233
anti-Petrine, 23–26, 28–31, 191
Arabic, 140–41
atomistic reading, 55
Austen, Jane, 54 66

balm, 58, 161, 169, 228, 232
barley. *See* Bread.
belief, believe, 11–12, 15, 20, 34–35, 37, 39–40, 42, 56–57, 65, 71, 73, 75–76, 81, 86, 95–97, 102, 109, 111, 130, 171, 178, 181–82 190–93, 195, 215, 221, 228, 247, 252–54, 262, 272, 277

Beloved Disciple, 10–11, 19, 21–30, 35, 39, 59, 73, 75, 175, 177, 180–82, 186–88, 189–91, 195–96, 221, 223, 235, 247, 250–51, 257, 271
Benjamin, 38, 47, 58, 82, 91, 100–101, 109–10, 113, 129, 132–33, 135, 137, 139, 144–46, 148, 150, 161–66, 186, 228, 241
bias, 77–78
biography, 20, 56, 75, 158, 163
boat, 2, 19, 175, 180, 185, 189, 198, 210, 213, 221–28, 233, 240, 259–61, 263–65
bread, 61, 82, 175–76, 181, 186, 198, 203–4, 215–16, 219–21, 229, 231–35, 244, 271–73
brevity. *See* Economy of detail.

Caiaphas, 65
Cana, 12, 183, 188–89
Canaan, 124, 131–34, 147, 162
Canaanite(s), 58, 104, 112, 232
centurion, 72
characters
    background, 67, 124
    cards, 67–68, 125
    characterization, ix, xiii, 17, 23, 26, 29–31, 46, 52, 54, 58, 65, 67–73, 76–77, 90, 105, 107, 109–112, 114–15, 117, 121, 129, 150, 154, 179, 181–82, 186–87, 189, 191–92, 194, 196–97, 238, 249, 254, 256, 265, 267, 270, 272, 277

characters (continued)
  development process, 123–32, 159, 166, 189, 194–96, 203, 234, 239, 271–72, 275
  dynamic, 26, 29
  ficelles, 67–68, 71, 124
  flat, 29, 66–68, 71–75, 77, 125, 212, 216, 230, 275
  in contrast. See Contrast.
  inner life, 6, 69, 74–76
  intermediate, 67–68, 125
  minor, 72–73, 76, 123
  protagonist, 67–68, 109, 124–26, 258, 274
  round, 66–75, 125, 178, 189, 191, 212
  serial aspect, 5, 13, 26, 29, 50–51, 72, 118, 120–23, 125, 128, 134, 138, 149, 150–51, 157, 160, 166–67, 193, 195–97, 253, 256
  static, 26, 44, 66–73, 77, 116–17
  unnamed, 46, 104, 187–88, 191
charcoal, 171, 175, 179–80, 225, 228–29, 233, 238, 251–52, 255–59, 272–73
chiasm, 20, 83
Cinderella, 169
Coleridge, Samuel Taylor, 56–57
contrast, 2, 7, 10, 12, 28–29, 48, 59, 61, 66, 70, 72, 76, 91, 106, 112–13, 116, 122, 125, 129–31, 181–82, , 188–89, 192–94, 215, 219, 225–26, 228, 231–33, 237, 249, 254–55, 257–59, 263–65, 271
cord. See Sign.
counter-manipulation, ix, xiii, 6, 46, 50–51, 106–8, 110, 112, 115, 117–20, 137, 142, 149–52, 154–55, 157–59, 161, 163–67, 179, 181, 184, 196–97, 199, 201–4, 222, 234, 236–37, 243–44, 251, 254–56, 258–59, 267–68, 270–71, 274–77
critical paradigm, in hermeneutics, 31, 55–57

dark, darkness, 44, 92, 98, 101, 107, 183, 186, 199

David, 63, 81, 83, 104, 126, 167
Dead Sea Scrolls, 11, 60, 141, 145,
deception. See manipulation.
déjà vu, 138, 147, 149, 166, 234, 256, 271–73
dénouement, 99, 107, 162, 165, 237, 255, 276
diachronic, 20, 26, 48
Dickens, Charles, 54, 66–68, 101
diminutives, x, xii, 52, 203–19, 226, 230–32, 236, 245–47, 259, 275–77, 279
  appurtenance nuances, 208–12, 229
  deteriorative duance, 207–8, 212, 215, 246
  faded, xii, 204–5, 210, 212–14, 217, 226, 229, 245
  food nuance, 208–10, 229, 230–34, 246,
  hypocoristic nuance, 208–9, 212, 218, 230, 247
  smallness, 206–15, 217–19, 226–27, 230–33, 246
Dinah, 84, 95, 97, 111–12, 114, 129–30, 157
discovery, 2–3, 5, 34, 44–45
disempowerment, 8, 98, 134, 136–38, 167, 199, 222, 234, 238, 271, 273–74
Documentary Hypothesis, 156
Dostoevsky, Fyodor, 69
double entendre, 250

Economy of Detail, 54, 58–60, 68, 70, 144, 179, 224
Eglon, 59, 82
Egypt, 5, 7, 12–13, 37, 42, 44, 47, 58, 91–93, 97, 100–102, 105, 110–11, 113, 119–21, 126, 131–33, 137, 139, 144–47, 150, 155, 160, 163, 165, 197, 222, 228, 255
Ehud, 82
Elisha, 203
Elohim, 91, 125, 133, 189
Eneglaim, 176
Engedi, 176
epilogue, 14, 19–22, 33
Er, 130

GENERAL INDEX

Esau, 5–6, 10, 13–14, 43, 59–62, 80–82, 85–87, 89–90, 92–94, 96, 98, 101, 103, 105–6, 110, 115, 119–20, 124–28, 132, 134, 153, 157, 160, 165, 184, 239, 241, 258
Esther, 203
Eve, 45–46, 109, 121, 123

fictive, 66, 75
fiction, fictional, 32, 44–45, 55, 66, 70
fish, large, 231
fish, small, 14, 233
fishing, 60, 175, 180, 183, 188, 195–200, 218–19, 225, 227, 237, 249–50, 252, 254, 259–60, 264, 272–73
form criticism, 55

gap(s), 41, 48, 57, 62–63, 70, 147
garment. *See* robe.
Gematria, 22, 176
girding, 192, 218, 223–25, 238, 248, 259–61, 263, 265, 272
goat, 60, 81, 85, 92, 99, 142–45, 151, 222, 256
Greek comedy, 75, 207
Greek drama, 2, 31–33, 38, 54
Greek tragedy, 17, 31–34, 38, 44, 75, 223
growth. *See* Characters, development process.
gum, 58, 161, 228, 232

Haman, 203
Hamor, 95, 102, 110–11, 121, 125, 129, 136
Hebraic, 5, 31–2, 43–44, 47, 51, 79, 142, 228
hellenism, hellenistic, 16, 31, 33, 40, 42, 168
hermeneutics, 55–57, 78
Historical Critical method, 16, 31, 53, 55, 70, 75, 77, 156
Horatian, Horace, 231
Hugo, Victor, 54

ignorance, ignorant, 3, 5–9, 11, 14–15, 44, 46, 96, 110, 139, 141–42, 144, 148, 151, 162, 167, 179–81, 185, 188–90, 192–95, 221–22, 235, 252–55, 267, 274
implicit commentary, 11–12, 25, 32, 44, 53, 61–64, 68–69, 93, 97, 108, 122, 127, 130, 136, 144, 150, 152,158,178–81, 184–85, 188–90, 196, 218–19, 225, 228, 235–36, 239, 242, 248, 254, 265
implied author, 32, 36, 57, 62–63, 108, 155, 260
implied reader, 4, 32, 54, 56–57, 62–65, 156–58, 172, 174, 196, 198, 202, 238–39, 250–51, 254–55, 259, 265–66
inclusio, 171, 176, 188–90, 239
indeterminancy, textual, 63, 91–92, 126, 148, 162, 196, 250–51, 256
intertextuality, 4, 12, 15, 42, 51, 59, 168–69, 172, 188, 216, 218, 221, 243, 244, 251, 263
intratextuality, 18, 59, 204, 220–21, 244–45, 248, 256, 258, 260, 263, 266–67, 275
irony, xiii, 28, 33–34, 53–54, 62, 64–66, 70, 107, 110, 114, 122, 128, 139, 141–44, 147, 150, 151, 158, 165, 194, 198, 200–4, 207, 227, 231–33, 237, 239, 249–50, 276–77
Isaac, 5–7, 13, 42, 49, 60, 80–81, 83–85, 89–94, 96, 98, 101, 103, 105–6, 110, 115–16, 119–21, 126–29, 131, 134–35, 142–43, 153–55, 157, 159, 184, 187, 212, 241
Ishmael, 126
Ishmaelites, 58, 104, 113, 147

Jacob
  characterization, 61, 69, 106–11, 113, 115, 125–26, 128, 130–31, 133–34, 150, 153, 159, 164, 189, 239, 267
  development process, transformation, 5, 29, 106–11, 113, 125–26, 128, 134, 164, 189, 234, 239, 267, 274
  in the Gospel of John, 4, 9–11, 52, 188, 190, 194, 238

Jacob *(continued)*
  lying, deceit, 10, 13, 29, 42–43, 50, 89, 92–95, 103, 110, 115, 122, 124, 127, 134, 139, 142–43, 150, 152, 155, 158–60, 190, 194, 239
  manipulation, 46, 81–87, 89–99, 101–8, 110, 115, 119–21, 123, 125, 128, 135–36, 139, 142–44, 150, 152–55, 157–60, 166, 183–84, 194, 201, 222, 237, 267, 274
  recognition or failed recognition by, 5, 37, 51, 65, 80–81, 93, 95, 101–2, 105, 139, 141–44, 183
  recognition or failed recognition of, 5, 7, 102, 106, 115
  stealing Esau's blessing, 6, 13, 42–43, 60–61, 80–81, 85, 89–94, 96, 98, 101, 103, 105–7, 115, 119–20, 125, 127, 138, 142–43, 153, 159–60, 184, 241
  taking Esau's birthright, 85–87, 96, 106, 120, 154
Jesus
  characterization, 185–86, 192–93, 198, 212, 224–25, 231, 232–33, 237, 254, 257–60, 263–65, 270, 276
  manipulation, 177, 179–81, 184, 201, 203, 236–37, 244, 251, 254, 258, 263, 267–68, 270–71, 273–77
  recognition or failed recognition of, 175–76, 178, 181–82, 185–86, 188–91, 196, 198, 200–4, 222–23, 235, 251, 254–55, 268, 271–73, 276
  resurrection, 175, 190, 235, 247
  withholding identity, ix, 13, 33–34, 180–81, 184–86, 201–2, 222, 271
Jew, Jews, Jewish, x, 4, 10–11, 15–16, 23–24, 33, 49, 58, 64, 73, 101, 116, 131, 143, 168, 170, 188, 190, 203, 212, 231–32, 238, 258, 262, 266
Joseph of Arimathea, 72
  characterization, 44, 59, 61, 109, 111, 121, 123, 125, 132–33, 163
  development process, transformation, 109, 111, 121, 125, 163
  manipulation, ix, 46, 82, 91, 96–98, 100–2, 111, 112, 117, 119–21, 123, 132–34, 137, 141–42, 148, 150, 152, 160–64, 167, 184, 197, 199, 201, 203, 222, 237, 277
  prefiguration or type of Christ, 12–13, 37
  recognition or failed recognition by, 5–6, 37, 80–81, 134, 139–42, 161
  recognition or failed recognition of, 3–5, 7, 13, 34, 41–42, 80–81, 101–2, 105, 134, 139–42, 161–62, 184, 186, 193
  withholding identity, 80–81, 120, 139–41, 143, 161, 184, 195
Joyce, James. Jocyean, 44
Judah
  and Jacob, 61, 65, 81, 119–21, 123–24, 142–43, 145–46, 159–60, 165–66, 241
  and Joseph, 13, 47, 59, 61, 65, 82, 92, 100–101, 110, 113, 119–21, 123, 125, 132–33, 137, 142, 144–46, 160, 162, 164, 165, 184, 197, 222, 241
  and Tamar, 47, 49, 58–59, 65, 81–82, 84, 87, 89, 95–99, 104, 110, 112–13, 116, 119–20, 123, 131, 136–37, 142–46, 151–52, 154, 157, 159–60, 163–65, 195, 197, 234–35,
  characterization, 3, 12–13, 46, 58, 61, 87, 100–101, 109, 112–13, 129–30, 133, 145, 151, 154, 165, 195, 197, 250
  comparisons to Peter, ix, 12, 13, 65, 190, 197, 234–35, 237, 250, 252, 273, 276–77
  development process, transformation, 13, 29, 45, 47, 100–101, 110, 112–13, 119–21, 125, 129, 131–33, 145, 148–50, 160, 162–65
  lying, deceit, 65, 82, 84, 124, 134, 142, 151, 158

manipulation, ix, 46, 51, 84, 87, 89,
    95–99, 112, 116, 119–21, 123,
    125, 129, 131, 136, 143, 145–46,
    151, 154, 157, 159–60, 163–64,
    167, 181, 197, 237
  pledge, 96, 99, 110, 136, 144–46, 149
  recognition or failed recognition
    by, 5–7, 12, 47, 58, 81, 101, 104,
    143, 151, 160, 164, 166, 181, 184
  self-recognition, 47, 58, 65, 104,
    164–65
Judaism, 11, 24, 40, 42, 73
Judas, 27, 75, 192–93, 257–58

Laban, 5, 46, 80–85, 89, 91–99, 102, 104,
    106–8, 110, 119–21, 124–25,
    127–28, 135, 137, 142–43, 150,
    152, 154–55, 158–60, 166, 178,
    183, 201, 222, 234, 237, 270
Lazarus, 190
Leitmotif. See Leitmotiv.
Leitmotiv, 44, 61, 139, 145–46, 257, 263,
    272
Leitwort, Leitwörter, 44, 61, 80, 110,
    138–39, 142–44, 146, 149, 161,
    166, 171, 180, 189–91, 233–34,
    256–57, 261, 266, 272–73
Levi, 89, 104, , 111, 129–30, 144–45,
    157, 173
Lex Talionis, Talion principle, 152, 154–
    58, 160, 162, 165, 180, 202, 222,
    237–38, 258–59, 268, 275, 277
lie, lying. *See* manipulation.
light, 171, 183, 186, 219
Literary Criticism, 32, 53, 55
litotes, 231
loaf, loaves. *See* Bread.
logos, 192
lying. *See* manipulation, deception.
lysis, 35

manipulation
  entrapment, 95, 98, 114–15, 135
  by camouflage, 89, 92–93, 98, 101,
    103, 114, 227, 269, 277
  by flight, 97, 114
  by masking, 92–93, 96–98, 101,
    114–15, 157, 180
  by objects of desire, 96–97, 114–15,
    118, 157
  by switching, 60, 94, 104, 106–7,
    110, 114–15, 117, 150, 158, 160,
    164, 234
  by theft, 80–81, 91, 94, 104–6, 110,
    114, 117, 119–20, 124, 133, 139,
    144, 152, 159, 270
  by trust building, 96, 114–15, 117
  deception, lying, 10, 14, 28–29, 62,
    81–82, 84–85, 87, 89, 92–98,
    105, 110, 114–15, 120, 122, 124,
    126–27, 129, 135, 154—55, 178,
    180, 194, 199, 201–2, 238–39,
    270, 273–74
  definition of, 89, 114
  effect on the plot or
    characterization, transforming
    effect, 6, 38, 90, 105–115, 122,
    149, 160, 163–67, 179, 182,198–
    99, 201–2, 237, 242, 244, 249,
    256, 258, 268, 271, 274–76
  kernels, 14, 90–93, 98, 103, 105, 114,
    115–16, 119, 121–23, 157,177–
    79, 182, 136, 269–71, 277
  statement or challenge in response,
    103–5, 114–15, 122–23, 128,
    179, 181, 237, 250, 269
  the manipulation kernel, 92–98,
    177–78
  the benefit achieved, 90, 98, 114–15,
    178, 181, 269, 271
  the desired benefit, 89, 90–91, 99,
    114–15, 117, 135, 157, 178,
    269–70, 277
  the recognition, moment of
    recognition, 4, 37, 41, 90, 93,
    101–2, 104, 114–16, 165, 181,
    184, 186, 203, 235, 255, 271, 276
  verbal, 92–, 93, 96, 114, 122
Martha, 10, 65, 174, 191
Mary Magdalene, 23, 34, 39, 174, 180,
    183, 236, 247, 277
Mary, mother of Jesus, 24
meiosis, 227–28, 231–32
metanarrative, 78
metaphor, 20, 198, 234, 246
Midianites, 146

Midrash, 49, 92, 101, 104, , 106, 108, 110, 113, 128, 131, 137, 143
mimesis, mimetic(s), 66—68, 72–76, 116
misunderstanding, 11, 20, 28, 42, 62, 65, 71, 73, 190–91, 193–95, 200, 202, 220, 253–54, 272
Mordecai, 203
Moses, 9, 33, 37, 216
myrrh, 58, 161, 228, 232

narrative criticism, xiii, 32, 52–57, 63, 75, 77–78
narrator, 29, 32, 48, 52, 57, 61–65, 72, 87, 90–91, 95, 97–99, 102–4, 106, 108, 111–13, 122, 126, 129–30, 138–39, 155, 160–61, 171, 174, 177–83, 187, 191, 195, 200, 222–23, 227, 229–32, 234–36, 239, 250–52, 259, 267, 271, 273
Nathanael, 4, 9–11, 19, 21, 61, 175, 183, 187–92, 194, 204, 272
Nicodemus, 65, 73–74

Odysseus, 2–3, 5, 38–39, 116, 270
Onan, 130
oral, orality, 7, 52, 59, 170–74

pathos, 35
Penelope, 38–39, 270
peripeteia, 2–3, 5–6, 13, 34–35, 47, 112, 251
Peter
 "do you love me", ix, xii, 3, 59–60, 63, 176–77, 202, 242–44, 250–53, 255, 268, 271–72, 275
 boast, 29–30, 59, 179, 189, 228, 237–38, 249, 251–52, 268, 270–73
 characterization, ix, 12–13, 15, 17, 23–31, 42, 59–60, 63, 66, 69–77, 179, 182, 187–96, 201, 223–24, 227–28, 235, 237–40, 244, 249–50, 252, 255, 257–60, 265–67, 271, 277
 comparisons to Judah, ix, 12, 13, 65, 190, 197, 234–35, 237, 250, 252, 273, 276–77

crucifixion or death, xiii, 27, 29, 177, 181–82, 218, 238, 249, 256, 258–68, 271–72, 274–75
denials, xiii, 10, 12, 28, 30, 47, 65, 163, 177–89, 200–202, 228–29, 237–39, 242, 249–54, 257–59, 268, 270–73, 275
development process, transformation, 15, 29, 45, 47, 194–96, 203, 236, 238, 242, 244, 248–49, 251, 264–65, 271–72, 275
lying, deceit, 7, 178–80, 270, 276–77
manipulation, ix, xiii, 7–8, 15, 123, 167,169, 177–82, 189, 197, 199, 201–2, 236–37, 267–68, 270–72, 274, 276
recognition or failed recognition by, ix, 1, 3, 11, 15, 181–82, 186, 200–201, 236, 239, 247, 250–51, 255, 260, 274–76
recognition or failed recognition of , 202, 249,
rivalry, 21, 23, 25–26, 30–31
self-recognition, 181, 276
Pharaoh, 5, 12, 62, 103, 121–22, 133, 163, 183
Pharisee, Pharisees, 62, 72, 199–200, 253, 277
Philippi, 26–27
pledge, 96, 99, 110, 136, 144–46, 149, 159, 165, 228, 256
plot. *See* Manipulation, effect on the plot.
poetics, 3, 34
poetry, 56, 103, 204
point of view, 32, 54, 57, 62–65, 75, 87, 91, 155, 187, 231
post-critical paradigm, in hermeneutics, 31, 57
Potiphar, 125, 133
Potiphar's wife, 59
primogeniture, 80, 115
prolepsis, 174, 181
prologue, 4, 19, 22

Qumran. *See* Dead Sea Scrolls.
Quran, Qur'ani, 140

Rachel, 5, 59, 80–81, 91, 93–98, 102–8, 112, 119–21, 125, 127–27, 135, 139, 142–46, 148, 150, 152, 159, 160, 162, 183, 232, 241, 255, 270

Rebekah, 5, 42, 60, 80–81, 83, 90–91, 93, 96, 103, 105–6, 115, 119–21, 125, 127, 134, 146, 149, 152–55, 158–59, 166

recognition. *See* manipulation.

repetition, 44, 53–54, 60–61, 80, 126, 132–33, 138–39, 151, 161, 171–72, 190, 223, 227, 231, 240, 247, 253, 256–59, 265

resurrection, 11, 20, 37, 56, 75, 175, 180–81, 183, 185–86, 190, 196–97, 199, 221, 245, 247, 262, 274

Reuben, 12, 100, 112–13, 126, 131, 144–45, 195

reversal, 2–3, 5–6, 25–26, 29, 29, 44, 4748, 58, 66, 77, 102, 105–7, 110–12, 115, 117, 132, 134, 137, 146, 160, 162, 164, 179, 181–82, 201, 236—38, 252, 259, 271, 274, 276, 277

rhetorical criticism, 52

robe, 5, 60, 81, 92–93, 95–96, 99, 105, 113, 131, 139, 142–43, 148, 151, 158–60, 192, 223–25, 233, 256, 260, 263

Robin Hood, 204, 207

Ruth, 140, 157, 167

Samaritan Woman, 4, 35, 63, 65, 73, 277

Samson, 35, 37, 111, 126, 151, 157, 188

Sarah, Sarai, 5, 103, 122, 149, 191

satire, 223, 231, 276

secrecy, secret, 89, 100, 102, 158

sequential episodes. *See* Serial aspect.

Seth, 123–24

σημεῖον, σημείων, 2, 40–41, 94, 233

Shechem, Shekhem, 4, 81, 84, 95, 97–98, 102, 104, 110–12, 114, 116, 119–21, 123, 125, 129–30, 135–36, 145, 157, 178, 270

signet ring. *See* signs.

signs, 2, 19, 21, 39, 40–41, 81, 99, 143–45, 165, 183, 223

silver, 92, 94, 103, 144, 146–50, 161–62, 190, 228, 251, 256–57

Simeon, 89, 92, 97, 100, 104, 111, 129–30, 144–45, 157, 161, 273

socio-rhetorical criticism, 52, 77

soldier(s), 34, 195, 200, 257–58, 263–64

Sons of Zebedee, 175, 187, 197

source criticism, 49, 55

staff. *See* signs.

story
  as a whole entity, 55, 171
  climax, 3
  components of, 54
  story time, 26
  story world, 6, 30–31, 38, 46, 77, 102, 105, 108, 125, 134, 155, 178, 238
  story-worthy, 151, 200

structuralism, 69

surprise, 3, 66–68, 71–72, 108, 157–58, 162, 178, 223, 234–35, 238

suspense, 63, 126, 162, 200

suspension of disbelief, 55–57

synchronic, 156, 205

Synoptic Gospels, 8, 12, 23, 25, 29–30, 170, 172–74, 178, 188, 200, 227, 238, 249, 251–52

Tamar, 5–7, 38, 47, 49, 58–59, 65, 81–84, 87, 89, 95–99, 101, 104, 110, 112–13, 116–17, 119–21, 123, 125, 129, 131, 136–37, 142–46, 151–52, 154, 157–60, 163–65, 167, 183–84, 195, 197 235, 237, 252, 273

tapeinosis, 231

Targum, Targumim, 49, 91, 102, 130, 136

telos, 37, 89

teraphim, 91, 110, 127, 135, 144

textual indeterminancy. *See* indeterminancy.

Thomas, 2, 11, 19–21, 27, 34, 38–39, 41, 53, 109, 145, 156, 175, 182, 185–91, 197, 221, 223, 240, 272

Token. *See* Sign.

tragedy. *See* Greek tragedy.

trickster, ix-x, xii, 6, 14, 17, 43, 46, 48–51, 79–84, 114–17, 126, 136–37, 149, 159, 164, 269, 276
turning, xiii, 6, 125, 131, 145, 154, 162–65, 167, 203, 252, 268, 270, 274, 276
type scene, 20, 35, 39, 43, 49, 60, 89–90, 97

unbelief, disbelief. *See* belief.

Wellhausen Hypothesis. *See* Documentary Hypothesis.
Weltanschauung, 55–56
woman at the well. *See* Samaritan Woman.
wordplay, 144, 184

Yahweh, 106, 108–9, 125, 128, 153–54, 188
Yehuda. *See* Judah.

Scripture Index

Gen

Ref	Pages
1–11	109
1–2	108
1:1	4
1:31	109
2:7	4
3	14, 121, 123
3:13	103, 109
3:14	109
4	109
4:26	109
5	14, 123
5	123
5:6–11	124
12	121, 124, 142
12:2–3	126
12:2	122, 155
12:3	62
12:10–20	60
12:13	126,
12:15	122,
12:16	62, 122, 142
12:18	103
13	124, 146
13:1–2	122
15	124
16:5	108
17	124, 146
17:5	239
17:18–19	109
18	35, 37
18:4–5	232
19	121
20	121, 142, 146, 239
20:1–17	60
20:8	103, 122
22	212
22:2	241
23	146
24	146
24:10–64	142
24:67	241
25	61, 166
25:21–34	109
25:22	154
25:23	106, 153
25:27	153
25:28	159, 241
25:29–34	86, 96, 106, 153
25:34	153
25:41	106
26	49, 119, 120, 121, 124, 142
26:1–10	60
26:6–11	154
26:10	103, 122
26:34–35	153
27:1—28:5	60
27	7, 13, 43, 80–81, 83, 90, 115, 119, 120, 124, 134, 142
27:1–46	60
27:4	90, 241

Gen *(continued)*

27:5–29	93
27:7	91
27:9	143, 159, 242
27:10	91
27:12	80
27:13	106
27:14	241
27:15	159
27:16	143
27:18–29	60
27:19–20	96
27:19	85, 93
27:20	93
27:23	80, 128, 138
27:24	93
27:27–29	98
27:30–40	93
27:30–35	93
27:30	101
27:33	14, 98, 101, 103
27:34	103
27:35	4, 9, 103
27:36	10, 98, 103, 125
27:37–41	103
27:41–46	103
28	124
28:1	98, 112
28:3	98
28:4	98
28:5	106
28:6–9	153
28:6	98
28:12	4, 10
28:13–15	127
28:13	128
28:14–15	98
28:14	155
28:18	128
28:19–22	130
28:20–21	189
29	81, 98, 119–20, 124, 150
29:7	243
29:15–30	60
29:15	96
29:16–17	91
29:18–19	106
29:18	241
29:19	94
29:20	241
29:21–27	159
29:21–30	135
29::25	183
29:23–24	98
29:23	92
29:25	81, 92, 98, 100, 102–3, 122
29:26	95, 106–7
29:27	106
29:28–29	98
29:28	234
29:30	98, 241
29:31—30:24	129
30–32	142
30	81, 119–20
30:25–43	127
30:25	99
30:27	91
30:28	96
30:32	94
30:34	96
30:35–36	94, 99
30:36	93
30:37–43	97
30:42–43	99, 107
30:43	135, 142
31	80–81, 119–20, 146, 150, 158, 201, 222
31:1	99, 102
31:6–16	159
31:7–9	150
31:7	108, 159
31:4–13	99
31:4	93
31:5	128
31:9	128
31:9–13	154
31:10–12	95
31:10–13	81, 127
31:11–13	128
31:14	159

31:15	146, 159	33:8	110, 128
31:16	135	33:13	110, 128, 217
31:17	142	33:14–17	110, 128, 239
31:18	150	33:14	110, 128
31:19	91, 93, 159	33:15	128
31:20	95, 97, 135	33:18–20	4
31:22–35	127	33:30	111
31:24	150, 154	34	81, 84, 97, 102, 104, 119–20, 123, 157
31:26	104		
31:27	97		
31:29	104, 135	34:1–4	97
31:30	91, 104, 135, 159	34:2	97, 112
31:32	91, 94, 128, 135, 144, 148, 159	34:3	241
		34:4	111
31:33	183	34:5	111
31:34	91, 112, 142	34:7	129
31:35	91, 95–96, 135	34:12	110
31:36–42	148, 154	34:13	129
31:36	135	34:14	129
31:41	104	34:15–16	95
31:42	91, 128, 135, 150, 154	34:19	130
		34:20–24	95
31:43	108, 150	34:23	110, 130, 136
31:46	93	34:24–25	97
31:49	108, 125	34:25–26	135
31:51–55	99	34:25	97, 109, 111, 130, 135
31:50	125		
31:54	128	34:27–29	111
32–33	110	34:29	109
32	128, 239	34:30–31	130
32:1	99	34:30	104, 109
32:5	110	35	124
32:7	142	35:16–19	129
32:10	128	35:22	145
32:13–15	142	35:23–26	129
32:15	142	35:25–28	113
32:18	110	37–45	201
32:20	110	37	81, 93, 102, 113, 119–20, 130–31, 137, 142, 144, 146–47, 165
32:28	239		
32:32	139		
32:34	93		
33	258	37:3	241, 242
33:2–3	110	37:4	113, 242
33:2	217	37:5–11	112
33:3–4	128	37:8	137
33:3	128	37:10	137
33:5	110, 128, 217	37:19–20	137

Gen *(continued)*

37:21	143
37:25	142, 228
37:26	131
37:28	146
37:30	112
37:31	143
37:32–33	128
37:32	112, 143
37–38	47
37–45	46
37:1–36	60
37:2	111
37:3	111
37:4	111, 241
37:5–11	132
37:5–9	133
37:11	111
37:12	243
37:26–27	13
37:31–35	136
37:31–32	94, 160
37:31	159
37:32–33	7
37:32	95–96
37:18	80, 113
37:21	138
37:22	113
37:25	58, 161
37:27–33	92
37:26	12
37:27	113
37:29	12
37:31	93
37:32	62, 92, 138, 151
37:33	105, 142
37:35	105, 111
38	12, 65, 81, 97, 104, 119–20, 131, 165
38:1–30	60
38:1–12	58
38:1	112
38:8	136
38:11	84, 95
38:7–10	130
38:11	250
38:12–13	93
38:13–15	157
38:14	99, 154, 157
38:16–18	59
38:16	13, 96, 131
38:17–18	110, 144
38:17	96, 160
38:18–19	99
38:18	144
38:23	136, 144
38:24–25	104
38:25–26	7, 101, 128
38:25	143, 160, 184
38:26	6, 62, 104, 112, 118, 130, 140, 151, 163, 181, 234
39:10	59
39:20	112
39:28	163
41:2	243
41:16	133
41:38—45:28	13
41–45	12
41:55	12, 183
42–46	120, 124
42–45	40, 42, 111
42–43	43
42	7, 81, 113, 120, 137, 145, 147
42:6–7	97
42:6	112
42:7–8	128, 139–40, 142
42:7	13, 80–81, 140–41, 161
42:8	80, 96, 138, 140
42:9	97
42:11	81
42:12	97, 124
42:13	100
42:14	97
42:15	91, 97
42:17	88, 97, 100, 112
42:18	97
42:21–22	100, 113
42:21	105, 113
42:22	113
42:23	97

42:24	100	44:33-34	100
42:25	147	44:33	13, 150, 217
42:27-28	94	44:34	164, 217
42:28	100, 103, 113, 122, 130, 132, 147, 190	44:35	222
		45	120, 222
		45:1-3	13
42:35	94, 100, 147	45:1	184
42:36-38	109	45:2	100
42:37	113, 144	45:3-5	13
43	147	45:3-4	101
43:2	144	45:3	13, 102, 105, 137, 222, 234, 255, 274
43:4	150		
43:8-9	144		
43:8	109	45:5-9	133
43:9	144	45:5-7	132
43:11	58, 166, 228	45:5	133, 165
43:11-14	113	45:7	165
43:11-13	161	45:8	165
43:11-12	232	45:15-28	93
43:13-15	109	45:15	105, 113
43:14	113, 128, 166	45:19	109, 217
43:15	228	45:23	142
43:18	148	45:26-27	102
43:23	92, 148	45:26	105
43:24	193	45:28	105
43:26	162	46:6-28	150
43:29-30	100	46:28-30	93
43:30	100	46:29	102
43:32	97	46:30	105
43:34	236	47:24	109
44	110, 148, 164	48:17-20	124
44:1	94	49:1-27	129
44:3—45:3	12	49:8-12	125, 165
44:9	139, 148	49:9-12	167
44:10	148	49:10	125
44:13	148, 190	49:11	142
44:14-16	163	49:13-26	165
44:14	129	49:22-26	165
44:15	222	50:1-21	165
44:16-34	13	50:15-21	105
44:16	100, 132, 148	50:15-18	44
44:17	101, 148	50:17	132, 163
44:18-34	137, 162	50:18	255
44:20	217, 241	50:20	155, 165
44:22	217	50:21	109, 165, 218
44:30	61	50:24-25	165
44:32	110, 145, 217	50:24	124

Exod

16:2–12	216
16:4	216
16:18–21	216
21:23–25	155
29:9	261

Lev

8:7	261
8:13	261
16:4	261
16:10	143
18:18	160
24:17–21	155, 156

Num

27:17	243

Deut

32:27	140, 141
19:21	155, 156
21:15–17	159

Judg

6	35
14:2	111
17:6	151
21:25	151

Ruth

2:10	140
4	167
4:12	167

1 Sam

20:1	104
24:12	108

2 Sam

5:2	243
6:14–21	63
13	83
14:1–28	83
14:28–33	83
14:31	83
15–18	83
22:27	102

2 Kgs

6:19	203
6:23	203
25:27–30	235

1 Chr

2	167
5:1–2	165, 167

2 Chr

18:16	243

Neh

8:3–18	171
8:3	170
8:18	170

Esth

5:4–5	203

Job

21:29	141
38:3	261
40:7	261

Ps

32:2	9
37:25	218
77:20	243
78:16	176
78:52	243
100:3	243

Prov

1:24–28	34
20:11	140–41
26:24	141

Song

2:15	199

Isa

11:5	261
34:17	243
53:6	243
63:11	243
64:6–7	35

Jer

9:4	10
11:18–19	247
19:4	141

Lam

4:8	141

Ezek

	37, 244
9:11	261
10	244
21	244
23:15	261

34	243, 263
34:2	243
34:3	243, 263
34:14	243
47	176
47:10	176

Hos

12:3–6	10

Zech

14:8	176

Matt

	8, 76, 173, 188, 220, 252
4	200
5:38–42	156, 238
5:38–39	238
7:6	212
9:22	77
9:36	243
13:47	176
14:17	230
14:19	230
15:24–27	232
15:26	212, 232
15:27	212
16:16	190
16:23	30
18:2–4	208
20:22–23	262
26:33	30, 249
26:72–74	30
26:74–75	251
26:75	12, 30, 178

Mark

	xiii, xvi, 8, 18, 28–29, 76, 173, 188, 220, 252

Mark *(continued)*

1	200
1:20	197
3:9	227
4:36	213
5:30	76
6:34	243
6:38	230
7:27	232
8:33	30
10:38–39	262
14:29	30, 249
14:68	253
14:71	30
14:72	12, 30, 178, 251
15	72
16:8	21

Luke

	8, 55, 76, 173, 188, 220, 252
5	173, 199–200
5:5–6	200
5:7	227
9:13	230
12:32	243
13:26	236
22:51	208
22:60–62	251
22:62	12, 30, 178
24	40
24:16	185
24:31	185
24:34	186

John

1–20	17, 18, 20, 183, 191, 194, 202, 276
1	9, 17, 19–21, 187–91, 239, 277
1–4	41
1:1–18	19
1:1	4, 11, 188
1:6	174
1:10–12	253
1:10–11	33
1:14–16	57
1:18	29
1:19	174
1:26	190, 253–54
1:31	178
1:34	10
1:35–51	190
1:38	4, 35
1:40–42	191, 198
1:42	188, 239
1:43–51	189
1:43–49	21
1:43–47	9
1:45—2:1	188
1:47	4, 9, 189
1:48	192
1:49	183, 189–90, 272
1:51	4, 9, 190
2	198, 203
2:1–11	223
2:20–22	63
2:24–25	192
2:4	63
2:5	12
2:11	183
2:17	212
2:25	254
3:24	174
4	220, 238, 277
4:5–6	52,
4:9	238
4:12	4, 64, 238
4:31	220
4:32	220
4:33	220
5–19	41
5:16–18	186
5:32	192
5:18	185
6	19, 28, 181, 198, 203, 213, 215, 217–21, 230, 232–35, 245, 248, 265, 267, 272–73

6:1–58	216	8:56	4
6:1–15	216	8:58	11
6:2	215	8:59	34–35
6:5	220	9	62, 72, 200, 253, 277
6:6	192, 221		
6:8	217	9:16	277
6:9	204, 213, 215, 219, 221, 229, 232	9:24	277
		9:29	62, 72, 277
		9:38	72
6:11	229, 236	9:39–41	277
6:15	221	10	234, 243–44, 248, 263, 266
6:16–21	198, 274		
6:17–21	226	10:11–18	263
6:17	227	10:11–15	243
6:19	180, 227	10:11	248, 265
6:22–25	226	10:16	247
6:22	226–27	10:27	247
6:23	220, 226–27	10:33	185
6:24	226–27	10:38	253
6:26	220	10:39	200, 274
6:27	219	11:1–2	174
6:31–33	235	11:2	174
6:31	220	11:6	190
6:35	235	11:16	190
6:41	235	11:24	191
6:48	235	11:27	10
6:49	220	11:35	212
6:50	220, 235	11:42	192
6:51	220, 235	11:50	65
6:52	220	11:57	200, 274
6:53	220	12	191, 275
6:58	235	12:3	174
6:61	192	12:32–33	266
6:64	192	12:33	266, 272
6:68	179 191, 272	12:50	192
6:69	189, 191, 272	13	19, 26, 30, 59, 192–94, 224–25, 237, 254, 259–61, 264–66, 273
6:70	271		
7	191		
7:29	192		
7:30–32	274	13:1–4	192
7:30	199	13:1–3	193
7:32	200	13:1	192–93
7:44	200, 274	13:2	193
8	231	13:3	192–93
8:14	192	13:3–5	259–60
8:20	200, 274	13:4–5	225, 260
8:33	64	13:4	193, 224, 265, 272
8:55	192		

John *(continued)*

13:6–11	272
13:7	193, 255
13:8	59, 193–94, 259
13:9	59
13:14	225, 258
13:15	256, 258
13:16	225
13:18	271
13:21–30	24
13:21	260
13:23–24	191
13:23	29
13:24–25	203
13:25	177
13:26	25
13:31–32	265
13:33	186
13:34	244
13:36–38	194
13:36	25, 29, 186
13:37–38	13
13:37	29, 179, 181, 189, 191, 242, 249, 272
13:38	179, 270
14	19, 190
14:5	190
14:21	185, 244
15:3	251
15:4–5	219
15:5	219, 254, 273
15:13	258, 260
15:16–19	271
16:2	258, 260
16:16	186
16:21	204
16:30	254
18–21	249
18–19	186
18	xiii, 8, 10, 15, 19, 27, 32, 177, 180, 189, 194, 201–3, 220, 236–37, 242, 250, 252, 254, 256–59, 265–66, 273–77
18:3	257
18:5	257
18:6	200
18:10–11	194, 249, 272
18:10	13, 179
18:12–27	257
18:12–14	257
18:12	200, 265
18:15–27	178, 189, 228, 249–50
18:15–18	191, 257, 262
18:15	178
18:16–27	29
18:17	178–79, 249
18:18	171, 179, 225, 257–58, 272
18:19–24	257
18:25–27	257–58, 272
18:25–26	191
18:25	178–79, 249, 257
18:27–28	251
18:27	12, 30, 178–79, 270
18:28	220, 257, 263
18:31–32	266
18:32	266
19	23, 187
19:2	263, 265, 272
19:7	188
19:13	250
19:15	64
19:16–18	265
19:17–18	265
19:17	263, 265, 272
19:20	59
20–21	21, 41, 186
20	19–21, 33, 175, 180, 188, 190–91, 196, 277
20:1–10	191
20:2–10	24
20:2	186
20:3	178
20:8–9	272
20:9	252
20:11–16	39
20:14	186
20:15	34, 180, 247

SCRIPTURE INDEX

20:16	39, 180	21:1	175, 181, 183, 185–86, 189, 203
20:19	182	21:2	187–88, 239
20:21	182	21:3	188, 195, 197, 199–200, 219, 226–27, 249, 252, 254, 264, 274
20:22	4		
20:23	196, 250, 252		
20:24—21:14	21		
20:24–29	190		
20:24–27	190		
20:26–29	223	21:4–5	65
20:26	182	21:4	12, 63, 186, 189, 191, 200–201, 234, 245, 247, 250–51, 254, 272
20:28	27, 41, 185 188–89, 272		
20:29–31	195		
20:29	20, 171	21:5–14	245–46
20:30—21:25	20	21:5–9	217
20:30–31	19–22, 57, 198	21:5	185, 201 203, 217, 219, 221, 244, 246–48, 259, 265
20:30	21, 56		
20:31	181		
21	x, xii, xiii, 4, 6–7, 10, 12–15, 17–26, 29–31, 33–34, 36, 41–43, 51–52, 59–60, 78, 113, 116–17, 120, 123, 149, 167–69, 173, 175, 177–80, 183–84, 186–88, 190–91, 195–96, 199, 201–6, 209–10, 216, 218–23, 225–27, 230, 234, 239, 243–44, 248, 254, 256–61, 263, 267, 270, 272–77	21:6	221, 226–27, 229, 254
		21:7	12, 21, 39, 175, 181–82, 191, 223–25, 250, 260, 265, 271
		21:8	180, 185, 225–26, 229
		21:9–14	228
		21:9–13	234, 275
		21:9	171, 203, 225, 229–32
		21:10	200–201, 221, 229, 234
		21:11	169, 176, 230–31
		21:12	12, 176, 181, 221, 234, 274
		21:13	229, 235
21:1–25	19	21:14	176, 183, 185
21:1–23	21	21:15–23	20
21:1–19	xii, 1, 12, 14, 15, 177, 205, 272	21:15–19	180, 237, 248, 265, 268
21:1–14	3, 7, 36, 168, 236, 244, 248, 265	21:15–18	182, 237, 264
		21:15–17	240–41, 244–46, 248, 251, 270, 272
21:1–12	246		
21:1–7	265		
21:1–5	183	21:15	60, 193, 213, 234, 239, 246, 250
21:1–4	272		
21:1–2	250	21:16–17	213, 245–46

John *(continued)*

21:16	245, 248
21:17	8, 12, 45, 63, 181, 192, 242, 245, 248, 251–55, 270, 274–75
21:18–19	264, 266, 268, 272, 274
21:18	177, 182, 218, 239, 248–49, 256, 260–63, 265
21:19	13, 21, 29, 218, 258, 260, 265–66, 275
21:20–25	177
21:20–21	191
21:20	180
21:22	21
21:24–25	21, 22
21:24	21, 57
21:25	21

Acts

	28, 76, 262
1:6	11
1:15	262
2	176, 196
2:4	262
2:10	262
3:1–11	262
3:7	199
5:1–16	262
8:27–30	171
9:32–43	262
12	262
12:4	199
12:8	261
15:7	262
20:28–29	243

Rom

1	232

1 Cor

	262
3:22	262
9:5	262
15:5	262

2 Cor

11:32	199

Gal

	262
2:7–8	262
2:11–14	262
4:19	211

Eph

	8
4:11	243

2 Tim

3:6	207

Heb

5:13	204

1 John

	4
3:16	260

1 Pet

2:25	243

Rev

	199, 213, 241

www.ingramcontent.com/pod-product-compliance
Lightning Source LLC
Chambersburg PA
CBHW052147300426
44115CB00011B/1556